Business Forecasting

WILEY AND SAS BUSINESS SERIES

The Wiley and SAS Business Series presents books that help senior level managers with their critical management decisions.

Titles in the Wiley and SAS Business Series include:

For more information on any of the above titles, please visit www.wiley.com.

Business Forecasting

The Emerging Role of Artificial Intelligence and Machine Learning

Edited by

Michael Gilliland
Len Tashman
Udo Sglavo

WILEY

Library of Congress Cataloging-in-Publication Data

Names: Gilliland, Michael, editor. | Tashman, Len, 1942- editor. | Sglavo, Udo, 1968- editor. | John Wiley & Sons, publisher.
Title: Business forecasting : the emerging role of artificial intelligence and machine learning / edited by Michael Gilliland, Len Tashman, and Udo Sglavo.
Description: Hoboken, New Jersey : Wiley, 2021. | Includes index.
Identifiers: LCCN 2021002141 (print) | LCCN 2021002142 (ebook) | ISBN 9781119782476 (hardback) | ISBN 9781119782599 (adobe pdf) | ISBN 9781119782582 (epub)
Subjects: LCSH: Business forecasting. | Artificial intelligence. | Machine learning.
Classification: LCC HD30.27 .B874 2021 (print) | LCC HD30.27 (ebook) | DDC 658.4/0355028563—dc23
LC record available at https://lccn.loc.gov/2021002141
LC ebook record available at https://lccn.loc.gov/2021002142

Cover Design: Wiley

SKY10025841_032621

"The future remains uncertain and so it should, for it is the canvas upon which we paint our desires. Thus always the human condition faces a beautifully empty canvas. We possess only this moment in which to dedicate ourselves continuously to the sacred presence which we share and create."

—Frank Herbert, *Children of Dune*

Contents

Foreword

The forecasting spring began with the M4 Competition, where a complex hybrid approach combining statistical and ML elements came first, providing a 9.4% improvement in its sMAPE relative to that of the Comb benchmark.

Makridakis and Petropoulos (2020)

On March 12, 2020, U.S. toilet paper sales ballooned 734% compared with the same day the previous year, becoming the top-selling product at grocery stores by dollars spent. Clearly, forecasting did not predict the huge surge in demand that created panic-buying – demand that became exaggerated once photos of empty store shelves began circulating on social and mass media. Worse, the scarcity lasted for several months even as manufacturers rushed to produce and ship more paper.

This story reveals two important facts about forecasting. The first relates to its phenomenal failure during the pandemic. The second, even more important one, confirms its astounding success for all other periods when there has always been toilet paper available to buy.

Moreover, it is not just toilet paper. Walmart sells more than 50 million items in its 12,000 stores and online, and it is rare that customers could not find an item they want to buy. Its sophisticated forecasting system accurately predicts the demand for all its products, avoiding stockouts in the great majority of cases. The same is true with essentially most retailers that manage their supply chain in such a way that their customers could buy whatever they want at practically all times when shopping. This achievement is made possible through the accurate forecasts of customer demand and a multitude of actions that make certain that the right items will be available in each store at the correct time to be purchased by the customer wanting to acquire it.

But even during the Covid-19 outbreak the number of products in shortage were limited to some, mostly food categories, hoarded for safety reasons just in case of future scarcities. There were also shifts in purchasing habits away from luxury items to necessities and from physical shopping to online purchases. Forecasting adjusted to the new pandemic reality and after some period of corrections managed to provide reasonably accurate predictions about the products consumers wanted to buy. What the virus has made clear is that our ability to accurately predict the future and be able to estimate the uncertainty of our predictions is straightforward during "normal" periods that account for the great majority of time. However, forecasting can fail, and uncertainty can increase tremendously during unusual periods like the Covid-19 pandemic, during recessions and when rare, unexpected events occur – particularly when people's actions greatly affect the future. It is important, therefore, to accept forecasting's advantages but also its limitations, avoiding unrealistic expectations of what forecasting can achieve.

To do so, executives must understand:

- The forecast is an estimation of a future situation. It is not a target. It is not a plan.

- Forecasting methods, from the simplest to the most sophisticated ones, do not possess any prophetic powers. Their predictions are based on identifying and estimating past patterns and/or relationships that are then extrapolated to forecast the future.

- All forecasts come with an error. All forecasts are uncertain.

- Forecasting accuracy and uncertainty can be estimated consistently in usual, everyday situations when established patterns/relationships remain fairly constant and can be extrapolated reasonably well.

- During periods of recessions/crises, or when unusual events occur, forecasting accuracy deteriorates – often significantly – while the level of uncertainty increases exponentially, and sometimes cannot be measured quantitatively.

- There are trade-offs between the achieved forecasting performance and the respective resources needed (such as data availability, computational cost, and personnel's time), so companies need to carefully choose an appropriate balance.

- When possible, forecasts should be assessed in terms of their utility (such as the decrease in the holding cost) instead of their forecasting performance.

Forecasting is a unique field in two distinct ways. First, it includes researchers and practitioners both interested in improving the accuracy of their predictions as well as the correct estimation of uncertainty. Second, it is a rare social science field where the equivalent of the experimentation, widely used in physical science, is possible and widely practiced through forecasting competitions. This means that the accuracy and uncertainty of available and proposed methods can be tested empirically, allowing firms to decide on what methods to utilize and researchers to strive to improve them by proving their value with real-life data. In the field of forecasting there are many established facts guiding practitioners and researchers on the most appropriate way to get the maximum benefits from its use, and so less need to rely on personal opinion. As in all fields there are potential problems but also available solutions. Many of these are covered in the first volume of *Business Forecasting: Practical Problems and Solutions* (published in 2015), which provides thorough and timely guidance for the forecasting problems facing executives, while the updated edition of the book embraces all new ones.

The field of forecasting just passed its 60th birthday since Robert Brown's pioneering book was published in 1959. His exponential smoothing methods were simple but powerful, and for a long time the most accurate of all available methods, including complex and statistically sophisticated ones, like the Box-Jenkins methodology for ARIMA models. Fortunately, during recent years, new developments originating in artificial intelligence (AI) and machine learning (ML) have opened some new prospects to not only improve forecasting accuracy but also to correctly estimate uncertainty. These advances commence a forecasting spring, with huge potential for revolutionizing the field. They are moving forecasting into new directions – exploiting new ideas from deep learning (DL), and utilizing information from countless series to predict individual ones with cross learning (CL).

In the M4 competition both the first and the second-best methods applied CL, not only achieving a close to 10% improvement in accuracy over the benchmark (a combination of three simple time series methods) but also attaining a phenomenal degree of correctly estimating the uncertainty in the provided forecasts. These new ML-based methods are still in their infancy. But they open huge opportunities for improvements not only in forecasting accuracy/uncertainty but also in the easiness of obtaining the predictions/uncertainty accomplished by AI, without the need of much human inputs.

During the last five years, data science has grown in importance and size, introducing brand-new ways to forecast and estimate uncertainty. In the M4 competition run in 2018, there were ~600 registrations of mostly statisticians and practitioners to participate, with 49 final submissions. In the M5, run two years later, there have been more than 40,000 registrations of mostly data scientists followed, we suspect, by statisticians and practitioners. The competition featured two tracks, one focusing on point-forecast accuracy (with 5,558 teams and 7,022 participants) and another one focusing on uncertainty (with 1,003 teams and 909 participants). Across both tracks, individuals and teams performed almost 100,000 submissions.

With such numbers involved, it is obvious that the forecasting field is being transformed to a new discipline dominated by data scientists that will grow it substantially in the future in unforeseen ways. The big challenge for the new field will undoubtedly be how to integrate data science and statistics and how the practice of forecasting can benefit from such merging. Will, for instance, simple statistical methods still be appropriate for forecasting at the stock-keeping-unit level, with DL used for products high up in the hierarchy, or vice versa? Will the estimation of uncertainty receive more attention from data scientists as it must supplement their point forecasts to determine, among other tasks, inventory levels and deal with the risks always present in all predictions? These and similar questions are being explored in this new book.

This second volume, *Business Forecasting: The Emerging Role of Artificial Intelligence and Machine Learning*, details the forthcoming big changes in the field of forecasting. Its first chapter, Artificial Intelligence and Machine Learning in Forecasting, provides ample treatment of how AI is revolutionizing the field, while its second chapter, Big Data in Forecasting, is concerned with the value of data and how it is being used to improve its importance. The remaining book includes model selection and monitoring, measuring forecasting performance, and covers the organizational aspects of forecasting and the use of judgment in the forecasting process. The Afterwords provide unique perspectives from over a dozen respected academics, consultants, vendors, and industry practitioners – all contributing essays on the issues, current status, and future direction of business forecasting.

Like the first volume, we expect this volume to become a must-read for practitioners. The editors did a fantastic job in delivering a diverse collection of articles and commentaries that offer important and contemporary aspects in forecasting which will help practicing managers to improve the forecasting within their organizations.

SPYROS MAKRIDAKIS
Institute for the Future, University of Nicosia
Nicosia, Cyprus

FOTIOS PETROPOULOS
School of Management, University of Bath
United Kingdom

Preface

In our 2015 compilation, *Business Forecasting: Practical Problems and Solutions*, we brought together 49 of the most interesting, important, and influential articles published in the field since 2000. The selection centered around fundamental issues in business forecasting, forecasting methods, performance evaluation and reporting, and forecasting process and politics. While these topics are just as relevant today as they were five years ago, we've seen a spectacular rise in interest in a new direction – in the role of artificial intelligence and machine learning in business forecasting. Hence the subtitle of this new volume.

Now in 2020, we are writing about forecasting against the backdrop of another spectacular forecasting failure – an unforeseen pandemic. The new compilation features over 60 articles, commentaries, and "op-ed" pieces – all either original or published since 2015. We are pleased to have assembled input from the top academics, consultants, vendors, and industry practitioners – many of the most recognized and respected names in the forecasting profession. Each provides their own unique vision of the issues, current state, and future direction of business forecasting.

There has been much progress in the last five years, and we have attempted to reflect that progress in the selected contributions. After an introductory review of business forecasting's "state of the art," the material is organized into five chapters:

1. Artificial Intelligence and Machine Learning in Forecasting

2. Big Data in Forecasting

3. Forecasting Methods: Modeling, Selection, and Monitoring

4. Forecasting Performance

5. Forecasting Process: Communication, Accountability, and S&OP

We close with a lengthy section of Afterwords (described below) from thoughtful contributors in the field.

Each chapter gets a brief introduction, and each article begins with an abstract summarizing its content and significance. Some articles also include commentaries that further expand upon – or argue counter to – the article's key points.

The authors wish to thank SAS Press and Wiley for initiating the idea of an updated volume, and for accepting the manuscript into the Wiley and SAS Business Series. We were assisted at SAS by Lauree Shephard, who initiated the book proposal, and by Catherine Connolly as Developmental Editor. At Wiley, Susan Cerra was our Senior Managing Editor, and Sheck Cho our Executive Editor.

As in the earlier volume, much of this book's content first appeared in *Foresight: The International Journal of Applied Forecasting*, and appears with permission from the International Institute of Forecasters. Len Tashman, co-editor of this compilation and

Foresight's editor-in-chief, extends special thanks to his staff: Liza Woodruff, Ralph Culver, Mary Ellen Bridge, Holly Lancaster, and Michelle Kitchens. In addition, we thank IIF Business Director Pam Stroud, for her critical support over the years.

We also, again, include several articles from the *Journal of Business Forecasting,* with permission graciously provided by its editor-in-chief, Dr. Chaman Jain, and the Institute of Business Forecasting. We look forward to the return of live events, and a chance to see our longtime IBF friends: Anish Jain, Stephanie Murray, and Latosha Staton.

This collection includes several adaptations from other previously published work, and we thank the authors and publishers:

- Jeff Baker, for adaptation of his MIT Master's thesis.
- Lora Cecere, for adaptation of her blog post.
- Charles Chase and SAS, for adaptation of his whitepaper.
- Paul Goodwin, for adaptation from his book *Forewarned: A Skeptic's Guide to Prediction.*
- Susan Kahler and Steven Mills, for adaptation of her blog post with his SAS Global Forum paper.
- Stephan Kolassa and Enno Siemsen (as well as publisher Scott Isenberg of Business Expert Press), for adaptation from their book *Demand Forecasting for Managers.*
- Steve Morlidge, for adaptations from two of his books, *Present Sense* and *The Little (Illustrated) Book of Operational Forecasting.*

We also wish to acknowledge and thank the Makridakis Open Forecasting Center (MOFC) of the University of Nicosia for funding open access to the important "Forecasting in Social Settings: The State of the Art" article, originally published by Elsevier in *International Journal of Forecasting.*

Rather than closing with a single Afterword, we realized there could be great benefit in sharing a diversity of perspectives, particularly from influential writers who might have had insufficient representation in the main body of the text. These individuals graciously followed our directive for delivering an original "opinion-editorial" piece, targeting 1,000–1,200 words, and within a very tight publication timeline. For these we thank Carolyn Allmon of Teleflex Inc., Jason Breault of LifeWork Search, Lora Cecere of Supply Chain Insights, Simon Clarke of Argon & Co, Robert Fildes of Lancaster University, Igor Gusakov of GoodsForecast, Jim Hoover of University of Florida, Rob Hyndman of Monash University, Chaman Jain of St. John's University, Jonathon Karelse of NorthFind Management, Bahman Rostami-Tabar of Cardiff University, Shaun Snapp of Brightwork Research & Analysis, Nicolas Vandeput of SupChains, Eric Wilson of IBF, and Dr. Davis Wu of Nestlé.

Finally, we wish to give very special thanks to Spyros Makridakis of the Institute for the Future at University of Nicosia, and Fotios Petropoulos of the School of Management at University of Bath. Amidst their busy academic schedules and the closing weeks of the M5 Competition, Spyros and Fotios contributed the Foreword. They also co-authored, with Rob Hyndman, our indispensable opening piece on the state of the art.

Just like last time, the editors wish to acknowledge all the authors whose work has been included in this book. We thank them for their continuing contributions to the advancement and better practice of business forecasting.

MICHAEL GILLILAND
SAS Institute
Seagrove, North Carolina

LEN TASHMAN
Foresight
Golden, Colorado

UDO SGLAVO
SAS Institute
Cary, North Carolina

State of the Art

We are about to embark on a journey through the last five years of business forecasting literature, with over 60 selections from journals, books, whitepapers, and original contributions written just for this collection. The biggest single topic area – reflecting the intense interest from practitioners and researchers alike – is the role of artificial intelligence and machine learning in business forecasting. But traditional forecasting topics like modeling, performance evaluation, and process remain vital, and are not ignored. We've sought to include the compelling new ideas, and the divergent viewpoints, to broadly represent advances in the business forecasting profession over the past five years.

But before we begin the journey, it is worth a few moments to review and reflect upon where we are at now – business forecasting's state of the art.

* * *

FORECASTING IN SOCIAL SETTINGS: THE STATE OF THE ART*

Spyros Makridakis, Rob J. Hyndman, and Fotios Petropoulos

This paper provides a nonsystematic review of the progress of forecasting in social (i.e., non-physical science) settings – which includes business forecasting. It is aimed at someone outside the field who wants to understand and appreciate the results of 2018's M4 Competition, and the M4's historical context and significance. As such, it forms a survey paper regarding the state of the art of the business forecasting discipline, and provides a perfect launch point for the chapters to follow.

The review discusses the recorded improvements in forecast accuracy over time, the need to capture forecast uncertainty, and things that can go wrong with predictions. It classifies the knowledge achieved over recent years into (i) what we know, (ii) what we are not sure about, and (iii) what we don't know. In the first two areas, this article explores the difference between explanation and prediction, the existence of an optimal model, the performance of machine learning methods on time series forecasting tasks, the difficulties of predicting nonstable environments, the performance of judgment, and the value added by exogenous variables. The article concludes with the importance of (thin and) fat tails, the challenges and advances in causal inference, and the role of luck.

Written by three of the very top contributors to the field, this article delivers an exceptional recap of our current knowledge about business forecasting, along with an extensive section of references for further study.

* * *

*This article originally appeared in the *International Journal of Forecasting* 36(1), January–March 2020 (https:// doi.org/10.1016/j.ijforecast.2019.05.011), published by Elsevier B.V. on behalf of the International Institute of Forecasters. © 2019 The Authors. This is an open access article under the CC BY license (http://creativecommons.org/licenses/by/4.0/). It has been modified slightly to fit the format of this book.

"There's no chance that the iPhone is going to get any significant market share."

—Steve Ballmer, CEO Microsoft, April 2007

I. THE FACTS

A Brief History of Forecasting

In terms of human history, it is not that long since forecasting moved from the religious, the superstitious, and even the supernatural (Scott, 2015) to the more scientific. Even today, though, old fortune-telling practices still hold among people who pay to receive the "prophetic" advice of "expert" professional forecasters, including those who claim to be able to predict the stock market and make others rich by following their advice. In the emerging field of "scientific" forecasting, there is absolute certainty about two things. First, no one possesses prophetic powers, even though many pretend to do so; and, second, all predictions are uncertain: often the only thing that varies among such predictions is the extent of such uncertainty.

The field of forecasting outside the physical sciences started at the end of the nineteenth century with attempts to predict economic cycles, and continued with efforts to forecast the stock market. Later, it was extended to predictions concerning business, finance, demography, medicine, psychology, and other areas of the social sciences. The young field achieved considerable success after World War II with Robert Brown's work (Brown, 1959, 1963) on the prediction of the demand for thousands of inventory items stored in navy warehouses. Given the great variety of forecasts needed, as well as the computational requirements for doing so, the work had to be simple to carry out, using the mechanical calculators of the time. Brown's achievement was to develop various forms of exponential smoothing that were sufficiently accurate for the problems faced and computationally light. Interestingly, in the Makridakis and Hibon (1979) study and the subsequent M1 and M2 competitions, his simple, empirically-developed models were found to be more accurate than the highly sophisticated ARIMA models of Box and Jenkins (Box, Jenkins, Reinsel, and Ljung, 2015).

As computers became faster and cheaper, the field expanded, with econometricians, engineers and statisticians all proposing various advanced forecasting approaches, under the belief that a greater sophistication would improve the forecasting accuracy. There were two faulty assumptions underlying such beliefs. First, it was assumed that the model that best fitted the available data (model fit) would also be the most accurate one for forecasting beyond such data (post-sample predictions), whereas actually the effort to minimise model fit errors contributed to over-parameterisation and over-fitting. Simple methods that captured the dominant features of the generating process were both less likely to overfit and likely to be at least as accurate as statistically sophisticated ones (see Pant and Starbuck, 1990). The second faulty assumption was that of constancy of patterns/relationships – assuming that the future will be an exact continuation of the past. Although history repeats itself, it never does so in precisely the same way. Simple methods tend to be affected less by changes in the data generating process, resulting in smaller post-sample errors.

Starting in the late 1960s, significant efforts were made, through empirical and other studies and competitions, to evaluate the forecasting accuracy and establish some objective findings regarding our ability to predict the future and assess the extent of the uncertainty associated with these predictions. Today, following many such studies/competitions, we have a good idea of the accuracy of the various predictions in the business, economic and social fields (and also, lately, involving climate changes), as well as of the uncertainty associated with them. Most important, we have witnessed considerable advances in the field of forecasting, which have been documented adequately in the past by two published papers. Makridakis (1986) surveyed the theoretical and practical developments in the field of forecasting and discussed the findings of empirical studies and their implications until that time. Twenty years later, Armstrong (2006) published another pioneering paper that was aimed at "summarizing what has been learned over the past quarter century about the accuracy of forecasting methods" (p. 583) while also covering new developments, including neural networks, which were in their infancy at that time. The purpose of the present paper is to provide an updated survey for non-forecasting experts who want to be informed of the state of the art of forecasting in social sciences and to understand the findings/conclusions of the M4 Competition better.

Some of the conclusions of these earlier surveys have been overturned by subsequent additional evidence. For example, Armstrong (2006) found neural nets and Box-Jenkins methods to fare poorly against alternatives, whereas now both have been shown to be competitive. For neural nets, good forecasts have been obtained when there are enormous collections of data available (Salinas, Flunkert, and Gasthaus, 2017). For Box-Jenkins methods, improved identification algorithms (Hyndman and Khandakar, 2008) have led to them being competitive with (and sometimes better than) exponential smoothing methods. Other conclusions have stood the test of time: for example, that combining forecasts improves the accuracy.

When Predictions Go Wrong

Although forecasting in the physical sciences can attain amazing levels of accuracy, such is not the case in social contexts, where practically all predictions are uncertain and a good number can be unambiguously wrong. This is particularly true when binary decisions are involved, such as the decision that faces the U.S. Federal Reserve as to whether to raise or lower interest rates, given the competing risks of inflation and unemployment. The big problem is that some wrong predictions can affect not only a firm or a small group of people, but also whole societies, such as those that involve global warming, while others may be detrimental to our health. Ioannidis, a medical professor at Stanford, has devoted his life to studying health predictions. His findings are disheartening, and were articulated in an article published in *PLoS Medicine* entitled "Why most published research findings are false" (Ioannidis, 2005).[1] A popular piece on a similar theme in *The Atlantic* entitled "Lies, damned lies, and medical science" (Freedman, 2010) is less polite. It summarizes such findings as: "Much of what medical researchers conclude in their studies is misleading, exaggerated, or flat-out wrong." Freedman concluded with the question, "why are doctors – to a striking extent – still drawing upon misinformation in their everyday practice?"

A recent case exemplifying Ioannidis' conclusions is the findings of two studies eight years apart of which the results were contradictory, making it impossible to know what advice to follow in order to benefit from medical research. In 2010, Micha, Wallace, and Mozaffarian (2010) published a meta-analysis that reviewed six studies which evaluated the effects of meat and vegetarian diets on mortality, involving a total of more than 1.5 million people. It concluded that all-cause mortality was higher for those who ate meat, mainly red or processed meat, daily. However, a new study published in 2018 (Mente and Yusuf, 2018), using a large sample of close to 220,000 people, found that eating red meat and cheese reduced cardiovascular disease by 22% and decreased the risk of early death by 25% (with such large sample sizes, all differences are statistically significant). If conflicting medical predictions, based on substantial sample sizes and with hundreds of millions of dollars having been spent on designing and conducting them, are widespread, what are we to surmise about studies in other disciplines that are less well funded, utilize small sample sizes, or base their predictions on judgment and opinion? Moreover, if the conclusions of a medical study can be reversed in a period of just eight years, how can we know that those of new studies will not produce the same contradictions? Recommendations about the treatment of disease are based on the findings of medical research, but how can such findings be trusted when, according to Ioannidis, most of them are false? Clearly, there is a predictability problem that extends beyond medicine to practically all fields of social science, including economics (Camerer et al. 2016, Dewald, Thursby, and Anderson, 1986). Fortunately, empirical studies in the field of forecasting have provided us with some objective evidence that allows us to both determine the accuracy of predictions and estimate the level of uncertainty.

There are several famous examples of forecasting errors, including Ballmer's forecast quoted earlier about the iPhone, which is possibly the most successful of all products ever marketed. In 1798, Malthus predicted that we were confronted by mass starvation, as the population was growing geometrically while food production was increasing only arithmetically. Today's material abundance and decreases in population growth in most advanced countries have been moving in the opposite direction to his predictions. In 1943, Thomas Watson, IBM's president, made his infamous prediction: "I think there is a world market for maybe five computers," missing it by about a billion times if all computers, including smartphones, are counted (see also Schnaars, 1989). However, even recent predictions by professional organisations that specialise in forecasting, using modern computers and well-trained, PhD-holding forecasters, can go wrong, as can be seen from the complete failure of these organisations to predict the great 2007/2008 recession and its grave implications. The same has been true with technological forecasting, which failed to predict, even a few decades earlier, the arrival and widespread usage of the three major inventions of our times: the computer, the internet, and the mobile phone. Judgmental predictions have been evaluated by Tetlock (2006), who has compared the forecasts of experts in different macroeconomic fields to forecasts made by well-informed laity or those based on simple extrapolation from current trends. He concluded that not only are most experts not more accurate, but they also find it more difficult to change their minds when new evidence becomes available.

After surveying past successes and failures in forecasting, what we can conclude is that there is a significant amount of uncertainty in all of our predictions, and that such uncertainty is underestimated greatly for two reasons. First, our attitude to extrapolating in a linear fashion from the present to the future, and second, our fear of the unknown and our psychological need to reduce the anxiety associated with such a fear by believing that we can control the future by predicting it accurately (known as the illusion of control, see Langer, 1975). Thus, it becomes imperative to be aware of the difficulty of accurate predictions and the underestimation of the uncertainty associated with them, in order to be able to minimise this bias. The field of quantitative forecasting has the potential advantage that it may be possible to assess the accuracy of forecasts and the level of uncertainty surrounding them by utilising information from empirical and open forecasting competitions.

Improving Forecasting Accuracy over Time

The scientific approach to forecasting in the physical sciences began with Halley's comet predictions in the early 1700s (Halleio, 1704), which turned out to be remarkably accurate. Other forecasts followed, including the somewhat less successful meteorological forecasts of Beaufort and FitzRoy in the late 1850s (Burton, 1986). These were highly controversial at the time, and FitzRoy in particular was criticised heavily, and subsequently committed suicide. Nevertheless, he left a lasting legacy, including the word "forecast," which he had coined for his daily weather predictions. Over the 150 years since, there has been extraordinary progress in improving the forecast accuracy not only in meteorology (Kistler et al., 2001; Saha et al., 2014) but also in other physical sciences, as the underlying physical processes have come to be understood better, the volume of observations has exploded, computing power has increased, and the ability to share information across connected networks has become available.

The social sciences are different. First, there is usually a limited theoretical or quantitative basis for representing a causal or underlying mechanism. Thus, we rely on statistical approximations that roughly describe what we observe, but may not represent a causal or underlying mechanism. Second, despite the deluge of data that is available today, much of this information does not concern what we want to forecast directly. For example, if we wish to predict the GDP next quarter, we may have an enormous amount of daily stock market data available, but no daily data on expenditures on goods and services. Third, what we are trying to forecast is often affected by the forecasts themselves. For example, central banks might forecast next year's housing price index but then raise interest rates as a result, thus leading the index to be lower than the forecast. Such feedback does not occur in astronomical or weather forecasts.

For these reasons, social science forecasts are unlikely ever to be as accurate as forecasts in the physical sciences, and the potential for improvements in accuracy is somewhat limited. Nevertheless, increases in computing power and a better understanding of how to separate signal from noise should lead to some improvements in forecast accuracy. However, this does not appear to have been the case, at least for macroeconomic forecasting (Fildes and Stekler, 2002; Heilemann and Stekler, 2013; Stekler, 2007).

On the other hand, time series forecasting has improved demonstrably over the last 30 years. We can measure the change through the published accuracies of forecasting competitions over the last 40 years, beginning with the first Makridakis competition (Makridakis et al., 1982), then the M3 competition (Makridakis and Hibon, 2000), and finally the recent M4 competition (Makridakis, Spiliotis, and Assimakopoulos, 2018a). In measuring the forecast accuracy improvement, we have applied the best-performing methods from each competition to the data from previous competitions in order to see how the methods have improved over time.

However, these comparisons are not straightforward because the forecast accuracy measures used were not consistent between competitions. In fact, there is still no agreement on the best measure of the forecast accuracy. We will therefore compare results using the MAPE (used in the first competition), the sMAPE (used in the M3 competition), and the MASE. The M4 competition used a weighted average of the sMAPE and MASE values. All measures are defined and discussed by Hyndman and Koehler (2006) and Hyndman and Athanasopoulos (2018).

In the first Makridakis competition (Makridakis et al., 1982), the best-performing method overall (as measured by MAPE) was simple exponential smoothing applied to deseasonalized data, where the deseasonalization used a classical multiplicative decomposition (Hyndman and Athanasopoulos, 2018); this is denoted by DSES. For non-seasonal data, DSES is equivalent to simple exponential smoothing.

In the M3 competition, the best method (as measured by sMAPE), and which is in the public domain, was the Theta method (Assimakopoulos and Nikolopoulos, 2000). We applied the Theta method using the thetaf() implementation from the forecast package for R (Hyndman et al., 2018), to ensure consistent application to all data sets.

In the M4 competition, the best-performing method (as measured by a weighted average of sMAPE and MASE) for which we had R code available was the FFORMA method (Montero-Manso, Athanasopoulos, Hyndman, and Talagala, 2020), which came second in the competition.

In addition to these methods, we also included, for comparison, the popular auto. arima() and ets() methods (Hyndman and Khandakar, 2008; Hyndman et al., 2002), as

Table I.1 Comparing the Best Method from Each Forecasting Competition against Each Other and against Benchmark Methods (Thanks to Pablo Montero-Manso for providing the FFORMA forecasts for the M1 and M3 data.)

Method	M1 Competition			M3 Competition			M4 Competition		
	MAPE	sMAPE	MASE	MAPE	sMAPE	MASE	MAPE	sMAPE	MASE
FFORMA	**15.9**	**14.4**	**1.3**	18.4	**12.6**	**1.1**	**14.3**	**11.8**	**1.2**
ETSARIMA	17.4	15.3	1.3	18.7	13.1	1.1	14.9	12.3	1.2
ETS	17.7	15.6	1.4	18.7	13.3	1.2	15.6	12.8	1.3
ARIMA	18.9	16.3	1.4	19.8	14.0	1.2	15.2	12.7	1.2
Theta	20.3	16.8	1.4	**17.9**	13.1	1.2	14.7	12.4	1.3
DSES	17.0	15.4	1.5	19.2	13.9	1.3	15.2	12.8	1.4
Naive 2	17.7	16.6	1.5	22.3	15.8	1.4	16.0	13.5	1.4
Naive	21.9	19.4	1.8	24.3	16.6	1.5	17.5	14.7	1.7

implemented by Hyndman et al. (2018), along with a simple average of the forecasts from these two methods (denoted "ETSARIMA"). We also include two simple benchmarks: naive and naive on the seasonally adjusted data (naive 2).

When we apply these methods to the data from all three competitions, we can see how the forecast accuracy has changed over time, as is shown in Table I.1. Note that the mean values of MAPE, sMAPE, and MASE have been calculated by applying the arithmetic mean across series and horizons simultaneously. Other ways of averaging the results can lead to different conclusions, due to greater weights being placed on some series or horizons. It is not always obvious from the published competition results how these calculations have been done in the past, although in the case of the M4 competition, the code has been made public to help to avoid such confusion.

There are several interesting aspects to this comparison.

- DSES did well on the M1 data and is competitive with other non-combining methods on the M3 and M4 data according to the MAPE and sMAPE, but it does poorly according to the MASE.

- While Theta did well on the M3 data (winner of that competition), it is less competitive on the M1 and M4 data.

- The most recent method (FFORMA) outperforms the other methods on every measure for the M1 and M4 competitions, and on all but the MAPE measure for the M3 competition.

- The ETSARIMA method (averaging the ETS and ARIMA forecasts) is almost as good as the FFORMA method in terms of MASE, and is easier and faster to compute.

- The results are relatively clear-cut across all competitions (in the order displayed) using the MASE criterion, but the results are less clear with the other accuracy criteria.

While there is some variation between periods, the good performances of FFORMA and ETSARIMA are relatively consistent across data sets and frequencies. Clearly, progress in forecasting methods has been uneven, but the recent M4 competition has helped to advance the field considerably in several ways, including: (1) encouraging the development of several new methods; and (2) providing a large set of data in order to allow detailed comparisons of various forecasting methods over different time granularities.

The Importance of Being Uncertain

No forecasts are exact, and so it is important to provide some measure of the forecast uncertainty. Unless such uncertainty is expressed clearly and unambiguously, forecasting is not far removed from fortune-telling.

The most general approach to expressing the uncertainty is to estimate the "forecast distribution" – the probability distribution of future observations conditional on the information available at the time of forecasting. A point forecast is usually the mean (or sometimes the median) of this distribution, and a prediction interval is usually based on the quantiles of this distribution (Hyndman and Athanasopoulos, 2018). As a consequence, forecasting has two primary tasks:

1. To provide point forecasts which are as accurate as possible;

2. To specify or summarise the forecast distribution.

Until relatively recently, little attention was paid to forecast distributions, or measures of the forecast distribution accuracy. For example, there was no measure of the distributional forecast uncertainty used in the M1 and M3 competitions, and it is still rare to see such measures used in Kaggle competitions.

Prediction Interval Evaluation

The simplest approach to summarising the uncertainty of a forecast distribution is to provide one or more prediction intervals with a specified probability coverage. However, it is well known that these intervals are often narrower than they should be (Hyndman et al., 2002); that is, that the actual observations fall inside the intervals less often than the nominal coverage implies. For example, the 95% prediction intervals for the ETS and ARIMA models applied to the M1 and M3 competition data, obtained using the automatic procedures in the forecast package for R, yield coverage percentages that are as low as 76.8%, and are never higher than 95%. Progress has been made in this area too, though, with the recent FFORMA method (Montero-Manso et al., 2020) providing an average coverage of 94.5% for these data sets. Figure I.1 shows the coverages for nominal 95% prediction intervals for each method and forecast horizon when applied to the M1 and M3 data. ARIMA models do particularly poorly here.

It is also evident from Figure I.1 that there are possible differences between the two data sets, with the percentage coverages being lower for the M1 competition than for the M3 competition.

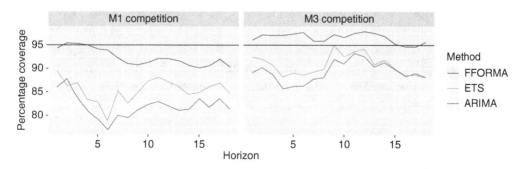

Figure I.1 Actual Coverages Achieved by Nominal 95% Prediction Intervals

There are at least three reasons for standard statistical models' underestimations of the uncertainty.

1. Probably the biggest factor is that model uncertainty is not taken into account. The prediction intervals are produced under the assumption that the model is "correct," which clearly is never the case.

2. Even if the model is specified correctly, the parameters must be estimated, and also the parameter uncertainty is rarely accounted for in time series forecasting models.

3. Most prediction intervals are produced under the assumption of Gaussian errors. When this assumption is not correct, the prediction interval coverage will usually be underestimated, especially when the errors have a fat-tailed distribution.

In contrast, some modern forecasting methods do not use an assumed data generating process to compute prediction intervals. Instead, the prediction intervals from FFORMA are produced using a weighted combination of the intervals from its component methods, where the weights are designed to give an appropriate coverage while also taking into account the length of the interval.

Coverage is important, but it is not the only requirement for good prediction intervals. A good prediction interval will be as small as possible while maintaining the specified coverage. Winkler proposed a scoring method for enabling comparisons between prediction intervals that takes into account both the coverage and the width of the intervals. If the $100(1-\alpha)\%$ prediction interval for time t is given by $[l_t, u_t]$, and y_t is the observation at time t, then the Winkler (1972) score is defined as the average of:

$$
W(l_t, u_t, y_t) = \begin{cases} (u_t - l_t) & l_t < y_t < u_t \\ (u_t - l_t) + \dfrac{2(l_t - y_t)}{\alpha} & y_t < l_t \\ (u_t - l_t) + \dfrac{2(y_t - u_t)}{\alpha} & y_t > u_t \end{cases}
$$

This penalises both for wide intervals (since $u_t - l_t$ will be large) and for non-coverage, with observations that are well outside the interval being penalised more heavily. However, although this was proposed in 1972, it has received very little use until recently, when a scaled version of it was used in the M4 competition. The lower the score, the better the forecasts. For a discussion of some of the problems with interval scoring, see Askanazi, Diebold, Schorfheide, and Shin (2018).

Forecast Distribution Evaluation

To the best of our knowledge, the only forecasting competitions that have evaluated whole forecast distributions have been the GEFCom2014 and GEFCom2017 energy forecasting competitions (Hong et al., 2016). Both used percentile scoring as an evaluation measure.

For each time period t throughout the forecast horizon, the participants provided percentiles $q_{i,t}$, where $i = 1, 2, \ldots, 99$. Then, the percentile score is given by the pinball loss function:

$$L(q_{i,t}, y_t) = \begin{cases} \left(1 - \dfrac{i}{100}\right)(q_{i,t} - y_t) & y_t < q_{i,t} \\ \left(\dfrac{i}{100}\right)(y_t - q_{i,t}) & y_t \geq q_{i,t} \end{cases}$$

This score is then averaged over all percentiles and all time periods in order to evaluate the full predictive density. If the observations follow the forecast distribution, then the average score will be the smallest value possible. If the observations are more spread out or deviate from the forecast distribution in some other way, then the average score will be higher. Other distribution scoring methods are also available (Gneiting and Raftery, 2007).

Without a history of forecast distribution evaluation, it is not possible to explore how this area of forecasting has improved over time. However, we recommend that future forecast evaluation studies include forecast distributions, especially in areas where the tails of the distribution are of particular interest, such as in energy and finance.

II. WHAT WE KNOW

On Explaining the Past versus Predicting the Future

Forecasting is about predicting the future, but this can only be done based on information from the past, which raises the issue of how the most appropriate information and the corresponding model for predicting the future should be selected. For a long period, and for lack of a better alternative, it was believed that such model should be chosen according to how well it could explain, that is, fit, the available past data (somewhat like asking a historian to predict the future). For instance, in the presentation of their paper to the Royal Statistical Society in London, Makridakis and Hibon (1979) had difficulty explaining their findings that single exponential smoothing was more accurate than the Box-Jenkins approach and that a combination of methods was more accurate than the individual methods being combined. Theoretically, with the correct model and assuming that the future is the same as the past, these findings would not be possible. However, this theoretical postulate does not necessarily hold, because the future could be quite different from the past. Both the superiority of combining and the higher accuracy of exponential smoothing methods relative to ARIMA models were proven again in the M1 and M2 competitions. However, some statisticians were still unwilling to accept the empirical evidence, arguing that theory was more important than empirical competitions, as was expressed powerfully by Priestley, who stated that "we must resist the temptation to read too much into the results of the analysis" (Makridakis and Hibon, 1979, p. 127).

The debate ended with the M3 Competition (Makridakis and Hibon, 2000), with its 3003 time series. Once again, the results showed the value of combining and the superior performances of some simpler methods (such as the Theta method) in comparison to other, more complicated methods (most notably one particular neural networks application). Slowly but steadily, this evidence is being accepted by a new breed of academic forecasters and well-informed practitioners who are interested in improving the accuracy of their predictions. Moreover, the accuracy of ARIMA models has improved considerably in the M3 and M4 competitions, surpassing those of exponential smoothing methods when model selection was conducted using Akaike's information criterion (Akaike, 1977).

As a result, the emphasis has shifted from arguing about the value of competitions to learning as much as possible from the empirical evidence in order to improve the theoretical and practical aspects of forecasting. The M4 Competition, which is covered in detail in this special issue, is the most recent evidence of this fundamental shift in attitudes toward forecasting and the considerable learning that has been taking place in the field. A number of academic researchers have guided this shift within universities. Determined practitioners from companies like Uber, Amazon, Google, Microsoft, and SAS, among others, present their advances every year in the International Symposium on Forecasting (ISF). They are focused on improving the forecasting accuracy and harnessing its benefits, while also being concerned about measuring the uncertainty in their predictions.

On the (Non)existence of a Best Model

Many forecasting researchers have been on a quest to identify the best forecasting model for each particular case. This quest is often viewed as the "holy grail" in forecasting. While earlier studies investigated the concept of aggregate selection (Fildes, 1989), meaning selecting one model for all series within a data set, more recent studies have suggested that such an approach can only work for highly homogeneous data sets. In fact, as Fildes and Petropoulos (2015) showed, if we had some way of identifying correctly beforehand which model would perform best for each series, we could observe savings of up to 30% compared to using the best (but same) model on all series.

Approaches for the individual selection of the best model for each series (or even for each series/horizon combination) include information criteria (Hyndman et al., 2002), validation and cross-validation approaches (Tashman, 2000), approaches that use knowledge obtained from the data to find temporary solutions to the problems faced (Fildes and Petropoulos, 2015), approaches based on time series features and expected errors (Petropoulos et al., 2014; Wang, Smith-Miles, and Hyndman, 2009), and approaches based on expert rules (Adya, Collopy, Armstrong, and Kennedy, 2001). However, all of these approaches are limited with regard to their input: they are attempting to identify the best model for the future conditional on information from the past. However, as the previous section highlighted, explaining the past is not the same as predicting the future. When dealing with real data, no well-specified "data generation processes" exist. The future might be completely different from the past, and the previous "best" models may no longer be appropriate. Even if we could identify the best model, we would be limited by the need to estimate its parameters appropriately.

In fact, there exist three types of uncertainties when dealing with real forecasting situations: model uncertainty, parameter uncertainty and data uncertainty (Petropoulos et al., 2018). In practice, such uncertainties are dealt with by combining models/methods. As George Box put it, "all models are wrong, but some are useful." Again and again, combinations have been proved to benefit the forecasting accuracy (Clemen, 1989; Makridakis, 1989; Timmermann, 2006), while also decreasing the variance of the forecasts (Hibon and Evgeniou, 2005), thus rendering operational settings more efficient. Current approaches to forecast combinations include, among others, combinations based on information criteria (Kolassa, 2011), the use of multiple temporal aggregation levels (Andrawis et al., 2011; Athanasopoulos et al., 2017; Kourentzes et al., 2014), bootstrapping for time series forecasting (Bergmeir, Hyndman, and Benítez, 2016) and forecast pooling (Kourentzes, Barrow, and Petropoulos, 2019).

Approaches based on combinations have dominated the rankings in the latest instalment of the M competitions. It is important to highlight the fact that one element of the success of forecast combinations is the careful selection of an appropriate pool of models and their weights. One explanation for the good performance of combinations is that the design of the M competitions requires the nature and history of the series to be concealed. This reduces the amount of background information that can be applied to the forecasting problem and may give combinations an advantage relative to models that are selected individually by series. In fact, as Fildes and Petropoulos (2015) have shown, model selection can outperform forecast combinations in certain situations, such as when a dominant method exists, or under a stable environment. Finally, the evidence in the M4 results suggests that hybrid approaches, which are based on combining simple time series techniques with modern machine-learning methods at a conceptual level (rather than a forecast level), perform very well.

On the Performance of Machine Learning

The hype publicizing the considerable achievements in artificial intelligence (AI) also extends to machine learning (ML) forecasting methods. There were high expectations that hedge funds that utilized ML techniques would outperform the market (Satariano and Kumar, 2017). However, new evidence has shown that their track record is mixed, even though their potential is enormous (Asmundsson, 2018).

Although some publications have claimed to show excellent accuracies of ML forecasting methods, very often they have not been compared against sensible benchmarks. For stock-market data, for example, it is essential to include a naive benchmark, yet often this is not done (see, for example, Wang and Wang, 2017). In addition, some studies claim high levels of accuracy by hand-selecting examples where the proposed method happens to do well. Even when a reasonably large set of data is used for the empirical evaluation and the time series have not been chosen specifically to favour the proposed approach, it is essential to consider the statistical significance of any comparisons made. Otherwise, conclusions can be drawn from random noise (Pant and Starbuck, 1990).

One advantage of large forecasting competitions is that they provide a collection of data against which new methods can be tested, and for which published accuracy results are available. The data sets are also large enough that statistically significant results should be able to be achieved for any meaningful improvements in forecast accuracy.

One disadvantage is that the series are a heterogeneous mix of frequencies, lengths and categories, so that there may be some difficulty in extracting from the raw results the circumstances under which individual methods shine or fall down.

In time series forecasting, the hype has been moderated over time as studies have shown that the application of ML methods leads to poor performances in comparison to statistical methods (though some ML supporters still argue about the validity of the empirical evidence). We are neither supporters nor critics of either approach over the other, and we believe that there is considerable overlap between the statistical and ML approaches to forecasting. Moreover, they are complementary in the sense that ML methods are more vulnerable to excessive variance, while statistical ones are more vulnerable to higher bias. At the same time, the empirical evidence to date shows a clear superiority in accuracy of the statistical methods in comparison to ML ones when applied to either individual time series or large collections of heterogeneous time series. In a study using the 1045 monthly M3 series (those utilized by Ahmed, Atiya, Gayar, and El-Shishiny, 2010) that consisted of more than 81 observations, Makridakis, Spiliotis, and Assimakopoulos (2018b) found, using accepted practices to run the methods, that the most accurate ML methods were less accurate than the least accurate statistical one. Moreover, 14 of the ML methods were less accurate than naive 2.

ML methods did not do well in the M4 Competition either, with most of them doing worse than the naive 2 benchmark (for more details, see Makridakis, Spiliotis, and Assimakopoulos, 2020). We believe that it is essential to figure out the reasons for such poor performances of the ML methods. One possibility is the relatively large number of parameters associated with ML methods compared to statistical methods. Another is the number of important choices that are related to the design of ML, which are usually made using validation data, as there is no standardised ML approach. The time series used in these competitions are generally not particularly long, with a few hundred observations at most. This is simply not sufficient for building a complicated nonlinear, nonparametric forecasting model. Even if the time series are very long (at least a few thousand observations), there are difficulties with data relevance, as the dynamics of the series may have changed, and the early part of the series may bias the forecasting results.

Machine learning methods have done well in time series forecasting when forecasting an extensive collection of homogeneous data. For example, Amazon uses deep learning neural networks to predict product sales (Salinas et al., 2017; Wen et al., 2017) by exploiting their vast database of the sales histories of related products, rather than building a separate model for the sales of each product.

We expect that future research efforts will work toward making these methods more accurate. Both the best and second-best methods of the M4 Competition used ML ideas to improve the accuracy, and we would expect that additional, innovative notions would be found in the future to advance their utilization.

III. WHAT WE ARE NOT SURE ABOUT

On the Prediction of Recessions/Booms/Non-stable Environments

One area of forecasting that has attracted a considerable amount of attention is that of extreme events, which include but are not limited to economic recessions/booms and natural disasters. Such events have a significant impact from a socioeconomic perspective, but also are notoriously tricky to predict, with some being "black swans" (events with no known historical precedent).

Take as an example the great recession of 2008. At the end of December 2007, *Business Week* reported that only 2 out of 34 forecasters predicted a recession for 2008. Even when the symptoms of the recession became more evident, Larry Kudlow (an American financial analyst and the Director of the National Economic Council under the Trump administration) insisted that there was no recession. Similarly, the Federal Open Market Committee failed to predict the 2008 recession (Stekler and Symington, 2016). Interestingly, after the recession, most economic analysts, victims of their hindsight, were able to provide detailed explanations of and reasons behind the recession, while the few "prophets" who did indeed predict the great recession were unable to offer equally good predictions for other extreme events, as if their prophetic powers had been lost overnight.

Two recent studies have taken some first steps towards predicting market crashes and bubble bursts. Gresnigt, Kole, and Franses (2015) model financial market crashes as seismic activity and create medium-term probability predictions, which consequently feed an early warning system. Franses (2016) proposes a test for identifying bubbles in time series data, as well as to indicate whether a bubble is close to bursting.

On the Performances of Humans versus Models

Judgment has always been an integral input to the forecasting process. Earlier studies focused on the comparative performances of judgmental versus statistical forecasts, when judgment was used to produce forecasts directly. However, the results of such studies have been inconclusive. For instance, while Lawrence, Edmundson, and O'Connor (1985) and Makridakis et al. (1993) found that unaided human judgment can be as good as the best statistical methods from the M1 forecasting competition, Carbone and Gorr (1985) and Sanders (1992) found judgmental point forecasts to be less accurate than statistical methods. The reason for these results is the fact that well-known biases govern judgmental forecasts, such as the tendency of forecasters to dampen trends (Lawrence et al., 2006; Lawrence and Makridakis, 1989), as well as anchoring and adjustment (O'Connor, Remus, and Griggs, 1993) and the confusion of the signal with noise (Harvey, 1995; Reimers and Harvey, 2011). On the other hand, statistical methods are consistent and can handle vast numbers of time series seamlessly. Still, judgment is the only option for producing estimates for the future when data are not available.

Judgmental biases apply even to forecasters with domain or technical expertise. As such, the expert knowledge elicitation (EKE; Bolger and Wright, 2017) literature has examined many ways of designing methods so as to reduce the danger of biased judgments from experts. Strategies for mitigating humans' biases include decomposing the task (Edmundson, 1990; Webby, O'Connor, and Edmundson, 2005), offering alternative representations (tabular versus graphical formats; see Harvey and Bolger, 1996) and providing feedback (Petropoulos, Goodwin, and Fildes, 2017).

The previous discussion has focused on judgmental forecasts that are produced directly. However, the judgment in forecasting can also be applied in the form of interventions (adjustments) to the statistical forecasts that are produced by a forecasting support system. Model-based forecasts are adjusted by experts frequently in operations/supply chain settings (Fildes et al., 2009, Franses and Legerstee, 2010). Such revised forecasts often differ significantly from the statistical ones (Franses and Legerstee, 2009); however, small adjustments are also observed, and are linked with a sense of ownership of the forecasters (Fildes et al., 2009). Experts tend to adjust upwards more often than downwards (Franses and Legerstee, 2010), which can be attributed to an optimism bias (Trapero, Pedregal, Fildes, and Kourentzes, 2013), but such upwards adjustments are far less effective (Fildes et al., 2009). The empirical evidence also suggests that experts can reduce the forecasting error when the adjustment size is not too large (Trapero et al., 2013).

Another point in the forecasting process at which judgment can be applied is that of model selection. Assuming that modern forecasting software systems offer many alternative models, managers often rely on their judgment in order to select the most suitable one, rather than pushing the magic button labelled "automatic selection" (which selects between models based on algorithmic/statistical approaches, for example, using an information criterion). The study by Petropoulos et al. (2018) is the first to offer some empirical evidence on the performance of judgmental versus algorithmic selection. When the task follows a decomposition approach (selection of the applicable time series patterns, which is then translated to the selection of the respective forecasting model), on average the judgmental selection is as good as selecting via statistics, while humans more often have the advantage of avoiding the worst of the candidate models.

Two strategies are particularly useful for enhancing the judgmental forecasting performance. The first strategy is a combination of statistics and judgment (Blattberg and Hoch, 1990). This can be applied intuitively to cases where statistical and judgmental forecasts have been produced independently, but it works even in cases where the managerial input could be affected by the model output, as in judgmental adjustments. Several studies have shown that adjusting the adjustments can lead not only to an improved forecasting performance (Fildes et al., 2009; Franses and Legerstee, 2011), but also to a better inventory performance (Wang and Petropoulos, 2016). The second strategy is the mathematical aggregation of the individual judgments that have been produced independently, also known as the "wisdom of crowds" (Surowiecki, 2005). In Petropoulos, Kourentzes, Nikolopoulos, and Siemsen's (2018) study of model selection, the aggregation of the selections of five individuals led to a forecasting performance that was significantly superior to that of algorithmic selection.

In summary, we observe that, over time, the research focus has shifted from producing judgmental forecasts directly to adjusting statistical forecasts and selecting between forecasts judgmentally. The value added to the forecasting process by judgment increases as we shift further from merely producing a forecast judgmentally.

However, given the exponential increase in the number of series that need to be forecast by a modern organisation (for instance, the number of stock-keeping units in a large retailer may very well exceed 100,000), it is not always either possible or practical to allocate the resources required to manage each series manually.

On the Value of Explanatory Variables

The use of exogenous explanatory variables would seem an obvious way of improving the forecast accuracy. That is, rather than relying only on the history of the series that we wish to forecast, we can utilise other relevant and available information as well.

In some circumstances, the data from explanatory variables can improve the forecast accuracy significantly. One such situation is electricity demand forecasting, where current and past temperatures can be used as explanatory variables (Ben Taieb and Hyndman, 2014). The electricity demand is highly sensitive to the ambient temperature, with hot days leading to the use of air-conditioning and cold days leading to the use of heating. Mild days (with temperatures around 20 °C) tend to have the lowest electricity demand.

However, often the use of explanatory variables is not as helpful as one might imagine. First, the explanatory variables themselves may need to be forecast. In the case of temperatures, good forecasts are available from meteorological services up to a few days ahead, and these can be used to help forecast the electricity demand. However, in many other cases, forecasting the explanatory variables may be just as difficult as forecasting the variable of interest. For example, Ashley (1988) argues that the forecasts of many macroeconomic variables are so inaccurate that they should not be used as explanatory variables. Ma, Fildes, and Huang (2016) demonstrate that including competitive promotional variables as explanatory variables for retail sales is of limited value, but that adding focal variables leads to substantial improvements over time series modelling with promotional adjustments.

A second problem arises due to the assumption that the relationships between the forecast variable and the explanatory variables will continue. When this assumption breaks down, we face model misspecification.

A third issue is that the relationship between the forecast variable and the explanatory variables needs to be strong and estimated precisely (Brodie, Danaher, Kumar, and Leeflang, 2001). If the relationship is weak, there is little value in including the explanatory variables in the model.

It is possible to assess the value of explanatory variables and to test whether either of these problems is prevalent by comparing the forecasts from three separate approaches: (1) a purely time series approach, ignoring any information that may be available in explanatory variables; (2) an ex-post forecast, building a model using explanatory variables but then using the future values of those variables when producing an estimate; and (3) an ex-ante forecast, using the same model but substituting the explanatory variables with their forecasts.

Athanasopoulos, Hyndman, Song, and Wu (2011) carried out this comparison in the context of tourism data, as part of the 2010 tourism forecasting competition. In their case, the explanatory variables included the relative CPI and prices between the source and destination countries. Not only were the purely time series forecasts better than the models that included explanatory variables, but also the ex-ante forecasts were better than the ex-post forecasts. This suggests that the relationships between tourism numbers and the explanatory variables changed over the course of the study. Further supporting this conclusion is the fact that time-varying parameter models did better than fixed parameter models. However, the time-varying parameter models did not do as well as the purely time series models, showing that the forecasts of the explanatory variables were also problematic.

To summarise, explanatory variables can be useful, but only under two specific conditions: (1) when there are accurate forecasts of the explanatory variables available; and (2) when the relationships between the forecasts and the explanatory variables are likely to continue into the forecast period. Both conditions are satisfied for electricity demand, but neither condition is satisfied for tourism demand. Unless both conditions are satisfied, time series forecasting methods are better than using explanatory variables.

IV. WHAT WE DON'T KNOW

On Thin/Fat Tails and Black Swans

Another misconception that prevailed in statistical education for a long time was that normal distributions could approximate practically all outcomes/events, including the errors of statistical models. Furthermore, there was little or no discussion of what could be done when normality could not be assured. Now, it is accepted that Gaussian distributions, although extremely useful, are of limited value for approximating some areas of application (Cooke, Nieboer, and Misiewicz, 2014; Makridakis and Taleb, 2009), and in particular those that refer to forecast error distributions, describing the uncertainty in forecasting. This paper has emphasized the critical role of uncertainty and expressed our conviction that providing forecasts without specifying the levels of uncertainty associated with them amounts to nothing more than fortune-telling. However, it is one thing to identify uncertainty, but quite another to get prepared to face it realistically and effectively. Furthermore, it must be clear that it is not possible to deal with uncertainty without either incurring a cost or accepting lower opportunity benefits.

Table I.2 distinguishes four types of events, following Rumsfeld's classification. In Quadrant I, the known/knowns category, the forecasting accuracy depends on the variance (randomness) of the data, and can be assessed from past information. Moreover, the uncertainty is well defined and can be measured, usually following a normal distribution with thin tails. In Quadrant II (known/unknowns), which includes events like recessions, the accuracy of forecasting cannot be assessed, as the timing of a recession, crisis or boom cannot be known and their consequences can vary widely from one recession to another. The uncertainty in this quadrant is considerably greater, while its implications are much harder to assess than those in Quadrant I. It is characterized by fat tails, extending well beyond the three sigmas of the normal curve. A considerable problem that amplifies the level of uncertainty is that, during a recession, a forecast, such as the sales of a product, moves from Quadrant I to Quadrant II, which increases the uncertainty considerably and makes it much harder to prepare to face it.

Things can get still more uncertain in Quadrant III, for two reasons. First, judgmental biases influence events; for instance, people fail to address obviously high-impact dangers before they spiral out of control (Wucker, 2016). Second, it is not possible to predict the implications of self-fulfilling and self-defeating prophecies for the actions and reactions of market players. This category includes strategy and other important decisions where the forecast or the anticipation of an action or plan can modify the future course of events, mainly when there is a zero-sum game where the pie is fixed. Finally, in Quadrant IV, any form of forecasting is difficult by definition, requiring the analysis and evaluation of past data to determine the extent of the uncertainty and risk involved. Taleb, the author of *Black Swan* (Taleb, 2007), is more pessimistic, stating that the only way to be prepared to face black swans is by having established antifragile strategies that would allow one to dampen the negative consequences of any black swans that may appear. Although other writers have suggested insurance and robust strategies for coping with uncertainty and risk, Taleb's work has brought renewed attention to the issue of highly improbable, high-stakes events and has contributed to making people aware of the need to be prepared to face them, such as, for instance, having enough cash reserves to survive a significant financial crisis like that of 2007–2008 or having invested in an adequate capacity to handle a boom.

Table I.2 Accuracy of Forecasting, Type of Uncertainty, and Extent of Risk

		Known	Unknown
Uncertainty	**Known**	**I. Known/known** (Law of large numbers, independent events, e.g. sales of toothbrushes, shoes or beer) Forecasting: Accurate (depending on variance) Uncertainty: Thin-tailed and measurable Risks: Manageable, can be minimized	**III. Unknown/known** (Cognitive biases, strategic moves, e.g. Uber reintroducing AVs in a super-competitive industry) Forecasting: Accuracy depends on several factors Uncertainty: Extensive and hard to measure Risk: Depends on the extent of biases, strategy success
	Unknown	**II. Known/unknown** (Unusual/special conditions, e.g. the effects of the 2007/2008 recession on the economy) Forecasting: Inaccuracy can vary considerably Uncertainty: Fat-tailed, hard to measure Risks: Can be substantial, tough to manage	**IV. Unknown/unknown** (Black swans: Low-probability, high-impact events, e.g. the implications of a total collapse in global trade) Forecasting: Impossible Uncertainty: Unmeasurable Risks: Unmanageable except through costly antifragile strategies
		Known	**Unknown**
		Forecast Events	

What needs to be emphasised is that dealing with any uncertainty involves a cost. The uncertainty that the sales forecast may be below the actual demand can be dealt with by keeping enough inventories, thus avoiding the risk of losing customers. However, such inventories cost money to keep and require warehouses in which to be stored. In other cases, the uncertainty that a share price may decrease can be dealt with through diversification, buying baskets of stocks, thereby reducing the chance of large losses; however, one then foregoes profits when individual shares increase more than the average. Similarly, antifragile actions such as keeping extra cash for unexpected crises also involve opportunity costs, as such cash could instead have been invested in productive areas to increase income and/or reduce costs and increase profits.

The big challenge, eloquently expressed by Bertrand Russell, is that we need to learn to live without the support of comforting fairy tales; he also added that it is perhaps the chief achievement of philosophy "to teach us how to live without certainty, and yet without being paralysed by hesitation." An investor should not stop investing merely because of the risks involved.

On Causality

Since the early years, humans have always been trying to answer the "why" question: what are the causal forces behind an observed result. Estimating the statistical correlation between two variables tells us little about the cause–effect relationship between them. Their association may be due to a lurking (extraneous) variable, unknown forces, or even chance. In the real world, there are just too many intervening, confounding and mediating variables, and it is hard to assess their impacts using traditional statistical methods. Randomised controlled trials (RCTs) have been long considered the "gold standard" in designing scientific experiments for clinical trials. However, as with every laboratory experiment, RCTs are limited in the sense that, in most cases, the subjects are not observed in their natural environment (medical trials may be an exception). Furthermore, RCTs may be quite impossible in cases such as the comparison of two national economic policies.

An important step towards defining causality was taken by Granger (1969), who proposed a statistical test for determining whether the (lagged) values of one time series can be used for predicting the values of another series. Even if it is argued that Granger causality only identifies predictive causality (the ability to predict one series based on another series), not true causality, it can still be used to identify useful predictors, such as promotions as explanatory variables for future sales.

Structural equation models (SEMs) have also been being used for a long time for modelling the causal relationships between variables and for assessing unobservable constructs. However, the linear-in-nature SEMs make assumptions with regard to the model form (which variables are included in the equations) and the distribution of the error. Pearl (2000) extends SEMs from linear to nonparametric, which allows the total effect to be estimated without any explicit modelling assumptions. Pearl and Mackenzie (2018) describe how we can now answer questions about 'how' or 'what if I do' (intervention) and 'why' or 'what if I had done' (counterfactuals). Two tools have been instrumental in these developments. One is a qualitative depiction of the model that includes the assumptions and relationships among the variables of interest; such graphical depictions are called causal diagrams (Pearl, 1995). The second is the development of the causal calculus that allows for interventions by modifying a set of functions in the model (Huang and Valtorta, 2012; Pearl, 1993; Shpitser and Pearl, 2006). These tools provide the means of dealing with situations in which confounders and/or mediators would render the methods of traditional statistics and probabilities impossible. The theoretical developments of Pearl and his colleagues are yet to be evaluated empirically.

On Luck (and Other Factors) versus Skills

A few lucky investing decisions are usually sufficient for stock-pickers to come to be regarded as stock market gurus. Similarly, a notoriously bad weather, economic or political forecast is sometimes sufficient to destroy the career of an established professional. Unfortunately, the human mind tends to focus on the salient and vibrant pieces of information that make a story more interesting and compelling. In such cases, we should always keep in mind that eventually "expert" stock-pickers' luck will run out. Similarly, a single inaccurate forecast does not make one a bad forecaster. Regression to the mean has taught us that an excellent landing for pilot trainees is usually followed by a worse one, and vice versa. The same applies to the accuracy of forecasts.

Regardless of the convincing evidence of regression to the mean, we humans tend to attribute successes to our abilities and skills, but failures to bad luck. Moreover, in the event of failures, we are very skillful at inventing stories, theories and explanations for what went wrong and why we did actually know what would have happened (hindsight bias). The negative relationship between actual skill/expertise and beliefs in our abilities has also been examined extensively, and is termed the Dunning-Kruger effect: the least-skilled people tend to over-rate their abilities.

Tetlock, Gardner, and Richards (2015), in their *Superforecasting* book, enlist the qualities of "superforecasters" (individuals that consistently have higher skill/luck ratios than regular forecasters). Such qualities include, among others, a 360° "dragonfly" view, balancing under- and overreacting to information, balancing under- and overconfidence, searching for causal forces, decomposing the problem into smaller, more manageable ones, and looking back to evaluate objectively what has happened. However, even superstars are allowed to have a bad day from time to time.

If we are in a position to provide our forecasters with the right tools and we allow them to learn from their mistakes, then their skills will improve over time. We need to convince companies not to operate under a one-big-mistake-and-you're-out policy (Goodwin, 2017). The performances of forecasters should be tracked and monitored over time and should be compared to those of other forecasts, either statistical or judgmental. Also, linking motivation with an improved accuracy directly could aid the forecast accuracy further (Fildes et al., 2009); regardless of how intuitive this argument might be, there are plenty of companies that still operate with motivational schemes that directly contradict the need for accuracy, as is the case where bonuses are given to salesmen who have exceeded their forecasts.

Goodwin (2017) suggests that, instead of evaluating the outcomes of forecasts based solely on their resulting accuracies, we should turn our attention to evaluating the forecasting process that was used to produce the forecasts in the first place. This is particularly useful when evaluating forecasts over time is either not feasible or impractical, as is the case with one-off forecasts such as the introduction of a significant new product. In any case, even if the forecasting process is designed and implemented appropriately, we should still expect the forecasts to be 'off' in about 1 instance out of 20 assuming 95% prediction intervals, a scenario which is not that remote.

V. CONCLUSIONS

Although forecasting in the hard sciences can attain remarkable levels of accuracy, such is not the case in the social domains, where large errors are possible and all predictions are uncertain. Forecasts are indispensable for decisions of which the success depends a good deal on the accuracy of these forecasts. This paper provides a survey of the state of the art of forecasting in social sciences that is aimed at non-forecasting experts who want to be informed on the latest developments in the field, and possibly to figure out how to improve the accuracy of their own predictions.

Over time, forecasting has moved from the domains of the religious and the superstitious to that of the scientific, accumulating concrete knowledge that is then used to improve its theoretical foundation and increase its practical value. The outcome has been enhancements in forecast accuracy and improvements in estimating the uncertainty of its predictions. A major contributor to the advancement of the field has been the empirical studies that have provided objective evidence for comparing the accuracies of the various methods and validating different hypotheses. Despite all its challenges, forecasting for social settings has improved a lot over the years.

Our discussions above suggest that more progress needs to be made in forecasting under uncertain conditions, such as unstable economic environments or when fat tails are present. Also, despite the significant advances that have been achieved in research around judgment, there are still many open questions, such as the conditions under which judgment is most likely to outperform statistical models and how to minimise the negative effects of judgmental heuristics and biases. More empirical studies are needed to better understand the added value of collecting data on exogenous variables and the domains in which their inclusion in forecasting models is likely to provide practical improvements in forecasting performances. Another research area that requires rigorous empirical investigation is that of causality, and the corresponding theoretical developments.

These are areas that future forecasting competitions can focus on. We would like to see future competitions include live forecasting tasks for high-profile economic series. We would also like to see more competitions exploring the value of exogenous variables. Competitions focusing on specific domains are also very important. In the past, we have seen competitions on neural networks (Crone, Hibon, and Nikolopoulos, 2011), tourism demand (Athanasopoulos et al., 2011) and energy (Hong, Pinson, and Fan, 2014; Hong et al., 2016; Hong, Xie, and Black, 2019); we would also like to see competitions that focus on intermittent demand and retailing, among others. Furthermore, it would be great to see more work done on forecasting one-off events, in line with the Good Judgment[2] project. Last but not least, we need a better understanding of how improvements in forecast accuracy translate into 'profit,' and how to measure the cost of forecast errors.

NOTES

1. Ioannidis' paper is one of the most viewed/downloaded papers published in *PLoS*, with more than 2.3 million views and more than 350K downloads.
2. www.gjopen.com/.

REFERENCES

Adya, M., Collopy, F., Armstrong, J. S., and Kennedy, M. (2001). Automatic identification of time series features for rule-based forecasting. *International Journal of Forecasting* 17 (2): 143–157.

Ahmed, N. K., Atiya, A. F., Gayar, N. E., and El-Shishiny, H. (2010). An empirical comparison of machine learning models for time series forecasting. *Econometric Reviews* 29 (5–6): 594–621.

Akaike, H. (1977). On entropy maximization principle. In: *Application of Statistics* (pp. 27–41). North-Holland Publishing Company.

Andrawis, R. R., Atiya, A. F., and El-Shishiny, H. (2011). Combination of long-term and short-term forecasts, with application to tourism demand forecasting. *International Journal of Forecasting* 27 (3): 870–886.

Armstrong, J. S. (2006). Findings from evidence-based forecasting: Methods for reducing forecast error. *International Journal of Forecasting* 22 (3): 583–598.

Ashley, R. (1988). On the relative worth of recent macroeconomic forecasts. *International Journal of Forecasting* 4 (3): 363–376.

Askanazi, R., Diebold, F. X., Schorfheide, F., and Shin, M. (2018). On the comparison of interval forecasts. https://www.sas.upenn.edu/ fdiebold/papers2/Eval.pdf

Asmundsson, J. (2018). The big problem with machine learning algorithms. Bloomberg News. https://www.bloomberg.com/news/articles/2018-10-09/the-big-problem-with-machine-learning-algorithms

Assimakopoulos, V., and Nikolopoulos, K. (2000). The theta model: A decomposition approach to forecasting. *International Journal of Forecasting* 16 (4): 521–530.

Athanasopoulos, G., Hyndman, R. J., Kourentzes, N., and Petropoulos, F. (2017). Forecasting with temporal hierarchies. *European Journal of Operational Research* 262 (1): 60–74.

Athanasopoulos, G., Hyndman, R. J., Song, H., and Wu, D. C. (2011). The tourism forecasting competition. *International Journal of Forecasting* 27 (3): 822–844.

Ben Taieb, S., and Hyndman, R. J. (2014). A gradient boosting approach to the Kaggle load forecasting competition. *International Journal of Forecasting* 30 (2): 382–394.

Bergmeir, C., Hyndman, R. J., and Benítez, J. M. (2016). Bagging exponential smoothing methods using STL decomposition and Box–Cox transformation. *International Journal of Forecasting* 32 (2): 303–312.

Blattberg, R. C., and Hoch, S. J. (1990). Database models and managerial intuition: 50% model + 50% manager. *Management Science* 36 (8): 887–899.

Bolger, F., and Wright, G. (2017). Use of expert knowledge to anticipate the future: Issues, analysis and directions. *International Journal of Forecasting* 33 (1): 230–243.

Box, G. E. P., Jenkins, G. M., Reinsel, G. C., and Ljung, G. M. (2015). *Time series analysis: Forecasting and control* (5th ed.). Wiley.

Brodie, R. J., Danaher, P. J., Kumar, V., and Leeflang, P. S. H. (2001). Econometric models for forecasting market share. In J. S. Armstrong (Ed.), *Principles of forecasting: A handbook for researchers and practitioners* (pp. 597–611). Springer US.

Brown, R. G. (1959). *Statistical forecasting for inventory control*. McGraw-Hill.

Brown, R. G. (1963). *Smoothing, forecasting and prediction of discrete time series*. Courier Corporation.

Burton, J. (1986). Robert FitzRoy and the early history of the Meteorological Office. *British Journal for the History of Science* 19 (2): 147–176.

Camerer, C. F., Dreber, A., Forsell, E., et al. (2016). Evaluating replicability of laboratory experiments in economics. *Science* 351 (6280): 1433–1436.

Carbone, R., and Gorr, W. L. (1985). Accuracy of judgmental forecasting of time series. *Decision Sciences* 16 (2): 153–160.

Clemen, R. T. (1989). Combining forecasts: A review and annotated bibliography. *International Journal of Forecasting* 5 (4): 559–583.

Cooke, R. M., Nieboer, D., and Misiewicz, J. (2014). *Fat-tailed distributions: data, diagnostics and dependence*. Wiley.

Crone, S. F., Hibon, M., and Nikolopoulos, K. (2011). Advances in forecasting with neural networks? Empirical evidence from the NN3 competition on time series prediction. *International Journal of Forecasting* 27 (3): 635–660.

Dewald, W. G., Thursby, J. G., and Anderson, R. G. (1986). Replication in empirical economics: The Journal of Money, Credit and Banking project. *The American Economic Review* 76 (4): 587–603.

Edmundson, R. H. (1990). Decomposition; a strategy for judgemental forecasting. *Journal of Forecasting* 9 (4): 305–314.

Fildes, R. (1989). Evaluation of aggregate and individual forecast method selection rules. *Management Science* 35 (9): 1056–1065.

Fildes, R., Goodwin, P., Lawrence, M., and Nikolopoulos, K. (2009). Effective forecasting and judgmental adjustments: An empirical evaluation and strategies for improvement in supply-chain planning. *International Journal of Forecasting* 25 (1): 3–23.

Fildes, R., and Petropoulos, F. (2015). Simple versus complex selection rules for forecasting many time series. *Journal of Business Research* 68 (8): 1692–1701.

Fildes, R., and Stekler, H. (2002). The state of macroeconomic forecasting. *Journal of Macroeconomics* 24 (4): 435–468.

Franses, P. H. (2016). A simple test for a bubble based on growth and acceleration. *Computational Statistics & Data Analysis* 100, 160–169.

Franses, P. H., and Legerstee, R. (2009). Properties of expert adjustments on model-based SKU-level forecasts. *International Journal of Forecasting* 25 (1): 35–47.

Franses, P. H., and Legerstee, R. (2010). Do experts' adjustments on model-based SKU-level forecasts improve forecast quality? *Journal of Forecasting* 29 (3): 331–340.

Franses, P. H., and Legerstee, R. (2011). Combining SKU-level sales forecasts from models and experts. *Expert Systems with Applications* 38 (3): 2365–2370.

Freedman, D. H. (2010, November). Lies, damned lies, and medical science. *The Atlantic.* https://www.theatlantic.com/magazine/archive/2010/11/lies-damned-lies-and-medical-science/308269/

Gneiting, T., and Raftery, A. E. (2007). Strictly proper scoring rules, prediction, and estimation. *Journal of the American Statistical Association* 102 (477): 359–378.

Goodwin, P. (2017). *Forewarned: A sceptic's guide to prediction*. Biteback Publishing.

Granger, C. W. J. (1969). Investigating causal relations by econometric models and cross-spectral methods. *Econometrica* 37 (3): 424–438.

Gresnigt, F., Kole, E., and Franses, P. H. (2015). Interpreting financial market crashes as earthquakes: A new early warning system for medium term crashes. *Journal of Banking & Finance* 56, 123–139.

Halleio, E. (1704). Astronomiae cometicae synopsis, Autore Edmundo Halleio apud Oxonienses. Geometriae Professore Saviliano, & Reg. Soc. S. *Philosophical Transactions of the Royal Society of London Series I* 24, 1882–1899.

Harvey, N. (1995). Why are judgments less consistent in less predictable task situations? *Organizational Behavior and Human Decision Processes* 63 (3): 247–263.

Harvey, N., and Bolger, F. (1996). Graphs versus tables: Effects of data presentation format on judgemental forecasting. *International Journal of Forecasting* 12 (1): 119–137.

Heilemann, U., and Stekler, H. O. (2013). Has the accuracy of macroeconomic forecasts for Germany improved? *German Economic Review* 14 (2): 235–253.

Hibon, M., and Evgeniou, T. (2005). To combine or not to combine: Selecting among forecasts and their combinations. *International Journal of Forecasting* 21, 15–24.

Hong, T., Pinson, P., and Fan S. (2014). Global energy forecasting competition 2012. *International Journal of Forecasting* 30 (2): 357–363.

Hong, T., Pinson, P., Fan, S., et al. (2016). Probabilistic energy forecasting: Global energy forecasting competition 2014 and beyond. *International Journal of Forecasting* 32 (3): 896–913.

Hong, T., Xie, J., and Black, J. (2019). Global energy forecasting competition 2017: Hierarchical probabilistic load forecasting. *International Journal of Forecasting* 35(4): 1389–1399.

Huang, Y., and Valtorta, M. (2012). Pearl's calculus of intervention is complete. arXiv preprint arXiv:1206.6831.

Hyndman, R. J., and Athanasopoulos, G. (2018). *Forecasting: Principles and practice* (2nd ed.), OTexts.

Hyndman, R., Athanasopoulos, G., Bergmeir, C., et al. (2018). Forecast: Forecasting functions for time series and linear models. http://pkg.robjhyndman.com/forecast

Hyndman, R. J., and Khandakar, Y. (2008). Automatic time series forecasting: The forecast package for R. *Journal of Statistical Software* 27 (3): 1–22.

Hyndman, R. J., and Koehler, A. B. (2006). Another look at measures of forecast accuracy. *International Journal of Forecasting* 22 (4): 679–688.

Hyndman, R. J., Koehler, A. B., Snyder, R. D., and Grose, S. (2002). A state space framework for automatic forecasting using exponential smoothing methods. *International Journal of Forecasting* 18 (3): 439–454.

Ioannidis, J. P. A. (2005). Why most published research findings are false. *PLoS Medicine* 2 (8): Article e124.

Kistler, R., Kalnay, E., Collins, W., et al. (2001). The NCEP–NCAR 50-year reanalysis: Monthly means CD-ROM and documentation. *Bulletin of the American Meteorological Society* 82 (2): 247–268.

Kolassa, S. (2011). Combining exponential smoothing forecasts using akaike weights. *International Journal of Forecasting* 27 (2): 238–251.

Kourentzes, N., Barrow, D., and Petropoulos, F. (2019). Another look at forecast selection and combination: Evidence from forecast pooling. *International Journal of Production Economics* 209, 226–235.

Kourentzes, N., Petropoulos, F., and Trapero, J. R. (2014). Improving forecasting by estimating time series structural components across multiple frequencies. *International Journal of Forecasting* 30 (2): 291–302.

Langer, E. J. (1975). The illusion of control. *Journal of Personality and Social Psychology* 32 (2): 311–328.

Lawrence, M. J., Edmundson, R. H., and O'Connor, M. J. (1985). An examination of the accuracy of judgmental extrapolation of time series. *International Journal of Forecasting* 1 (1): 25–35.

Lawrence, M., Goodwin, P., O'Connor, M., and Önkal, D. (2006). Judgmental forecasting: A review of progress over the last 25 years. *International Journal of Forecasting* 22 (3): 493–518.

Lawrence, M., and Makridakis, S. (1989). Factors affecting judgmental forecasts and confidence intervals. *Organizational Behavior and Human Decision Processes* 43 (2): 172–187.

Ma, S., Fildes, R., and Huang, T. (2016). Demand forecasting with high dimensional data: The case of SKU retail sales forecasting with intra- and inter-category promotional information. *European Journal of Operational Research* 249 (1): 245–257.

Makridakis, S. (1986). The art and science of forecasting: An assessment and future directions. *International Journal of Forecasting* 2 (1): 15–39.

Makridakis, S. (1989). Why combining works? *International Journal of Forecasting* 5 (4): 601–603.

Makridakis, S., Andersen, A., Carbone, R., et al. (1982). The accuracy of extrapolation (time series) methods: Results of a forecasting competition. *Journal of Forecasting* 1 (2): 111–153.

Makridakis, S., Chatfield, C., Hibon, M., et al. (1993). The M2-competition: A real-time judgmentally based forecasting study. *International Journal of Forecasting* 9 (1): 5–22.

Makridakis, S., and Hibon, M. (1979). Accuracy of forecasting: An empirical investigation. *Journal of the Royal Statistical Society, Series A* 142 (2): 97–145.

Makridakis, S., and Hibon, M. (2000). The M3 competition: Results, conclusions, and implications. *International Journal of Forecasting* 16 (4): 451–476.

Makridakis, S., Spiliotis, E., and Assimakopoulos, V. (2018a). The M4 competition: Results, findings, conclusion and way forward. *International Journal of Forecasting* 34 (4): 802–808.

Makridakis, S., Spiliotis, E., and Assimakopoulos, V. (2018b). Statistical and machine learning forecasting methods: Concerns and ways forward. *PloS One* 13 (3): Article e0194889.

Makridakis, S., Spiliotis, E., and Assimakopoulos, V. (2020). The M4 competition: 100,000 time series and 61 forecasting methods. *International Journal of Forecasting* 36 (1): 54–74.

Makridakis, S., and Taleb, N. (2009). Decision making and planning under low levels of predictability. *International Journal of Forecasting* 25 (4): 716–733.

Mente, A., and Yusuf, S. (2018). Evolving evidence about diet and health. *The Lancet Public Health* 3 (9): e408–e409.

Micha, R., Wallace, S. K., and Mozaffarian, D. (2010). Red and processed meat consumption and risk of incident coronary heart disease, stroke, and diabetes mellitus: A systematic review and meta-analysis. *Circulation* 121 (21): 2271–2283.

Montero-Manso, P., Athanasopoulos, G., Hyndman, R. J., and Talagala, T. S. (2020). FFORMA: Feature-based forecast model averaging. *International Journal of Forecasting* 36 (1): 86–92.

O'Connor, M., Remus, W., and Griggs, K. (1993). Judgmental forecasting in times of change. *International Journal of Forecasting* 9 (2): 163–172.

Pant, P. N., and Starbuck, W. H. (1990). Innocents in the forest: Forecasting and research methods. *Journal of Management* 16 (2): 433–460.

Pearl, J. (1993). Comment: Graphical models, causality and intervention. *Statistical Science* 8 (3): 266–269.

Pearl, J. (1995). Causal diagrams for empirical research. *Biometrika* 82 (4): 669–688.

Pearl, J. (2000). Causality: *Models, reasoning, and inference*. Cambridge University Press.

Pearl, J., and Mackenzie D. (2018). *The book of why: The new science of cause and effect*. Allen Lane.

Petropoulos F., Goodwin P., and Fildes, R. (2017). Using a rolling training approach to improve judgmental extrapolations elicited from forecasters with technical knowledge. *International Journal of Forecasting* 33 (1): 314–324.

Petropoulos F., Hyndman, R. J., and Bergmeir, C. (2018a). Exploring the sources of uncertainty: Why does bagging for time series forecasting work? *European Journal of Operational Research* 268 (2): 545–554.

Petropoulos, F., Kourentzes, N., Nikolopoulos, K., and Siemsen, E. (2018b). Judgmental selection of forecasting models. *Journal of Operations Management* 60: 34–46.

Petropoulos, F., Makridakis, S., Assimakopoulos, V., and Nikolopoulos, K. (2014). 'Horses for courses' in demand forecasting. *European Journal of Operational Research* 237, 152–163.

Reimers, S., and Harvey, N. (2011). Sensitivity to autocorrelation in judgmental time series forecasting. *International Journal of Forecasting* 27 (4): 1196–1214.

Saha, S., Moorthi, S., Wu, X., et al. (2014). The NCEP climate forecast system, version 2. *Journal of Climate* 27 (6): 2185–2208.

Salinas, D., Flunkert, V., and Gasthaus, J. (2017). DeepAR: Probabilistic forecasting with autoregressive recurrent networks. arXiv preprint arXiv:1704.04110.

Sanders, N. R. (1992). Accuracy of judgmental forecasts: A comparison. *Omega* 20 (3): 353–364.

Satariano, A., and Kumar, N. (2017). The massive hedge fund betting on AI. Bloomberg News. https://www.bloomberg.com/news/features/2017-09-27/the-massive-hedge-fund-betting-on-ai

Schnaars, S. P. (1989). *Megamistakes: Forecasting and the myth of rapid technological change* (29th ed.). The Free Press.

Scott, M. (2015). *Delphi: A history of the center of the ancient world.* Princeton University Press.

Shpitser, I., and Pearl, J. (2006). Identification of conditional interventional distributions. In: *Proceedings of the 22nd Conference on Uncertainty in Artificial Intelligence* (pp. 437–444). UAI 2006.

Stekler, H. O. (2007). The future of macroeconomic forecasting: Understanding the forecasting process. *International Journal of Forecasting* 23 (2): 237–248.

Stekler, H., and Symington, H. (2016). Evaluating qualitative forecasts: The FOMC minutes, 2006–2010. *International Journal of Forecasting* 32 (2): 559–570.

Surowiecki, J. (2005). *The wisdom of crowds: Why the many are smarter than the few* (new ed.). Abacus.

Taleb, N. N. (2007). *The black swan: The impact of the highly improbable.* Penguin.

Tashman, L. J. (2000). Out-of-sample tests of forecasting accuracy: An analysis and review. *International Journal of Forecasting* 16 (4): 437–450.

Tetlock, P., Gardner, D., and Richards, J. (2015). *Superforecasting: The art and science of prediction* (unabridged ed.). Audible Studios on Brilliance.

Tetlock, P. E. (2006). *Expert political judgment: How good is it? How can we know?* (new ed.). Princeton University Press.

Timmermann, A. (2006). Forecast combinations. In: G. Elliott, C.W.J. Granger, and A. Timmermann (Eds.), *Handbook of economic forecasting,* vol. 1 (pp. 135–196). Elsevier.

Trapero, J. R., Pedregal, D. J., Fildes, R., and Kourentzes, N. (2013). Analysis of judgmental adjustments in the presence of promotions. *International Journal of Forecasting* 29 (2): 234–243.

Wang, J., and Wang, J. (2017). Forecasting stochastic neural network based on financial empirical mode decomposition. *Neural Networks* 90: 8–20.

Wang, X., and Petropoulos, F. (2016). To select or to combine? The inventory performance of model and expert forecasts. *International Journal of Productions Research* 54 (17): 5271–5282.

Wang, X., Smith-Miles, K., and Hyndman, R. (2009). Rule induction for forecasting method selection: Meta-learning the characteristics of univariate time series. *Neurocomputing* 72 (10–12): 2581–2594.

Webby, R., O'Connor, M., and Edmundson, B. (2005). Forecasting support systems for the incorporation of event information: An empirical investigation. *International Journal of Forecasting* 21 (3): 411–423.

Wen, R., Torkkola, K., Narayanaswamy, B., and Madeka, D. (2017). A multi-horizon quantile recurrent forecaster. arXiv preprint arXiv:1711.11053

Winkler, R. L. (1972). A decision-theoretic approach to interval estimation. *Journal of the American Statistical Association* 67 (337): 187–191.

Wucker, M. (2016). *The gray rhino: How to recognize and act on the obvious dangers we ignore.* St. Martin's Press.

CHAPTER **1**

Artificial Intelligence and Machine Learning in Forecasting

I t is five years since publication of our initial collection, *Business Forecasting: Practical Problems and Solutions* in 2015. Since that time the forecasting landscape has undergone a major transformation, and is now dominated by the explosion of interest in the role of artificial intelligence (AI) and machine learning (ML).

These five years have been a very exciting time of experimentation – applying existing AI/ML methods to time-series problems, and research into creating entirely new or hybrid methods. Research endeavors such as the M4 (2018) and M5 (2020) Forecasting Competitions provide important data to help evaluate the key questions we need to ask:

- Will AI/ML fundamentally change the way we do forecasting?
- Will AI/ML fundamentally improve our forecasting performance (both accuracy, and our understanding of forecast uncertainty)?
- Can AI/ML address the psychological and process issues that so greatly impact the real-life practice of forecasting?

This last question is not the least important. The value of better forecasting is delivered through better decision making (and the resulting better outcomes). So solving the statistical side of forecasting, alone, does not solve the business forecasting problem.

This chapter begins with three somewhat technical discussions of ML and deep learning, including neural networks, with examples of their application in online retail and energy. These three, along with Kolassa's critical assessment of deep and machine learning, are meant to provide objective tutorials on the use of these methods in forecasting, without hiding the critical issues users will face.

The next two pieces (and their accompanying commentaries) revolve around a forward look at the impact of artificial intelligence by Spyros Makridakis, originally published in a five-part series in *Foresight: The International Journal of Applied Forecasting*. Here, we get competing perspectives on what AI will be able to deliver to affect our lives.

The next four pieces delve into other areas impacted by AI/ML, including implications for supply chain and the forecasting process. We know, for example, that the review and manual override of computer-generated forecasts can be a considerable drain on management resources, with overrides often resulting in a degradation of forecast accuracy. Chase and Baker illustrate alternative ways ML can augment the role of a demand planner by identifying which forecasts are likely to benefit from adjustment, and which should be left alone. This "ML-assisted demand planning" can both save the planner time and also result in more accurate forecasts.

This chapter ends with a recap of findings from the M4 competition – the key takeaways for practitioners. We encourage readers to find more complete M4 coverage in a special issue of the *International Journal of Forecasting* 36(1), January–March 2020, which includes 35 articles on results, analysis, and commentary.

* * *

1.1 DEEP LEARNING FOR FORECASTING[*]

Tim Januschowski, Jan Gasthaus, Yuyang Wang, Syama Sundar Rangapuram, and Laurent Callot

While the term **deep learning** (DL) wasn't widely used until the 2010s, the techniques it refers to have been in development since the 1950s, namely artificial neural networks (NN or ANN for short). DL has scored major successes in image recognition, natural language processing (e.g., machine translation and speech recognition), and autonomous agents such as Google Deep Mind's AlphaGo. It is often used as a synonym for artificial intelligence (AI), by which name it has received extensive press coverage.

Deep learning has the potential to make forecasting systems both simpler and more robust while improving forecast accuracy relative to "classical" approaches. This first of two installments from Tim Januschowski et al. presents a tutorial on the basics of DL with illustrations of how it has been applied for forecasting Amazon product sales and other variables.

"Fears about the implication of the 'black box' are misplaced: compared to human intelligence, AI is actually the more transparent. Unlike the human mind, AI can be interrogated and interpreted. Human intelligence is and has always been the real 'black box.'"

– *Vijay Pande*, New York Times, *January 25, 2018*

---

*This article originally appeared in *Foresight: The International Journal of Applied Forecasting* (Summer 2018) and appears here courtesy of the International Institute of Forecasters.

Introduction

The forecasting case one would likely associate with Amazon is that of the demand for products available for purchase on its websites. The products are organized in a catalog that includes a wealth of metadata, such as product descriptions, images, and customer reviews.

The demand for many of these products is highly seasonal or driven by external events or internal decisions (e.g., price changes or promotions), and new products are continually added to the catalog. In addition, many products have sparse and intermittent demands, adding to the forecasting challenge.

Many of these problems are especially challenging for traditional forecasting methods such as ARIMA, exponential smoothing (ES), and linear models, and some even more advanced modeling techniques (Seeger, Salinas, and Flunkert 2016).

Limitations of the Classical Methods

Due to diverse data characteristics, successfully addressing the entire forecasting landscape with a single method is unrealistic. Models that operate on individual time series, such as ARIMA and ES, perform well in situations where the data exhibit clear, regular patterns and a behavior compatible with the structural assumptions of the model. The number of real-world forecasting problems that match this ideal case is limited. Rather, one is often faced with situations where individual time series do not provide enough information to identify predictable dynamics such as seasonality or the influence of causal factors. Common reasons for this are inadequate data history (i.e. new products), intermittency, and factors with weak signals.

The classical approach focuses on the time series that handle orderly data well, and to perform data preprocessing steps when needing to deal with irregularities. Preprocessing includes seasonal adjustments, Box-Cox transformations, and corrections for causal effects. The chain of preprocessing and modeling procedures to deal with the variety of data characteristics is called a *forecasting pipeline*. With the classical time-series approaches, forecasting pipelines can quickly become complex (Böse et al. 2017), making them hard to manage, maintain, and improve.

An area where ARIMA and ES fall short but where linear regression models are often successful in industry is in the incorporation of drivers such as price changes and promotional activities, as well as the metadata in catalogs and additional qualitative information. Incorporating these variables into linear regression models seems straightforward; however, it does present practical challenges, such as selecting the right variables and preprocessing them appropriately. This is also true for methods such as ARIMA with regression variables, ARIMAX, and the Bayesian state space forecasting model that our group at Amazon recently proposed (Seeger et al. 2016): these are hybrids between time-series and linear regression models.

The process of preparing the input data so that the model can learn the desired effects is referred to in the machine learning community as *feature engineering* and *feature selection*. In determining forecast accuracy, the data preparation process is often as important (if not more important) as the choice of the core forecasting model.

The Deep-Learning Alternative

Deep learning (DL) offers an alternative to complex forecasting pipelines. With DL, only a limited amount of data preprocessing is necessary and feature engineering is included in the DL model itself. Training the end-to-end model will automatically optimize the implicit feature-engineering steps, with the end goal of producing the best possible forecast. In practice, DL forecasting pipelines rely almost exclusively on what the model can learn from the data, in contrast to traditional pipelines that rely heavily on heuristics such as expert-designed components and feature processing.

Before we address the use of DL for forecasting, the next section provides a primer on DL core concepts and techniques. For a fuller (and more technical) coverage, we recommend the 2016 book by Goodfellow, Bengio, and Courville.

What Is a Neural Network?

While the term *deep learning* goes back only a few years, most of the techniques it refers to have been in development since the 1950s, namely artificial neural networks (NN or ANN for short). For an extensive summary of the history of deep learning, we refer the reader to Schmidhuber (2015). Although forecasting was never at the core of the neural network research efforts, neural networks have regularly been applied to forecasting problems throughout their development, long before the recent resurgence.

A neural network is a complex mathematical function that is composed of simpler building blocks. The mathematical function is defined by the topology of a given neural network and has free parameters that can be *trained* to best approximate the desired output.

Layers, Neurons, and the Activation Function

The building blocks of NNs are called *layers*. Each layer consists of individual computational units called *neurons*. Each neuron usually contains a linear and a nonlinear function. The linear function performs a simple mathematical calculation, typically a weighted sum of the input data (with trainable weights). The result is then transformed by a nonlinear *activation function* to produce an output. The output then becomes an input to neurons in the next layer. Figure 1.1 is a graphical representation of a single neuron.

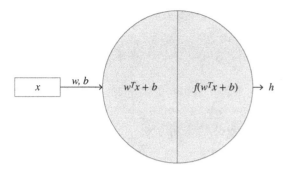

Figure 1.1 Composition of a Neuron

In Figure 1.1, x is the input vector, w is a vector of weights, and b is another vector of "offsets," also called "bias" (analogous to the intercept in a regression equation). f is a nonlinear "activation function" that transforms the weighted (by w, using a scalar product $w^T x$) and shifted (by b) input into an output. f is specified by the modeler, and w and b are parameters that are optimized for each neuron when the entire network is trained.

Networks, Edges, and Layers

Neurons are structured in *networks*, as illustrated in Figure 1.2.

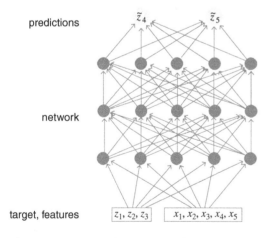

Figure 1.2 Example of a Feed-Forward Neural Network for Forecasting

Each neuron is a node in the network. The connecting lines, called *edges*, represent data flow through the network.

The rectangles at the base of the network represent the *input layer*, whose values are the input data series. The inputs in Figure 1.2 consist of the observed time series z (of length 3) and of time-varying *features* x. Such features might include product price, promotion, availability, and other predictors, as well as metadata such as product type. The circles at the top represent the *output layer*, the predictions computed by the network. The two nodes there are forecasts for the next two time periods.

Layers in between are called the *hidden layers*. Each contains neurons whose output is connected to the inputs of other neurons and is therefore not visible as a network output. Figure 1.2 contains three hidden layers and each of these consists of five neurons, represented by the solid dots.

Deep versus Wide Networks

The term *deep* refers to the number of hidden layers: the more hidden layers a neural network has, the deeper it is. A network with many neurons in each hidden layer is called a *wide network*. We use the term *"architecture* of the NN" to refer to the number, type, and arrangement of the neurons, layers, and connections to each other.

Even a shallow NN with a single hidden layer can approximate any function if it is wide enough: this is called the "universal approximation theorem." However, deep neural networks enjoy certain computational advantages over wide networks in that they can approximate similarly complex functions with fewer neurons.

In addition, deep networks are able to model the complex hierarchies of building blocks that are omnipresent in nature. For example, a time series can often be decomposed into simple building blocks like seasonality components, trends, level, and noise, with the latter potentially varying over time. Their combination, however, can yield complex patterns, and a deep NN could identify such components and learn how to recompose them.

How Do We Forecast with Neural Nets?

The forecasting task has two phases: *training* and *prediction*.

Training a Neural Network

During the training phase, the historical time series is split into two segments, the first segment comprising the training data that are fed into the network. A *learning algorithm* adjusts (i.e., optimizes) the weights and bias parameters in the neurons so that the output predictions best fit the historical data.

In the prediction phase, we feed an observed time series as well as any predictors and other features into the trained neural network, and the network outputs a continuation of the time series: the forecasts. Although the terms are different, the training and prediction data are traditionally called the in-sample and out-of-sample data.

Neural networks can also be trained to quantify the uncertainty in their predictions, so that prediction intervals or Monte Carlo samples can be obtained. For example, we can use a neural network to learn the parameters of a probability function, such as the mean and variance of Normal distribution, which would then allow us, via Monte Carlo sampling, to estimate prediction intervals.

A technical detail: the training phase is commonly based on statistical principles such as maximum likelihood estimation, and the optimization is performed using well-established methods such as *stochastic gradient descent*.

The training proceeds iteratively. First, the data flow from the input layer to the output layer in what we call a *forward propagation step*. In Figure 1.2, the propagation is from bottom to top: it takes the input, a time series, and accompanying features and transforms the series using the weights into a forecast.

In the training phase, we know what the actual time series looks like so we can calculate the prediction errors. We then adjust the weights to decrease the error in what is called a *back-propagation step*. Intuitively, we propagate the error in the opposite direction of the data flow (hence "backward," top to bottom in Figure 1.2) and compute the influence of a change in a weight on the error. The learning algorithm stops once a satisfactory degree of accuracy has been obtained.

There is a great deal of research on how to make the training of the neural network efficient and stable. We will discuss this in Part 2 of our article.

Types of Neural Nets

While a large number of different NN architectures exist, the most basic architecture is the *feed-forward* neural network, also called a *multilayer perceptron* (MLP). This is the architecture depicted in Figure 1.2. Here the inputs are mapped through multiple hidden layers of neurons, each of which computes a nonlinear function of the weighted average of its inputs, as in Figure 1.1. This allows the MLP to model complex nonlinear relationships.

Linear regression can be viewed as an MLP composed of a single hidden layer with an identity activation function. In the nomenclature of Figure 1.1, the input data x corresponds to a single row of the linear regression design matrix w to the estimated regression coefficients, and the bias b to the intercept parameter. As an MLP, linear regression is trained to minimize the mean squared error loss function.

Other popular architectures are *convolutional neural nets* (CNNs) and *recurrent neural nets* (RNNs). CNNs are similar to MLPs in their basic structure, but contain additional layers called *convolution layers*. A convolution operation on a time series is the computation that creates a new time series where each point of the new series is a weighted combination of points from the original time series (from a window around the same point in time).

Figure 1.3 illustrates a convolution operation. The convolution filter slices over the input series, multiplying the weights and input data, and summing the result into weighted averages.

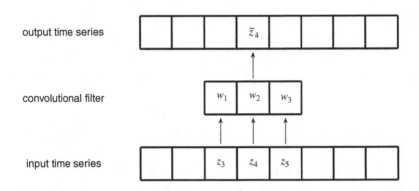

Figure 1.3 A Convolution Operation

CNNs have proven successful for image classification, where they encode the assumption of *translation invariance*, meaning that an object occurring anywhere in an image can be recognized by the same convolutional filter. In image processing, the convolution occurs over more than one dimension: for example, there are multiple dimensions to account for the height, width, and color of an image. In practice, they have additional desirable properties such as stability and speed of training, especially on modern GPU hardware. Compared to MLPs, CNNs strike a balance between a relatively low number of parameters and high prediction accuracy.

RNNs, shown in Figure 1.4, explicitly model the sequential nature of time-series data and are thus a natural fit for forecasting. Industrial forecasting success stories (e.g., at Uber, Amazon, and Zalando) use RNN architectures. In RNNs, the output of the hidden layers (referred to as the *hidden state*) evolves over time, and the hidden state of the network at the current time step is fed back to the network on the next time step. This structure allows us to model the data sequence and correlation across time. The recurrent nature of these models can make them harder to train in practice, but a number of techniques exist, most prominently long-short-term-memory (LSTM) cells, that make these RNNs trainable.

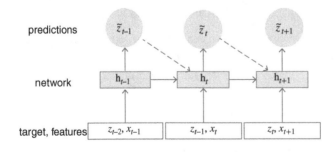

Figure 1.4 A Basic RNN Architecture for Forecasting

In Figure 1.4, at time step t, the input of the network consists of features (x) as well as observed target value (z) at previous time step $t - 1$. The network is then trained to output the forecast for time step *t*. For time steps in the prediction range, the previous target value is not available, so the forecast of the previous time step (dotted line) is used instead (which is a common procedure as well in some classical time-series methods).

A large number of variants and combinations of these basic architectures exists, and it is an ongoing research topic to improve existing architectures and invent better ones.

Examples of Neural Forecasting Models

Figures 1.5 and 1.6 illustrate NN models for a pair of highly regular time series: hourly electricity consumption of two households in Figure 1.5, and hourly traffic-lane usage on San Francisco Bay–area freeways in Figure 1.6.

The historical time series are in black. The forecast start date is marked by the black vertical line and the forecasts are to the right. The central line is the median forecast, and the shaded region corresponds to the prediction interval bounded by the 90th percentile forecast (the upper line) and the 10th percentile forecast (the lower line). These neural forecasts were produced by a variant of DeepAR, an RNN/LSTM architecture. For these data sets, the DeepAR forecasts were more accurate than classical methods.

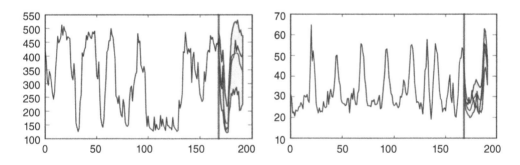

Figure 1.5 Hourly Electricity Consumption of Two Example Households

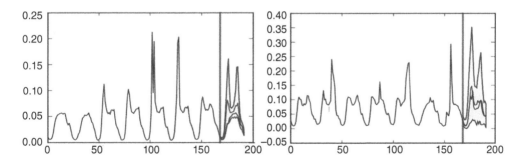

Figure 1.6 Hourly Occupancy Rates for San Francisco Bay–Area Freeways

Figure 1.7 shows forecasts for sales of selected Amazon products with short histories. In the first frame, there are virtually no data points, while the second has limited historical sales data that cannot explain the future behavior.

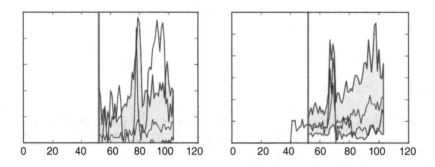

Figure 1.7 Sales and Forecasts of Two Amazon Products by DeepAR

The black line corresponds to actual sales, and the vertical line divides past from future (i.e., DeepAR does not see the data to the right of the vertical line). The shaded region marks a central 80% prediction interval, and the dark line the median forecast.

It is striking that the same NN that produced reasonable forecasts for the good historical data in Figures 1.5 and 1.6 produces reasonable forecasts in these data-limited cases. The neural network is able to do so because, during training, it has been shown many similar time series at different stages of evolution, particularly at the beginning, and thus can extrapolate from them.

Notice too how the prediction intervals grow over time (which is expected, as there is more uncertainty at longer horizons), but not in a regular way. This reflects the fact that during certain times of the year, forecasting is more difficult due to seasonally higher variance. While it is possible to model this pattern with classical techniques, it is challenging from a practical standpoint.

The examples in Figures 1.5–1.7 cover many real-word forecasting scenarios: we have positive real numbers (electricity consumption), ratios or 0-1 values (traffic lane usage), and count data (product sales).

In Part 2, we will explain the pros and cons of deep-learning methods and discuss the challenges in applying DL to forecasting problems.

References

Böse, J.-H., Flunkert V., Gasthaus, J., et al. (2017). Probabilistic demand forecasting at scale. *Proceedings of VLDB* 2017.

Goodfellow, I., Bengio, Y., and Courville, A. (2016). *Deep learning (adaptive computation and machine learning)*. MIT Press.

Januschowski, T., Arpin, D., Salinas, D., et al. (2018). *Now available in Amazon SageMaker: DeepAR Algorithm for More Accurate Time Series Forecasting*, AWS Machine Learning Blog. https://aws.amazon.com/blogs/machine-learning/now-available-in-amazon-sagemaker-deepar-algorithm-for-more-accurate-time-series-forecasting/

Schmidhuber, J. (2015). Deep learning in neural networks: An overview. *Neural Networks* 61, pp. 85–117.

Seeger, M., Salinas, D., and Flunkert, V. (2016). *Bayesian intermittent demand forecasting for large inventories*. NeurIPS Proceedings.

1.2 DEEP LEARNING FOR FORECASTING: CURRENT TRENDS AND CHALLENGES*

Tim Januschowski, Jan Gasthaus, Yuyang Wang, Syama Sundar Rangapuram, and Laurent Callot

In this second installment, Januschowski and colleagues describe the pros and cons of forecasting through neural networks. They discuss the considerable research ongoing in the deep-learning community, and report on progress in several important areas, including more efficient training methods for neural models; fusing model-driven and data-driven approaches; leveraging unstructured metadata; metalearning and AutoML; and reinforcement learning.

The authors observe that while neural networks are a comparatively data-hungry method for forecasting, many forecasting problems face relatively few data points. Thus, their preferred way to maximize use of limited data is through global models, in which training occurs over multiple, related time series. They advise that neural modeling can be considered for many forecasting problems, but there are advantages and drawbacks, and so should be considered judiciously.

Applying Neural Nets as Global Forecasting Models

At Amazon's Machine Learning Forecasting group in Berlin, we've found it helpful to differentiate between *local* and *global* models. In the former, a separate model is trained for each time series. This is the typical case for many time-series models such as ARIMA and exponential smoothing: the parameters of these models are optimized for *one* time series. Local models often work very well if the time series is lengthy (e.g., at least two years of weekly data to learn seasonality correctly). For forecasting multiple time series (e.g., multiple products of a supermarket), we would have as many models as there are time series.

---

*This article originally appeared in *Foresight: The International Journal of Applied Forecasting* (Fall 2018) and appears here courtesy of the International Institute of Forecasters.

In contrast, a global model is one where the free parameters (the weights in the neural network) are trained jointly over a *set* of closely related time series. A linear regression could also be a global model if trained on more than one time series – an approach often referred to as *multivariate forecasting*.

A global model works well if we have available a large number of time series with similar structural patterns. The major advantage is that it can identify patterns that are not distinguishable in a local model but become so when aggregated over multiple series. Two caveats: normalization of each series is typically necessary to ensure that all are comparable in scale during training, and correlations between the time series still need to be incorporated and modeled appropriately (a nontrivial task for which research is ongoing).

Historically for forecasting applications, neural networks have usually been implemented as local models. While these have had some success in forecasting long time series, we believe that the real strength of neural networks lies in global models. When training such models with a large set of related time series as well as metadata on how the time series relate, we can obtain results that consistently and convincingly outperform local models. The performance gap increases further with the richness of the available metadata and the number of related time series used during training.

Figure 1.8, which reproduces Figure 1.7, offers a good illustration of the benefit of global models. The sales histories of these two Amazon products are short, virtually nonexistent for that in the first frame. Training a local model on just these series would be essentially pointless, but the global model used here was trained on many new-product time series as well as other series at various phases of their life cycle. As you can see, the global model elicited forecasts that are rich in detail despite the absence of history on the products in question.

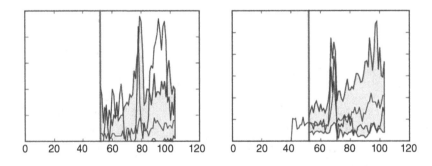

Figure 1.8 Sales and Forecasts of Two Amazon Products by DeepAR

Local and global forecasting models are two extremes of the spectrum. Hybrids are often employed in practice, e.g., by applying a global model to the residuals of a local model, or by training certain parameters of local models across different time series, or by reconciling local models globally via hierarchical forecasting techniques.

Pros and Cons of Neural Forecasting

Neural networks are a fundamental part of the forecasting toolbox at Amazon. We believe their application should be considered for many forecasting problems; however, they should be considered judiciously. There are advantages and drawbacks.

Advantages

As discussed, NN can simplify complex *forecasting pipelines* – the steps from data preprocessing through model formulation – since fewer such procedures are required, which is to say these steps are integrated into the model-training process.

Importantly, NNs allow the incorporation of the kind of rich metadata that is becoming increasingly available. In industrial forecasting applications, time series come with a host of metadata such as categorizations, product descriptions, reviews, and images. By combining NN architectures designed for text and images with architectures for forecasting, this metadata can be leveraged effectively.

The different layers of a neural network learn data transformations that in traditional models have to be handcrafted and/or selected using additional data sets. Metadata permits groupings: a product belonging to a certain product category can be encoded as a dummy variable (say 0 = the product belongs to the category, 1 = it does not belong to the category). The NN can then use this feature to differentiate one product category from another and go on to learn which categories may be more closely related than others. Even when explicit groupings are not available, the network can learn effects such as "products with similar images exhibit similar seasonality patterns."

These are core advantages for applying NN to forecasting problems. But there are a number of more subtle virtues, some directly related to NN, others to the framework of modern deep-learning software.

- **A neural network learns a representation (an "embedding") of a time series internally, allowing for groupings that are trained with forecast accuracy as the goal.** Contrast this to more traditional methods such as using k-means on time series to find group-seasonality curves (Mohammadipour, Boylan, and Syntetos 2012). This approach decouples the identification of seasonal indices from the forecasting steps and, while intuitive, may not yield the clustering with the best forecasting accuracy.

- **NNs show great flexibility in modeling data distributions.** In many forecasting situations, the observed time series does not match the assumptions made by classical techniques (e.g., normally distributed and homoscedastic errors). To the contrary, real-world data is often sparse, heavy-tailed, and bursty, as is true for many Amazon products. NN modeling allows for using weaker assumptions and can be flexible in the way it represents underlying distributions.

▪ **Sophisticated DL software packages (such as Tensorflow and MXNet) make it easy to build, train, compose, and extend forecasting models.** Features such as autodifferentiation are built in, which greatly simplifies the creation of custom models or model components. These frameworks have converged on common programmatic concepts (e.g., how to construct NN, how to train them effectively), and they are flexible and robust enough to handle experimentation and production-use cases.

▪ **By slicing a time series into randomly selected windows, the NN can be trained to see the time series at different points in its evolution.** Figure 1.9 contains an illustration. This could be at the introduction of the product, during its regular life cycle, and toward its end. The neural network learns how time series behave across their entire life cycles and the model becomes independent of the time interval chosen.

In Figure 1.9, the observed time series, z, and the accompanying features x (e.g., price, promotions, availability) are sliced into the three windows. During training, the left part of the vertical line is fed into the model in the forward propagation step and the right part is used to compute the prediction error.

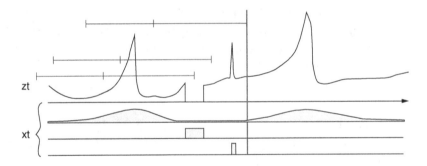

Figure 1.9 Three Window Slides (top three lines) Cut from a Single Time Series as Training Data – The x_t Are Covariates (Explanatory Variables)

Contrast this with exponential smoothing (ES), where the parameters are optimized for a particular time segment. Since the NN is trained over a set of time series as well as different forecast start times, we can use the same model for longer periods of time. Closely related to this is the reusability of pretrained neural nets for other forecasting cases. We use an already trained network and feed in training examples from a new but related domain (e.g., the same data from a different country) to achieve better results than training on the new domain alone.

Disadvantages and Caveats

Neural networks are hardly a silver bullet for forecasting. Their application requires statistical understanding and at least as much rigor in experimentation as classical models do.

- **Because NNs learn from, and only from, the data, they struggle with extrapolation and are not robust towards outliers.** NNs impose very little a priori structure on the forecast. A structure (e.g., a type of trend) that is known to exist in the data could be imposed in exponential smoothing but can be challenging to impose upon a neural network. Controlling long-horizon forecasts by, say, limiting the amount of growth or imposing stationarity is not straightforward. There is promise that the model-driven and data-driven approaches can be brought into harmony. In the recently completed M4 competition, the winning methodology from Uber's Slawek Smyl was a combination of model- and data-driven approaches: https://eng.uber.com/m4-forecasting-competition/

- **For single time series, as typically considered in econometrics, neural networks would not be the first option to try.** Neural networks work well when we have a large set of related time series or a lengthy single time series where we train a single "global" model on each time series (in contrast to exponential smoothing, where one trains an individual model for each time series in the set). A recent Kaggle competition on forecasting page hits on Wikipedia was won by a neural forecasting method: https://www.kaggle.com/c/web-traffic-time-series-forecasting

  In the event of a single-time-series case, there are more free parameters in the neural network than there are observations of the time series, so achieving a reasonable forecast requires modern neural-network regularization techniques. In contrast to classical models, there are few theoretical guarantees on the performance of neural networks. They are, at this stage, an empirical tool.

- **It is often unclear why certain NN architectures or parametrizations work – and when they work, it is hard to explain why they predict the way they do.** NN research currently relies much on intuition and experimentation and less so on theory. We expect this to change over time. The reason for this is the complexity and nonlinearity of the function that a neural network represents. This strength becomes a weakness when it comes to explicability. We do note, however, that interpretability of pure linear models is often overrated.

- **Training neural networks is time consuming and computationally intensive.** While modern implementations of exponential smoothing (such as the ETS implementation in the R Forecast package) produce robust forecasts almost instantly, the training of a neural network on a large set of time series can take hours. Because it takes so long, it must happen offline; that is, a number of past time series are used to train a model, which is then stored. At prediction time, the trained model is loaded and used for predicting. Thus, the most recent data in a time series may have not been available for training the neural network. However, the assumption is that the data distribution does not change radically between training the neural network and using it for forecasting. Understanding whether the computational cost outweighs the benefit of potentially increased accuracy is therefore a key point.

Note that once resource-intensive training is terminated, prediction itself is typically not computationally intensive and can be deployed even in settings that require real-time forecasts.

Finally, for the many time-series models, training recurrent neural networks (RNNs) is problematic in that careful weight initialization is required, and repeated training on the same data can lead to differing results. Recent advances have enabled RNNs to be more stable and robust.

Current Trends and Challenges

There is much ongoing research in the deep-learning community, and here we speculate on how it might affect neural-forecasting models. We've ordered the topics roughly from near to long term.

Making training and prediction more stable and more (energy) efficient is an area of immediate impact. Recurrent neural networks (which explicitly model the sequential nature of time-series data and are thus a natural fit for forecasting) and convolutional neural networks (or CNNs, which transform a time series into one where each point is a weighted combination of points from the original time series) have had a number of breakthroughs in sequence-data domains such as language and speech. Compared to RNNs, CNNs offer a higher degree of stability and have led to even better results in other sequence-domain fields (even though they do not model the sequential nature of the data). It is likely that the successes of CNNs will extend to forecasting applications.

The fusion between model-driven and data-driven approaches is an active area of research. The M4 competition's winning entry is currently the most prominent example, but we expect to see much more work in this direction. The underlying motivation is to bring the robustness and stability of classic time-series models together with the rich data and feature processing capabilities of an NN.

The amount of data for forecasting applications is increasing, and there is a desire to leverage unstructured metadata. We can now store data in disaggregated form, a benefit for companies that wish to forecast at the lowest aggregation level possible. However, at these lower levels, as the data are sparser, noisier, and more irregular than at higher levels of aggregation, there is a greater need to be able to learn effects from *related items*. Metadata plays a crucial role here, and this is where global models – in particular, multimodal, deep-neural networks with flexible, data-driven data-distribution models – will increasingly be applied.

Meta-learning and AutoML have received considerable attention in the scientific literature for using related prediction problems to solve new ones. We can imagine taking a trained neural network for product-demand forecasting in one country and then retraining it for another country. In some cases, doing so could be better than training a model for the new country from scratch. The more closely related the countries (e.g., similar holidays and weekly seasonality), the more effective this approach could be, because we are essentially feeding the model more data. Moreover, the network architecture and configuration to use for a given forecasting problem could itself be learned from similar forecasting problems.

Generative adversarial networks (GANs) have emerged over the last few years as a powerful technique for image recognition. GANs consist of two neural networks, one *generative* network and one *adversarial* network, and the two engage in a competition. The adversarial network is tasked with discriminating between examples produced by the generative network and real-world examples. The generative network's task is to try to fool the adversarial network by producing and imitating the real data set (and thereby the data distribution) as closely as possible. For forecasting, the adversarial network may not be needed as there are good mathematical functions available to distinguish time series (contrast this to the task of deciding whether two images represent the same object).

We could consider the goals of the forecasting task to be the production of forecasts that are indistinguishable from the true time series; that is, the model perfectly captures the future realizations of a time series. This provides a nonparametric, purely data-driven way of learning the forecast distribution.

Reinforcement learning has received a lot of popular attention due to pioneering work in board games such as go and chess. Reinforcement learning is concerned with those tasks in which a series of actions has to be taken before feedback is received. Based on the delayed feedback, reinforcement learning methods find good sequences of action. In games, the feedback or reward is "win/lose game" and the series of actions are the moves executed.

In theory, reinforcement learning offers a framework that unifies the typical division between forecasting and a decision-making problem. With reinforcement learning, instead of forecasting, you directly model the action that you're interested in (buying decisions). Inventory management, for example – for which demand forecasting is typically a key input – could be considered as a reinforcement-learning problem. The actions available at any point in time are to buy a certain product in a certain quantity from a certain vendor, to leave the inventory unchanged, or even to mark down or promote a given item, and the resulting reward would be a function of, say, inventory health, cash-flow, or profit. Note that designing a suitable reward function is nontrivial and one of the hardest components when formalizing a reinforcement-learning problem.

In this setting, we do not need to follow the typical two-stage approach in which we forecast demand first and then solve an optimization problem to make optimal decisions. In the "classical" approach, prediction and optimization are decoupled: first a predictive distribution is generated by the forecasting model; then an optimal decision is computed given the predictive distribution and the loss function of the decision problem. Reinforcement learning offers a theoretical avenue out of this by treating the combination of forecasting and decision problem as a single problem.

A disadvantage is that our current approaches to reinforcement learning with NNs are data hungry and rely on quick experimentation and feedback loops, prerequisites that are not so onerous in many application areas of forecasting, such as supply-chain optimization.

Having covered some basic NN background, its applications in forecasting, pros and cons, and recent research trends, we want to leave you with a simple recommendation: try it! It is not difficult to make first steps in DL in general and in DL for forecasting. Here are some recommendations on how to get started.

DL Software for Forecasting

For software-development engineers and a tech-savvy audience, there are many excellent online courses, such as Andrew Ng's "Deep Learning" course on coursera. org. Python seems to have emerged as the dominant programming language for deep learning, but there are R packages as well. The major deep-learning frameworks such as Tensorflow and MxNet all offer good tutorials on DL techniques and first steps and come with excellent documentation.

At Amazon, we mainly work with MxNet due to its computational speed. Introductory level material on how to use MxNet for forecasting can be found in the community-effort book "MxNet – The Straight Dope" on github.com.

Our group at AWS AI Labs recently launched a neural forecasting model called DeepAR as part of the company's general-purpose machine-learning service, Amazon SageMaker. When we developed DeepAR, we found it could meet many of the challenges of real-world forecasting problems laid out in this article. It has robust out-of-the-box performance, yet enough bells and whistles to be tuned to improve performance.

References

Mohammadipour, M., Boylan, J., and Syntetos, A. (2012). The application of product-group seasonal indexes to individual products. *Foresight* 26 (Summer 2012): 20–26.

The M4 Competition. https://www.m4.unic.ac.cy/the-m-competitions-and-their-far-reaching-contributions-to-the-theory-and-practice-of-forecasting/

1.3 NEURAL NETWORK–BASED FORECASTING STRATEGIES*

Steven Mills and Susan Kahler

Recent literature – such as from the M4 Forecasting Competition – indicates that hybrids of machine learning and classical time-series models are among the top contenders in accurately forecasting the future. Classical linear models are parsimonious and often perform well, but they are unable to capture nonlinear relationships in the data. On the other hand, machine learning models such as neural networks (NNs) are very good at modeling nonlinear effects.

*This article is an adaptation of Steven Mills's SAS Global Forum paper "Neural Network-Based Forecasting Strategies in SAS® Viya®" (2020) and Susan Kahler's blog post "Using Deep Learning to Forecast Solar Energy" (2018) and appears here courtesy of SAS.

Mills and Kahler argue that while knowing when and how to use machine learning models might seem difficult, these decisions can be distilled down to best practices that any analyst can use with little experience. This article discusses several NN-based modeling strategies available in SAS® Visual Forecasting software and the important factors to consider in choosing and training a model.

Discussion includes key features of the data that inform the decision to use machine learning models, feature generation options to augment the training process, and best practices to fit a robust model. Methods are illustrated with case studies in predicting ozone levels and energy forecasting for a solar farm.

Introduction

Machine learning and hybrid modeling strategies have emerged as top contenders in time series forecasting because of the volume of data and processing power brought about by the information age. Neural networks have become particularly popular because they are able to approximate any functional relationship and they are very well suited for modeling nonlinear relationships between the dependent (target) variable and independent (predictor) variables. See, for example, Box (1976); Yoshio, Hipel, and Mcleod (2005); Taşpınar (2015); and Crone and Häger (2016).

SAS Visual Forecasting implements three forecasting strategies that are based on neural networks (NNs): panel series neural network, stacked model, and multistage model. Neural networks might seem mysterious or even intimidating because they have many parameters, but the guidelines in this paper will enable you to successfully apply NNs to forecasting problems and increase your forecasting accuracy.

The first section explains how each of the three NN-based modeling strategies is customized for time-series forecasting and what types of data work well. Next, a case study shows predictions of ozone levels in Chicago by using an NN-based strategy that easily outperforms classical models. Finally, some effective-use strategies not covered in the example are discussed. We also include a case study on using deep learning (DL) for forecasting energy generation at a solar farm.

After reading this paper, you will understand what types of data work well with these modeling strategies and you will be able to effectively apply these strategies to your own forecasting problems. Whether the volume of data is medium size, big, or huge, these modeling strategies can help identify complex relationships between variables and increase the predictive power of your models.

Background

Some basic knowledge of neural networks is presented here in order to provide a foundation for the concepts discussed later. A neural network is composed of an input layer, one or more hidden layers, and an output layer. An example of an NN with one hidden layer is shown in Figure 1.10(a). Each input node has a connection to every node in the first hidden layer. Likewise, every node in the hidden layer has a connection to the node in the output layer.

Figure 1.10(b) expands the hidden node n_4 to illustrate how the output of a node is calculated. (Nodes n_3 and n_5 are omitted for clarity.) The input layer simply passes through the values in the input vector X such that the output of node n_1 is the value x_1 and the output of n_2 is the value x_2. The output of each node is multiplied by a connection, w_{jk}, where j and k represent the nodes being connected. The hidden node adds up the input values and a bias parameter, b_k, and feeds the sum into a nonlinear activation function to produce the hidden node output. The output from n_4 is multiplied by the corresponding connection weight, w_{46}, and fed forward to node n_6.

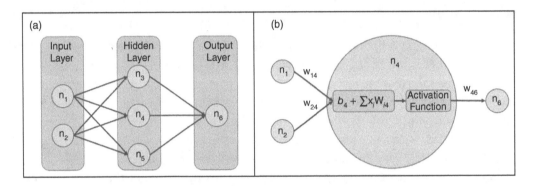

Figure 1.10 (a) Example Neural Network Architecture and (b) Functionality of a Node

Neural networks learn through an iterative cycle of training and validation. Training data are fed forward through the NN to calculate an output value. Then back propagation is used to update the connection weights and reduce the error. The details of back propagation are outside the scope of this paper, but they can be summarized succinctly as follows: The error is measured with respect to the training data, and partial derivatives are calculated with respect to each connection weight. The aggregated partial derivatives are used to update the connection weights and reduce the error (Goodfellow, Yoshua, and Courville 2016). The error with respect to the validation data is measured periodically to validate the model training process.

Neural Network Modeling in SAS Visual Forecasting

Some special considerations are required to successfully use NN-based models in time series forecasting. Fortunately, the modeling strategies in SAS Visual Forecasting take care of a lot of the details by structuring the data and generating additional features before training the model. However, it is important to understand how the data are interpreted and when to use the extracted features. This section describes how the NN-based strategies in SAS Visual Forecasting structure interpret the data compared to classical forecasting and machine learning.

Data Structure

In classical time series forecasting, BY variables are used to delineate a panel of related time series and find the best model for each series individually. This approach is intractable for NNs because they require significantly more data to train than classical models require. A single time series is typically not enough.

The neural network modeling strategies in SAS Visual Forecasting are designed for panel data that consist of multiple related time series. For example, a retail chain might have many time series that are delineated by BY variables (such as STORE and SKU) and independent variables (such as promotions, number of shoppers, and calendar events).

The time series are concatenated together as shown in Figure 1.11 and modeled as a single series with the BY variables included as categorical independent variables. The resulting input table is a concatenation of all the series.

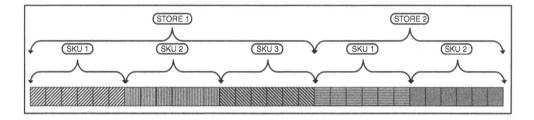

Figure 1.11 Five Concatenated Time Series Delineated by the BY Variables STORE and SKU

Data Partitioning

A typical machine learning algorithm randomly partitions the data into training, validation, and test partitions. Model fitting is accomplished through alternating cycles of using the training data to minimize the training partition error and validating the progress by checking the validation partition error. This cycle continues until some stopping criterion is met.

The training and validation partitions are analogous to the training and holdout samples in time series forecasting where the holdout portion is used to select the model that best generalizes to new data. The out-of-sample (test) data are used to measure how well the model predictions generalize to new data.

Random sampling in order to partition data is acceptable for machine learning applications, but in time series the most recent data usually have a larger impact on predicted values. To adjust for this, the NN-based forecasting strategies use ordered sampling. Random and ordered sampling are illustrated in Figure 1.12 for a single time series. In ordered sampling, the oldest data are placed in the training partition and more recent data are placed in the holdout (validation) partition. The out-of-sample (test) partition contains the most recent data leading up to the forecast horizon.

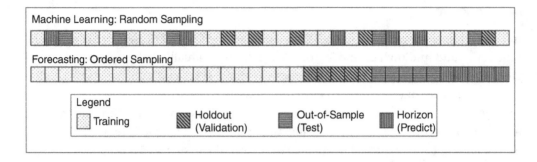

Figure 1.12 Partitioning for Machine Learning (Random Sampling) vs. Forecasting (Ordered Sampling)

Modeling Strategies

Panel Series Neural Network

The panel series neural network (PSNN) can be used to implement a neural network like the one described in the introduction. Figure 1.13 illustrates the general flow of operations in the PSNN modeling strategy. The input data first go through a preprocessing step where data are partitioned, transformed, and/or standardized. Next, salient features are extracted. After preprocessing and feature extraction, the NN learns how to fit a model to the data. Finally, the output data are reverse-transformed and destandardized back to the original scale to produce the final forecast.

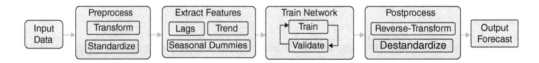

Figure 1.13 Panel Series Neural Network Modeling Strategy

Stacked Model

The stacked model uses the PSNN to create an initial forecast of the target variable and then models the residuals by using a classical time series approach. The forecasts of the input data and the residuals are then added together to generate the final forecast, as shown in Figure 1.14.

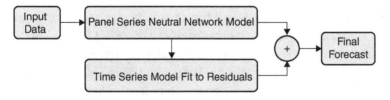

Figure 1.14 Stacked Modeling Strategy

Multistage Model

The multistage model is a twist on hierarchical forecasting. The lowest levels in a time series hierarchy are often intermittent or display more nonlinear characteristics that challenge time series models. Figure 1.15(a) shows the block diagram, and Figure 1.15(b) shows an example hierarchy. The lower levels are modeled by using regression or a neural network, whereas the higher levels are fit to time-series models. The forecasts are reconciled at a user-specified level of the hierarchy to produce the final forecast.

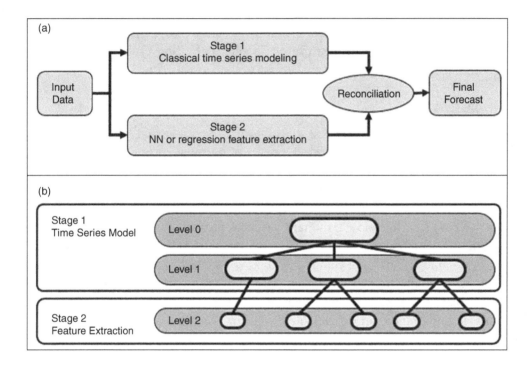

Figure 1.15 (a) Block Diagram of Multistage Modeling Strategy and (b) Example Division of Hierarchy Levels

When Should You Use a Neural Network Model?

Neural networks are not an all-purpose magic tool to replace classical models (Zhang 2003). To quote George Box, "All models are wrong, but some are useful" (Box and Draper 1987). For a neural network to be useful, you need more training data than classical time-series models require, and you need independent variables that have complex nonlinear relationships to the dependent variable (Box 1976; Yoshio, Hipel, and Mcleod 2005; Crone and Häger 2016).

Typical data for which neural networks work well have the following characteristics:

- Large data volume, such as a panel of time series
- Historical data length of at least 300 time ID values

▪ At least three independent variables, which ideally have nonlinear relationships to the target

▪ Few (or zero!) missing values

Case Study: Ozone Prediction

Data Description

The data set that is used in this example was obtained from Chicago's Array of Things (AoT) project. The data consist of one month of sensor output from modules that are placed around the city to measure air quality, light, and other environmental conditions.

Data Preparation

Cleaning the data is an important first step to ensure that the model can make accurate predictions, but this process is outside the scope of this paper. Note that the AoT data had many missing values and broken or malfunctioning sensors.

Columns for irrelevant variables and sensors that were clearly malfunctioning are removed, and the important independent variables are chosen. You might be wondering why you should choose important variables instead of including everything. It is true that NNs require a large amount of data, but the data quality is important too. Extraneous variables and multicollinearity among variables can reduce forecast accuracy and increase the training time significantly, so unimportant variables should be excluded (Diaconescu 2008; Christ, Kempa-Liehr, and Feindt 2016).

Variable importance can be evaluated by using machine learning methods or an ARIMAX model if required, or you can use domain knowledge about ozone formation, which indicates that UV light, temperature, humidity, and the presence of other pollutants (such as nitrogen oxides from combustion engine exhaust) are important factors. Gas sensors require calibration and exhibit signal drift over time, so it would be best not to use other gas sensors to predict the output of the ozone sensor. In this case study, the chosen predictors are temperature, humidity, and infrared, ultraviolet, and visible light.

Feature Extraction

Now that the data are prepared, you are ready to choose the features to extract. The following sections describe how you can select the appropriate number of lags, the seasonal dummy variables, and the type of trend component.

It is important to understand how feature extraction impacts the effective number of input variables and model parameters. For example, generating three lags of 10 variables results in a total of 40 variables and 40 nodes in the input layer. If there are five hidden nodes in the first hidden layer, then there are 200 connection weight parameters to solve. A NN model can quickly become very complex, which causes the training time to increase dramatically.

Lags

Neural network theory assumes that each observation is independent from any other observation. This assumption makes it difficult to learn autocorrelated features that are common in time series, such as trends and seasonality. Generating lags of the dependent and independent variables helps the model understand the local level and trend in a series similarly to the way an ARIMA model uses an autoregressive (AR) term.

It is important to realize how missing values affect the generation of lagged variables. Consider the example shown in Table 1.1, which consists of six observations. The independent variable, X, has one missing value, and three lags have been generated for both X and Y.

Notice that the first three observations contain missing values in the lags of the dependent variable (Y) because the historical data before January 1 is not available. Also notice that the missing value for the independent variable (X) on January 3 propagates downward, resulting in missing values for the last three observations. Every observation in this data set has a missing value, so none of them can be used in the neural network model. If your data have many missing values or you use many lags (or both), then you quickly run out of complete observations for training the NN.

Seasonal Dummy Variables

Generating lags of variables quickly increases the volume of data and the time required to train a neural network. In addition, some data are sacrificed at the beginning of each series as shown previously. Imagine generating a seasonal lag for monthly data, which results in a whole year of data that can't be used because of missing values. Sacrificing a large portion of the historical data is usually a bad idea.

Seasonal dummy variables can be included to help capture seasonal fluctuations in the data without any data loss. In addition, the seasonality can be specified

Table 1.1 Example of Missing Values Propagating When Lags Are Generated

Date	Y	Lag1(Y)	Lag2(Y)	Lag3(Y)	X	Lag1(X)	Lag2(X)	Lag3(X)
1-Jan	16				4			
2-Jan	25	16			6.25	4		
3-Jan	21	25	16			6.25	4	
4-Jan	22	21	25	16	5.5		6.25	4
5-Jan	14	22	21	25	3.5	5.5		6.25
6-Jan	17	14	22	21	4.25	3.5	5.5	

Table 1.2 Weighted MAPE Calculated for the PSNN and Hierarchical Models

Model	In-sample WMAPE	Out-of-sample WMAPE
Hierarchical forecasting	23.0136	10.9508
PSNN	10.9310	9.7429

independently of the time series seasonality. For example, if the time series is accumulated to a weekly interval, then the default behavior would generate 52 seasonal dummy variables to cover the 52 weeks in a year. Specifying "month" or "qtr" as the seasonal dummy interval results in fewer dummy variables and faster convergence when training a neural network.

The AoT data in this example are accumulated to an hourly interval, so 24 seasonal dummy variables are generated, one for each hour of the day. This could be very useful because certain times of the day have increased traffic or sunlight to contribute to ozone generation. Seasonal dummy variables allow capturing information about the hour of the day without creating many lagged variables. Avoiding the use of many lagged variables results in a smaller data table and a faster training process.

Trend Component

A trend component can be extracted from the data to help the model learn. You can choose a linear trend, a damped trend, or an exponential smoothing model (ESM) of the dependent variable to include as an independent variable. The linear and damped trends are special cases of the ESM, so only one of these options should be selected. If an ESM is selected, then the time-series forecasting engine chooses the best ESM type on the basis of the training and holdout data partitions. For more control over the extracted model, you can choose between a linear or damped trend on the basis of the length of the holdout and forecast periods. When forecasting further into the future, linear trends often overestimate a series. A damped trend will yield better results.

Viewing the results shows that the PSNN performs substantially better than hierarchical forecasting on in-sample data. Keep in mind that the NN training process depends on random initialization and that race conditions in parallel processing threads can also cause variation in output. Therefore, you might see slightly different numbers for the PSNN weighted mean absolute percentage error (WMAPE) measurements.

The WMAPE values are summarized in Table 1.2, and the last two days of forecasts are plotted in Figure 1.16 for a representative sensor node. The shaded region in the right half of Figure 1.16 is the forecast horizon.

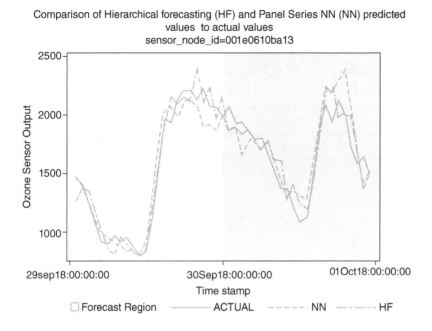

Figure 1.16 Forecast Comparison between PSNN and Hierarchical Forecasting

Scaling

Training time for neural networks is heavily influenced by the amount of data, the available processing power, and the training specifications. Figure 1.17 shows the training time dependence for the AoT data as the number of BY groups increase 10×, 50×, and 500×. These additional data are simulated by creating another BY variable and duplicating the original data. The plot displays a nice linear trend as the data size increases.

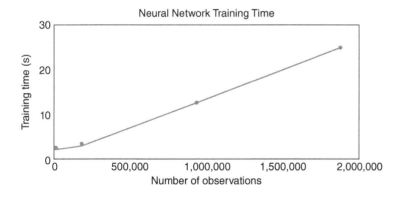

Figure 1.17 Scaling of Neural Network Training Time with Number of Observations

Scaling the data down provides insight into the minimum amount of data required. The effect of reducing the length of the historical record is shown in Figure 1.18. Using the full month of data (720 observations in each series) provides the data in Table 1.2. The WMAPE increases approximately linearly as data are discarded until around 50% (360 observations) remain. Further reduction of the historical record length results in a more drastic increase in WMAPE. Be cautious if you have only a few hundred historical time points to work with.

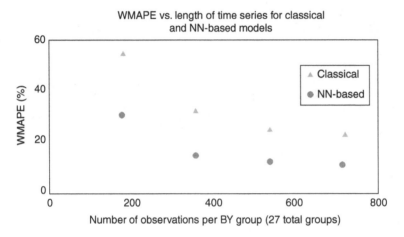

Figure 1.18 WMAPE as a Function of Historical Record Length for Classical and NN-Based Models

Reducing the number of BY groups and holding the series length constant does not necessarily impact the error measurement the same way. Figure 1.19 shows the lowest error measurement for seven BY groups. Increasing the number of BY groups causes an increase in WMAPE for both classical and NN-based models. Further increasing the number of series shows a slight reduction in WMAPE for NN-based models, whereas the classical models display higher WMAPE with no clear trend. These data indicate that additional BY groups might help reduce forecasting error, but also indicate that a small number of similar series might produce better results. The small number of series has less variation (allowing for a tighter fit), but the model would likely be less accurate if it were used to forecast the other series.

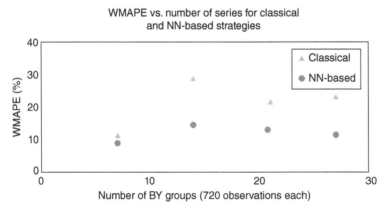

Figure 1.19 WMAPE as a Function of the Number of BY Groups for Classical and NN-based models

Case Study: Solar Energy Forecasting

Incorporating solar energy into an electrical grid is an important step in sustainable business practices – but this requires the accurate forecasting of solar power generation. Due to the volatility of weather conditions, however, it is a challenging forecasting problem.

This case study examines the application of deep learning in forecasting the solar farms at SAS. SAS has two solar farms, located on 12 acres at corporate headquarters in Cary, NC. These farms have a combined 2.3 MW in capacity, and the photovoltaic (PV) solar arrays generate around 3.5 million kilowatt-hours of clean, renewable energy each year.

SAS has collected a wealth of data about solar energy across various weather conditions, providing data that are appropriate for use in deep learning models, as these models are data hungry and require huge volumes of data for training. In this example, we have used around 60,000 data points collected from the two solar farms over a period of eight years.

Deep Learning Models

Prior to delving into the time series forecasting model used, we need to take a step back and look at deep learning models. Deep learning is a type of machine learning that trains a computer to perform humanlike tasks, such as recognizing speech, identifying images, or making predictions. Instead of organizing data to run through predefined equations, deep learning sets up basic parameters about the data and trains the computer to learn on its own by recognizing patterns using many layers of processing. Deep learning methods use neural network architectures to process data, which is why they are often referred to as deep neural networks.

As the number of hidden layers within a neural network increases, deep neural networks are formed. In this context, "deep" refers to the number of hidden layers in the network. A type of deep learning network is a recurrent neural network (RNN). RNNs use sequential information such from a sensor device (time series) or a spoken sentence (sequence of terms). Unlike traditional neural networks, all inputs to a recurrent neural network are not independent of each other since the output for each element depends on the computations of its preceding elements. Hence, connections between the nodes form a directed cycle, creating an internal memory within the networks. These networks are recurrent because they perform the same task for every element of a sequence. RNNs are used in forecasting and time-series applications, sentiment analysis, text categorization, and automatic speech recognition.

Time-Series Forecasting with Recurrent Neural Networks

In this example, we want to predict the solar power, which is the hourly power output from the solar farm, using a recurrent neural network. The predictors include the following:

- Hour, which is the hour of the day.
- Solar Elevation Angle, which is the angle between the horizon and the center of the Sun's disc.

- Daytime Indicator, which equal to 1 if it is daytime.
- Global Horizontal Irradiance (GHI), which is the solar irradiance intensity at the solar farm.

In this data set, the first three predictors are known in advance – we know their future values. However, GHI is not known in advance, but is measured in real time at the solar farm. Note that GHI will vary widely depending on weather and cloud patterns, and is the largest determinant in a solar array's output. (If not measuring it yourself, you can get GHI data from weather providers.)

The lags for all the predictors as well as response variables are created. We are generating sequences each spanning a 5-hour time window (five time steps), since the temporal dependency is relatively short-term in this data set. In general, the appropriate length of sequence will depend on the properties of the data set and application.

In our example, we created models for both one-step-ahead forecasting (1-hour ahead) and multistep-ahead forecasting (24-hours ahead); those differences are explained in Figure 1.20.

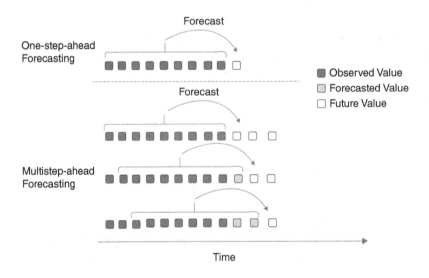

Figure 1.20 Illustration of One-step-ahead versus Multistep-ahead Forecasting

In a one-step-ahead forecasting model, we forecast only the immediate next step, so all of the information used in the model consists of observed values. In multistep forecasting, we fed the value from the one-step-ahead forecast model back into the model as input and did this recursively until we reached the forecast horizon. Since forecasted values are fed back into the multistep-ahead model, those values can contribute to higher forecasting errors. This may be reflected as a higher error rate in both Weighted Absolute Percentage Error (WAPE) and Root Mean Squared Error (RMSE).

We created a two-layer deep RNN. The performance metrics for the deep learning model are shown in Table 1.3 for the 1-hour- and 24-hour-ahead models. These are compared to a naïve ("no change") model (using the actual value from 1 hour and 24 hours in advance). Twenty-four-hour-ahead forecasting is a common practice for solar forecasting.

It is worth noting the considerable accuracy improvement in the DL-RNN model compared to the naïve model. The magnitude of this improvement (80–90% lower error than the naïve) would be very uncommon in, for example, supply-chain forecasting. Such a degree of improvement should normally raise suspicions about the methods or measurement. However, in this situation, there is a reasonable explanation.

It is known that the GHI variable typically accounts for over 70% of the variation in solar-power output. While the naïve model takes no account of GHI (or any other variables), it is therefore at a disadvantage compared to the DL-RNN model. Reasonably accurate forecasts of GHI can be generated 1 and 24 hours in advance, so any model that incorporates the forecasted GHI value should have a significant advantage over models that don't use it.

Summary

Based on these metrics, a recurrent neural network is a viable forecasting strategy for forecasting solar energy output when there is a large amount of historical data available.

One needs to give careful consideration to how the RNNs are configured, with a key parameter being the number of layers used in the model. Other parameters include the type of RNN used, the number of neurons per recurrent unit, and how the weights are initialized in the model. One caveat is that if response variables at previous time steps are used as input, then different forecasting strategies need to be made for one-step and multistep-ahead forecasting. RNNs are another tool to add to the forecasting toolbox for suitable business applications, such as solar forecasting.

Best Practices and Other Tips

Neural network strategies have many parameters to set up and initialize. This section discusses some common pitfalls that are related to the different parameters. Data standardization and activation functions must be chosen along with architectural choices such as the numbers of hidden layers and nodes and the initial neuron connection weights. Model training options such as the optimization algorithm, number of tries, and stopping criteria must also be specified.

Table 1.3 Performance of Naïve and DL-RNN Models

MODEL	1 hour ahead		24 hours ahead	
	WAPE	RMSE	WAPE	RMSE
Naïve	33.67	93.93	71.08	185.79
DL-RNN	5.51	17.45	7.17	21.55

Out-of-Sample Testing

Neural networks and other machine learning models are prone to overfitting during the training process. Overfitting causes the models to make very accurate predictions in the training data but generalize poorly to new data. SAS Visual Forecasting includes a robust early-stopping option that does a good job of preventing overfitting, but reserving part of the data for out-of-sample testing is still a good practice.

Neural Network Architecture

Choosing the number of hidden layers and neurons is the primary way that you can specify the NN architecture. As in time-series models, parsimony is your friend here. Smaller neural networks often perform better than those that have many nodes and layers for two reasons: First, the training time and the number of model parameters increase rapidly with the number of nodes and layers, thus requiring longer times to train. Second, as the network size grows, it is more likely to learn more complex interactions, which eventually leads to overfitting (Diaconescu 2008). It is recommended that you start with a single layer containing 10 nodes and adjust from there if you are not satisfied. Autotuning can also be applied, but it has an even more drastic effect on the training time and is often not necessary. The distribution of connection weights should also be specified. The Xavier and normal distributions are good choices.

Activation Functions and Standardization

Not all activation functions and data standardization methods are compatible with each other. Two options are available for standardization of the input and output data: z-score and mid-range. Z-score standardization scales values to a zero mean and standard deviation equal to 1, whereas mid-range standardization scales values to fall within the range $(-1,1)$. Each activation function also has some range of output values, as shown in Table 1.4.

The activation function for the output layer must be compatible with the output standardization method. Consider an example that uses the tanh function on the output layer and z-score standardization for the output values. In this case, the output tanh

Table 1.4 Activation Function Ranges

Activation Function	Input Range	Output Range
Sigmoid	$[-\infty,\infty]$	$(0,1)$
Logistic	$[-\infty,\infty]$	$(0,1)$
Tanh	$[-\infty,\infty]$	$(-1,1)$
Rectifier	$[-\infty,\infty]$	$[0,\infty]$
Identity	$[-\infty,\infty]$	$[-\infty,\infty]$
Sine	$[-\infty,\infty]$	$(-1,1)$

function is trying to map its (−1,1) output to data with a range of (−σ, σ), which results in loss of information for |σ| > 1, where σ is the standard deviation.

Neural networks for time series generally work well by using a rectifier activation function for hidden layers and an identity activation function on the output layer. This configuration allows any standardization method for the input and output variables. If you try different activation functions, then you must ensure compatibility between the output layer activation function and the output standardization.

Algorithm

Two algorithm options are available for training the PSNN and stacked model. Historically, stochastic gradient descent (SGD) has been used often for neural networks, but SGD frequently requires subtle tuning of its parameters such as the learning rate and annealing rate. If your data set is large (over 100,000 rows), then SGD might be a good option. However, for most applications, the limited-memory Broyden-Fletcher-Goldfarb-Shanno (LBFGS) algorithm converges faster and is easier to use.

Overfitting

Regularization is one technique to avoid overfitting because it penalizes large connection weights. L1 and L2 regularization terms can be specified, but they should be used sparingly because incorporating lagged variables into the training data can also have a regularizing effect and lead to an underfitted model. You can start with 0 for both L1 and L2 regularization and try increasing them if your out-of-sample fit is much worse than the in-sample fit.

The early-stopping mechanism is very effective at stopping the training/validation cycle when the validation fit stops improving. However, the error that is measured over the input space is almost always nonconvex, which means that multiple local minima can be found. The stagnation property specifies how many training iterations can complete with no improvement in the validation fit before ending the training/ validation cycle. This helps the solver find its way out of local minima so that it can continue searching for better solutions.

Conclusion

This paper introduces the neural network-based modeling strategies available in SAS Visual Forecasting and provides guidelines for using them effectively. It explains important considerations for using machine learning strategies for time-series forecasting, including structuring of the input data and extraction of features from the input data to aid in modeling. Guidelines for determining when to use a machine learning model are shown, and an example panel series neural network model was fit to data from Chicago's Array of Things environmental monitoring project. The example was shown to significantly outperform hierarchical forecasting, as evidenced by a WMAPE error measurement about half the size of that for the classical model. A deep learning–recurrent neural network was also demonstrated, forecasting energy generation by a solar farm. Other details and pitfalls not covered in the examples are explained, including architecture considerations, regularization, and compatibility of activation functions with data standardization techniques. Finally, the algorithm scaling is evaluated, showing that training time increases linearly with the number of observations.

Acknowledgments

Special thanks go out to the Array of Things team, the City of Chicago, the National Science Foundation, and any other contributors to the Array of Things project for their hard work and for making the data available to the public.

References

Box, G. E. P. (1976). Science and statistics. *Journal of the American Statistical Association* 71 (356): 791–799.

Box, G. E. P., and Draper, N. R. (1987). *Empirical model-building and response surfaces.* New York: Wiley.

Christ, M., Kempa-Liehr, A. W., and Feindt, M. (2016). Distributed and parallel time series feature extraction for industrial big data applications. *ArXive Pre-Print.* arXiv:1610.07717v3.

Crone, S. F., and Häger, S. (2016). *Feature selection of autoregressive neural network inputs for trend time series forecasting.* IEEE International Joint Conference on Neural Networks.

Diaconescu, E. (2008). The use of NARX neural networks to predict chaotic time series. *WSEAS Transactions on Computer Research* 3 (3): 182–191.

Goodfellow, I., Yoshua, B., and Courville, A. (2016). *Back-propagation and other differentiation algorithms.* Cambridge, MA: MIT Press.

Kahler, S. (2018). Using deep learning to forecast solar energy [SAS Data Science Blog]. https://blogs.sas.com/content/subconsciousmusings/2018/07/05/deep-learning-forecasts-solar-power/

Mills, S. (2020). Neural network-based forecasting strategies in SAS® Viya®. SAS Global Forum 2020, Paper SAS4493-2020.

SAS (2019). How to do deep learning with SAS. [White Paper]. https://www.sas.com/content/dam/SAS/en_us/doc/whitepaper1/deep-learning-with-sas-109610.pdf

SAS (2020). SAS 2019–2020 annual report. https://www.sas.com/content/dam/SAS/documents/corporate-collateral/annual-report/company-overview-annual-report.pdf

Taşpınar, F. (2015). Improving artificial neural network model predictions of daily average PM10 concentrations by applying principle component analysis and implementing seasonal models. *Journal of the Air & Waste Management Association* 65 (7): 800–809.

Yoshio, K., Hipel, K. W., and Mcleod, A. I. (2005). Forecasting nonlinear time series with feed-forward neural networks: A case study of Canadian Lynx data. *Journal of Forecasting* 24 (2): 105–117.

Zhang, G. (2003). Time series forecasting using a hybrid ARIMA and neural network model. *Neurocomputing* 50: 159–175.

1.4 WILL DEEP AND MACHINE LEARNING SOLVE OUR FORECASTING PROBLEMS?*

Stephan Kolassa

Researchers have made incredible progress in artificial intelligence (AI) and machine learning (ML) in past years, and the three previous articles have provided sober examples of this progress. However, AI and ML are still hyped in many quarters, but as yet are nowhere near as good as the hype might make you think. The problems, as Stephan Kolassa points out, include data hunger, opacity, brittleness, dubious input data, fickle trust by users, and straightforward project-management issues.

While AI/ML are important additions to a forecaster's toolbox, they will not automatically solve our forecasting problems. This conclusion is underscored by 2018's M4 competition, which was dominated by hybrid and combination approaches, while "pure" AI/ML methods were not competitive.

Great success in some fields does not automatically carry over to an unrelated field like forecasting. Even if AI/ML methods become more accurate, other considerations such as computation time and understandability may outweigh the benefit. As stated by Robert Fildes in a quote to close this piece, "The notion that off-the-shelf ML methods will automatically produce improvements in accuracy . . . must be regarded as fanciful."

Introduction

Anyone who has not spent the past 10 years under a rock is aware of the giant strides that have been made in machine learning (ML) and artificial intelligence (AI). Deep learning (DL) and other AI/ML methods surpass humans at image recognition and at tasks that were traditionally considered "too hard for computers," like the Asian game of Go, also known as *Weiqi* (Chinese) or *Baduk* (Korean). And in forecasting, AI/ML methods have shown a strong performance in the recent M4 forecasting competition.

Thus, the question on everyone's lips: Will AI/ML solve our forecasting problems?

Let's start by clarifying nomenclature. It seems like everyone has their own pet definition of "ML" and "AI," and of their relationship to each other. Without going too deeply into semantics here, one possibility would be to use "AI" as a more general term that encompasses automating activities like planning, reasoning, searching, as well as knowledge representation and ML, whereas "ML" could be used to mean more specific model-based approaches that aim at learning relationships in data.

*This article originally appeared in *Foresight: The International Journal of Applied Forecasting* (Spring 2020) and appears here courtesy of the International Institute of Forecasters.

Examples for ML tools would be probabilistic learning, decision trees, genetic algorithms, neural networks, and DL. As such, there doesn't seem to be much difference between algorithms commonly associated with the label "ML" and established forecasting algorithms, like ARIMA and exponential smoothing. As a matter of fact, I very much recommend the commentary on the M4 competition penned by Tim Januschowski et al. (2020), who essentially argue that a classification of forecasting methods as "ML" versus "statistical" misses the mark and offer alternative classifications.

The Good and the Bad

Just in case you have indeed recently emerged from a 10-year hibernation under that rock, here is a short summary of the successes AI/ML have had over the past years.

- Amazon's Alexa routinely understands us well enough to control our entertainment electronics and tell us the weather forecast for Timbuktu. (It doesn't have a very large repertoire of German-language mathematician jokes, though.)
- Google's AlphaGo and AlphaZero routinely beat top professional players at Go, a situation inconceivable only a few years ago when even a lowly amateur player would easily win against the top Go programs of the day.
- Google Translate does a reasonable, though not great, job at translating texts between pretty much any two languages. I would certainly not trust it to provide a watertight translation of a legal document, though, or a decent rendering of a literary text. (If you speak a foreign language and feel masochistic, feed Edgar Allan Poe's "The Bells" to Google Translate, but be prepared for a painful experience!)
- Similarly, product recommendation engines and navigation systems make our lives enormously easier – although, are basket analyses and graph-optimization algorithms "ML"?

So much for the good parts. What about the not-quite-so-good aspects of AI/ML?

Pull up Google Images and search for "Tesla Crash Autopilot." Go ahead, do it now. I'll wait.

Well, now we have seen a number of examples of how AI/ML can – quite literally, and sometimes fatally – crash and burn, which should give us pause in an overly optimistic attitude about the inexorable march of AI/ML towards perfection. As a matter of fact, once you dig a little deeper into investigations of car crashes that involve autopilots, your apprehension will only grow. My favorite quote comes from an IEEE report (Harris 2019) on the NTSB's investigation into a fatal crash by an Uber car on autopilot: "The car's self-driving system did not have the capability to classify an object as a pedestrian unless they were near a crosswalk." Better use crosswalks when self-driving cars are on the prowl.

Of course, this argument is a straw man. Nowhere did Uber, Tesla, or others advertise an "autopilot" that could autonomously drive your car in normal street traffic.

Instead, what they are offering is an "assistant" that will *support* the driver, who still needs to be on board, with their hands on the steering wheel. Most of the crashes we found in our image search occurred because the driver was *not* paying attention, but was trusting the system to be a true "autopilot," while the driver could do anything from chatting to watching a movie.

Does this mean that everything is fine, and that any problems are simply due to an incorrect use of the systems? To a degree, yes. However, this is precisely what I want to argue here: AI/ML systems are nowhere near as good as you might think based on breathless news pieces and marketing materials. In particular, they still require a lot of very specific hand-holding. And if you trust them blindly and fail to provide this domain knowledge input and safety railings, even very simple challenges can lead to major problems. Unfortunately, the current hype provides an environment that may promote exactly this kind of overconfidence.

The Problems

There are different challenges for AI/ML. A few general ones can be found in *Rebooting AI* by Marcus and Davis (2019) – my review of the book also appears in this issue of *Foresight*. The authors identify the following three major problems: AI is data hungry, it is opaque, and it is brittle.

Data Hungry

AI is data hungry. Image-classification software is trained on millions of labeled pictures. Getting these *labeled* training data in the first place is actually a problem all by itself. You may need to use humans via Amazon Mechanical Turk to create it, or use CAPT-CHAs, as in asking humans to detect street signs in pictures. There are large labeled data sets of certain object classes, e.g., of dog breeds, so research proceeds quickly on automatic classification of dog breeds – but neural-network architectures that have been optimized on this very particular task may or may not generalize to other object classification tasks.

The success of AlphaGo and AlphaZero is another example of data hunger. Most game-playing ML is nowadays a case of *reinforcement learning*. For instance, AlphaZero is provided with the bare rules of a game and then proceeds to play against itself many, many, *many* times. Each game played is another data point from which it learns what worked well and what didn't. In reinforcement learning, the training data is created *during training*. The end result for AlphaZero is a system that has played many more games than any human Go player could ever do.

In forecasting, we may also have large numbers of time series, and indeed, ML algorithms typically perform well when they can learn across many such series. Janus-chowski and colleagues (2020) call this approach "global" modeling. However, each separate time series may be very short, and the relationships between the series may be complicated, as in a multilevel product hierarchy. In addition, forecasting typically requires extracting more "signal" from our time series than a classification task, namely one or even multiple forecast values for each of multiple future time periods. And, of course, a reinforcement learning approach, which has shown itself to be extremely powerful in learning how to play board and computer games, cannot be applied in forecasting.

Opaqueness

AI is opaque. AI/ML systems and their output are extremely hard to explain. This has implications on two different levels. The first level is debugging. When AI/ML breaks – and we have seen above that it does – it is often completely unclear why, and where to even start looking to debug it. Marcus and Davis give a couple of examples, like a street sign that was defaced by stickers and was described by an automatic system as "a refrigerator filled with lots of food and drinks." We can deal with a system misclassifying a cat as a dog, but where do we start looking when a street sign is mislabeled as a fridge?

The second level where AI's opacity is problematic is in building trust. Not everyone is fine with a black-box model, or they may be fine with it only in noncritical applications. In areas where critical processes feel the impact, people often need to understand why a system gives the kind of output it does before they can trust it. Some systems are good at this, like checklists in medical or aviation environments, or decomposition approaches to forecasting. Other systems, like neural networks and random forests, typically are far harder to understand. Recently, Yelland, Baz, and Serafini (2019) noted the key importance of understandability in building a forecasting system driving a major retailer's operations.

Fortunately, this aspect is not lost on AI/ML researchers (who are, by and large, very intelligent people). Much effort is being devoted to a new research direction called "explainable AI." Approaches include, for example, evaluating how much attention an image-classification network pays to particular regions in an image. (One finding was that in classifying dog breeds, huskies were detected not through their physical characteristics, but because pictures of huskies far more often included a lot of white in the background – namely, snow.) Alternatively, one can apply a small perturbation to the input, examine the resulting change in the output, and hope for enlightenment. This is a very praiseworthy endeavor, but the more complex AI/ML methods will always *inherently* be harder to understand. There is a reason why there is no research agenda on "explainable" exponential smoothing!

Brittleness

AI is brittle. As noted above, AI/ML can fail by changing the input in small and seemingly innocuous ways (e.g., by adding stickers to street signs). AI/ML simply cannot reason outside its programmed framework – recall Uber's car not being able to classify something as a pedestrian unless it was near a crosswalk. Any human would be able to perform this small feat of generalization, but AI/ML may not be, depending on whether or not the programmer anticipated specific kinds of potentially necessary generalization.

There is an entire research stream devoted to making AI/ML methods break in the most entertaining way possible, which has also spawned bona fide advances in AI/ML itself, in the form of so-called *generative-adversarial networks* (GANs). This is good, but the problem remains: while we can reasonably trust a human not to be fooled by a few stickers into believing a street sign is a refrigerator, there is no guarantee our AI/ML system won't start making completely nonsensical errors.

As I've noted, Marcus and Davis go into much more detail on all these problems. For the time being, I would like to add a few more problem dimensions to the three explained earlier. Specifically, *input data are dubious, trust is easily lost,* and *AI projects are projects, too.*

A Few More Problems

Input data are dubious. In my experience in retail forecasting, the best hope for improving forecast accuracy is not in using a more complicated system, or in adding more layers to your DL network, or (more sophisticatedly) in tweaking our regularization setup. Rather, it lies in better understanding the relevant causal drivers. In a retail environment, these may be promotions, prices, and calendar events. Thus, understanding input data – and cleaning it appropriately – is supremely important in forecasting.

However, our capacity for *leveraging* data has far outpaced our capacity for *cleaning and organizing* it. Part of the problem is that AI/ML sounds far more impressive than database schemas and writing sanity checks, and partly because software and database vendors propagated a mindset of collecting data *now* and worrying about cleaning it later. Unfortunately, many companies never found the time and the resources for the "cleaning" part. Sound familiar?

Accordingly, the vast majority of problematic retail forecasts I see are cases where a new promotion type has been introduced that we simply have no experience with, or – prosaically – the system was fed wrong prices or a promotion's duration was wrongly specified. Garbage in, garbage out, whether there is a linear regression or a deep network between the input and the output. These kinds of problems will not be solved by AI/ML alone, but by a conscious effort to clean up data.

Trust is easily lost. In creating a forecasting system, we typically deal with large numbers of time series that we need to forecast automatically and quickly. In contrast to long-term forecasts ("futurist" is a great career: the best forecasts are the ones that can only be evaluated in a hundred years), operational forecasters get very quick feedback, in a matter of days or hours – or even sooner, if the forecast is so *obviously* wrong that we don't even need to wait for the actual outcome.

Unfortunately, really bad forecasts have a way of sticking out like the proverbial sore thumb: as a single misforecasted time series may be just one out of 100,000 series, your thumb is just a tiny part of your body. Until, of course, you hit it with a hammer, at which point in time it becomes the focal point of your earthly existence for a few memorable moments. For the practicing forecaster, explaining an obviously wrong forecast to a business user may be a comparable experience. And misforecasting badly may very quickly erode your users' trust in the entire "newfangled system," and they may return to their old spreadsheet forecasts after just a few such problems.

No, this is not a problem that is specific to AI/ML. However, just as with all the other problems noted here, these issues interact and reinforce each other.

- If your forecasting method is not opaque, trust may not be so easily lost – you may be able to explain a bad forecast and how you will make sure it doesn't occur again.

- If your method is not brittle, or if your input data were not dubious, the bad forecast might not have happened in the first place.

- If your system was not so data hungry, you might have been able to vet your smaller inputs more carefully.

Here is a quote from Marcus and Davis (2009, p. 185) that encapsulates the essence of their analysis: "AI scientists must actively do their best to stay far away from building systems that have the potential to spiral out of control."

AI projects are projects, too. Marcus and Davis touch on IBM's Watson system and how Watson projects were stopped at multiple medical establishments. Part of the problem was that Watson simply didn't deliver better clinical accuracy than the alternatives. But, importantly, other stumbling blocks included classic, well-known project management issues: scope creep, missed milestones, disappearing budget, changing priorities. The takeaway: just because a project involves AI/ML does not mean that project management gets any easier. More to the point, AI/ML will not work straight out of the box – even if, as you'd expect, vendors' ad copy has a vested interest in suggesting that it does.

What about the M4 Competition?

"Okay," I hear you say, "this is all well and good, but what about the M4 forecasting competition? Wasn't it won by a neural network?"

Actually, that's a great question! The M4 competition makes for enormously interesting reading, and I recommend that you take a look at the findings and the commentaries yourself. All the material is currently free to download in Volume 36, Issue 1 of the *International Journal of Forecasting*. And when you look a little more closely, you find that the key findings are a little more complicated than "NNs won the M4 competition." Specifically:

- The winning method featured a combination of straightforward exponential smoothing and LSTM networks.

- Second place was taken by combining standard forecasting methods using gradient boosting.
- The method in third place again combined standard forecasting methods using pooling and weights derived from in-sample performance – no ML required (unless you count clustering as ML).
- Overall, the M4 competition was dominated by combination and hybrid approaches.
- A number of extremely simple combinations performed very competitively – and quickly!
- "Pure" ML methods were not competitive at all.

Conclusion

There is no question that AI/ML have made giant strides. Judging by results, Alexa understands me better than my kids, and I will never again beat a state-of-the-art Go program, which I used to do easily 10 years ago. However, we should be careful: great success in one field (like Go) does not automatically carry over to an unrelated field (like forecasting) just because there is the same "AI/ML" sticker on the box. Yes, AI/ML is now a force to be reckoned with in forecasting, but the M4 competition has shown that it is not necessarily a game changer. Even if AI/ML methods are more accurate – and it is by no means certain that they automatically are – other considerations such as understandability may outweigh this higher accuracy (Yelland et al. 2019).

Here, I will let Robert Fildes (2020) have the last word: "The notion that off-the-shelf ML methods will *automatically* produce improvements in accuracy, which has been propagated by some software suppliers, must be regarded as fanciful."

References

Fildes, R. (2020). Learning from forecasting competitions (invited commentary on the M4 forecasting competition). *International Journal of Forecasting* 36 (1): 186–188.

Harris, M. (2019). NTSB investigation into deadly Uber self-driving car crash reveals lax attitude toward safety. https://spectrum.ieee.org/cars-that-think/transportation/self-driving/ntsb-investigation-into-deadly-uber-selfdriving-car-crash-reveals-lax-attitude-toward-safety

Januschowski, T., Gasthaus, J., Wang, Y., et al. (2020). Criteria for classifying forecasting methods (invited commentary on the M4 forecasting competition). *International Journal of Forecasting* 36 (1): 167–177.

Marcus, G., and Davis, E. (2019). *Rebooting AI: Building artificial intelligence we can trust*. New York: Pantheon Books.

Yelland, P., Baz, Z. E., and Serafini, D. (2019). Forecasting at scale: The architecture of a modern retail forecasting system, *Foresight* 55 (Fall); 10–18.

1.5 FORECASTING THE IMPACT OF ARTIFICIAL INTELLIGENCE: THE EMERGING AND LONG-TERM FUTURE*

Spyros Makridakis

This is the final installment of a five-part series on forecasting the impact of artificial intelligence by Spyros Makridakis, published in consecutive issues of *Foresight* (Fall 2017–Fall 2018). Here, Makridakis assesses AI's ongoing influence on human culture and commerce by focusing on 10 technological trends that stand to have a profound impact on our lives. These 10 trends are Supercomputing, Nanotechnology, Medicine and Genomics, Renewable Energy and Energy Storage, Autonomous Vehicles (AVs) and Drones, Advanced Robotics, Advanced Materials, 3D Printers, Augmented and Virtual Reality, and Sophisticated Virtual Assistants.

The effects of a few of these trends are already being felt in our day-to-day affairs, while others might seem to have sprung from the imaginations of the most audacious science fiction writers. One thing appears certain: it is truer now than ever before that, as the author noted at the outset of this series, the challenge will continue to be to predict forthcoming technologies without falling into the trap of shortsightedness, which has plagued so many of the previous forecasts.

This series provoked a lengthy commentary by Owen Davies, along with a separate discussion of the topic by Lawrence Vanston. Both of these follow, along with a response from Makridakis.

"Whether we are based on carbon or on silicon makes no fundamental difference; we should each be treated with appropriate respect."

—Arthur C. Clarke, author of *2001: A Space Odyssey*

"Anything you dream is fiction, and anything you accomplish is science – the whole history of mankind is nothing but science fiction."

—Ray Bradbury, author of *Fahrenheit 451*

Introduction

The famous French economist Jean-Baptiste Say stated in 1828 that cars could never substitute for horses in a busy, great city. Of course, Say couldn't be blamed for his prediction as the cars of that time had no resemblance to modern ones and were hardly going faster than horses, even at the end of the 19th century when a person with a red flag had to walk before a car to warn of its coming. Could Say, in his wildest imaginings,

---

*This article originally appeared in *Foresight: The International Journal of Applied Forecasting* (Fall 2018) and appears here courtesy of the International Institute of Forecasters.

have believed that 190 years later there would be driverless cars cruising the streets of Phoenix, Arizona, in what promises to become the greatest disrupted technology of all time?

But even in 1900, less than a decade before Henry Ford's Model T was produced, French futurologists celebrating the arrival of the 20th century created a series of "sketches" entitled *Life in the Year 2000,* where there were barely a handful of cars on a major Paris boulevard but plenty of airplanes and other flying objects. Driverless vehicles were not within the realm of possibility even in the 1950s and 1960s, while there were still plenty of predictions about flying cars, jet-packs, and domed cities.

Accurate predictions about the long-term future are rare and highly uncertain. They usually underestimate reality considerably by linearly extrapolating the present. Even the predictions for 2014 made in 1964 by Isaac Asimov, the celebrated science fiction writer, that appeared in the *New York Times* were shockingly conservative (Rosen 2013), and (together with some correct forecasts!) included underwater homes, underground cities, and moon colonies. Asimov, the same as many others, did not envision the widespread utilization of computers, the Internet, or mobile phones, never mind driverless cars. Thomas Watson, IBM's president at the time, made his infamous prediction in 1943 that "there will be a world market for maybe five computers"; Ken Olson, the founder and CEO of Digital Equipment Corporation, said in 1977 that "there is no reason for any individual to have a computer in his home." (Now we not only have several at home, but also one in our pocket, with a smartphone.) These are well-known examples of the shortsightedness of human prediction.

Any attempt to predict the long-term future of humanity is a big challenge on two grounds: not being too conservative in our predictions of new technological developments and their impact, and not falling on the other side of the fence and forecasting things that will never materialize. This is particularly true for AI, where there is very little agreement about its future path and potential impact. For these reasons, I will follow a different approach. First, I will separate the near future from the long term and consider four interrelated indicators to determine how potential, emerging technologies will affect us. I will then extrapolate the most critical of these technologies to predict the long term, believing that what could be considered science fiction (SF) today will probably be the reality of tomorrow. Maybe keeping Jean-Baptiste Say in mind can help us to accept some far-fetched predictions.

The 10 Major Emerging Trends

The emerging trends of this section are in addition to those of AI, intelligence augmentation (IA), and blockchain (BC), and their integration already presented in a previous part of this series. The potential of these emerging trends packs considerable power, enough to affect all aspects of our lives, our work, our organizations. Because of space restraints, I will not cover them all in great detail, but I will highlight what I see as their major impacts.

Here are the 10 major emerging trends:

1. Supercomputing

2. Nanotechnology

3. Medicine and Genomics

4. Renewable Energy and Energy Storage

5. Autonomous Vehicles (AVs) and Drones

6. Advanced Robotics

7. Advanced Materials

8. 3D Printers

9. Augmented and Virtual Reality

10. Sophisticated Virtual Assistants

The speed at which the above 10 trends will advance in the future will depend upon the four factors listed below, as well as their interaction. In a decade or less, however, they will result in some fundamental changes in practically all aspects of our lives, work, and society.

1. *The X (improvement) Factor:* The number of times that the expected benefits of the proposed technology will be greater than those of the existing one.

2. *Amount of Investment and Number of Startups Being Funded:* Clearly, the more money being invested and the more startups being funded, the higher the probability that the proposed new technologies will succeed.

3. *Expected Growth in Spending:* The greater the expected growth in spending, the higher the chance that a potential technology will materialize.

4. *Existing Problems and the Urgency of Solving Them:* Consider, for instance, the critical need to deal with pollution and global warming; urgency at this level will affect the previous three factors and contribute to achieving technological improvements at faster rates.

Supercomputers, High-Speed Networks, and the Cloud

On March 19, 2018, IBM announced that it had made the world's smallest computer, designed from the ground up to work with the blockchain. The computer itself was smaller than a single grain of salt, coming in at 1 millimeter by 1 millimeter and reportedly having about the same computing power as a 1990s-era CPU.

This is a remarkable achievement on four counts. First, it proves the great advances of nanotechnology. Second, it demonstrates that incredibly cheap, amazingly tiny computers will be available for a wide range of applications, provide sophisticated processing power everywhere it's needed, and eventually be used instead of RFIDs to tag materials and products. Third, the trend of producing smaller and smaller gadgets will continue in the future, reaching eventually the level of single atoms. Lastly, the trend toward supercomputing will also continue and may even accelerate with the appearance of quantum computing that will be millions of times faster than conventional machines. The obvious implications of Trends 1 (supercomputing) and 2 (nanotechnology) will be practically free computing and unlimited storage, affecting all remaining trends and accelerating AI, IA, and their integration.

The trends toward faster/smaller computers, practically unlimited and cheaper memory, and speedier/cheaper network connections have been fundamentally transforming the landscape of computer applications. The iPhone X today has the speed and memory of a mid-1990s supercomputer while incorporating face-recognition technology that at that time was considered impossible to develop. These improvements in technology are leading to the wide utilization of cloud computing, which enables access to storage and data-transfer sites like Dropbox. The cloud will facilitate integrated computing services, mostly over the Internet, that in addition to storage would provide processing power as well as all the programs required for all computer needs of individuals/organizations. Such cloud services are already offered today by Amazon, Microsoft, IBM, and many others.

This means that instead of owning expensive computers, IT infrastructure, and software programs, organizations and individuals can utilize (rent) all services required for fulfilling their computing needs, thus avoiding up-front costs and having access to such services with minimal effort and little expert knowledge, simply "paying as you go." Some of the most advanced computer applications, such as AI, ML, and BC as well as specialized software for various industries and firms, will be offered through cloud providers. Hospitals, for instance, can utilize advanced AI image-recognition algorithms in the cloud to diagnose cancer in X-rays instead of owning expensive equipment and specialized and expensive algorithms to do so in-house. Similarly, the many dedicated programs for optimizing the inputs from IoT gadgets will not have to be located on each premise but can be run in the cloud, avoiding complex setups and expensive equipment.

The potential of the cloud as a utility service can be confirmed by the strong competition evidenced among the big players and a number of promising startups. Cloud services have the ability to revolutionize computer usage, costs, and ease of accessing applications. It will be the equivalent of not having to own and operate a personal generator for getting electric power. Instead, superfast and reliable networks will allow Computing as a Service (CaaS), avoiding the need to own expensive equipment/software and employ expert personnel. Furthermore, using the cloud would not require anything more than a digital watch (at least for individuals) to be able to utilize all computing services from smartphones to sophisticated AI applications. Eventually, using the cloud could become as easy as using electricity.

Medicine and Genomics

The trend toward more effective medicine will continue exploiting information from genomics while utilizing AI to improve diagnostics, discover more effective drugs, and reduce preventable medical errors, now the third-highest cause of death. As the cost of medical care has been exploding and the population graying, there is a growing need for efficient and affordable medical services, and that means attracting new startups entering the medical field and offering innovative service.

At the same time, established firms like Amazon, Berkshire Hathaway, and JPMorgan (Reuters 2018) are planning partnerships to cut health costs and improve services for their employees, with an eye from Amazon to offer such improved services to the general public. Medical improvements could reduce costs substantially, improve the quality of our health, and further extend our life expectancy. Such improvements will be the motivation for fundamental changes in the entire medical industry that will lead to a new era of unimaginable progress.

Renewable Energy and Energy Storage

A new report by the International Renewable Energy Agency, or IRENA (2016), concluded that the global weighted average cost of electricity could fall by 26% from onshore wind, by 35% from offshore wind, by at least 37% from concentrating solar power (CSP) technologies, and by 59% from solar photovoltaics (PV) by 2025. With these trends also reducing pollution and the exhaustion of natural resources, there are strong benefits for investing in renewable energy while at the same time increasing the motivation for research on how to store generated energy for later use when the wind and sun are unavailable. If the trends toward greater energy conversion and superior storage ability continue, all our energy needs could be easily satisfied from renewables and create a world of cheap and clean energy affordable to everyone, everywhere.

AVs and Drones

AVs (once they're in mass production) will disrupt not only automobile usage and ownership, but also garages, taxis, and trucks, among other concerns. At present, the usage of cars is at about 5%, meaning that 95% of the time they are in garages or parked outside. Moreover, when cars are moving, the average number of passengers per car is less than 1.5.

Not only are cars underutilized, they also require huge infrastructure (garages, refueling stations, etc.) in the center of cities to accommodate the cars of those working during the day, plus others in houses and apartment buildings. Affordable AVs that can be called by telephone when transportation is needed will eliminate the need for owning a car and, together with ride sharing, will noticeably reduce traffic jams and pollution, as well as the size of parking accommodations in apartment and office buildings that at present make up around 30% of the total construction cost. Most important, however, they will reduce traffic accidents together with deaths and bodily injuries by more than 90%, according to some reports.

Drones will ultimately influence the ways goods are delivered and provide personalized transportation through the air similar to that of today's helicopters. As the trend toward cheaper, more reliable self-operating drones will continue, they will become part of our lives and be used in numerous applications.

Greater Wealth and More Comfort

I've grouped the remaining five emerging trends (advanced robotics, superior materials, 3D printers, virtual and augmented reality, and sophisticated virtual assistants) together, as they would all be contributing to greater material wealth and more comfort to people's lives. Advanced robotics will accelerate the pace of automation and further increase productivity. Superior materials will enhance construction and improve the life and usage of durable goods, while 3D printers have even now opened up new opportunities for the creation of prototypes to print toys, specific parts made out of plastic, and, more recently, even full-scale houses. Augmented reality will provide new dimensions for entertainment and education while sophisticated assistants will become initially our personal secretaries and, eventually, someone to interact with as a trusted companion.

The "Science Fiction" Type of Technological Developments

Ray Kurzweil, a director of engineering at Google (and the premier technological optimist), is using the following three "bridges" to describe the future world (Garma 2015):

1. Bridge 1 is the current medical technology aimed at keeping people healthy and slowing down aging by improving our diet, exercise, use of personalized medicine, and other innovations.
2. Bridge 2 will utilize biotechnology widely and be capable of reprogramming our biological system to make us resistant to disease. The objective of the second bridge is to sufficiently reduce or even eliminate disease or genetic propensities so that we can live long enough to get to the third bridge.
3. Bridge 3 will use nanotechnology to merge biology with machines, increasing our life span significantly, and eventually connecting our brains to the cloud, expanding human memory and intelligence at least to the level of AI.

Other SF-type inventions mentioned in the literature are telepresence, telepathy, and – further out in the future – brain implants, brain/computer interface (BCI), brain emulations (Ems), and transhumanism, embracing technology to enhance our skills/capabilities (Hanson 2016), and finally interplanetary travel beyond our solar system (Kaku 2018).

What will become reality and what will remain in the domain of science fiction? I will leave this question to the reader to answer – keeping in mind Jean-Baptiste Say in 1828 and his prediction about cars and horses, Isaac Asimov's *New York Times* forecasts in 1964 for the year 2014, and Olson's conviction that we would not need personal computers at home.

Conclusions

This five-part article has covered advances in AI, how they will affect all of us, and what can be done to exploit the availing opportunities while avoiding the lurking dangers by correctly predicting these revolutionary changes and planning for them.

- In the first installment I looked at predictions I made in 1995 to identify my successes and failures and to present what I now see as the forthcoming achievements in AI.

- In Part 2, I presented four major AI possibility scenarios and showed how they might have an impact on us, as well as the actions needed to avoid their potentially negative consequences.

- In the third installment I probed into how these technologies will affect the competitive landscape to which our business models will have to adapt.

- In Part 4, I investigated blockchain technology, its integration with AI, and the challenges and potentialities of intelligence augmentation.

- In this fifth and concluding section I've examined emerging technological trends and advances with an eye toward both near-term and long-term forecasts.

What we *can* predict with certainty in all of this is that, for the first time in our long history, we humans will have a worthy opponent to compete with – one that we created ourselves. While there is rarely agreement about the outcome of such competition, we've seen that AI is superb in winning all sorts of games and in image, speech, and text recognition, where it has far surpassed human performance. However, in a study we just published (Makridakis, Spiliotis, and Assimakopoulos 2018) comparing machine learning (ML) and statistical methods, we found that "the accuracy of the best of ML methods was worse than the least accurate of statistical ones." Our findings and other similar conclusions support Moravec's paradox, which is often stated as "Robots find the difficult things easy and the easy things difficult."

This paradox reinforces the complementarity of AI and IA and provides a positive note to the gloom of pessimists predicting the end of humanity. IA – even if the sci-fi type of predictions are downplayed – would allow us to stay at least on par with AI, and even stay ahead of it if some form of direct contact with computers is achieved beyond the keyboard interface and the faster but still inadequate voice communications. Direct brain-to-computer connections are the hope to stay competitive in this race, and ways to achieve this type of linkage will have to be found, given its great importance for the future of humanity.

My strong belief is that the 10 emerging trends mentioned above will continue to affect all aspects of our lives, work, and society in general, and that we will experience significant breakthroughs in the next couple of decades. In all likelihood, initially a wristwatch will be the only gadget we will need to communicate, using voice commands, with cloud computers and storing/retrieving all information (personal or stored in Google-type services) from the cloud and processing it at lightning speed. Computer screens will not be needed, as our watches will be capable of projecting and making available any information we require while blending virtual and augmented reality in a harmonious manner. Our holographic communications will also be done through our watches in an augmented-reality manner. At a later time there will be some forms of BCI, allowing us unlimited access to computer power. Teaching, working, and interacting socially will all be affected, while personal assistants and robots will be doing all the boring, uninteresting work. We will, of course, live healthier, longer, and more comfortable lives.

The major concerns are the resulting great wealth inequality, both between people living within the same country and among AI/IA leaders and the rest of the world; the probability of a race among nations to stay ahead in technological advancements – similar to the arms race of the mid-to-late 20th century; and the challenge of exploiting AI/IA to capitalize on its greatest advantages.

In conclusion, I want to refer one more time to my prediction of our wristwatch of the future being the only gadget we will need to communicate and connect with computers using the cloud. I thought this reality would be far out into the future, and even worried that it resembled more of a sci-fi effort. Well, three days after I had originally written about it, there was the following story in the Kurzweil AI newsletter (2018):

Three radical new user interfaces

Holographic videoconferencing, a smart wall, and a smartwatch projector offer new ways to interact with data and each other.

I felt that, in just those three days, science fiction had become reality right before my eyes and that BCI cannot be too far away.

References

Angel.co. https://angel.co/supply-chain-management

Garma, J. (2015). *Are Ray Kurzweil's "three bridges" to immortality insane?*, GarmaOnHealth.com. https://www.garmaonhealth.com/ray-kurzweils-three-bridges-immortality/

Hanson, R. (2016). *The age of Em: Work, love, and life when robots rule the Earth*. Oxford University Press.

IRENA.org (2016). *The power to change: Solar and wind cost reduction potential to* 2025. http://www.irena.org/DocumentDownloads/Publications/IRENA_Power_to_Change_2016.pdf

Kaku, M. (2018). *The future of humanity: Terraforming Mars, interstellar travel, immortality, and our destiny beyond Earth*. Allen Lane.

Kurzweil Accelerating Intelligence News (2018, April 27). http://www.kurzweilai.net/three-radical-new-user-interfaces?utm_source=KurzweilAI+Weekly+Newsletter&utm_campaign=1ebec2faf2-UA-946742-1&utm_medium=email&utm_term=0_147a5a48c1-1ebec2faf2-282225629

Makridakis, S., Spiliotis, E., and Assimakopoulos, V. (2018). Statistical and machine learning forecasting methods: Concerns and ways forward. *PLOS ONE* (March 27). https://doi.org/10.1371/journal.pone.0194889

Reuters.com (2018). *CEO to be named soon for Berkshire, Amazon, JPMorgan Healthcare Venture*. https://www.reuters.com/article/us-berkshire-buffett-healthcare/ceo-to-be-named-soon-for-berkshire-amazon-jpmorgan-healthcare-venture-cnbc.html

Rosen, R. J. (2013, December 31). In 1964, Isaac Asimov imagined the world in 2014, *The Atlantic*. https://www.theatlantic.com/technology/archive/2013/12/in-1964-isaac-asimov-imagined-the-world-in-2014/282728/

COMMENTARY: SPYROS MAKRIDAKIS'S ARTICLE "FORECASTING THE IMPACT OF ARTIFICIAL INTELLIGENCE"*

Owen Davies

> By 2005 or so, it will become clear that the internet's impact on the economy has been no greater than the fax machine's. . . . As the rate of technological change in computing slows, the number of jobs for IT specialists will decelerate, then actually turn down; ten years from now, the phrase 'information economy' will sound silly."
>
> – Paul Krugman, Nobel laureate economist, in 1998

Long-Term Forecasts

Some years ago I had the opportunity to chat with Sergei Sikorsky, son of Igor and probably the go-to person for insight into vertical-lift technology and markets. He mentioned an essay his father had written in the 1930s and kindly sent me a copy. In it, the helicopter's inventor looked ahead to life as it might be some decades on. It was fascinating reading. There were no Jetsons-style personal aircraft, no highways miraculously twined among skyscrapers hundreds of feet in the air (then a favorite of science-fiction illustrators), neither so much as a single robot. Not everything Sikorsky envisioned has come to pass, of course; he missed developments such as the personal computer, which arrived during the period he considered. Yet overall, his description of urban life in the late 20th century was remarkably easy to recognize. Those of us who lived in New York, or Chicago, or London or Tokyo at the time would have been at home in his city. In all, it was a forecast that most of us, looking so far into the future, can only envy.

Which of course is why it comes to mind after reading "Forecasting the Impact of Artificial Intelligence" by Prof. Spyros Makridakis. As Prof. Makridakis points out in the first of his five installments, accurate long-term forecasts are rare indeed and seem likely to grow even less common in the future for reasons that become

---

*This commentary originally appeared in *Foresight: The International Journal of Applied Forecasting* (Summer 2019) and appears here courtesy of the International Institute of Forecasters.

clear as we read on. However, that comes as a backdoor implication of this article. We should acknowledge what Spyros has accomplished and consider the issues that remain to be resolved.

Credit where it is due: Spyros has done a better job than most in providing a snapshot of this broad and fast-moving subject of artificial intelligence. His first segment (Fall 2017) traced the history and current state of AI development, hitting the high points without getting lost in needless detail. This primer alone would justify spending time with his essay.

The remaining four installments are devoted to looking ahead. They both explain and demonstrate what a hard job it is to anticipate where this critical technology will lead. "The difficulty is in knowing which of the AI technologies will provide the greatest benefits," he notes – and hence the soundest investments.

Forecasts of the Impacts on Jobs

Spyros writes: "The question everyone asks, however, is will the new jobs being created compensate for or even augment those lost by AI technology, as was the case in the past. . .. Some have considered both sides of the argument and concluded that there are no obvious answers."

TechCast (www.techcastglobal.com) has been following AI for some 20 years. In late 2017, after reading many conflicting estimates, we tried to work out for ourselves how AI technology will affect employment. Per our standard practice, we conducted a Delphi poll among our panel of experts.

We first asked them how soon machines would replace the human mind in 30% of routine mental activities. (We try to make these targets as quantifiable as possible, leaving no ambiguity about when they are met.) Some 85% of the experts believed that machines will replace the human mind in 30% of routine mental activities by 2027. Just over half of those respondents put the target beyond 2022. Another third expected to reach it sooner. Overall, the most likely year was 2025.

Then we asked how AI would affect four categories of employment activity: routine manual tasks, nonroutine manual tasks, routine cognitive tasks, and nonroutine cognitive tasks. Predictably enough, the experts found routine mental tasks most likely to be automated in the near future. Routine manual tasks have been largely mechanized already, and automating nonroutine tasks, whether manual or cognitive, seemed to them beyond the abilities of today's AI.

The experts did believe that AI will trigger a wave of job creation. However, it will not quite replace all the positions technology automates out of existence. When the 30% target is reached, they expected to see a net loss of roughly 5 million jobs. This is enough to be noticed, but should be manageable in an economy that had about 130 million full-time jobs as of mid-2018.

A report from the Federal Reserve Bank of St. Louis seems to confirm that automation already is eroding the market for routine occupations. From mid-1983 to mid-2015, when the study ended, nonroutine manual and nonroutine cognitive jobs have grown steadily. The number of routine jobs, both manual and cognitive, has been essentially unchanged since 2008. Both categories remain several million jobs below their prerecession levels.

It will be interesting to know how many routine occupations have appeared since 2015, as hiring has accelerated and begun to exhaust the candidate pool. However, these categories seem unlikely to have improved much on their recent performance. As a fraction of the workforce, they are in decline. We can expect their slide to accelerate as AI becomes more powerful and companies adjust their business processes to take advantage of it.

Blockchain Technology

Makridakis views blockchain as a complement to AI. For each application, today's deep-learning software requires training on enormous quantities of high-quality data, and in many fields there just aren't enough data to work with. He believes that blockchain repositories will be able to supply the training material not yet available.

I don't believe there's a sound basis on which to accept or reject this suggestion; it is strictly a personal insight. Yet, a counterargument comes to mind: the task of moving business, medical, and especially government data (outside tech-forward Estonia) from conventional databases into blockchains will take years, assuming it is done at all. Even before that effort seriously begins, many scientists are working to help AI master new skills with much less preparation. Several groups already have reported enough success to offer hope that greater reductions lie ahead. Before blockchains offer much help in training AI applications, we may no longer require the masses of data that are needed today.

Intelligence Augmentation (IA)

Intelligence augmentation is the route Makridakis believes humanity will use to avoid obsolescence when AI eventually becomes as smart as we are and incomparably faster. Hook our brains to the AI's computer and all the world's knowledge will be as available as our natural memories, while the software's mimicry of reason will amplify our own cognitive power. In effect, AI is no longer a useful tool, but becomes part of us – "enhancing the way we combine perceptual data into concepts, thus achieving hitherto impossible intellectual feats." If anything can save human jobs from the threat of automation – as well as our sense of personal worth – this should.

At TechCast Global, we have been watching the development of the brain-computer interfaces that IA would require. Our team of about 140 expert forecasters predicts that 30% of the public will use them for ordinary tasks in 2031. However, like general AI itself, this requires significant technological development and probably breakthroughs in our understanding of the mind. Much remains to be accomplished in this field before the IA that Spyros envisions becomes practical.

At least, that is our default position. We could be mistaken. Serial inventor Elon Musk has frequently warned that humanity is likely to find itself displaced by AI. Like Spyros, he believes that intelligence augmentation offers our best hope of remaining relevant, and perhaps even of remaining viable, in the age of intelligent machines.

This September, Musk announced that Neuralink, one of his many companies, will soon reveal exactly the product IA needs, an interface that connects the human brain to computers. It will be "better than anyone thinks possible," he declared on a podcast called "Joe Rogan Experience." "Best-case scenario, we effectively merge with AI." And in that case: "It will enable anyone who wants to have superhuman cognition."

Musk believes IA will give humans their best chance to remain relevant in a world of artificial intelligence. "The merge scenario with AI is the one that seems like probably the best," he said. "If you can't beat it, join it."

We remain to be convinced that practical IA is only months away. Elon Musk has a substantial history of overpromising and underdelivering, at least in the short term. Yet his accomplishments at Tesla and SpaceX and his invention of the Hyperloop make it difficult to discount anything he says about technology. We will be watching this possible advance with great interest.

The Art of Technological Forecasting

What emerges most clearly, from Spyros Makridakis's articles and from our own experience, is how much more difficult the art of forecasting is becoming each day.

Painful experience verifies just how hard forecasting can be even without the complicating factor of technology. I entered forecasting under the tutelage of my mentor and friend Dr. Marvin Cetron, of Forecasting International. Late in 1988, we published a daring forecast that within five years East and West Germany would be reunited as a single country. To our knowledge, that possibility was on no one's horizon ("You heard it here first!"). Of course, it happened in less than one year, before the book reached the stores, but too late for us to amend it. After several similar experiences – fortunately less significant, much less public, and reported by others – I grumbled that it was becoming impossible to predict something that hadn't already happened.

This was not entirely a joke. It is much less so 30 years on. In an age of computers and the internet, tech billionaires with an urge to reshape the world and the money to do it, and endless other factors, a long-term technology forecast that seems reasonable almost certainly is behind the times.

As science-fiction writer William Gibson famously observed, "The future is already here. It's just not very evenly distributed." This is nowhere truer than in AI research.

In considering this issue, Spyros reminds us of Amara's law, which states that we overestimate the effects of new technologies in the short term but underestimate them in the long term. As it happens, this law had been quantified even before Amara formulated it.

In the late 1950s and early 1960s, Dr. Cetron was head of technology forecasting for the U.S. Department of the Navy. It was a busy operation with a long history. Over the years, they had made enough forecasts to permit a valid statistical analysis of the results. It turned out their predictions fell into three groups:

- Four to 15 years was the sweet spot. Forecasts of developments within that range proved correct more often than not. A technology might become available, or its applications significant, a year or two sooner or later than expected, but within reasonable limits their predictions were accurate. Outside that range, forecast accuracy dropped off sharply.

- With target dates of three years or less, things took twice as long to materialize. The basic technology might have been demonstrated that soon, but engineering slowed the development of practical applications. Organizational inertia probably did not help.

- Beyond 15 years, developments took half as long as expected. Either some unpredictable breakthrough in that field brought the target much closer, or a new technology made it obsolete.

So many decades later, in a world where Chinese companies routinely reverse-engineer consumer electronics and bring a knockoff to market in two weeks or less, the timeline surely has changed. The internet spreads discoveries across the globe at light speed. Computers have accelerated engineering and design, and they also have flattened organization charts, so good ideas have fewer layers of management to penetrate before someone in authority can decide they are worth pursuing. It is this characteristic that makes tech companies so mobile and profitable. In an age of accelerating change, we can expect forecasting's long-term horizon to grow ever nearer in the years ahead.

As Spyros Makridakis rightly observes, trying to project where technology will lead us a few decades ahead quickly degenerates into science fiction. In the age of AI, it appears to be doing that faster than ever.

Conclusion

And that brings us full circle. Prof. Makridakis has done as good a job as anyone can of attempting to figure out where AI will lead. If his conclusions are limited and perhaps not entirely satisfying, it is in no way his fault. We simply need better ways to project technology more than a few years ahead – and we will need them ever more urgently as AI becomes more powerful and its applications more widespread. This "drive-by" insight may, in fact, be the most significant lesson we take away from "Forecasting the Impact of Artificial Intelligence."

1.6 FORECASTING THE IMPACT OF ARTIFICIAL INTELLIGENCE: ANOTHER VOICE*

Lawrence Vanston, President, Technology Futures, Inc.

In the previous article, Spyros Makridakis provided his forecast of the impact of artificial intelligence. Now, technology forecaster Lawrence Vanston adds his perspective on the topic, along with his reaction to the views of Makridakis. Areas meriting additional emphasis, per Vanston, are AI performance forecasts, AI's impact on employment, and the dangers of AI. Areas where the two differ are in brain-computer interfaces, blockchain, and AI for forecasting. Makridakis follows with a commentary in response to Vanston's points.

Forecasting AI's Computational Power

My first reaction to the AI performance forecasts cited by Spyros was "Is that all there is?" For a field as important to humanity as AI, I was expecting more. We can't really blame Spyros, because when his series appeared there weren't many compelling forecasts of AI performance that I could find either. Since then I have made some progress on forecasting AI performance, which I shared last summer at ISF2018 (Vanston 2018) and will highlight in this section.

A key component of forecasting AI performance is forecasting computational power. Although Ray Kurzweil has argued for a future of superexponential improvement in computer performance (Kurzweil 2005), the actual evidence supports continued exponential progress along the lines of Moore's law (see Sidebar A for a primer on growth curves).

Exponential progress is typical of technologies unless there is a fundamental limit that cannot be overcome, further improvement has no utility, or there is a fundamental change in technological approach. The last often results in a discontinuity or a change in the rate of improvement. The transition from discrete circuits to integrated circuits is an example. That transition increased the rate of improvement and confirmed Moore's law, but it is not evidence of a superexponential trend, as Kurzweil argues. Another example of a discontinuity is the transition from analog modems to broadband, where we saw a dramatic bump in data rates and then a return to the previous rate of improvement. Even when two exponential trends combine, as happened for a while when we increased clock rates and wavelengths simultaneously in optical transmission systems, the combined trend is still exponential. Setting aside a major discontinuity from quantum computing, for example, or the oft-predicted but yet-to-happen death of Moore's law, the logical working forecast is exponential at historical rates.

'This article originally appeared in *Foresight: The International Journal of Applied Forecasting* (Spring 2019) and appears here courtesy of the International Institute of Forecasters.

Sidebar A: Growth Rate Primer

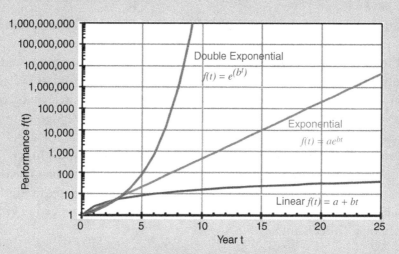

With linear growth, performance increases by a constant **b** units each year. Linear growth is not typical of performance improvement in high tech, but as we discuss in the text, there is evidence that progress in many AI applications is linear.

With exponential growth, performance increases by a constant percentage **r** each year, where $r = e^b - 1$. Exponential growth implies a constant doubling time, $d = \ln 2 / b$. Moore's law is the classic example of exponential growth with a doubling time of two years and an annual growth rate of 41%. Exponential growth yields a straight line when performance is plotted on a log scale as shown in the graph.

With double exponential growth, the annual growth increases exponentially, so it plots on a log scale like an exponential would on a linear scale. This is the curve to use if you want to forecast insane future performance improvement, but such improvement is unsustainable in the long run. It's easy to mistake one-time increases in the exponential growth constant **b** for double exponential growth, especially if you're looking for it.

One-time changes in **b** can occur when the technology approach changes (as when we went from discrete to integrated circuits), or when two exponentially improving processes are combined. The latter results in a new exponential curve since the product of two exponential curves is another exponential: $f(t) = a_1 e^{b_1 t} * a_2 e^{b_2 t} = ae^{bt}$ where $b = b_1 + b_2$.

A trove of data has been compiled by the Electronic Frontier Foundation for AI applications such as games, image recognition, speech recognition, machine translation, natural language processing, and computer programming (Electronic Frontier Foundation 2018). These data, along with insightful analyses in blogs by Miles Brundage (2018) and Sarah Constantin (2017), reveal that, in some areas, AI has passed human performance, while in others it has a long way to go. In some cases, deep learning has caused a discontinuity in performance improvement; in others, it simply enabled continuation of the trend. Surprisingly, when measured in the customary units applied to a specific application (for example, the Elo rating for chess or BLEU score for machine translation), AI progress has typically not been exponential, but *linear* (Vanston 2018).

This suggests that for those AI applications still far below human performance, AI parity may be years away, barring breakthroughs. This probably explains why 92.5% of the AI fellows in Oren Etzioni's survey (Etzioni 2016) cited by Spyros said superintelligence wouldn't be achieved for 25 years, if ever. And why almost every speech I hear from an AI expert starts with "Forget about AI and human intelligence, current AI has the IQ of a slug. Nothing to worry about here!" – before they move on to whatever they're selling.

Is there really nothing to worry about? See Sidebar B for my thoughts on that topic, but we are flying blind until we have better technology forecasts than those provided by Kurzweil (who is a great visionary relying on a highly questionable forecast) and the offhand opinions of experts (who know everything about AI, but may not know much about technology forecasting).

AI's Impact on Employment

Spyros does a balanced job of laying out the arguments regarding the impact of AI on employment. This issue, and how we handle it, may be as important and more immediate than our existential concerns about AI. Before you continue, note that I lean optimist/realist even though I sound like a pessimist!

Optimists argue that we have had technological revolutions before, and each time we have ended up with more, but different, jobs. That's true, but each of those revolutions was unique and there have not been so many to make broad generalizations. We can indeed say based on this experience that we *could* end up with more jobs, but saying we *will* without specifics is speculative. It is argued that we just can't imagine the jobs yet. Perhaps . . . but if you can't imagine it, you can't count on it. Same for happy historical examples such as still having bank tellers in spite of ATMs.

Even if we do end in a happy place of full employment, there's no guarantee it will be a smooth transition. The impacts of employment dislocation can be substantial and consequential. The last American presidential election turned on a few states where the displacement of industrial jobs by technology or offshoring is either a reality or a realistic fear. What's it going to be like when the factories return home, but the parking lots are empty?

AI will doubtless generate many jobs in AI and managing AI, but realistically, how many compared to the jobs lost? And not everyone is suited by talent, disposition, or inclination for those jobs. Optimists say that creative and intellectual jobs are not threatened and that AI will supplement, not replace, them. I don't doubt that AI will help doctors be better doctors and architects be better architects. But suppose AI makes architects twice as efficient at designing buildings. Does that mean we will have twice as many buildings or half as many architects?

Optimists who concede that jobs will be lost look on the bright side and offer the prospect of more leisure time to pursue their personal interests, perhaps with the benefit of a Universal Basic Income. I will never run out of creative, productive, fulfilling things to do, but that's not true for everyone; witness people on unemployment who fall prey to opioids. Economists would say that if you must do income redistribution, it's most efficient to just give people cash. I'm not so sure. Perhaps pushing the money through programs (grants, microloans, fellowships, etc.) and institutions (schools, charities, churches, nonprofits, sports leagues, etc.) makes more sense for some individuals.

Lastly, while AI will impact employment, it likely won't be dramatic in the next 10 years. So we may have some time for forecasters to forecast, analysts to analyze, planners to plan, entrepreneurs to entrepreneur, and think tanks to develop policy positions consistent with their politics. If there are indeed problems, I believe there are solutions. The question is whether we pay enough attention to them.

Sidebar B: Is There Nothing to Worry About?

AI multiplies the potential for surveillance and control. Are Elon Musk and the late Stephen Hawking, not to mention the other authors cited by Spyros, wrong to be deeply worried about AI? In my opinion, absolutely not, but perhaps for different reasons. My reasons are independent of when and whether computers achieve human intelligence or human consciousness.

1. Rather than the threats of single computers, you should worry about the interactions of millions of interconnected computers, the actions of each dictated by an AI algorithm optimized for its own purposes. Really smart humans managed to design complex derivatives that were impossible for really smart humans to unwind, almost bringing down our financial system. At least we know how those algorithms reasoned. Is the same true for AI?

2. Emerging technologies provide computers with the types of inputs and outputs that heretofore only humans and fellow animals had. This not only provides data fodder for machine learning, but assumes you can just pull the plug or take out the battery. (Try that with your iPhone!)

3. Further, AI is advancing to the point of being able to use those skills in spite of the second half of Moravec's Paradox (Moravec, 1988) – that it's "difficult or impossible to give them [computers] the skills of a one-year-old when it comes to perception and mobility." Our machines are already approaching a one-year-old's level in many ways. Consider this list of "easy for one-year-olds, hard for computers" skills: "recognizing a face, moving around in space, judging people's motivations, catching a ball, recognizing a voice, setting appropriate goals, paying attention to things that are interesting; anything to do with perception, attention, visualization, motor skills, social skills" (Wikipedia, 2018). On some of these measures our machines seem equal to a one-year-old and working on the terrible twos.

4. This brings us to the other half of Moravec's Paradox: "It is comparatively easy to make computers exhibit adult-level performance on intelligence tests or playing checkers." As machines begin to reach fundamental levels of sensory perception, motor skill, rudimentary language skills, learning ability, and pseudo-reasoning, how far is it really to human

intelligence? If what sets us apart from other vertebrates is massive amounts of pliable, general-purpose wiring, is that really so hard to duplicate? Add in the human knowledge base, already conveniently compiled, and we could be a lot closer than is now apparent.

5. Finally, AI doesn't need human intelligence or human consciousness to be dangerous. Microbes with sub-slug intelligence kill millions of us and theoretically could kill us all, so AI *isn't* the first intelligence to challenge humans! Once we leave programming decisions to AI we don't know what intelligence – possibly far inferior to ours, but just as dangerous – will emerge. Nor do we know whether its evolution will be on pace with vertebrate evolution or microbal evolution.

These concerns exist in the absence of human greed, malice, and bias, intentional or otherwise. In their presence, they are deeply troubling. There are indeed ways to address these problems. My fear regards the will, not the way. It's hard to say *no* to useful, cool technology. In the United States we have seen our own technology used against us to influence the fundamental course of events, including our global alliances and trade relationships, even without AI. The problems arising from AI may be harder to fix. Will we be quick enough? And, in the current winner-take-all world, what are the consequences if we don't?

Blockchain, IA, and Forecasting

Most of Part 4 of the Makridakis series is devoted to blockchain. That Spyros put block-chain on the same plane as AI surprised me, and I disagree with so many of his observations and conclusions that the margins of my copy are full. Here are my main objections:

AI doesn't need blockchain. Neither does IoT or any other cutting-edge tech-nology, so why link them? Blockchain is an interesting character, but it is not crucial to the AI story.

Blockchain claims to have the potential to replace banks and other financial inter-mediaries, even government institutions. This outcome assumes that the recording of transactions is the most important aspect of the financial entity's business. However, anyone who has bought a house knows that recording the deed at the county court-house (or the equivalent in your country) is a tiny part of the transaction. The institu-tions involved – agents for the buyer and seller, the title company, the lending bank, federal lending agencies, etc. – provide expertise, broad trust, fiduciary responsibility, insurance, money in the form of loans and loan guarantees, and force of law.

Similarly, the main function of Amazon and the source of its "monopolistic/oli-gopolistic power" is not the recording of the financial transactions. If it were, Amazon could easily be replaced, with or without blockchain. The reason it has not is that for a reasonable price Amazon provides a host of useful services and a form of trust that is far broader than blockchain's narrow definition of trust.

Blockchain is basically a narrow technology attempting to replace existing technol-ogies that are already providing transaction documentation quickly, reliably, and cheaply. Maybe it will be widely adopted, maybe it won't, but it won't change the world. And if it does change the world, it may be for the worse; the Internet is a dangerous place.

Intelligence Augmentation

Part 4 ends with a discussion of intelligence augmentation, in which Spyros views AI and humans helping each other, leveraging each other's strengths. Nothing new or controversial there – the future is an extension of the past. He then links the future of IA with direct human-machine interfaces. The latter technology may be closer than we think and may have immediate medical, military, and other benefits. However, the risks and benefits of direct human-machine interfaces need to be assessed on their own, regardless of AI. In fact, this technology may increase our susceptibility to AI domination as much as ameliorate it.

The Long-Term Future

Part 5 of the series starts with a discussion of the pitfalls of long-term forecasting and the top 10 emerging trends. I find a lot here to agree with. I absolutely believe in the necessity of steering between the shoals of being too conservative or too optimistic. That's why I never start a forecast without doing a *drivers and constraints analysis* (see Sidebar C) that usually includes the four factors Spyros lists, among others. Along with AI itself, half of his top 10 trends are on my own list of top information/communications technology trends, and the others are areas I know well enough to agree with their presence on the list.

Sidebar C: Drivers and Constraints

This simple method is a great tool for navigating the shoals of overoptimistic and overpessimistic technology forecasts. It's been likened to forcefield analysis, but it emphasizes the dynamic instead of the static, which is the whole point of forecasting. Basically, it is a series of questions begetting more questions until you have an answer, or at least an informed opinion!

  ▪ What are the drivers for adoption?

How strong are they?

  ▪ What are the constraints on adoption?

How strong are they? Can they be overcome?

  ▪ What is the balance of drivers and constraints?

Will this change?

  ▪ What are the important areas of uncertainty that need to be resolved?

How can these be addressed to everyone's satisfaction?

Incidentally, besides preventing avoidable shipwrecks, the exercise of going through these questions provides a foundation for quantitative forecasts as well as a research agenda for both forecasting and the technology itself. For more information on drivers and constraints, see Vanston (2008).

While we are on the topic of long-term forecasting, I will take the opportunity to plug my own field, technological forecasting (or technology forecasting) – which includes the kinds of "not so statistical forecasting" that we need when we require rigor and proven methods, but don't have much data. These methods include alternative scenarios, expert opinion, Delphi, substitution analysis, performance analysis, analogies, cross-impact analysis, and ideation tools like nominal groups and impact wheels, to name a few. *Technological Forecasting and Social Change* is the field's classic journal. Martino (1983) and Porter et al. (2011) are a couple of the classic texts. Technological forecasting was essential in the 1960s as the digital revolution began, it was essential for the forecasting we did during the 1990s and early 2000s for the last wave of new technology (Vanston and Hodges 2004), and it will be essential for forecasting AI and other new-wave technologies in the future.

A few selected cautions regarding some of Spyros's specific conclusions:

- Don't assume that all computing will end up in the cloud. Computing has a long pendulum when it comes to centralization and decentralization. "Easy as using electricity" sounds a lot like the "computing utility" mantra from the late 1970s, right before the PC revolution decentralized computing. Currently, *edge computing* is as much a trend as cloud computing. With edge computing, information is stored and processed close to the user (thus, at the network's edge) to serve applications such as autonomous vehicles that require high reliability and low latency. Most likely there will continue to be local, edge, and cloud computing in some combination.

- I think Spyros sticks his neck out unnecessarily when he predicts that a wristwatch will be the interface of choice for communicating with computers. It might be, but AR/VR using glasses or headsets may reemerge as a contender as well. Or maybe a drone will fly beside us! Or maybe our current array of laptops, pads, smartphones, and big screens will survive. Choosing among alternative technologies that do the same thing is high on the list of the risky forecasting tasks (Vanston 2008). Better to avoid it if possible!

- As I've noted above, brain-computer interfaces may have a place, but they are not necessary to survive AI. We should ask for more analyses of drivers/constraints and risks/benefits before agreeing with Spyros's optimistic conclusion regarding this technology. Otherwise, we risk having another unfortunate example of forecasts gone wrong. And it's very odd that he ends his opus on AI on this point!

AI for Forecasting

Spyros makes one other point in Part 5 that I'd like to challenge vigorously. He cites the alleged slow progress in using AI for forecasting as an example of the weaknesses of AI. First, it's not a representative example. More important, it masks some fundamental changes in forecasting. The M competitions measure the ability to forecast the next few numbers in a long series of numbers with no contextual information except the frequency of the data. Years of research and prior contests have honed statistical methods so that they would be hard to be beat by any emerging technology. By not having labeled or contextual information, the strengths of AI forecasting are missed. The advantages statistical methods have in these contests are such that some AI forecasting experts have refused to participate.

Even then, the top finisher in the 2018 M4 competition, Slawek Smyl of Uber Technologies, used a hybrid of AI and conventional forecasting (Smyl, Ranganthan, and Pasqua 2018). This is more an example of teaching AI to use statistical forecasting so it doesn't have to learn it on its own than an example of happy machine/human collaboration. ISF2018 this summer was instructive. Four major presentations on AI for forecasting were authored by employees of Amazon, Microsoft, and Uber, leaders in the application of technology. All of these presentations were positive regarding AI for forecasting and optimistic that the constraints on AI (e.g., that it's data and computation intensive and that it's prone to overfitting and instability) will be overcome. Reading the article by the Amazon team, ironically in the same issue of *Foresight* as Part 5, reinforces this position (Januschowski et al. 2018).

Will AI eventually replace most statistical forecasting? It's too soon to tell, but it's possible: parity has been reached in some applications, improvements in AI are likely, and constraints on AI can likely be overcome. Some of the objections to AI I've heard remind me of those raised by people engaged with prior old technologies such as traditional telephony, dial-up modems, and circuit switching. I'd mention slide rules, but that would date me. And then there are the classic examples: steam locomotives and prop planes. Maybe forecasters need to sponsor their own long-range technology forecast, starting with a good drivers and constraints analysis! Even if the news is bad, I think the skill sets are highly transferable with a little training, and job security will be more like that of doctors than architects.

Summary

Spyros has done a masterful job covering a complex, wide-ranging subject. I'm genuinely impressed. I have highlighted the areas of disagreement rather than the much broader areas of agreement because those are the ones that need to be talked about more. For the same reason, I have also addressed the more controversial concerns and dangers of AI more than its immense benefits. Forecasters of all stripes have a crucial role to play in helping sort these issues for the benefit of our clients and humanity. As my mentor the late Ralph Lenz once told me: "The highest value of a forecast is to raise the level of discussion." Let's talk.

References

Brundage, M. (2018). Blog posts. https://www.milesbrundage.com/blog-posts

Constantin, S. (2017). *Performance trends in AI*. Otium. https://srconstantin.wordpress.com/2017/01/28/performance-trends-in-ai/

Electronic Frontier Foundation (2018). AI progress measurement. https://www.eff.org/ai/metrics

Etzioni, O. (2016, September 20). *No, the experts don't think superintelligent AI is a threat to humanity. MIT Technology Review.* https://www.technologyreview.com/s/602410/no-the-experts-dont-think-superintelligent-ai-is-a-threat-to-humanity/

Januschowski, T., Gasthaus, J., Wang, Y., et al. (2018). Deep learning for forecasting: Current trends and challenges. *Foresight* 51 (Fall): 42–47.

Kurzweil, R. (2005). *The singularity is near*. Viking Books.

Martino, J. (1983). *Technological forecasting for decision making* (2nd ed.). North-Holland.

Moravec, H. (1988). *Mind children*. Harvard University Press.

Moravec, H. (1998). When will computer hardware match the human brain? *Journal of Evolution and Technology* 1.

Porter, A. L., Cunningham, S. W., Banks, J., et al. (2011). *Forecasting and management of technology* (2nd ed.). *Wiley*.

Smyl, S., Ranganthan, J., and Pasqua, A. (2018, June 25). *M4 Forecasting Competition: Introducing a new hybrid ES-RNN model*. Uber Engineering. https://eng.uber.com/m4-forecasting-competition/

Vanston, L. (2008). *Practical tips for forecasting new technology adoption. Telektronikk* 3/4. http://tfi.com/pubs/forecasting-tips.pdf

Vanston, L. (2017). *Forecasting issues for the New World, 23rd IIF Workshop on Predictive Analytics and Forecasting (20–25).* Munich: International Institute of Forecasting. http://predictiveanalyticsandforecasting.com/wp-content/uploads/2017/10/MUNICH-WORKSHOP-VANSTON-Sepember-2017.pdf

Vanston, L. (2018). *Forecasting AI performance, 38th International Symposium on Forecasting*, Boulder, CO: International Institute of Forecasters.

Vanston, L., and Hodges, R. (2004). Technology forecasting for telecommunications. *Telektronikk* 100 (4), 32–42. http://tfi.com/pubs/w/pdf/telektronikk_peer.pdf

Wikipedia (2018). *Moravec's paradox*. Wikipedia. https://en.wikipedia.org/wiki/Moravec%27s_paradox

COMMENTARY: RESPONSE TO LAWRENCE VANSTON

Spyros Makridakis

I'm extremely flattered that two futurists as distinguished as Owen Davies and Lawrence Vanston have thought well to comment on my five-part *Foresight* paper "Forecasting the Impact of Artificial Intelligence." My sincere thanks to both for their insightful remarks and the opportunity they provided me to update my thinking about AI and check the rationality of my predictions. Their commentaries have considerably improved my original article, and I'm pleased that there is a fair amount of agreement among us. This response is devoted to Larry's commentary, as Owen's was a coda to my original paper with additional expert opinion gathered by TechCast's Delphi forecasts.

The Nobel laureate Paul Krugman in 1998 made some profoundly off-the-mark predictions that Owen Davies used as an epigraph to his coda in the Winter 2019 issue – including Krugman's statement that the Internet's effect on the world economy would be no greater than that of the fax machine – illuminating the shortsightedness of forecasters. Of course Krugman did not notice that a year earlier IBM's Deep Blue computer had beaten world chess champion Garry Kasparov, or that algorithms in 1998 could read handwritten characters in what were preludes to AI.

At the other extreme, forecasters should not fall into the trap of the science-fiction hype advocating that General Purpose AI (GAI) and singularity are just around the corner, competing with us and threatening our human dominance. I would like to reiterate my position that while AI is superb in games and image, speech, and text recognition, it is incapable of understanding meaning, making causal links, and exhibiting common sense. Many experts, to paraphrase Lawrence Vanston, say that "current AI has the IQ of a slug." My own prediction is that AI will take a long time to achieve the abilities of a one-year-old child to interact with its external world.

My main comments center on Larry's four major disagreements with what I have written, and present my reasoning as to why I believe I'm on the right track, although it will be many years before we know who's right and who's mistaken. Additionally, I will outline my view of the two biggest AI/IA issues facing humankind and explain why dealing with them may prove extremely difficult.

The Four Disagreements

Blockchain

Larry states that blockchain is basically a narrow technology trying to become mainstream. I disagree. I believe blockchain possesses three major advantages of great value that are not available in the traditional Internet:

- It provides trust among unknown participants who can interact with each other with confidence;
- It ensures enlarged safety in transactions;
- It permits the construction of fast, trusted, and safe local networks.

These may not seem like much, but let's consider the implications of hacking houses that are connected to the Internet of Things (IoT), smart contracts, autonomous vehicles, and even the possibility of getting your thoughts stolen through a BCI (brain-to-computer interface). Unless perfect safety could be assured, the operation of IoT, smart contracts, and AVs, not to mention BCI, might be impossible. The same would go for local networks that could re-create the equivalent of the village square where neighbors can share communications and services. They must operate in a trusted and safe environment; otherwise, they would be shunned.

The Cloud

The second and third disagreements are about the cloud and its accessibility without a computer, say through a digital watch or other device. I understand Larry's objections, but I still believe that we are at the very beginning of the utilization of cloud computing.

Two factors would contribute to moving the future toward my prediction. First, G5 and higher-level communication networks will bring wi-fi to all places, facilitating connections from anywhere to the cloud. Second, once voice commands become widespread and reliable, they would make keyboards obsolete: this would substantially increase the utilization of the cloud, whether this would be done by a cheap computer, a smartphone, or a digital watch. In my view, there will be no reason to own and maintain an expensive computer if the same service can be obtained more cheaply and easily from the cloud, allowing one to access and process information from any place at any time without having to carry a big device or worry about where such information is stored.

Forecast Accuracy

Will AI improve forecasting accuracy? My strong view is that improvements, if any, will be limited and will be due not to AI learning to forecast more accurately but rather to the ability of computers to optimize the parameters of the forecasting model more precisely. The top two winners of the M4 Competition (Smyl's model from Uber, and Montero-Manso from University of A Coruña, Spain) did not learn to forecast more accurately by studying past patterns or analyzing historical data. Rather, they simply found more effective ways to choose the most appropriate model and/or compute the best weights to combine the various forecasting methods used. AI forecasting models cannot work well when there are structural changes in the data or when patterns change. Our own experience has indicated that there is still a long way to go before AI forecasting models will be able to improve their accuracy through such learning.

Other Major Issues

AI will give rise to two major, interrelated issues. The first will have to do with the "winner takes all" syndrome. AI applications, once developed, could be exploited at a global level at little additional expenditure, providing a huge advantage to their inventor(s).

The second will have to do with the income inequality created by such a syndrome as a single firm, or a very few firms, in some advanced countries would dominate the AI market. Furthermore, income inequality will become much worse between advanced AI nations and the rest of the world that would not have the specialized scientists or the vast research funds required to keep up.

Worse, as AI will be automating more and more repetitive labor tasks it will reduce the advantage of less-developed countries to attract firms through low labor costs, as robots and machines will be capable of operating the factories of advanced countries at similar or even lower costs. The big challenge will be to reduce income inequality within advanced AI countries through some form of guaranteed minimum income. However, it may be much harder to do so between countries. People seem unwilling to help poorer countries/regions economically while, at the same time, remaining unwilling to allow immigrants to enter their wealthier countries.

1.7 SMARTER SUPPLY CHAINS THROUGH AI*

Duncan Klett

Supply-chain management is a complex control system in which latency (delay) in the control can lead to instability. While there are many other sources of instability in a supply chain, delay in responding to changes in supply or demand is perhaps the largest and easiest to manage. In this article, Duncan Klett sees a broad role for AI/ML in furthering this goal of reducing response delay, through automating processes, validating data, segmenting items, and generating forecasts.

*This article originally appeared in *Foresight: The International Journal of Applied Forecasting* (Winter 2020) and appears here courtesy of the International Institute of Forecasters.

Traditional supply-chain planning systems consist of several unconnected processes such as Sales and Operations Planning (S&OP), Master Scheduling, Demand Planning, Order Promising, Supply Planning, Production Planning, Production Scheduling, Material Requirements Planning (MRP), and more. Each of these operates in isolation, adding delay to supply-chain response.

Removing control-system latency improves a system's responsiveness and reduces its instability, but there is no single approach to supply-chain management that will provide good results across all products and customers. Therefore, Klett argues, we should also segment supply-chain strategies to align with the characteristics of the different products, even for different customers of the same products. The concept is to match execution and planning strategies with the characteristics of specific products and markets.

The areas of potential improvement from AI/ML lie in automating processes, validating and correcting data, generating forecasts, segmenting items and customers for appropriate management strategies, managing changes, recommending actions, and mitigating risks.

Introduction

Every demand forecast has its flaws. Newer methods, such as AI and ML, can provide better forecasts, but even these will never be perfect. There is always some difference between predicted sales and actual customer demand. Still, an imperfect demand forecast is better than no forecast at all.

If we accept that a demand forecast is just a road map of future demand, then our goal should not be only to minimize forecast error but to improve supply-chain execution – what you do with the forecast matters! The more important metrics relate to supply-chain execution, such as projected and actual inventory, on-time delivery in-full, and counts of stock-outs. Put another way, if the "plan" is not executed through operations, then the forecast is of little value. Alternatively, supply-chain design, such as structure of the bill of materials or inventory policies, can exaggerate or mitigate the impact of inaccurate forecasts.

Supply-chain execution can be improved by recognizing that supply-chain management is really a control system, similar in concept to an automobile's cruise control. A principle of control-system theory is that delays in a control process can lead to instability.

Execution can also be improved by applying different strategies and methodologies to different segments of products, markets, and customers. Various forecasting methods, inventory strategies, and replenishment strategies can be tuned to different products and markets. In addition, AI/ML techniques are beginning to be used to manage supply chains. The right strategies applied to the right product segments, and generally reducing latency can enable organizations to respond to supply-chain variability more effectively to achieve business success.

Supply-Chain Challenges

Supply-chain management is really common sense: get the right stuff to the right place at the right time. The goals are almost always variations of

- Assuring customers on-time delivery
- Minimizing costs in purchase, inventory, scrap/waste, and overhead.

There are really only two types of output from supply-chain planning:

- Replenishing supply (consisting of source selection, transportation routing, replenishment quantity, and releasing orders); and
- Allocating resources (including materials and capacity) to meet demands.

In addition, you can manage various parameters and strategies, such as

- Inventory
- Demand "shaping"
- Product offerings, setting expectations, and product design

However, reality creeps in to add innumerable complexities to these simple concepts. For a single supply chain, there can be thousands or millions of parts to manage, perhaps in hundreds of different locations (or even thousands, if managing out to retail locations). Products become more and more complex in both function and manufacturing complexity. In many cases, the actual manufacturing processes required to produce a product are at the outer limits of current technology, resulting in highly variable yields and lead times.

A sense of the difficulty of managing a supply chain becomes immediately evident through a simple calculation. Consider an assembly that requires 100 different component parts. If each individual component is available 99% of the time, then the likelihood of having all 100 components available at the same time is $0.99 \wedge 100 = 0.37$ or 37%. Not a very good customer-service level!

In addition to product complexity, customer expectations have become more demanding and more difficult to meet. Customers often expect close to immediate delivery of "personalized" products, sometimes 12 time zones away from the actual factory! It is becoming increasingly difficult to meet these expectations, while also minimizing costs.

Product complexity and customer expectations are not even the end of the story. Supply chains operate globally and so are subject to disruption from natural and human-created events. Storms can disrupt transportation, tariffs can change cost structures and times for materials to cross borders, and global supply and demand for commodities change frequently.

In the end, supply-chain management is like any other business process in that it relies on a combination of people, process, and technology. Any change in the capabilities of one of these elements will often present risks and opportunities in overall system performance through corresponding changes in either or both of the other two.

Control-System Theory for Supply-Chain Management

Figure 1.21 is a simplified representation of a classic control system in which feedback from errors in achieving a target leads to adjustments in the production process.

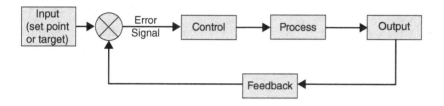

Figure 1.21 Classic Control System with Feedback

There are many sources of variability (change) in a supply chain:

- Lot sizes (order quantity minimums and multiples). Mismatches between typical demand quantities and replenishment lot sizes can be particularly problematic.
- Demand fluctuations and misalignment of actual and forecasted demand.
- Supply fluctuations such as actual lead times and yields.

However, perhaps the largest and easiest-to-manage factor is *delay* in responding to changes in supply or demand.

If we think of supply-chain management processes as a complex control system, the impact of delay (latency of response) becomes very clear. Control systems are commonly understood and used extensively in engineering (https://en.wikipedia.org/wiki/Controlsystem). Their objective is to adjust various controls so that the actual process perfectly tracks to the desired target. Furthermore, the process should instantaneously track to changes in either the target setting or in the operation of the process. For example, an automobile's cruise control represents a simple control system that consists of a target (desired speed), a control (throttle setting and, more recently, braking), a process (the vehicle), and an output (actual vehicle speed). The difference between the target speed and the actual speed is an error signal which is used as a feedback loop to adjust the throttle setting.

Clearly, modern cruise controls show the effectiveness of such control systems.

Delay and the Instability Problem

Instability is a common problem with multiple levels in a supply chain, a result often attributed to the bullwhip effect (https://en.wikipedia.org/wiki/Bullwhipeffect).

Control-system theory reveals that delays in the control-to-feedback path lead to instability, and that instability can only be reduced by reducing the magnitude of the feedback signal. Such reduction is often called "damping." Unfortunately, reducing the feedback signal makes the system less responsive. The theory also shows that the system overreacts (bullwhip) unless the damping factor is less than 1/delay.

Supply-chain delays are introduced in three primary ways:

- Time for "system" to react to a change in supply or demand for a part.
- Time for "control" to react to a change in supply or demand for a part.
- Time to propagate a change at one level to the next (e.g., through the product structure, between supply-chain systems, between different entities in a complex supply chain).

Multilevel Supply Chains

Figure 1.22 shows a simplified view of several levels in a typical supply chain.

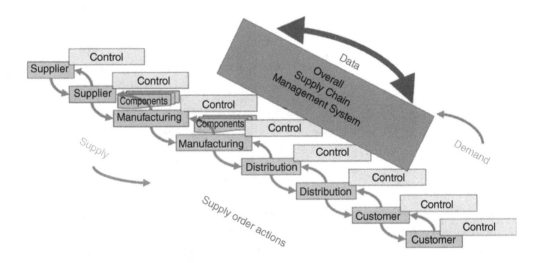

Figure 1.22 Multi-Level Supply Chain

Each level in the supply chain adds to the time it takes for the entire supply chain to react to a change. As discussed above, each extra delay contributes to instability.

Disjointed Supply Planning

As illustrated in Figure 1.23, traditional supply-chain planning systems consist of several unconnected processes such as Sales and Operations Planning (S&OP), Master Scheduling, Demand Planning, Order Promising, Supply Planning, Production Planning, Production Scheduling, Material Requirements Planning (MRP), and more. Each of these operates in isolation. Data from one process is then passed to another process, often manually, using Excel or another tool such as a data warehouse. Each interface adds further delay to supply-chain response.

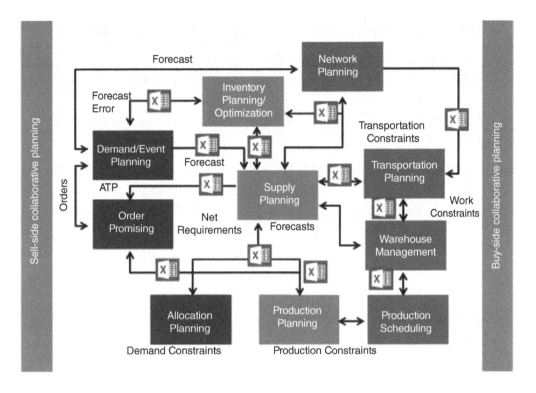

Figure 1.23 Disjointed Supply Chain Management

A Digital Model to Overcome Delays

An extension to control-system theory, designed specifically to overcome delay (latency) in system response, is named a Smith Predictor Model (https://www.controleng.com/single-article/process-modeling-feedback-controllers/8d97811eab2a09c44f1be0c03e5 d1b55.html). This approach, as illustrated in Figure 1.24, uses a model of the physical process to predict its output prior to the actual process response. The process-model prediction is then combined with the actual system response to become the feedback input to control-system logic. In terms of a supply chain, a digital model of the supply chain can be used to predict supply-chain response at all levels and through all elements at once, thereby removing the latency.

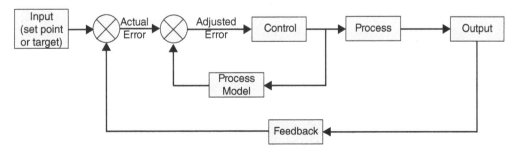

Figure 1.24 Control System Using Process Model

Removing control-system latency improves a system's responsiveness and reduces its instability. Therefore, a digital model of the supply chain can significantly improve supply-chain responsiveness and reduce or eliminate the bullwhip effect. A companion digital model can provide higher on-time delivery (increased customer satisfaction) and lower inventory requirements.

Applying AI/ML

So how should we apply AI/ML to achieve improvements? For this discussion, I define AI as any system where a machine replaces or augments human activity. Even ML (machine learning) should be broadly defined to include any machine that gets better (learns) as it processes more data.

Several areas for potential improvement from AI/ML lie in Automating processes

- Validating and correcting data.
- Generating forecasts (including forecasts other than of demand).
- Segmenting items and customers for appropriate management strategies.

Remember, though, that the most important input to any system that uses data, including AI, is clearly the data. Therefore, processes must be in place and used to achieve as accurate and timely data as practical.

Automating Processes

Automation occurs when a specific action (which can include "do nothing") is triggered based upon observed data and some combination of calculations or rules. This requires that a programmer, user, or learning algorithm recognizes a pattern and then triggers an action. For example, when the projected inventory at a distribution center (DC) for a set of parts falls below a specified level and if the supplying site has sufficient inventory to satisfy this demand, a stock transfer order (STO) is created automatically to prevent the below-target situation. The STO would have an associated due date, transfer quantity, and other information.

Material requirements planning (MRP) is actually a form of automation that has been in general use since the mid-1960s. MRP recommends replenishment orders based on projected demand, current supply, and new planned supply.

An extension of process automation would use machine learning (ML) to recommend or perform actions based on its observations of human activity and the ensuing results. A machine could be trained to learn which actions are most successful in improving the results from various situations. Think of computers already beating human masters in chess and Go. Similar learning approaches might be applicable to managing supply chains.

In addition, AI/ML approaches might even be better used in setting planning parameters (rules and data involved in source selection, lot sizes, transport routes, etc.) than in managing the individual transactions. Given more effective planning parameters, standard processes could then manage most of the transactions.

Demand Sensing

Statistical models for forecasting demand rely on historical data to predict future demand. The past, however, is not always a good predictor of the future. In those cases, the dream is to find other data sources – leading indicators – that are better predictors of future demand. Some such data, such as national holidays and recognizing which days fall on the weekend, are known well in advance. Other data such as weather and weather forecasts, product promotions, and internet search trends can also be included in the calculations (or learned response) to generate better demand forecasts.

In one case, the company's challenge was to manage daily delivery of product to numerous retail stores, such that inventory was minimized while always having product available to sell. Learning historical trends with holiday information, the simulated result reduced stock-outs from five days to one, and did this using 10% less inventory.

However, our experience has shown that the "smarter" (i.e., more complicated) an algorithm, the more resistance there is from users to actually employ it. Simply put, if they don't understand it, they don't trust it, and they won't use it! To overcome this resistance, we have utilized processes that allow users to set thresholds as to when a recommendation is accepted. Visualization techniques such as Shapely analysis (https://arxiv.org/abs/1705.07874) can also help users understand the significance of the different data (features) as they affect a particular prediction.

In Figure 1.25, "until holiday" and "weekday" add to the initial forecast quantity for a specific period while "month," "week," and "since holidays" reduce it. Thus, the revised forecast is 17.26 compared to the base forecast of 20.89.

Figure 1.25 Impact of Features on Forecast

Remember, though, that a better forecast does not ensure better supply-chain results. The supply chain must still execute in order to get the right stuff to the right place to satisfy the actual demand.

Beyond Demand Forecasting

Most discussions of forecasting for supply chains deal with demand. A demand forecast is important, but so are other factors, such as production times, shipping times, and yields. Models and techniques for forecasting these can be quite different from those for forecasting demand. For example, demand data is often aggregated by adding the observed quantities in a period to generate a single historical number for that period. Clearly, shipping times for receipts on the same day should not be added together when predicting future lead times. Further, for predicting yields there is a physical maximum of 100%.

For predicting future values for some of these factors, we have found it is better not to aggregate the historical data at all. Each observation is then used for learning and subsequent predictions of future values.

Segmentation

Reiterating a comment above, supply-chain management does just two things: replenishment and allocation. Behind these two functions, though, are a myriad of supporting operations, such as

- Policies (including inventory targets, replenishment).
- Supply order management.
- Demand prioritization and sequencing.
- Demand forecasting.
- Sales promotions.

There is no single approach to supply-chain management that will provide good results across all products and customers. The Pareto Principle (also known as the 80/20 rule) is well known. A lesser-known extension of that principle is the Glenday Sieve (www.repetitiveflexiblesupply.com). Glenday's research has found that while 20% of a company's products represents 80% of its business, just 6% of the products typically represents 50% of its business. At the other extreme, the last 30% of products represents just 1% of its business. Therefore, it makes sense that strategies for production and inventory for the top 6% would be different than those for the bottom 30%.

For example, for high-runner products, even a few days of inventory might represent a significant investment, so replenishment should occur frequently. But for these parts, forecasts based on history often have less error due to the significance of large data volumes to time-series forecasts. Furthermore, with frequent replenishment, only a relatively small percentage of demand is needed in buffers to achieve desired service levels. The risk of carrying extra inventory is small because it will be needed in the next period.

On the other hand, products with infrequent and irregular demand are difficult to forecast. However, carrying enough supply to cover even a year's expected demand for these products might not represent a large investment. Also, depending on product commonality and distribution requirements, it might be preferable to hold inventory at "upstream" locations where different finished goods might use common components.

From a holistic perspective, balance the value of incremental improvements in forecast accuracy against the cost of achieving that improvement, or of carrying additional inventory to overcome forecast errors. The concept is to match execution and planning strategies with the characteristics of specific products and markets.

AI cluster analysis (https://en.wikipedia.org/wiki/Clusteranalysis) can be used to help identify groups of products and customers that exhibit similar demand, supply, and other characteristics that might therefore be managed using similar strategies.

Lessons Learned

From our work with many customers over many years, we have identified rules of thumb that should be helpful to supply-chain professionals and to researchers wishing to provide theoretical frameworks for managing supply chains.

Supply-chain management systems should strive to reduce the time required for supply-chain execution to respond to changes.

- Apply AI/ML processes in steps from detection, prediction, recommendations, and then to automation.
- Allow people to understand what the system is recommending or doing and why.
- Facilitate people to add their insight to make incremental system improvements and to adjust automated recommendations or automated actions.

References

https://en.wikipedia.org/wiki/Controlsystem
https://en.wikipedia.org/wiki/Bullwhipeffect
https://www.controleng.com/single-article/process-modeling-feedback-controllers/8d 97811eab2a09c44f1be0c03e5d1b55.html
https://arxiv.org/abs/1705.07874)
https://en.wikipedia.org/wiki/Cluster_analysis
www.repetitiveflexiblesupply.com

1.8 CONTINUAL LEARNING: THE NEXT GENERATION OF ARTIFICIAL INTELLIGENCE*

Daniel G. Philps

Automated machine learning could become an indispensable tool for forecasters, as it has for data scientists, but practitioners first need to take a pragmatic view of the perceived complexity/disadvantages of machine learning (ML). In this article, Dan Philps provides an introduction to automated machine learning and its possible next-generation realization, continual learning (CL).

*This article originally appeared in *Foresight: The International Journal of Applied Forecasting* (Fall 2019) and appears here courtesy of the International Institute of Forecasters.

Continual learning advances the state of the art by attempting to automatically learn different tasks while retaining knowledge from previous model implementations. This is shown through an application of CL to guide investment decisions. Philps also offers the interesting perspective that complexity is not simply a technical characteristic of a model formulation, but also a resultant of the application of human judgment. Although CL may be more technically complex than many forecasting models, it reduces if not eliminates the complexity from judgmental human inputs.

Introduction

Go simple or go complex? For an applied-data scientist, simplicity wins every time (although with just enough "complexity-veneer" to hedge the next promotion).

There is considerable evidence that undue complexity reduces forecasting accuracy (Green and Armstrong 2015). It also detracts from interpretability and costs more in time, tech, and resources. So how can it be that machine learning (ML), generally considered to be complex, presents forecasters with an unmissable opportunity?

Answer: while ML is generally perceived to be complex, it can actually reduce complexity in model development by avoiding human behavioural biases and by automating intermediate steps. In addition, if complexity serves to encompass a richer variety of information and if learning from this information can be automated, complexity is a price worth paying. For these reasons, ML has started to become a powerful resource for forecasters. This article discusses the potential benefits of two types of ML: automated (autoML) and continual learning (CL). Both can be described as end-to-end approaches, meaning they can directly convert input data into an output forecast, bypassing traditional intermediate steps.

Eliminating Our Own Complexities

The subjectivity and behavioral biases we as forecasters tend to introduce to a modeling process are only partly tempered through experience. Biases include confirmation bias (Hergovich, Schott, and Burger 2010) towards our latest favored approach; cognitive dissonance (Festinger 1957), where we rework past errors to fit a competent perception of ourselves; and the availability heuristic (Tversky and Kahneman 1973), where we bias our approach to cues that happen to be at the forefront of our minds. While the perception of ML is one of complexity, ML may actually be a way of automating away the greater complexity of our own inductive biases.

Following on from Spyros Makridakis's excellent series of articles in *Foresight* (Makridakis, 2017–2018), this piece first describes automated machine learning (AutoML), and then what is likely to be the most disruptive end-to-end ML technology you have never heard of, continual learning (CL). This piece then explains why both are likely to become indispensable tools for forecasters.

AutoML

AutoML attempts to automate the steps an expert human would take to complete a forecasting project, thereby reducing the complexity in model development. AutoML's big advantage is that it allows forecasters to tap into the power of ML with minimum engagement in the underlying ML algorithms.

The original motivation for AutoML was to increase the productivity of researchers and reduce the probability of errors. However, AutoML has now exceeded these initial aims by becoming capable of learning from past operations (Feurer et al., 2015). For instance, some commercial AutoML systems now learn to associate different shapes of input data – metadata – with preprocessing and model selection choices that have been effective in the past. This is described as learning to learn, or meta-learning.

Figure 1.26 displays an AutoML system; input data is passed in with a forecasting target specified (Ytest). The system then attempts to build an appropriate solution. First, meta-data is extracted (i.e., information that describes the input data) from which the system may attempt to guess options and settings to use. Many different learners are also tested, which can range from linear regression through to ARIMA, multilayered perception, and support vector machines (SVMs). Gradient boosting trees and random forests are popular choices. The winning approaches (and associated settings) are generally chosen using fairly traditional statistical model selection combined with brute force grid searches. The most effective algorithms are shortlisted and then, typically, an ensemble of these approaches is formed to perform a final forecast.

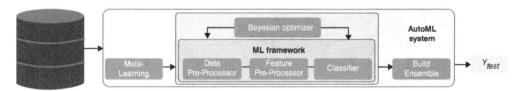

Figure 1.26 A Simple AutoML System
Source: An AutoML system for classification based on Auto-sklearn.

AutoML gives forecasters wide-ranging access to a broad toolbox of learners in a packaged pipeline – a neat way of consolidating existing algorithms and ML approaches while reducing the complexity of model development.

Continual Learning

While AutoML is a powerful tool, it is mainly just a consolidation of first-generation ML approaches. The next generation of ML, while drawing on similar building blocks, offers much greater potential. An example is continual learning – but is it mature enough to use in a forecasting process?

In ML, once a new model is learned, all previous models tend to be forgotten, an effect called catastrophic forgetting. In contrast, CL attempts to extract knowledge from a stream of information over time, to then build memories (a knowledge base) that can be used to improve future forecasting, as illustrated in Figure 1.27. The idea is to have a system that generalises across different forecasting tasks (Tn) and perhaps modes of data, and retains the task-specific knowledge of what works best for each. This knowledge can then be recalled and applied if a similar task is encountered again in the future.

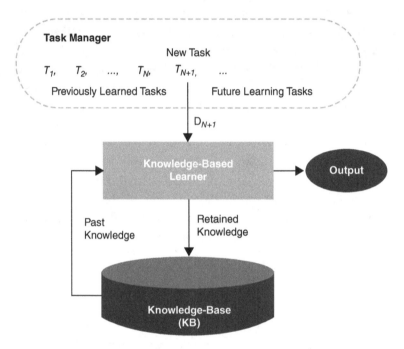

Figure 1.27 A Simple CL System
Source: Based on Lifelong Machine Learning, Chen et al., 2018.

Research into CL commenced in the 1990s from a desire to construct knowledge-accumulating machines to avoid the catastrophic forgetting of traditional approaches (Silver, 2015). However, enabling machines to learn over time faces the serious challenge known as the stability-plasticity dilemma (Mermillod, Bugaiska, and Bonin 2013), in that a system should learn over time but not at the expense of corrupting older knowledge.

A number of solutions have been proposed. In the late 1990s, Sepp Hochreiter and Jurgen Schmidhuber (1997) introduced the long short-term memory (LSTM) approach, which allows a recurrent neural network (NN) to forecast sequences – words in a passage of text, for example. (For a *Foresight* tutorial on neural network architecture basics, see Batchelor (2005), and for a more recent review of NN, see Januschowski and colleagues (2018). Alex Graves and his team at DeepMind (2016) made a start in overcoming catastrophic forgetting, and subsequent researchers focused on how the extensive memories created by CL could be compressed into a knowledge base using elastic weight consolidation (Kirkpatrick et al., 2017). However, there is only so much information you can squeeze into even a deep neural net before an information saturation point is reached.

An analogy of continual learning is how a child learns to ride a bike: wobbly at first, and then as skill develops with practice the neural pathways are reinforced and harden in the brain. Once learned, this skill is difficult to forget; in addition, it can be augmented if the child graduates to mountain biking, or transferred in learning to ride a unicycle. Simulating this effect with technology is challenging because the stability-plasticity problem must be addressed. Fortunately, real-world progress is being made through continual learning augmentation (CLA).

Continual Learning Augmentation

A team I belong to from City University of London (Philps, Weyde, Garcez, and Batchelor 2018) developed an end-to-end learning system that acquires knowledge of different states (regimes) from multiple time series and then applies this to a forecasting process that guides investment decisions. We call it continual learning augmentation (CLA), and it is applied as an open-world approach, belonging to a class of deep ML algorithms called memory-augmented neural nets (MANNs).

A base learner is chosen to drive CLA – for example, linear regression or a multilayered perceptron. This selected approach is run in a conventional way, stepping forward through time, forecasting time steps ahead. We then add a memory structure to this base learner. CLA's memory structure is designed to contain its base learner's parameters, which are remembered and recalled to improve future forecasting. Two observations allow us to develop this approach. First, we found it is possible to remember the most effective base learner parameterizations (model memories) over time, as patterns in the input data changed. Second, as Figure 1.28 shows, we found it is possible to recall these model memories at a future time by recognising reoccurring patterns in the input data.

We tested the system in a trading simulation using multivariate time-series data from recent financial history, including the period leading up to the subprime crisis, the "quant quake," the post-quantitative easing (QE) era, and the (first) eurozone crisis. Base-learner parameterizations that appeared to best identify good (and bad) investments during these periods were stored as model memories that could be recalled when current events seemed to echo the past. For example, the approach recalled the QE-driven recovery in 2009 and identified this knowledge as the most pertinent to apply in stock-selection decisions during the stimulus-driven stock market rally in China in 2017.

We found the system would have significantly outperformed the investment returns of the simple, unaugmented base learners we tested in a global equities investment

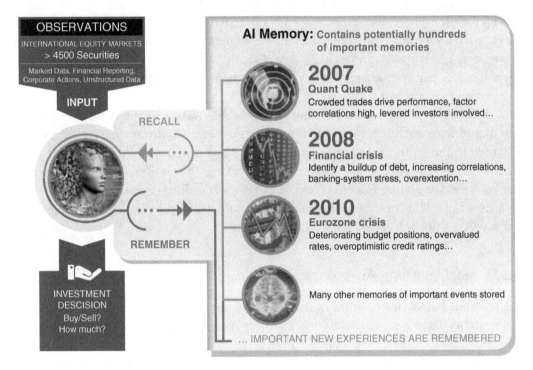

Figure 1.28 A CLA System to Guide Investment Decisions
Source: Philps, Weyde, d'Avila Garcez, and Batchelor, 2019.

simulation between 2003 and 2017. We believe these returns would have put a CLA-driven investment strategy in the top 25% of managed funds by return over the study period.

Although CLA does not overcome the stability-plasticity dilemma, we have shown that CL can be effectively applied to specific, complex, real-world tasks.

Conclusion

In spite of its perceived complexity, end-to-end machine learning is likely to become an indispensable tool for forecasters. It will reduce human involvement in model development and, in doing, make outcomes more objective. Additionally, the complexity of ML approaches is a price worth paying if the result is richer information and automated learning.

This article has addressed the potential benefits of two advances in machine learning: AutoML and continual learning (CL). While AutoML is now a reality, offering forecasters a powerful, automated approach, the next generation of ML promises to be more powerful still.

CL will allow machines to learn over time, enabling generalizations across many tasks. While key research questions behind CL remain unanswered, this has not stopped the successful development of applied CL, of which continual learning augmentation (CLA) is an important example. So the seemingly simple question as to whether we "go simple or go complex" is not as simple as it seems.

Acknowledgment

The author thanks Peter Simon, Data Scientist at DataRobot, for his advice and fact-checking on AutoML, and Professor Roy Batchelor of the City University of London for inspiring this entire endeavor.

References

Batchelor, R. (2005). A primer on forecasting with neural networks. *Foresight* 2 (October): 37–43.

Chen, Z., and Liu, B. (2018). Lifelong machine learning. *Synthesis Lectures on Artificial Intelligence and Machine Learning* 12 (3): 1–207.

Festinger, L. (1957). *A theory of cognitive dissonance*. Palo Alto, CA: Stanford University Press.

Feurer, M., Klein, A., Eggensperger, K., et al. (2015). Efficient and robust automated machine learning. *Advances in Neural Information Processing Systems* 28 (NIPS 2015): 2962–2970.

Graves, A., Wayne, G., Reynolds, M., et al. (2016). Hybrid computing using a neural network with dynamic external memory. *Nature* 538 (27 October): 471–476.

Green, K.C., and Armstrong, S. (2015). Simple versus complex forecasting: The evidence. *Journal of Business Research* 68, 1678–1685.

Hergovich, A., Schott, R., and Burger, C. (2010). Biased evaluation of abstracts depending on topic and conclusion: Further evidence of a confirmation bias within scientific psychology. *Current Psychology* 29 (3): 188–209. doi:10.1007/s12144-010-9087-5

Hochreiter, S., and Schmidhuber, J. (1997). Long short-term memory. *Neural Computation* 9 (8, November 15): 1735–1780.

Januschowski, T., Gasthaus, J., Wang, Y., Rangapuram, S. S., and Callot, L. (2018). Deep learning for forecasting. *Foresight* 50, 35–41.

Kirkpatrick, J., Pascanu, R., Rabinowitz, N., et al. (2017). Overcoming catastrophic forgetting in neural networks. *Proceedings of the National Academy of Sciences* 114 (13): 3521–3526.

Mermillod, M., Bugaiska, A., and Bonin, P. (2013).The stability-plasticity dilemma: Investigating the continuum from catastrophic forgetting to age-limited learning effects. *Frontiers in Psychology* 4: 504.

Philps, D., Weyde, T. d'Avila Garcez, A., and Batchelor, R. (2018). Continual learning augmented investment decisions. https://arxiv.org/abs/1812.02340

Silver, D. (2015). Consolidation using sweep task rehearsal: Overcoming the stability-plasticity problem. *Canadian AI 2015: Advances in Artificial Intelligence*, 307–322.

Tversky, A., and Kahneman, D. (1973). Availability: A heuristic for judging frequency and probability. *Cognitive Psychology* 5 (2): 207–232. doi:10.1016/0010-0285(73)90033-9. ISSN 0010-0285.

1.9 ASSISTED DEMAND PLANNING USING MACHINE LEARNING*

Charles Chase

As Chapter 1 has illustrated, there is considerable interest in the role of AI and ML in business forecasting. Both academic researchers and industry practitioners are exploring ways to exploit the developing technologies, with most of the attention focused on modeling and forecast generation. In particular, the recent M4 and M5 forecasting competitions have encouraged innovations – such as hybrid and combination models using both ML and traditional time-series methods – and provide a wealth of data for researchers.

In this adaption of his SAS whitepaper, Charles Chase takes a different angle. Chase explores the use of ML to augment the human demand planner, by helping guide the review and override of computer-generated forecasts. As we know from prior research (such as the frequently cited Fildes and Goodwin study from 2007), the review and override of statistical forecasts can consume considerable management resources, without always improving the accuracy of the forecast.

The new ML method presented in this article was tested on data from a large consumer products company. It shows promise in both reducing the amount to time spent reviewing forecasts, and at improving the accuracy of adjustments.

The Life of a Demand Planner

Demand planning at most commercial organizations is a repeating, week- (or month-) long, multistep process that includes an array of manual workflow processes. An important and time-consuming step is the review and manual override of the statistical forecast generated by the forecasting software.

Demand planners may override the statistical forecast when they have relevant information (such as a new promotion) not included in the forecasting model. They may override the statistical forecasting due to pressures from management, who wish to have the forecast express aspirations (such as a sales target) rather than being an unbiased "best guess" at what is really going to happen. Or they may override the forecast simply because they think they have a better number.

The percentage of statistical forecasts being manually overridden can be quite high, averaging 75% in a study of four UK supply chain companies by Fildes and Goodwin (2007). Overriding forecasts consumes an expensive resource (the demand planner's time), and frequently does not result in more accurate forecasts. It would be quite beneficial, therefore, to be able to identify, in advance, which statistical forecasts should be reviewed and adjusted, and which can be left alone. The following describes a new patented method that uses machine learning to do just that (Valsaraj et al. 2019). This

---

*This article is adapted from the whitepaper "Assisted Demand Planning Using Machine Learning for CPG and Retail" and appears here courtesy of Charles Chase and SAS.

approach shows promise at guiding demand planners to where they can add value with their overrides, and reducing the number of forecasts they need to review.

What Is Forecast Value Added?

Companies have been searching for a performance measurement that can effectively measure and improve the demand forecasting process, reduce cycle time, and minimize the number of touch points. The best approach is to implement a methodology called Forecast Value Add (FVA) analysis, or lean forecasting (Gilliland 2013).

FVA is a metric for evaluating the performance of each step and participant in the forecasting process. Simply put, FVA is the change in forecast accuracy after each touch point in the process. Measurement can be based on any specific forecast performance metric, such as percentage error (PE), absolute percentage error (APE), mean absolute percentage error (MAPE), or weighted mean absolute percentage error (WMAPE).

FVA determines whether manual adjustments to the forecast have improved accuracy. If those manual adjustments increase the accuracy of the statistical forecast, then those changes "add value" and should remain in the process. However, if the manual adjustments do not improve the accuracy, they should be eliminated or minimized (simplified) to reduce cycle time and resources, thereby improving forecast process efficiency.

Figure 1.29 is an example of a "stairstep" report, which provides pairwise comparisons between each step on the forecasting process. Starting with a naïve forecast that has achieved forecast accuracy of 60%, we see that the statistical forecast (generated by forecasting software) achieves 65% accuracy, so it has added value. However, management overrides have reduced accuracy to 62%. In this example, based on real-life data presented by a large consumer products company, overrides not only consumed resources (management time), they on average reduced accuracy of the forecast by three percentage points.

Process Step	Forecast Accuracy	FVA vs. Naive	FVA vs. Statistical
Naïve Forecast	60%		
Statistical Forecast	65%	+5%	
Management Override	62%	+2%	−3%

Figure 1.29 FVA "Stairstep" Report

FVA is a common-sense approach that is easy to understand. The idea is simple – it's basic scientific method. What are the results of doing something versus doing nothing? FVA can be either positive or negative, telling you whether your efforts are adding value by making the forecast more accurate, or whether you are making things worse. FVA analysis consists of a variety of methods that have been evolving through industry practitioners' applications around this innovative performance metric.

FVA is used to improve not only forecast accuracy, but to reduce non-value adding touch points in the demand planning process, thus improving process efficiency. According to a recent analyst report (Griswold 2016), FVA is the second-most widely used performance metric to measure the effectiveness of a company's demand forecasting and planning process. Weighted MAPE (WMAPE) is the No. 1 performance metric, while the former standard, MAPE, is now the third-most widely used.

Mid-sized and large organizations can have thousands, or even millions of forecasts to create and manage. Manually reviewing and overriding even a modest percent of these forecasts would require an army of demand planners – and is simply not feasible. But what if this process could be automated – guiding demand planners to which forecasts should be reviewed (and which should be left alone)? Further, what if there could be additional guidance on the direction (up or down) and amount of the override? These are the objectives of a new approach utilizing machine learning, seeking to reduce time spent making forecast overrides, while simultaneously improving the FVA.

The Need for Intelligent Automation

Not all forecast overrides add value. In fact, many add no value, or even make the forecast worse. The challenge is to distinguish likely value adding overrides from those that are unlikely to add value.

Distinguishing potential value added from nonvalue added overrides becomes more difficult when you have thousands of SKUs across brick-and-mortar stores, mobile, online, Amazon, and other related e-commerce channels in multiple countries. This could represent millions of forecasts. It would be impossible for demand planners to review and manually adjust all those forecasts. So demand planners often rely on aggregate-level adjustments that are then disaggregated down their business hierarchies. In many cases, mass aggregation of overrides is not an accurate way of manually adjusting statistical forecasts. This is true even when the aggregate overrides are accounting for sales and marketing activities not considered in the original forecast.

Using Intelligent Automation to Improve a Demand Planner's FVA

Assisted Demand Planning

The following describes an intelligent automation technique that uses ML to boost FVA. It has been tested with data from a large global consumer packaged goods company, using ML to learn from past demand planners' overrides. The test focused on two main objectives:

- Identify forecast entities that need overrides.
- Provide demand planners with the direction (up or down) and range of suggested overrides.

ML analyzes past statistical forecasts and overrides, learning from successful and unsuccessful adjustments to identify the most appropriate candidates to review. The method then provides guidance to demand planners about where, and by how much, to either raise or lower the statistical forecast.

A Process Approach

In the example below, a minimum of two-and-a-half years of historical overrides based on an 18-month rolling forecast were collected for five product categories in two geographic areas for more than 700 items. A 60-day future forecast was used for FVA purposes. In-sample and out-of-sample training and validation periods were used to choose the appropriate ML model. A three-step approach was implemented:

1. **Enrich**: Enrich the process by identifying value-add and nonvalue-add overrides made by several demand planners, and add any other attributes that are available.

2. **Model**: Build ML models using neural networks, gradient boosting, and ensemble random forest training models in a competition to determine the champion model.

3. **Assess**: Assess models using the out-of-sample validation data and report the levels of accuracy.

It is possible to enhance these steps by adding causal factors like sales promotions, pricing strategies and others, but causal factors were not included in this example. Smart rules can also be added – such as not making overrides if forecasts have historically been quite accurate (e.g., MAPE < 10%).

Results

The assisted demand planning process reduced the number of manual overrides by 47%, allowing the demand planners to focus only on those products and periods that would benefit the most from overrides. As a result, it improved the value added to the forecast by 6.3%.

The user interface (a portion of which is shown in Figure 1.30) guides demand planners in making manual overrides, in what direction, and within what volume

	JAN History	FEB History	MAR Current	APR Future	MAY Future	JUN Future	
Actual	17.48	18.90	-	-	-	-	
SAS Statistical Forecast			8.83	10.48	9.73	11.50	
Recommended Adj Direction			⇧		⇧	⇧	**Override Legend:**
Override	-	-	9.78	10.48	9.87	11.60	Value entered is out of recommended bounds
Lower Bound	17.48	18.90	8.83	10.48	9.73	11.50	Recommend an override
Upper Bound	17.48	18.90	10.85	12.42	13.17	14.83	No override recommended

Figure 1.30 User Interface for Entering Overrides

range (bottom two rows). Up arrows for March, May, and June indicate the direction of the suggested override. User enters the adjustment in the Override row.

For April there is no arrow up or down, indicating no manual overrides are suggested for that month because the statistically derived forecast is expected to be accurate. Demand planners can scroll up or down the hierarchy for customer and product. Note that there is no limitation to the number of levels in the hierarchy. It is based on available data.

If a demand planner chooses to make a manual override for a month not recommended by intelligent automation, a default warning appears to indicate that overriding the statistical derived forecast is not recommended. Demand planners can be blocked from making overrides in those cells, or you can flag those cells with warning messages but still allow the demand planner to make an override.

Conclusion

Overall, ML helped to improve forecast accuracy (on average) across all the product groups, items and geographies in this study – results demonstrating that ML can augment the role of demand planner. ML helps automate the repetitive work of managing enormous amounts of data in a forecasting process. ML provides targeted intelligence to pinpoint where, when, and by how much to manually adjust the statistical forecast. And, this approach saves management time by recommending when *not* to adjust statistical forecasts that have proven to be more accurate than prior overrides. In short, intelligent automation reduces the time spent reviewing and overriding forecasts and improves accuracy.

Intelligent automation does not replace the demand planner with a machine. Rather, it helps the demand planner work smarter. Intelligent automation lets demand planners ingest massive amounts of forecast information and boost the FVA of their forecasting process.

References

Fildes, R., and Goodwin, P. (2007). Good and bad judgment in forecasting: Lessons from four companies. *Foresight* 8, 5–10.

Griswold, M. (2016, 22 December). Market Guide for Retail Forecasting and Replenishment Solutions. Gartner.

Gilliland, M. (2013). FVA: A reality check on forecasting practices. *Foresight* 29, 14–18.

Valsaraj, V., Aral, B., Yi, J., Baldridge, R., and Gallagher, B. (2019). Interactive graphical user interface with override guidance. United States patent US10255085B1.

1.10 MAXIMIZING FORECAST VALUE ADD THROUGH MACHINE LEARNING AND BEHAVIORAL ECONOMICS*

Jeff Baker

We know that the manual adjustment of statistical forecasts can fail to improve accuracy by any meaningful degree, and frequently makes the forecast less accurate. So it is in the forecaster's interest to reduce this wasted effort, and only make adjustments that are likely to provide meaningful accuracy improvements.

The previous article by Chase showed how machine learning could provide guided assistance for the forecaster in making overrides. This article illustrates an alternative method with a similar aim. Baker introduces the notion of a "demand scaled override" (DSO) which considers the size of an override with respect to the underlying volatility of the time series data. He then describes a classification tree to influence adjustment behavior by providing what behavioral economics calls a "nudge."

Dictating the forecaster's behavior – such as preventing manual override of forecasts meeting specified criteria – could be achieved through a restrictive user interface. But rather than dictate behavior, the "nudge" is meant to influence behavior by providing information that should be included in a decision. Combining machine learning methods with behavioral economics provides a new path for increasing process efficiency while simultaneously improving the value added by manual forecast adjustments.

Introduction

Business forecasting frequently combines statistical time-series techniques with qualitative expert opinion overrides to create a final forecast. Minimizing forecast error is critical, as it enables key supply chain objectives such as safety stock reduction, customer service improvement, and manufacturing schedule stability.

One of the most common forecasting performance metrics is Mean Absolute Percent Error (MAPE). In addition to measuring MAPE of the "final" forecast, MAPE can also be recorded at intermediate process steps, such as for the original statistical forecast before any management overrides, and for a naïve forecast. Measuring MAPE (or any other error or accuracy metric) at each process step is known as Forecast Value Added (FVA) analysis (Gilliland 2010). FVA analysis lets you identify process steps that are "adding value" by improving forecast accuracy, or process waste (steps that are failing to improve forecast accuracy or are just making it worse).

*This article is an adaptation of the author's Master's thesis, "Effect of Override Size on Forecast Value Add" (Massachusetts Institute of Technology 2018) and appears here courtesy of the International Institute of Forecasters. An updated version will appear in *Foresight: The International Journal of Applied Forecasting* (Winter 2021).

The FVA between the statistical forecast and the final forecast is of critical importance, as it measures the value of the qualitative overrides provided by business experts from the sales, marketing, and other functional areas. However, overrides often fail to improve final forecast accuracy. At best, this wastes the time of scarce forecasting resources. At worst, it seriously impacts business performance. Under-forecasting leads to revenue loss from stock outs, reduced customer service, and excessive cost due to instability in manufacturing, warehousing, and transportation operations. Over-forecasting leads to excessive inventory, additional warehousing costs, and exposure to obsolescence.

The impact of judgmental overrides on final forecast accuracy has been studied by Fildes, Goodwin, Lawrence, and Nikolopoulos (2009). A key finding in their work was the relationship that often occurs between the size of the override and its direction, which indicated either over- or under-forecasting (Figure 1.31). Several interesting patterns emerge:

- The smallest overrides failed to add significant value.
- Positive adjustments frequently made forecast accuracy worse.
- Negative overrides usually improved forecast accuracy.

While these patterns hold across the five groups studied, the differences indicate that the results are also a function of the company. For example, Groups A–C are better at guarding against overly positive bias, so they do not see the same accuracy degradation that impacts Groups D1 and D2 when the forecast is adjusted upwards.

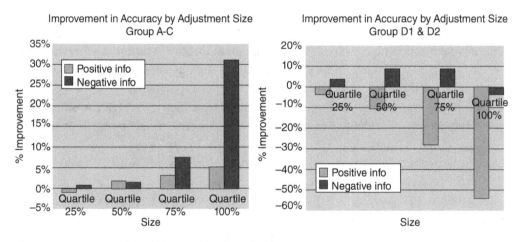

Figure 1.31 Forecast Value Add by Override Size and Direction

Predicting Forecast Value Add

Because behavior differed company to company, there remains a key unanswered question: Can we create a framework to classify overrides which were likely to add value based on the FVA metric? Under such a framework, small adjustments would be ignored, and potentially value-destroying overrides could be flagged and vetted. This would reduce the number of overrides made and simultaneously improve forecast accuracy, thereby increasing the efficiency and effectiveness of the supply chain.

Master's thesis research by the author (Baker 2018) sought to answer this question, and extended the research in several areas. The first was the concept of a critical threshold FVA value, FVA_{crit}, to create two classification categories. While technically any FVA value above 0% improves upon the statistical forecast, FVA_{crit} takes into consideration the cost of resources (e.g., management time) consumed in making overrides, versus the value of the override. Thus, efforts that result in $FVA < FVA_{crit}$ are time wasters that do not truly add value once the effort required is considered. Incorporating FVA_{crit} allows each company to determine their own threshold value that draws the line between value added and non-value added.

Three variables were then used to drive the classification prediction. As found in previous studies, the direction of the override is relevant. Overforecasting is a problematic bias in business, which makes this a key driver. The other predictors of value add are override size and forecastability.

Override Size

Percentage change is often used as an indicator of adjustment size. Computationally this is straightforward. However, it does not consider the underlying variation of the forecast.

Consider two products, A and B, with identical statistical forecasts (flat lines at 1,000) and identical overrides (dots at 1,050) as shown in Figure 1.32.

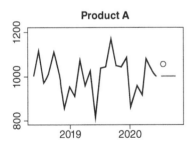 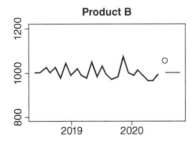

Figure 1.32 Identical Forecast Overrides for Products A and B

In both cases the overrides represent the same percentage increase (+5%) and appear identical. However, consider that the variability of Product A's forecast is larger than the variability of Product B's forecast. If we re-display with prediction intervals (PIs) added (Figure 1.33), a different picture arises.

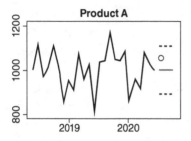 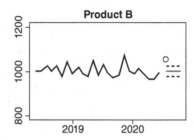

Figure 1.33 Forecast Overrides, with Prediction Intervals

The first override is within the PI of the statistical forecast. Given the dispersion of the statistical forecast, the two are indistinguishable from one another other – the override "signal" is within the "noise" of the statistical forecast. The second override is outside the PI, indicating a true signal that this is different from the underlying variation.

To reflect this relationship, a new metric called the Dispersion-Scaled Override (DSO) was created. DSO measures the ratio of override signal to the underlying statistical forecast noise. The actual demand time series is decomposed into trend, seasonal, and residual components using the seasonal trend decomposition using Loess technique (Cleveland et al. 1990).

From the residual component, three measures of dispersion – standard deviation, mean absolute deviation, and median absolute deviation – were calculated. The override was divided by these measures of dispersion, creating three signal-to-noise metrics which relate the override to the underlying variability. Different dispersion metrics were considered due their varying responsiveness to outliers in the residuals. Standard deviation is known to be impacted by outliers, whereas median absolute deviation is more robust to outliers.

Forecastability of Demand

In addition to override direction and DSO, the third and final type of predictor was forecastability. Forecastability measures the theoretical maximum achievable accuracy.

If forecastability is low, the statistical model will likely fail to achieve the level of accuracy desired by management. In these cases, expert intervention using overrides would likely reduce forecast error. Conversely, it is unlikely that the statistical forecast of a highly forecastable time series may be meaningfully improved upon, especially through small overrides.

In-sample weighted mean absolute percent error (WMAPE) was used as a proxy for forecastability. The relevant demand history is fitted, without a hold-out period, and the best forecast is chosen. This is similar to the automatic forecast selection process used by many software packages. By eliminating any hold-out data, the model will be over-fitted; this is desired, as it is improbable that any future forecast will have lower error.

The observed forecast accuracy will then be plotted against in-sample WMAPE as seen in Figure 1.34. In theory, the upper limit of accuracy should be dictated by the in-sample WMAPE. In practice, the actual results will likely be less. All things being equal (forecasting technique, underlying demand pattern), the only way to break above the theoretical limit is to manually adjust the forecast.

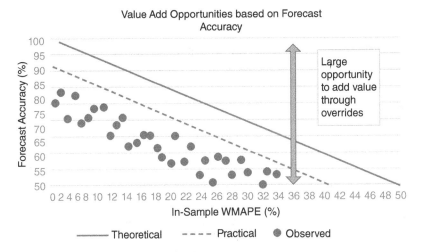

Figure 1.34 Forecast Accuracy vs. In-Sample WMAPE

Override Classification Techniques

The FVA_{crit} response variable, along with the three predictor variables (override direction, forecastability, and DSO size) were then analyzed using machine learning classification techniques to classify an override as value added or not (Figure 1.35).

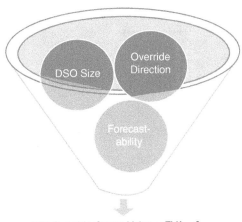

Will Override Create Value > FVA_{crit}?

Figure 1.35 Machine Learning Classification

Classification tree, boosted tree, random forest, and logistic regression machine learning techniques were utilized in the evaluation. These classification techniques have several advantages, including automatic variable selection, robustness to outliers, and no assumptions regarding linearity of relationships between predictor variables and the response variable. Each technique resulted in approximately the same accuracy in properly classifying an override, which was approximately 80%.

Classification Trees

Classification trees are particularly attractive because their graphical nature makes them easy to explain to non-technical business personnel. The variable of primary importance shows on the top level. Logic tests at nodes create branches based on responses. A yes response indicates you branch right, while a no response indicates you branch left. The lowest level logic test leads to the classification – in this case either forecast value added (FVA) or non-value added (NVA).

The example tree shown in Figure 1.36 can be used to trace the logic flow. Consider a small, positive override. By inspecting the tree, we see positive override direction as the top-level driver. Because our override was positive, we follow the logic branch to the right. The next logic test would be dispersion-scaled override size. If the dispersion-scaled override was less than 2.5, we again follow the right branch, and see that the override is likely to be non-value added. This coincides with our expectation for small, positive overrides being subject to bias. Also, any small override will, at best, result in a small improvement in forecast accuracy that may not be worth the effort.

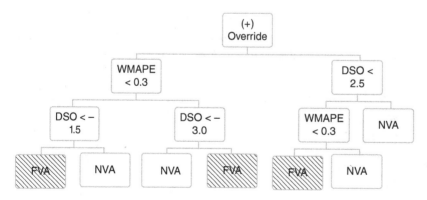

Figure 1.36 Classification Tree Example

Analysis

Classification was approximately 80% accurate in predicting whether an override would create forecast value add above a user defined threshold. This suggests a framework should be used during the consensus forecasting process to evaluate any override to the baseline statistical model (Figure 1.37).

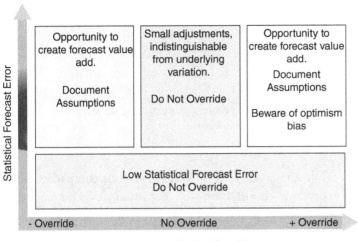

Figure 1.37 Override Evaluation Framework

Overrides flagged as non-value adding require additional vetting. The forecast adjustment behavior will become self-correcting. Previous bad decisions will increase the likelihood of an override being flagged as non-value adding, which will increase the need to document and discuss underlying assumptions. Documentation and discussion will in turn increase forecast value-add. This will maximize the value that experts add to the business forecasting process.

Three key, interrelated factors drive the probability of creating a value-added override.

Forecastability

The first factor is the accuracy of the baseline statistical model. If the statistical forecast was performing poorly, it was more likely that there were opportunities to improve upon it. Conversely, a well-performing statistical model was difficult to improve upon.

Dispersion Scaled Override Size

The second factor was the size of the override scaled by the residual variation of the time series – a new class of metrics called Dispersion-Scaled Override (DSO). Small overrides which are indistinguishable from the underlying random noise variation are unlikely to add value. Larger overrides with a clear signal-to-noise have a better opportunity to improve accuracy.

Reducing the number of small overrides and overrides to forecastable demand will reduce the burden on the forecaster, allowing them to concentrate on more important opportunities where they can add value.

Override Direction

The final factor was the direction of the override. Downward adjustments of the statistical forecast were more likely to add value due to increased scrutiny. Upward adjustments, often driven by a biased desire to match financial goals, are more likely to degrade forecast accuracy. This directional bias is consistent with previous studies and is a clear opportunity for improvement in the business forecasting process.

Framework Adaptability

It is important to note that while there are general trends between companies, each company will generate its own, unique classification tree. For instance, a company that diligently guards against bias may not have positive override direction as a primary driver.

Another conclusion is that even within the same company, these drivers may change. Changes in the underlying demand pattern, better statistical forecasting techniques, and improved override quality could all impact classification.

Behavioral Economics: How to Influence Forecaster Behavior

Once an override is classified, it is important to leverage that information to improve forecast accuracy. One approach could be to systematically ignore any override flagged as non-value added. A more sophisticated technique might attempt to auto correct the override based on the quality of past overrides.

The challenge with either approach is that they do not address the root cause of the override error. In response to auto-correction, the forecaster may respond by amplifying their entries, getting caught up in an endless loop of adjustments and counter-adjustments.

A better approach is to influence behavior, not dictate it. In behavioral economics, this concept is known as the nudge (Thaler and Sunstein 2009). With a nudge, we provide information which should be included in the decision – think about a restaurant menu which provides information on calories and saturated fat. Unlike the systems described above, there is no penalty for ignoring the nudge.

There are two critical elements to influence – data and questions. Visually representing past results and actively questioning current decisions will drive improved forecasting.

Nudge Data

Several data elements are useful in supporting better overrides. Utilizing these metrics will draw attention to counterproductive forecasting behaviors.

1. Percent of forecasts overridden. In its simplest form, this is a single number representing total overrides divided by total forecasts. A more sophisticated approach is to calculate this using a 2×2 Volume-Forecastability matrix. As a rule of thumb,

the greater value add opportunities would be for items with high volume and low forecastability. Trying to improve the accuracy of a highly forecastable item just wastes time.

2. **Percent positive versus percent negative.** A properly specified statistical model is just as likely to over-forecast as it is to under-forecast, so too many positive overrides indicate bias.

3. **Override size (dispersion scaled).** Understanding the distribution of dispersion scaled overrides will indicate if small, non-value adding adjustments are prevalent.

4. **Percent of forecast overrides which have added value.** This metric is the cumulative effect of the others and would be an ideal final measure of the override process effectiveness.

Nudge Questions

In conjunction with data on past performance, questioning during a consensus review can be used to influence behaviors that are more likely to lead to final forecast improvement.

1. Is this positive override overly influenced by budget goals, or sales "best case" optimism?

    a. Is this consistent with year-over-year and month-to-month trends?

2. Is this small override based on new information?

3. Is this override of a highly forecastable product based on significant new information?

4. Will you be able to explain this change in Executive Business Review?

The answer to one or more of these questions should be documented at the time of the override. The act of documenting clarifies the reasoning and may be reviewed in later months to evaluate its effectiveness. This will focus forecast improvement analysis on assumptions, which will drive improved decisions in the future. Also, if documentation of all overrides is *required*, this may discourage small or other frivolous overrides because forecasters will not want to make the extra effort of providing their reasons.

Summary

A multi-disciplined approach will improve final forecast accuracy. Machine learning can be utilized to identify and understand underlying drivers of inaccuracy. The process missteps like small or biased adjustments and overrides to forecastable products can be surfaced. Behavioral economics can then be used to influence the desired override discipline. Nudges will influence, but not dictate, the proper approach to overrides. The combination of the two will lead to more accurate forecasts, laying the foundation for optimal safety stock, improved customer service, and stabilized manufacturing and distribution schedules. Ultimately, this will drive bottom-line improvements to business profitability.

References

Baker, J. A. (2018). *Effect of override size on forecast value add*. Master's Thesis, Massachusetts Institute of Technology, Cambridge.

Cleveland, R., Cleveland, W., McRae, J., and Terpenning, I. (1990). STL: A seasonal-trend decomposition procedure based on Loess. *Journal of Official Statistics* 6 (1): 3–73.

Fildes, R., Goodwin, P., Lawrence, M., and Nikolopoulos, K. (2009). Effective forecasting and judgmental adjustments: An empirical evaluation and strategies for improvement in supply-chain planning. *International Journal of Forecasting* 25 (1): 3–23.

Gilliland, M. (2010). *The business forecasting deal*. Hoboken, NJ: Wiley.

Thaler, R., and Sunstein, C. (2009). *Nudge: Improving decisions about health, wealth, and happiness*. New York: Penguin Books.

1.11 THE M4 FORECASTING COMPETITION – TAKEAWAYS FOR THE PRACTITIONER*

Michael Gilliland

2018's M4 Forecasting Competition involved 61 competitors and benchmarks forecasting 100,000 time series with frequencies ranging from hourly to yearly. The competition led to a wealth of analysis and commentary on the relevance and implications of the results, including publication of 35 articles in a dedicated issue of the *International Journal of Forecasting* (36 (1), 2020). This article and the accompanying commentary provide background history and motivation for the M4, competition results, and important takeaways for business forecasting practitioners.

The M4 was organized, in part, to evaluate claims in the machine learning literature that ML methods improved upon traditional time-series forecasting methods. M4 found, instead, that pure ML methods fared worse than traditional methods, failing in most instances to surpass even simple benchmarks. However, when machine learning was used in a combination or hybrid model with traditional time-series methods, results were favorable – although the improvement came at a prohibitive cost in computational time.

Among other important findings for practitioners, the M4 confirmed previous compelling evidence that forecast combinations improve accuracy. Also, methods for accurately calibrating prediction intervals were demonstrated, but only by the costly ML/time series methods. Although such competitions (including 2020's M5) don't reflect all the complexities of real-life business forecasting, they are more than just a scholarly exercise, and practitioners can learn from the results.

---

*This article originally appeared in *Foresight: The International Journal of Applied Forecasting* (Spring 2020) and appears here courtesy of the International Institute of Forecasters.

M4 Background

The M4 competition (2018), like its predecessors M (1979), M2 (1983), and M3 (1998), was not meant as either a horse race or beauty contest. The M competitions were designed as research endeavors intended to advance our knowledge of forecasting – and they have succeeded in doing so. Rob Hyndman's "A Brief History of Forecasting Competitions" (2020) provides a fascinating review of the findings and impact of prior competitions, including a sometimes humorous look at the motivation behind the first M competition.

The original M competition grew out of a contentious presentation by Spyros Makridakis and Michele Hibon (1979) at the Royal Statistical Society. In the 1970s, an era smitten with the newly invented Box-Jenkins ARIMA modeling as the forecaster's panacea, Makridakis and Hibon had the audacity to report that simpler methods (such as exponential smoothing) could actually forecast better!

Highlights of the ensuing discussion – including insults questioning the competence of the presenters – are captured in Hyndman's article. In response to this general hostility, the first M competition was born, involving 1,001 time series. The most consequential findings were that complex methods typically did not produce more accurate forecasts than simpler ones, and that combining various methods generally outperformed the individual methods being combined (Fildes et al. 1998).

Today, after nearly 40 years, Machine Learning (ML) is being offered as the panacea for forecasting. In a widely downloaded PLoS|One article by Makridakis, Spiliotis, and Assimakopoulos (2018a), the authors evaluated popular ML methods using a subset of the M3 data and compared post-sample accuracy to eight traditional forecasting methods. Motivation for this analysis was the growing body of academic literature advocating the use of ML methods in forecasting, yet providing scant evidence of improved performance versus traditional methods.

The PLoS|One article (available online at https://doi.org/10.1371/journal.pone.0194889, so results won't be reproduced here) goes into considerable detail on the data used, methods compared, and performance across multiple metrics (sMAPE and MASE). In short, the ML methods performed worse than the traditional statistical methods across both accuracy metrics, for all forecasting horizons examined. And worse for ML advocates, the computational requirements for the ML methods were considerably greater.

The authors' main critique of the academic ML forecasting literature was that "the majority of published studies provide forecasts and claim satisfactory accuracies without comparing them with simple statistical methods or even naïve benchmarks. Doing so raises expectations that ML methods provide accurate predictions, but without any empirical proof that this is the case." The way forward, they suggested, was through a new research effort – the M4 competition – which ran January through May, 2018.

M4 Results

The M4 utilized 100,000 real-life time series across a variety of domains, with frequencies ranging from hourly to yearly. Sixty-one methods (49 competitors plus 12 benchmarks) were compared. Six of the methods were considered pure ML, while two were hybrid/combinations of ML with traditional statistical methods. An overall summary is provided by Makridakis, Spiliotis, and Assimakopoulos (2020) in an issue of the *International Journal of Forecasting* dedicated to M4 results, discussion, and commentary. (The full issue of 35 articles is available online at https://www.sciencedirect.com/journal/international-journal-of-forecasting/vol/36/issue/1.)

Here are four of the key findings.

Point Forecast (PF) Accuracy

The pure ML methods fared poorly, all falling below the main benchmark "Comb" – a combination model averaging Single, Holt, and Damped Trend exponential smoothing. However, the two methods that used ML in conjunction with traditional statistical methods, either in a hybrid model (Smyl 2020) or in a combination referred to as FFORMA (Montero-Manso, Athanasopoulos, Hyndman, and Talagala 2020), performed at the top. Overall, Smyl's method was approximately 9% more accurate than the main benchmark. This is noteworthy, because in M3 the top performing Theta method was just 3.8% more accurate than the same Comb benchmark.

The benefit of combining models was reaffirmed, as nine of the best 10 performers were combination (or hybrid) methods, and the 10 worst (least accurate) performers were all individual statistical or ML models. Tables of the full results are in Makridakis, Spiliotis, and Assimakopoulo (2020).

Prediction Interval (PI) Precision

For the first time in M competitions, prediction intervals were requested along with the point forecasts. PIs assert, for example, that there is a 95% chance the forecast will fall within the specified band about the point forecast. Correct PIs provide very useful information to the planner, as knowing the forecast is 100+/–10 could lead to very different decisions than if the forecast is 100+/–100.

Earlier methods for computing PIs tended to greatly underestimate future forecast errors. In M4, the winning Smyl and FFORMA methods also succeeded in specifying the 95% PIs precisely. Per Makridakis, Spiliotis, and Assimakopoulo (2018b), "These are the first methods we are aware of that have [specified PIs correctly], rather than underestimating the uncertainty considerably."

Run Time

While M4 showed that the complex methods utilizing ML with traditional statistical methods were able to generate more accurate PFs (and achieve unprecedented precision in their PIs), this came at considerable cost. One of the major innovations of the M4 was having participants provide their code, allowing for replication on a standard hardware configuration. Table 1.5 shows the run time for selected methods.

Table 1.5 Running Time of Selected Methods and Comb Benchmark

Method	Error Metrics			Run Time
	sMAPE	MASE	OWA	(minutes)
Smyl	11.374	1.536	0.821	8056.0
FFORMA	11.720	1.551	0.838	46108.3
Legaki & Koutsouri	11.986	1.601	0.086	25.0
Theta	12.309	1.696	0.897	12.7
Comb (benchmark)	12.555	1.663	0.898	33.2
ARIMA	12.669	1.666	0.903	3030.9
Naïve2	13.564	1.912	1.000	2.9
Naïve1	14.208	2.044	1.058	0.2

As expected, the main benchmark (Comb), random walk (Naïve1), and seasonal random walk (Naïve2) required little processing time. Comb took 33 minutes to forecast the 100,000 series, and Naïve1 took just 12 seconds! Contrast this with 6 days for the Smyl hybrid approach, and 32 days for FFORMA's ML and statistical combination approach.

Performance of Machine Learning Methods

The M4 competition was organized, in part, to test the excessive, unjustified claims about the ability of ML methods to forecast. It found that when ML methods were used creatively with existing statistical methods, meaningful accuracy improvements were demonstrated (albeit at high cost). However, pure ML methods, used on their own, performed considerably worse than even low-cost benchmark methods, and at much higher cost in run times.

Takeaways for Forecasting Practitioners

Should practitioners care about the M4? Does it reflect any of the complex realities faced by business forecasters? Or was it just a scholarly exercise of interest only to forecasting academics?

As Petropoulos and Makridakis (2020) state in their introduction to the *IJF* issue, "... there will never be a 'perfect' forecasting competition . . . . Nevertheless, forecasting competitions, similarly to laboratory experiments, can enhance our understanding of what affects the accuracy of forecasting methods and become catalysts in the development of unique approaches that advance the art and science of forecasting" (p. 3).

I concur. There seems no practical way to fully reproduce the vacillating data and conditions under which we perform real-life business forecasting. But a research endeavor such as this, however imperfect a reflection of reality, can still deliver insights of practical importance. What follows are what I see as the most compelling lessons practitioners can draw from the M4.

The High Cost of Complexity

M4 revealed, contrary to much of the previous evidence, that complex methods can possibly lead to greater forecast accuracy than simpler methods. The combination/hybrid methods of the two winners showed that utilizing machine learning with traditional time-series forecasting techniques can add value. But as we've seen from the run-time data, this improvement came at huge cost.

For practitioners, the cost of forecast accuracy improvement is a relevant concern. No organization can afford days of processing time to eke out a few percentage points of forecast accuracy. Decisions must be made and plans executed in a timely manner. The practitioner needs forecasts that are "good enough" to make better decisions than are made from poor quality forecasts.

The business world has no shortage of poor-quality forecasts, as evidenced by the excellent Morlidge studies published in *Foresight* (2014, 2016). When 30–50% of the real-life forecasts – the forecasts organizations are using to run their businesses – are less accurate than Naïve1 (a random walk, aka "no change model), there is ample room for improvement. We learn from M4 that significant improvement over Naïve1 is readily available via several simple time-series options, including the Comb benchmark (approximately 18% more accurate than Naive1, with a manageable 33-minute run time). Or better still, the promising approach by Legaki and Koutsouri (a variation of the M3-winning Theta method), which showed an additional 4.5% improvement over Comb – with only 25 minutes run time to forecast 100,000 series!

The Benefit of Combining Models

Combination models continued to shine, as they have in prior M competitions. Hyndman (2020) calls it "patently absurd" to believe a single model can be found to describe the data-generating process when ". . . real data come from processes that are much more complicated, non-linear, and non-stationary than any model we might dream up" (p. 8). The compelling evidence that forecast combinations improve accuracy suggests that software vendors should make it easy for practitioners by making combination models (rather than a single model) the default. Perhaps these findings will lead customers to demand the availability of combination models from their forecasting software vendors.

Raising Awareness of Prediction Intervals

PIs are an invaluable addition to point forecasts by providing decision makers with a sense of the uncertainty around their PFs (even though this uncertainty has typically been underestimated). But the usefulness of PIs is not widely recognized.

Part of the reason is that not all forecasting software packages provide PIs (or other ways of expressing uncertainty, such as fan charts or full predictive densities). But there are also many psychological reasons – explored in Goodwin (2014) – why PIs, even when provided, may be ignored.

Goodwin cites and summarizes the body of research on this topic and the two conflicting objectives of accuracy and informativeness, noting the quality of the calibration of the PIs does not appear to be related to the motivation to use them. "An interval forecast may accurately reflect the uncertainty, but it is likely to be spurned by decision makers if it is too wide and judged to be uninformative" (p. 5).

The Smyl and FFORMA methods showed that properly calibrated PIs are now possible. But as the psychological research shows, when there is great uncertainty and the interval is wide, decision makers may (wrongly) consider that useless information.

Shrinking Role for ARIMA Modeling

The saga of ARIMA modeling continues to be written. The ARIMA methodology certainly allows for tight fitting of the model to history. What early users of ARIMA failed to account for – until exposed by Makridakis and Hibon – was that fit to history can be a poor indication of the quality of a forecast about the future. ARIMA models tended to be "overfit" – reacting to noise in the history and projecting that forward.

The overfitting problem is now recognized and largely addressed using information criteria in the modeling steps. However, even though ARIMA performance has been improving relative to benchmarks since the first M, in M4 it is essentially only as good as Comb. Yet ARIMA's run time is much longer, and the models are not easily explainable to decision makers who may want to know where the forecasts are coming from.

Something that is difficult to explain, has longer run time, and is still a mediocre performer should not be the primary modeling choice. ARIMA should only be used in circumstances where the method demonstrably improves over simpler alternatives.

Exposing the ML Hype . . .

ML methods, on their own, failed to meet the accuracy of even simple benchmarks. Since these methods were not originally developed to do time-series forecasting, the results may not be surprising. Yet bad forecasting performance should not reflect badly on the usefulness of ML methods for other types of data science problems where they are appropriate. Also, ongoing research to adapt traditional ML methods to time-series forecasting is showing real promise (witness Smyl and FFORMA).

Ma and Fildes (2018) note that ML methods have been shown to work on specific data sets, and that careful application of ML can produce substantially better forecasts than standard benchmarks. In his M4 discussion paper, Fildes (2020) decries the ML hype, reaffirming the call for rigorous validation (versus benchmarks) as a requirement of good science. He states, ". . . the notion that off-the-shelf ML methods will *automatically* produce improvements in accuracy, which has been propagated by some software suppliers, must be regarded as fanciful" (p. 187).

. . . But Opening New ML Opportunities

M4 examined the application of ML methods directly to time-series forecasting. But there is also a clear role for ML in peripheral forecasting processes, such as review and override of the computer-generated forecasts.

Food company Kellogg's (Pineda and Stevens 2018) and SAS research and development (Valsaraj, Gallagher, and Chase 2018) have independently utilized ML to guide manual overrides to statistical forecasts. Both report favorable results in reducing the number of overrides being made (thus saving management time) and improving the quality of the overrides. While much research remains, these examples illustrate ML's relevance and broad application beyond just time-series forecasting.

Criticism of the M4

There were many valid criticisms of the M4. Foremost, it did not reflect the hierarchical nature of most business forecasting problems. Also, there was a dearth of weekly time series – often used in retail and manufacturing – yet weekly were only 359 of the 100,000.

From Google, Fry and Brundage (2020) argued for more emphasis on daily, hourly, or even shorter (e.g., 5-minute) intervals, as business cycles speed up and automation enables faster and more agile planning. They also note that forecasters rarely work with time-series data in isolation: "We almost always have a much richer set of information about the time series" (p. 157), such as attributes, external events, or constraints.

The selection of error measures will always generate debate, as it is well recognized that competition results (the ranking of participants) depend on the error measure being used. Kolassa (2020) reviews this topic in detail. And Goodwin's (2020) discussion asks for the addition of a bias metric and assessment of the consistency of a method's performance across different series and forecast horizons.

Looking Ahead to the M5

When this article appears, the M5 competition will already be in progress, run using the Kaggle Platform. To improve the value of the competition as a research endeavor, it has been designed to address many of the suggestions noted by M4 commentators. The notable changes, from the M5 website (https://mofc.unic.ac.cy/m5-competition/):

- First, it uses hierarchical sales data, generously made available by Walmart, starting at the item level and aggregating to that of departments, product categories, stores, and three geographical areas: the U.S. states of California, Texas, and Wisconsin.

- Second, besides the time-series data, it also includes explanatory variables such as price, promotions, day of the week, and special events (e.g., Super Bowl, Valentine's Day, and Orthodox Easter) affecting sales and used to improve forecasting accuracy.

- Third, in addition to point forecasts, the distribution of uncertainty is being assessed by asking participants to provide information on four indicative prediction intervals and the median.

- Fourth, the majority of the more than 43,000 time-series display intermittency (sporadic sales including zeros).

No such competition has ever been perfect, nor will the M5 be. Yet we should eagerly await its results, and our next step in the advancement of forecasting knowledge.

References

Fildes, R. (2020). Learning from forecasting competitions. *International Journal of Forecasting* 36, 186–188.

Fildes, R., Hibon, M., Makridakis, S.G., and Meade, N. (1998). Generalizing about univariate forecasting methods: Further empirical evidence. *International Journal of Forecasting* 14, 339–358.

Fry, C., and Brundage, M. (2020). The M4 Competition – A practitioner's view. *International Journal of Forecasting* 36, 156–160.

Gilliland, M. (2020). The value added by machine learning approaches in forecasting. *International Journal of Forecasting* 36, 161–166.

Goodwin, P. (2014). Getting real about uncertainty. *Foresight* 33 (Spring): 4–7.

Goodwin, P. (2020). Performance measurement in the M4 competition: Possible future research. *International Journal of Forecasting* 36, 189–190.

Hyndman, R.J. (2020). A brief history of forecasting competitions. *International Journal of Forecasting* 36, 7–14.

Kolassa, S. (2020). Why the "best" point forecast depends on the error or accuracy measure. *International Journal of Forecasting* 36, 208–211.

Ma, S., and Fildes, R. (2018). *Customer flow forecasting with third-party mobile payment data*. Working Paper, Lancaster: Lancaster University.

Makridakis, S.G., and Hibon, M. (1979). Accuracy of forecasting: An empirical investigation (with discussion). *Journal of the Royal Statistical Society, Series A* 142, 97–145.

Makridakis, S.G., Spiliotis, E., and Assimakopoulos, V. (2018a). Statistical and machine learning forecasting methods: Concerns and ways forward. *PLoS One* 13 (3): 1–26.

Makridakis, S.G., Spiliotis, E., and Assimakopoulos, V. (2018b). The M4 Competition: Results, findings, conclusions, and ways forward. *International Journal of Forecasting* 34, 802–808.

Makridakis, S.G., Spiliotis, E., and Assimakopoulos, V. (2020). The M4 Competition: 100,000 time series and 61 forecasting methods. *International Journal of Forecasting* 36, 54–74.

Montero-Manso, P., Athanasopoulos, G., Hyndman, R.J., and Talagala, T.S. (2020). FFORMA: Feature-based forecast model averaging. *International Journal of Forecasting,*36, 86–92.

Morlidge, S. (2014). Forecast quality in the supply chain. *Foresight* 33 (Spring), 26–31.

Morlidge, S. (2016). Using error analysis to improve forecast performance. *Foresight* 41 (Spring), 37–44.

Petropoulos, F., and Makridakis, S.G. (2020). The M4 Competition: Bigger. stronger. better. *International Journal of Forecasting* 36, 3–6.

Pineda, B., and Stevens, R. (2018). How machine learning boosts statistical forecasting for better demand planning at Kellogg's. https://www.sas.com/en_us/events/analytics-conference/watch-live.html#formsuccess

Smyl, S. (2020). A hybrid method of exponential smoothing and recurrent neural networks for time series forecasting. *International Journal of Forecasting* 36: 75–85.

Valsaraj, V., Gallagher, B., and Chase, C. (2018). How demand planning will benefit from machine learning. https://www.sas.com/en_us/webinars/machine-learning-for-demand-planning.html

COMMENTARY: THE M4 COMPETITION AND A LOOK TO THE FUTURE

Fotios Petropoulos

Mike Gilliland has written a very insightful overview of the latest Makridakis Competition, the M4, the outcome of which is of great value to practitioners and academics alike. I widely agree with the points that he raises and would like both to reinforce some arguments and highlight several additional elements of the competition.

Prediction Intervals

Mike correctly notes the welcome evaluation of prediction intervals in the competition. Estimating the uncertainty around the forecasts is invaluable and can inform the preparation of contingency plans. However, I would personally like to see future competitions go one step further and directly link the uncertainty in the forecasts to the setting of safety stocks and proper inventory/utility evaluation of the forecasts. Such an exercise would allow us to gain an empirical understanding of the cost of the forecast error: how 1% in accuracy translates to monetary savings.

Trade-off of Accuracy and Cost

I also agree that we need to trade off improved accuracy with the added computational cost of achieving it. A translation of forecasting performance into monetary terms, as noted above, would allow for a direct comparison of the cost of forecast error with the computational cost of the procedures utilized. There are now a plethora of available-to-rent cloud computing services such as Amazon Web Services or Microsoft's Azure Cloud Computing.

Winning Formulas

It is worth noting that the top-ranked methods share several elements. As Mike correctly points out, there are benefits from forecast combinations. Additionally, five of the top six entries in the M4 competition (including my own submission) use at least one variant of the Theta method, which was the winning submission at the M3 competition. (For an introduction to the Theta method, see Petropoulos and Nikolopoulos 2017). So participants cautiously chose methods that have repeatedly performed well. One notable exception is the winning submission (https://eng.uber.com/m4-forecasting-competition), whose underlying basis is Holt-Winters, a method that did not perform well on its own in previous competitions (at least for longer forecasting horizons).

Another important element of the M4 competition is the use of global models. Instead of focusing on a series-by-series modeling approach, the two top-ranked submissions applied cross-learning, which allows a series to get information from other series, either in terms of selecting the parameters of the model or selecting combination weights. This technique has been widely used in machine learning solutions in several Kaggle competitions, and Bojer and Meldgaard (2020) predict that it will be an important approach to be tested in the forthcoming M5 competition.

Applicability to Forecasting Practice

I have heard many comments questioning the applicability of the M4 results to forecasting practice. While I agree that the absence of intermittent data and hierarchical structures is an important limitation – and one that will be addressed by the M5 competition – the data in the M4 are nevertheless quite representative of business forecasting efforts, especially in comparison to data sets from industry-specific Kaggle competitions (see Bojer and Meldgaard 2020, for more details). Moreover, if practitioners are interested in a single-data frequency (such as monthly or daily), it is possible to decompose the results of the M4 for that particular frequency and take forward insights from the top performing methods in that cluster.

Performance Measures

One element with which I'm not entirely in agreement in Mike Gilliland's article is that different error measures result in different rankings. The Spearman's rank correlation coefficient for the overall values of sMAPE and MASE (the two measures used to evaluate forecast accuracy in the M4 competition) is very strong, at 88.5%. Methods that performed well based on the sMAPE are also very likely to perform well with regards to MASE. I understand the limitations when translating these results into practice, with different companies focusing on different KPIs, but I believe that appropriately specifying the cost function to fit the purpose will do the trick. This, for instance, was done by the second-best performing method in the M4 competition, which adopted the M4 competition's main cost function (Ordered Weighted Average/OWA) to estimate the methods' combination weights.

The Value of Participation

I would like to emphasize the importance of participating in forecasting competitions. When a task is challenging, as was the case with the M4 competition where participants had to submit forecasts for 100K series, I view participation as a marathon rather than a sprint. While the rankings are obviously important, participation itself is an achievement that should be celebrated, and I hope that more forecasting researchers and practitioners embrace entering future competitions. At the end of the day, we cannot call ourselves forecasters if we are afraid to forecast. We must, as they say, have skin in the game.

Conclusion

Despite some limitations and criticisms, my personal view of the M4 is that we gained valuable insights that advance the theory and practice of forecasting. I am confident that many forecasting researchers and practitioners will benefit from the availability of open-access code for most of the submissions in the M4 and use this information to improve upon their own approaches.

Last but not least, I believe the M4 competition managed to bring together two communities: traditional statistical/econometrics experts with experts from the machine learning world. As demonstrated by the winning entry, exciting things can happen when these two worlds work together.

REFERENCES

Bojer, C.S., and Meldgaard, J.P. (2020). Learnings from Kaggle's forecasting competitions. *ResearchGate*, 10.13140/RG.2.2.21579.75046.

Petropoulos, F., and Nikolopoulos, K. (2017). The Theta method. *Foresight* 6 (Summer): 11–17.

CHAPTER 2

Big Data in Forecasting

A major objective of this book is to provide sober, measured guidance on the practice of business forecasting and the current trends being hyped in the media and vendor marketing. One such trend, starting well before 2015, is the notion of *big data*, and how (like AI/ML after it), big data will alter forecasting in meaningful and positive ways. But just as we asked about AI/ML in Chapter 1, will big data have this positive effect?

Prior to M4 results in 2018, there was a large body of evidence supporting a simple and parsimonious approach to forecast modeling. Going as far back as the original M-competition in 1979, it was found that even simple and time-worn methods like exponential smoothing could perform on par with the latest, complex innovations – with fewer data and computational requirements. In a comparison of simple versus complex methods in 2015 (*Journal of Business Research* 68: 1678–1685), Green and Armstrong went so far as to assert that complexity harms accuracy.

It was not until the M4, with the two top performers being hybrids/combinations of ML and traditional statistical methods, that a more positive view of model complexity has emerged. But as we saw in the M4 analysis, this modest improvement in forecast accuracy came at prohibitive cost. These new methods, at least for the moment, have limited practical consequence.

In the two articles (and accompanying commentaries) in this chapter, we find contrasting views of the potential for big data in forecasting. Snapp takes a mostly dismissive view, focusing on the excessive and unwarranted marketing hype. But there is harm in this hype as well. He argues that the big data message distracts organizations from focusing on real solutions that are already available to them.

Boone et al., however, provide a more positive view of the potential for big data to impact supply-chain planning. They argue that big data can improve forecasting through better understanding of customer behavior, better forecasting models, and more efficient supply-chain execution. But they also recognize the challenges of managing the scale of the data, becoming skilled in the new methods and techniques, the effect on demand planner behavior, and unintentional biases.

Perhaps commentator Peter Catt summarizes the situation best, imploring "In the spirit of bridging evidence-based research with practice, we should keep an open mind on these technological developments."

2.1 IS BIG DATA THE SILVER BULLET FOR SUPPLY-CHAIN FORECASTING?*

Shaun Snapp

Will big data alter the nature of supply chain forecasting for the better? That is the claim by some loud voices in the field, but here, Shaun Snapp lays out the reasons for his dissent.

Proponents argue that big data will improve forecasting by letting us forecast at more granular levels, and will enable more causal forecasting. But, according to Snapp, this thinking is incorrect. It is based on assumptions that more granular (e.g., item-customer) forecasts are needed for supply-chain planning (they aren't), and that causal forecasting is more accurate (it need not be). What's worse, companies already have a difficult enough time implementing proven good forecasting practices. Adding the distraction of big data will almost certainly misdirect attention, funding, and focus away from actually improving their forecasting applications.

Snapp's points are supported and extended in the five Commentaries that follow this article. While the bottom line seems to be "Don't fall for the big hype," the discussion illuminates critical issues in forecasting for the supply chain, including the roles of product versus customer forecasting, the nature of causal forecasting models, and whether these models can supersede traditional time-series forecasts.

The "Big Data" Bubble

Big data has become one of the hottest concepts in IT. It is now seen as a magic elixir for a wide variety of problems, and technology and consulting companies with big-data products and services to sell have put enormous marketing muscle behind them. All one has to do during a pause in a presentation is utter something nonspecific like "It's big data," or "It's really all about the big data," and the audience nods approvingly.

Conferences are awash with energetic optimism regarding the potential benefits of big data. The phrase has become a huge buzz among CEOs, who may not even know what big data is. This hype allows conference or corporate presenters, pundits, and bloggers to say things that don't actually make any sense, but seem visionary. Since there is so much hype around big data, almost any comment can seem reasonable.

*This article (and the following Commentaries) originally appeared in *Foresight: The International Journal of Applied Forecasting* (Spring, 2017) and appears here courtesy of the International Institute of Forecasters.

This article will focus on recent statements made by software vendor Blue Ridge, statements that are quite typical in content for other market buzz on big data. Once we become more specific about how big-data proponents think the phenomenon will improve forecasting, it comes down to the following forecasting types:

- *Customer Forecasting:* The first prediction is that big data will be used to switch forecasting focus away from the product and more towards the customer.
- *Causal Forecasting:* The second is that big data will lead to far more causal forecasting.

So let's begin with the first topic by reviewing a direct quotation from a Blue Ridge publication (Blue Ridge 2016). In fact, the company distributed a Gartner document with Blue Ridge's addition of several pages. However, these added pages have Gartner's name in the lower left-hand corner, making it confusing as to whether Gartner is endorsing these views. The endnotes state that the "editorial content supplied by Blue Ridge is independent of Gartner analysis." However, many if not most readers will overlook this disclaimer and assume that Blue Ridge's content is actually Gartner's content. As Blue Ridge writes:

> Nearly everyone talks about the item's demand, and building a forecast based on what the item is doing. But what if you've been forecasting the wrong thing? The fact is, items don't really "do" anything. They don't sell themselves. They don't make decisions. They don't really even have a history. It's the customer who has history, who buys, who makes decisions, who influences your stock levels. Any statistics you have on the item do not derive from the item, but from the customer. The customer's behavior is what you should be tracking. But until the era of big data and sophisticated analytics, tracking and predicting behavior was not possible. Big data and the ability to analyze customer transactions have revolutionized the understanding of customer demand, providing visibility and precision on a whole new level.

While this line of thinking may come across as high concept, the most charitable way to describe it is as inaccurate, in a word. So let's get into the detail of why this statement regarding transitioning from forecasting products to gaining deeper insights into customers is incorrect.

Forecasting by Item or Consumer

Blue Ridge is suggesting that instead of forecasting by item, it is more sensible and ultimately more accurate to forecast total volume by customer – that is, forecast a different "attribute" (customer grouping) – and that big data is what makes this possible. But in doing so, we have lost sight of the fundamental requirement for supply-chain forecasting: that the company is actually stocking *products*, and it therefore must (at some point) generate a product forecast in order for inventory management to work properly. As with supply-chain forecasting systems, supply-planning systems produce a supply plan in the form of products and quantities to be ordered, and this means a product forecast at a location. Let us assume for the moment that a forecast of total customer demand is "more accurate." Where is Blue Ridge's evidence that the *product* forecast (item and location) derived from it for inventory management is more accurate than a product forecast calculated directly without a detour over customer forecasts?

Big data does nothing to change this foundational rule of supply-chain planning.

The Complication of Customer Forecasts

Today, in many companies, forecasting by customer is performed by the Sales and Marketing department. In practice, these forecasts do little or nothing for supply-chain planning. No matter what hierarchy Sales and Marketing chooses to use to produce its forecast (by product group, by sales group, by region, etc.), the supply-chain forecast must be focused on the product, and more specifically at the product × location combination. Eventually, the Sales/Marketing forecast must be disaggregated to a product location and aggregated over customers. It should be acknowledged, or at least understood, that the primary reason Sales creates forecasts by customer is that they use their knowledge of customers to make manual adjustments to the forecast. It is not in many situations that the customer is being used to generate a better "automated" forecast.

The Normalcy of Using Customer Data

Customer data and their association to products have been used in forecasting applications for quite some time. Any forecasting application that has the ability to apply attributes or a hierarchy can use the customer as an attribute to perform a top-down forecast, which can then be analyzed and used to drive the influence of the customer down to the lowest level of the forecast hierarchy. The effect can be tested against other attributes (color of the product, product group, etc.), and then the impact of each attribute can be measured. None of this has anything at all to do with big data, as I do this work comparing customer attributes versus other attributes in a forecasting application without any involvement from big data.

Forecasting "at the customer" is the general term, but in many cases a company has multiple ship-to locations for a single customer. Therefore, forecasting at the customer ship-to location is another option. Sometimes people will recommend switching the forecast from the product to the customer or customer ship-to location. The company then begins thinking in terms of forecasts at those levels, assuming that the change is improving forecast accuracy. This does not work, for several reasons:

■ Multiple customers may be stocked from a single location. By moving to a customer forecast we reduce the volume that is forecasted. A forecast generated at one location will almost always be more accurate than one based upon multiple forecasted customers that are recombined at the location, because the sales history at the location includes customers that vary strongly per week or month, but are offset by other customers.

- Forecasting for a large customer is easier, but what about all the smaller customers? The problem of developing independent forecasts for every single customer is there's a great deal of work involved, and customer demand will show far higher variability than the forecast for the stocking location. Blue Ridge never really gets to this level of detail, but it's a problem for everything else the company has to say on this issue.

- It requires a great deal of adjustment to get the forecast eventually back to a product-location level, which is used by supply planning. This is not to say that "customer" may not be used as an attribute in a top-down forecast, but this is not the same as forecasting "by customer." However, proponents of big data for forecasting have been emphasizing the opposite, that companies should be forecasting the customer rather than the stocking location.

Here are more comments from Blue Ridge (2016):

Stores, distribution centers, and suppliers each need to have their own distinct demand forecast. The forecast must represent how demand will occur in these locations. For that reason, DC and supplier forecasts will never be accurate if they are a statistical average based upon sales in the store or shipments from the DC.

It is difficult to see what is meant here by "statistical average." Therefore, it is difficult to contradict the claim of the use of averages. Is this the statistical average of all the customers whose demand flows through the DC? Sales history is presented as it is incurred to a planning bucket, and this is used to drive the statistical forecast. It is not an "average." But clearly Blue Ridge is saying that one should not be performing statistical forecasting based upon sales history.

A Conspicuous Lack of Academic Work

Blue Ridge is making a very bold claim that big data is going to transform forecasting to be far more customer based. They are also saying that time-series statistical forecasting is no longer the right way to proceed. Yet no references or other evidence are provided that big data is currently being used to improve customer forecasts.

I performed a search into a comprehensive academic-paper database, and I found 28 total results from the search "Big Data Customer Forecasting." Upon review, however, most of these papers were not real hits on the topic, but false positives. I have been researching topics for quite some time, and I can say it would be strange for there to be no (or close to no) articles on a topic in academics that Blue Ridge is claiming either is actually happening or very close to happening.

Big Data and Causal Forecasting

While, in my view, Blue Ridge's prediction on customer forecasting with big data is not accurate, they were not yet finished proposing how big data would improve forecasting.

Next they moved on to making a prediction regarding something called *causal forecasting*. This is very similar to the prediction we just covered in that it sounds very enticing, particularly to people who are less familiar with forecasting. Let's take a look at that, because it shows a pattern of Blue Ridge referencing big data for forecasting improvement.

> When it comes to improving demand forecast accuracy, it hinges heavily on your ability to understand the customer better and to translating that deeper understanding of the customer into precise supply chain planning that improves both sales and margin. . . . Every single customer transaction is influenced by causal factors. The truth is that causal simply identifies what causes or influences a shopper to buy something. When you know "why," you have a much better chance at accurately forecasting "what," "when," and "how much."

Blue Ridge is expressing a preference for using causal forecasting over time-series statistical forecasting. They do so again in the following quotation:

> Rolled up point-of-sale data, or historic sales orders – even with an understanding of stores inventory excess or shortage – is fundamentally the wrong data for producing a demand signal to generate a forecast at any DC.

This is an enormous claim. It states that the time-series forecasting approach – the one used to produce forecasts by very nearly every supply-chain company – is wrong.

Blue Ridge versus the History of Causal Forecasting

These statements are problematic in a number of ways. The first one is that predicting the customer is not the holy grail of forecasting, as we have seen above. But to get to the meat of it, here Blue Ridge is proposing that big data will allow forecasts to be created that are causal, which they make sound like something new. Causal forecasting is not at all new to supply-chain forecasting. Quite the contrary: the ability to create causal models has existed for many years in many supply-chain forecasting applications. There are a virtually unlimited number of academic papers written on the topic. The areas where causal forecasting is applied are much greater than those using simply supply-chain forecasting.

In fact, in supply-chain forecasting, causal models are very rarely used regardless of the availability of causal forecasting functionality. And the implied assumption by Blue Ridge that the limiting factor in using causal forecasting has been *not having access to big data* is not true. Here's why:

- **Unrelated Limitations to Causal Forecasting:** The definition of *big data* applies when data sets that are processed are so large or complex that traditional data processing techniques are inadequate. This means using applications like Hadoop, NoSQL, and so on to manage enormous amounts of unstructured data. However, being unable to process enormous amounts of data using traditional processing techniques has never been the limiting factor in creating causal models.

- ▪ ***Actual Limitations in Causal Forecasting:*** The limiting factors have ranged from not having access to causal factors (because the data is not maintained or is not of sufficient quality to use) to not having the time or expertise to build causal models.

- ▪ ***When Causal Forecasting Tends to Be Used:*** Causal models are often used where the number of forecasted items is small, and the financial benefit (or assumed financial benefit) to forecasting is very large. A good example of this is forecasting in the financial-services industry, where investment banks have few forecasted items and very big budgets. Big data does nothing to address the limitations that have caused causal forecasting to be so infrequently used in supply-chain forecasting.

Blue Ridge may say that big data now allows for these causal factors to be more readily found. That would certainly be true. However, it does not address how powerful these causal factors are (or will be) and how effectively they can be put to use to improve the forecast. There is also the small matter of finding evidence for this effect of big data. But they are not making this point. Their clear emphasis is that big data is now revolutionizing supply-chain forecasting, that big data is right now being used to very significantly improve the supply-chain forecast, and that this effect is so powerful that it has antiquated the use of statistical time-series forecasting.

Distractions Galore

The really unfortunate thing in this case is that companies greatly underuse the functionality that is available to them in the forecasting applications they have already purchased. Furthermore, businesses often end up with inappropriate forecasting software because it's unclear to them how to perform proper software selection.

Companies already have major issues in implementing and maintaining their current forecasting applications. The investment made by companies to improve forecasting accuracy is low, particularly in proportion to what unnecessary forecast error costs companies in operational inefficiencies, waste, etc. Companies in most cases are not applying well-established and tested approaches for improving forecasting accuracy. There are exceptions, but often knowledge of the fundamentals of forecasting in businesses is weak, making many of them particularly susceptible to the erroneous information of the type we have been reviewing here. Focusing on big data will almost certainly misdirect the limited attention, funding, and focus they do have away from actually improving their forecasting applications or choosing better ones.

Conclusion

When businesses follow commonly heard advice on investigating big data for purposes of improving forecasting accuracy, they move away from focusing on the real solutions that are already available to them. It is a distraction that in all likelihood will have an amazingly low probability of improving actual forecast accuracy.

REFERENCES

Blue Ridge (2016). How to supercharge product availability without inflating inventory. http://www.slideshare.net/BlueRidgeInventory/blueridgegartnersupplychainplanningmagic-quadrant2016report

Snapp, S. (2014). *Sales and statistical forecasting combined: Mixing approaches for improved forecast accuracy.* SCM Focus Press.

COMMENTARY: BECOMING RESPONSIBLE CONSUMERS . . . OF BIG DATA

Chris Gray

Shaun Snapp brings a refreshingly skeptical voice to the overhyped subject of big data, and particularly to the application of big data to forecasting and demand planning. Anyone responsible for enterprise profit and loss, or for technology investments, or for marketing, sales, forecasting, and sales planning would be well advised to understand both the claims and the realities of big data for their organizations. And an excellent place to start would be with Shaun's article "Is Big Data the Silver Bullet for Supply-Chain Forecasting?"

While big data is one of the current crazes in technology, it isn't the first, and it's unlikely to be the last. It will be advantageous to some and perhaps many companies, and it may well have important positive effects on forecasting and forecasting processes. But it may also cause some wild goose chases, as companies pursue ideas that "read well but work lousy." Everyone needs to be realistic about where big data may help management improve performance and where it probably won't. And to the degree possible this needs to be based not on how it *might* work but instead on proven benefits and concepts.

Shaun mainly focuses on two ways in which big data is said by Blue Ridge and others to revolutionize supply-chain forecasting:

1. Big data will make possible a shift to forecasting customers rather than forecasting products.
2. Big data will allow companies to identify the causal factors that underlie their sales data, and make it possible to eliminate traditional time-series forecasting, moving instead to some form of causal forecasting (apparently using something like regression analysis).

BIG DATA ENABLES CUSTOMER FORECASTING?

The first claim, "Big Data Enables Customer Forecasting," is particularly odd regardless of whether you interpret it as "forecasting total demand for all products ordered by a customer" or as "forecasting future demand by product/customer combination."

Shaun interpreted the first claim to mean "forecasting total demand for all products ordered by a customer." He then correctly points out that the forecasting process will be ignoring some (most) of the primary objectives of forecasting in an integrated supply chain or for a manufacturing enterprise, and that forecasting total demand by customer creates additional complications in many related supply-chain processes.

What he doesn't point out is that, in this situation (forecasting total demand by customer), the only sensible unit of measure is a financial unit (dollars, euros, pounds sterling, etc.). Not all products have the same primary unit of measure, and for most companies the only common unit for all products sold to any particular customer is dollars, so the forecast must be done in dollars.

Forecasts are supposed to help predict future financial results (tick the box on this one), but also to help determine the product-stocking levels and safety stocks required to properly satisfy customer needs. Forecasts are needed as well to predict the capacity requirements for labor and machinery needed to produce the mix and volume of specific products that the customer wants or needs. While a customer forecast might produce a reasonable result in terms of future financial performance, it fails to help with the other objectives and will require further translation (to the product or product/location) to be useful for inventory and capacity management.

If this "total demand for all products ordered by a customer" is what is meant by "customer forecasting," then an additional step – translating the individual customer forecasts to product forecasts using some kind of proration logic – will be necessary to get to product demand. So apparently, we are to believe that the benefits of forecasting total dollars and then forecasting the proration percentages to get to product demands gives us a better, more accurate picture of future needs and/or results.

Forecasting Product/Customer Combinations

Conversely, if the claim were interpreted as meaning that the forecasts need to be done by product/customer combination, it's hard to see how this is different from the capabilities already available for most companies today. Nearly every modern forecasting software system allows product/customer combination forecasting. And even when this capability exists in forecasting systems, there are serious questions about the degree to which it should be used, based on past performance, market and product characteristics, degree of integration of the supply chain, and more.

Claiming that forecasting is properly done only by product/customer combination is overly broad and ignores:

- The types of industry and/or market and/or supply chain in which the forecasting is happening (for example, forecasting consumer products versus forecasting industrial equipment versus forecasting industrial components).
- The number of customers and how much volume each one represents as a percentage of total product demand.
- The degree of connectedness of the supply chain, etc.

Differentiating Forecasting Environments

Not differentiating the environments in which forecasting must be done and then making a blanket statement like this one is simply a bridge too far.

For example, in a manufacturer of polyester films used in industrial processes, any given product may have two or three dominant customers, with hundreds or even thousands of small-volume customers. If the two or three dominant customers represent 80 or 90 percent of total demand for the item, there may be situations where it makes sense to forecast these product/customer combinations individually. But the remaining customers should unarguably not be forecasted individually and instead should be grouped together for forecasting purposes. There is a reason why supply-chain professionals believe that forecasts are more accurate for larger, rather than smaller, groups of products or groups of customers.

For products produced and sold, perhaps via mail order or over the Internet to the ultimate consumer, it's hard to see how customer forecasting makes any sense at all. Should Amazon forecast which book it will sell to every single customer next month, in order to aggregate all book × customer forecasts per book, to decide on target stock levels? In this situation, it may make sense to forecast by product and market, or product and market within stocking location, but even this may be arguable based on specific circumstances.

For a highly "vertically integrated" company producing construction equipment that also produces, at a different location, the diesel engines for that equipment, and that produces, at yet another location, the fuel injectors used in the diesel engines, there should be a forecast for the different pieces of construction equipment – and depending upon how and to whom they are sold, it may or may not make sense to forecast by customer. But all the lower levels of demand – including engines and fuel injectors – are best derived, not forecasted at all.

Item Histories

Finally, this claim that forecasting should be done by customer and not by item is "justified" by questionable statements like "items have no history, but customers do." Attention grabbing? Yes. Thought provoking? Again, yes. An effective marketing gimmick? Maybe. But *true*? No.

Many items do have a history, and a long and detailed one. Not to mention the fact that outrageous claims don't help with the real issues that face product managers and product forecasters trying to anticipate demand, or supply-chain or material planners trying to anticipate supplies of material and capacity to produce the exact products that are likely to be ordered.

BIG DATA ENABLES CAUSAL FORECASTING?

What we know today about comprehensive forecasting methods and where they can and can't be applied was developed over many years of experience in working with forecasting systems. For a long time, there were two major misconceptions about forecasting. One was that it was possible to develop a "single right number," and that by developing more and more sophisticated and complicated forecasting algorithms it would be possible to compute this right number.

The other misconception was that it was possible to develop a single technique that would work to forecast all items. Now, apparently, there is a new, third misconception: that "causal forecasting," i.e., some kind of regression analysis, can completely replace traditional time-series forecasting and that the use of big data can identify all the causal factors that underlie customer demand.

Today, even without big data, companies have the ability to develop and apply causal indices and develop causal forecasts. Historically, companies have produced causal indices using classical statistical inference through the scientific method. Causal factors, each independent of the other, are proposed, and a model is fit and analyzed statistically to build specific cause-and-effect models. This is a straightforward process and can be done with or without big data.

Problems with Causal Models

Big data adds an additional capability – data mining – to identify causal factors. In data mining as it is typically applied, statistical or machine learning algorithms look for explanatory factors that can predict demand with some degree of accuracy. However, this sometimes results in multiple redundant explanatory variables, often numbering in the thousands, potentially complicating the forecasting process for the humans who manage it.

The fact that we can identify n different sets of variables, each with multiple, say m, redundant factors, that can explain some dependent aspect of the forecast may not actually help us understand true cause and effect. In other words, one might ask "at what point are we sacrificing clarity or usability for the sake of 'completeness?'" As Wells and Rey (2016) point out, "Building adequate *prediction* models does not necessarily mean an adequate *cause-and-effect* model." Taken together, these two consequences of data mining may actually reduce the applicability or usefulness of causal forecasting.

Causal forecasting is not the dominant form that is the basis for manufacturing and supply-chain demand planning today. While big data and data mining, when applied sensibly, may allow more detailed analysis and better application of causal factors to baseline forecasted demand, it seems far-fetched to believe that time-series forecasting will be replaced entirely by causal forecasting. Even in situations where known external factors drive product demand, an important question will be, "Are the external factors used to predict the forecast themselves predictable?" For example, replacing time-series forecasting completely with causal forecasting based on future weather or economic conditions may take a simple forecasting problem and replace it with something much more complicated, and perhaps create an impossible forecasting situation.

Where Big Data Can Help

Having said that, it does seem clear that the tools of big data, perhaps coupled with the proven scientific method for analyzing causal factors, have potential for more effective analysis of historical events. There will be situations where it provides better visibility to the effects of:

- **Management decisions.** What is the effect of a price increase or decrease? What disruptive effects, if any, will be caused by introduction of a new technology? What is the historic effect of an end-of-season promotion? What is the product life cycle for this product, and where is the product in its life cycle?
- **External but known future events.** When is Easter and how does it affect demand timing? When does a specific law go into effect?
- **Forecasted external events.** What are weather effects on product demand, if any? How do increased housing starts affect our products? What population growth/birth rate can we expect and how will this affect demand?

In my view, some modified form of data mining using the *scientific method for analyzing hypothesizing causal factors* promises a better path forward than a massive assault on the data to find thousands of potential explanatory factors. If sensible and practical methods can be applied to identify real causal factors, then it's reasonable to expect that companies *will* be able to better anticipate the effects of management decisions, known future events, and reasonably forecastable external events to the baseline time-series forecast.

But without some practical method for reducing the number of *potential* explanatory factors to a smaller subset of *real* explanatory factors – that is, reducing the factors that correlate to changes in demand to the factors that cause the demand to change – big data may be long on promise and short on results. It's certainly not the kind of forecasting panacea being presented in the bold claim that "big data enables causal forecasting."

ANOTHER QUESTIONABLE CLAIM ABOUT BIG DATA AND FORECASTING

I found one additional claim to be odd, based on the experience of implementing and operating effective distribution planning systems. Blue Ridge states that "Stores, distribution centers (DCs) and suppliers each need to have their own distinct demand forecast. . ." – and then goes on to suggest that the root problem is forecasting itself and that companies are simply computing forecasts incorrectly.

In fairness, this is correct in the sense that forecasting each product/location produces the wrong results – but the reason isn't what they apparently believe. Instead, it's because forecasting the DCs and the suppliers *independently* is flat-out wrong in most situations. While each stocking location across the supply chain needs to have its own demand plan, the one for distribution centers is dependent on the replenishment plan for stores (which is dependent on the forecast and the inventory position there), and the demand plan for suppliers is dependent on the replenishment plan for the DCs.

We learned about the interconnectedness of the supply chain in Forrester's (1961) explanation of the *bullwhip effect*, and the pioneering work done by Landvater and Martin (1983) on *distribution resource planning* (application of dependent demand planning through distribution networks) in the 1980s and *flowcasting* – the application of dependent demand planning through a wholesale/retail/store-level supply chain (Martin, Doherty, and Harrop 2006) in the 21st century.

Instead of thinking that big data will be a cure-all for forecasting problems, and then enabling less effective forecasting throughout the supply chain, in a wholesale/retail/store-level environment we should be using the power of modern computers to process massive amounts of data:

- Forecasts by SKU at each store netted against inventory levels;
- Projected replenishments a year or more into the future and then cascading this replenishment plan to the DCs;
- Repetition of the process with the generated demand from store replenishments to project replenishments at the DC and so forth through the supply chain down to the suppliers.

Almost no big data connection is required to improve the quality of demand plans in this situation! And even in an industrial supply chain, where one company or location produces components for another, it is often preferable to link suppliers to customers via their planning systems rather than forecasting each independently of the other.

CONCLUSIONS

While I believe that big data is an important concept and useful for improving many processes – including forecasting – I also am skeptical that the advertised effects will be as often presented. However, the message to those who may want to apply "big data" concepts to forecasting process is that you should be responsible consumers: understand the concepts of big data, understand the claims being made as well as the possible applications of big data to your specific situation, investigate its proven benefits to the areas where you would like to apply it, and proceed cautiously, with eyes wide open.

REFERENCES

Forrester, J.W. (1961). *Industrial dynamics*. Waltham, MA: Pegasus Communications.

Landvater, D., and Martin, A. (1983). DRP distribution resource planning: Distribution management's most powerful tool. Oliver Wight Limited Publications.

Martin, A., Doherty, M., and Harrop, J. (2006). Flowcasting the retail supply chain. Essex Junction, VT: Factory 2 Shelf.

Wells, C., and Rey, T. (2016). Data mining for forecasting: An introduction. In Gilliland, Tashman, and Sglavo (Eds.), *Business forecasting: Practical problems and solutions,* 112–119.

COMMENTARY: CUSTOMER VERSUS ITEM FORECASTING

Michael Gilliland

Through his many books and blog postings, Shaun Snapp has earned a reputation for independent and critical reviews of software, supply-chain practices, and the industry analysts who cover this territory. In this piece, Shaun takes on the notion that big data will radically change the way we do forecasting. I tend to agree with his skeptical assessment.

Citing a publication by software vendor Blue Ridge (which itself cites Gartner's 2015 Magic Quadrant on Supply Chain Planning System-of-Record solutions), Shaun focuses on two assertions:

- With big data, we should be forecasting customer behavior rather than items;
- Big data facilitates causal forecasting, so we will understand the reason for demand.

I will examine just the first point.

FORECAST CUSTOMER BEHAVIOR – NOT ITEMS

While it is certainly true that items don't sell themselves or make decisions (two claims made in the Blue Ridge publication), I struggle with their statement that items "don't really even have a history." I have utilized item sales history my entire career, and suspect other business-forecasting practitioners have as well. Shaun points out that supply chains work by making, stocking, and selling *items*. Thus a forecast by item (and location) does seem to be needed at some point in the planning process.

So let's excuse the claim that items don't have a history as a bit of marketing histrionics.

The substantive argument is that by forecasting items we are forecasting the wrong thing. Instead, we should be analyzing customer behavior (not item sales), and that "until the era of big data and sophisticated analytics, tracking and predicting [customer] behavior was not possible."

The availability of big data (more variables, and at a more granular level) certainly opens up a broader range of models that can be used to predict customer behavior. But as is well understood in the forecasting community, more "sophisticated" models don't necessarily entail more accurate forecasts. A recent study by Green and Armstrong (2015) even suggests that "complex" models harm accuracy.

Furthermore, you could always create a forecast of customer behavior by management judgment alone, or with simple time-series models – even before big data. So customer-level forecasting is possible whether you have big data or not. It remains a question for research as to whether big-data models will improve accuracy. This is not something that is "true" just because it has been asserted.

WHAT IF BIG DATA DOES IMPROVE CUSTOMER FORECASTS?

If research proves that big data does *not* improve the accuracy of customer forecasts, then for cost and simplicity's sake we should not bother using it. But what if it's shown that big data *does* improve customer-forecast accuracy? Will this help us with supply-chain planning and overall company performance?

The answer isn't clear.

As Shaun points out, we still need to convert customer forecasts to item/location forecasts for supply-chain planning. Blue Ridge says this is done by translating customer demand "into a forecast of fully calculated inventory replenishment orders from the stores, DCs, or other serviced tier" (p. 3), but the mechanism for this translation is not precisely defined. Shaun brings up several reasons why this process can be problematic, raising doubts as to the practical benefit of improved customer forecasting.

IS BIG DATA JUST A DISTRACTION?

In 2013, big data was near the "peak of inflated expectations" in Gartner's *Hype Cycle for Emerging Technologies*. By 2014, it was falling into the "trough of disillusionment," before disappearing in 2015, when it was considered no longer an emerging technology (Woodie 2015).

Shaun Snapp has expressed his own disillusionment with big data's potential for improving forecasting, and considers it a distraction. The unfortunate result is that focus on dubious big-data approaches may limit the funding and effort put toward alternative approaches that have a better chance of improving performance.

Blue Ridge is not the first to advocate for customer-level forecasting, but is perhaps the first to base their argument on using big data to create more accurate forecasts. Previous advocates did so because salespeople – who (presumably) had the best insight into customer buying behavior – could directly update a customer forecast and make it (again presumably) more accurate. The problem is that presumption is not proof, and advocacy in itself is not evidence. It remains to be determined whether big data is the silver bullet for supply-chain forecasting, and Snapp is right to raise the question.

REFERENCES

Blue Ridge (2016). How to supercharge product availability without inflating inventory.

Green, K., and Armstrong, J.S. (2015). Simple versus complex forecasting: The evidence. *Journal of Business Research* 68, 1678–1685.

Woodie, A. (2015). Why Gartner dropped big data off the hype cycle. Datanami (August 26). https://www.datanami.com/2015/08/26/why-gartner-dropped-big-data-off-the-hype-curve/

COMMENTARY: BIG DATA OR BIG HYPE?

Stephan Kolassa

Shaun Snapp has written a rather biting commentary on Blue Ridge's prediction that big data will revolution-ize forecasting. Overall, I agree with his critique, but I'd like to add a few comments, concentrating first on how big data changes or does not change statistical realities, and second, on the current state of causal forecasting.

BIG DATA AND STATISTICS

On the first point, it has been claimed that big data makes theory, statistics, and the entire scientific method obsolete. For instance, Anderson (2008) writes:

"With enough data, the numbers speak for themselves."

Unfortunately, as David Hand (2016) said in a presentation I recently attended, the data may speak for themselves, but what they are telling us may not be the truth. Hand concentrated on the effects of *selection bias*, which is a very real problem. For instance, I have seen quite a number of proposals to leverage Facebook and/or Twitter data to improve forecasting, but few of those proposals address the fact that Facebook and Twitter are still only used by a subset of your target market, and – more to the point – the people posting and tweeting about your particular product will form a heavily self-selected sample from the Facebook/Twitter user base, one that is likely not very representative. Thus, classical statistical issues are still alive and well in the era of big data, and turning a hose of a limitless stream of data at them will not wash them away.

However, big data, and more particularly social media, offer a few challenges that are absent from "tradi-tional" data. For instance, there are actual feedback loops. *Crime maps* have been proposed as ways you can easily determine the amount of crime in certain areas, which will certainly be interesting if you plan on buying a house in a specific locale. However, homeowners are not stupid, and they respond to incentives. Indeed, they may be less likely to report crime for fear of harming their property values (Direct Line 2011). And this in turn will have an impact on crime forecasting, as well as on forecasting property values.

CAUSAL FORECASTING NOW

As Shaun writes, Blue Ridge makes it seem like the factor preventing businesses from including causal effects in their forecasts was the unavailability of big data (or of the infrastructure and computational resources to deal with it). This has not been my impression. Over the years, I have seen customers – mostly retailers, who have a vested interest in good causal forecasts that include the effects of price changes and promotions – who forecasted base-line sales with extremely simple methods and included the effects of promotions via very ad hoc judgmental or blanket adjustments ("this promotion always gives a 20% uplift" – regardless of the specific product or location).

As Shaun writes, this is not because methods were lacking that included such clear and obvious causal factors. Instead, the limiting factors, in my opinion, are twofold. On the one hand, there is a general unwilling-ness of businesses to engage with modern forecasting methods, as has recently been pointed out by Fildes (2017), which in turn may be connected with the fact that most forecasters come from business or IT, not from statistics (Kolassa 2016b).

On the other hand, businesses still surprise me with the quality of their very own data – and *not* in a good way. They may not have historical promotion information, since nobody ever thought of keeping this data. Or their systems may contain all promotions that were ever *considered*, but no information on which promotions actually *went live* at the point of sale. Retailers' stock information is notoriously unreliable (DeHoratius and Raman 2008), so historical demands may be heavily censored through out-of-stocks.

Bottom line: if businesses don't even capture clear and obvious causal effects through established and known methods because of a lack of familiarity with the relevant tools or of good data in-house, how can big data, which is only tenuously connected to a particular company's business, suddenly dramatically improve forecasts?

In addition, the impact of promotion, price, and inventory data on forecasting and planning is typically strong and obvious. In the era of big data, people increasingly turn to data whose connection to your sales is far more tenuous – like whether a particular product is trending on social media, as derived from a few tweets, likes, or blogs by a handful of users (after extensive automated text mining and data cleansing, which is never perfect and will introduce noise of its own). I recently illustrated (Kolassa 2016a) how modeling a weak-but-present signal can actually *harm* your forecasts, through the statistical but very real effect of the bias-variance tradeoff. Of course, the same situation holds for other weak effects – like the connection between social-media trends and your sales. Pouring more data into your forecasting software will not automatically improve forecasts, and we have known about the perils of overfitting for a long time now. Overfitting will not go away with big data.

In conclusion, I agree that more data – big data – can be an opportunity for better forecasting (for instance, because it drives better recognition of the role statistics and machine learning can play in a data-driven enter-prise). However, big data is not a silver bullet, and it will not magically make known issues disappear.

REFERENCES

Anderson, C. (2008). The end of theory: The data deluge makes the scientific method obsolete. *Wired.* https://www.wired.com/2008/06/pb-theory/

DeHoratius, N., and Raman, A. (2008). Inventory record inaccuracy: An empirical analysis. *Management Science* 54, 627–641.

Direct Line (2011). Fear of crime maps hits reporting of crime. https://www.directline.com/media/archive-2011/news-11072011

Fildes, R. (2017). Research into forecasting practice. *Foresight* 44 (Winter): 39–46.

Hand, D. (2016). So you think you have all the data? Causes and consequences of selection bias. Presentation at the Swiss Data Science Day, Winterthur.

Kolassa, S. (2016a). Sometimes it's better to be simple than correct. *Foresight* 40 (Winter): 20–26.

Kolassa, S. (2016b). Commentary: That feeling for randomness. *Foresight* 42 (Summer): 44–47.

COMMENTARY: BIG DATA, A BIG DECISION

Niels van Hove

Every so many years, a new supply-chain terminology takes the front page and dominates the conversation in magazines and conferences. In the last decade or two we've seen JIT (Just in Time), TQM (Total Quality Management), Six Sigma, S&OP (Sales and Operations Planning), Lean, Agile, Demand-Driven Supply Chains . . . to name just a few.

Often it is for good reasons that these concepts draw attention, as they have proven to provide value in certain companies or industries. What frequently happens next is that the marketing machines of commercial expert analysts, research institutes, consultancies, and IT vendors run overtime to capitalize on them. Usually the result is that the supply-chain concept is generalized as a solution for everything, accompanied by a simplified interpretation of the complexity involved in implementation. Risks and costs of implementation are hardly ever mentioned, only the benefits. On top of this, a sense of urgency and fear of being left behind is created, often pressuring companies to decide rapidly and adapt the new concept.

Big data has been one of the concepts to dominate the supply-chain scene for a while. There is no denying that we're getting more connected, we consume more and more data, and we produce exponentially more data, but like any concept, big data is not a holy grail for every supply chain. One of the premises Shaun Snapp's article examines in this issue of *Foresight* is that big data will be used to switch forecasting from the product and more towards the customer. This might be true in some cases, but in many supply-chain cases it will not.

INDUSTRY SPECIFICS

Some industries are more supply driven rather than demand driven. We've recently seen the oil industry creating a glut in oil, whilst knowing that oil demand is hardly increasing. Similarly, in the mining industry, production often continues to pay off fixed asset costs, even when demand stagnates or drops. While these industries might use big data for exploration or other purposes, they are unlikely to use it for customer forecasts.

Supply-driven industries focus less on the customer and so hardly require a customer-driven forecast. On top of this, in some industries, the ability to respond to customer demand is limited. In the agricultural industry, connected technology that produces masses of data is used for pest control. However, a tomato plant will produce tomatoes for nine months, regardless of customer demand. This limits the need for big data or customer-based forecasting.

The value of big data also depends upon where in the supply chain a business operates and what the influence is on the end-to-end value chain as well as the final customer. If a business has limited influence on these fronts, customer data will not add value to its forecasts. A contract manufacturer that supplies a car or a phone manufacturer who is dependent on a yearly tender doesn't need big data.

THE CUSTOMER-ORDER DECOUPLING POINT

To understand the potential of big data in forecasting for a supply chain, let's start with a basic understanding of the *customer order decoupling point* (CODP). This is the point in the value chain where the product is linked to a customer order.

In an Engineer-to-Order (ETO) environment, a company will work with the customer to design and make a product – for example, luxury yachts or specialized machinery. Supply chains with this type of CODP have long order lead times and only a few customers.

In a Make-to-Order (MTO) environment, the customer product is made from raw materials, parts, and components. The commercial airline industry operates in an MTO environment. And although some jet engines produce 10 GB of data each second and apply artificial intelligence to optimize fuel consumption, there is no need for big data in customer forecasting.

ETO and MTO environments have few customers. This is similar for companies that sell services. SpaceX, which delivers commercial payloads to space, has only a few customers. Big data might be useful for these companies in other areas, but not to forecast their customer demands.

In a make-to-stock (MTS) environment, a manufacturer will produce physical products to be held by a wholesaler or retailer, who then sells them to the final customer. The manufacturer might support 100,000 customer ship-to locations like DCs, retail outlets, hotels, hospitals, or restaurants. There is value in understanding this customer demand through point-of-sale (POS) information and including this in your forecast. Using POS data isn't new in forecasting. Over a decade ago, I included POS information from retail stores four times a day in the production forecast for a meat manufacturer. What's a more recent development is to apply *demand sensing* – automatic algorithm changes to short-term forecasts – to every ship-to and product combination. To apply demand sensing to 100,000 ship-tos that all hold 1,000 SKUs, an algorithm needs to work through 100 million combinations. It is questionable to call this scale of information big data.

The final decoupling point is to sell from stock. This is the closest point where the order is linked to the customer, who is also the final customer. Traditionally, this is the brick-and-mortar retailer. The largest retailers collect significant amounts of data from their POS and customer-loyalty cards. This data collection can be across tens of millions of customers; however, data collection is still restricted to the geographical network, the number of retail outlets, and the customer behaviour within the retail outlet. The online retailers of today don't have these restrictions anymore. Amazon has over 300 million active accounts. Account holders can be anywhere in the world; every smartphone or laptop is a retail outlet, and online consumer behaviour can be followed whenever the consumer is online.

Also in the last decade traditional MTS manufacturers started to apply other distribution models. Nike once produced running shoes with an MTS model, supplying retailers. Now it sells online direct to customers from stock and also gives customers an Assemble-to-Order (ATO) option to design their own shoes. So, the traditional MTS manufacturers that started online stores are now online retailers. If you're an online retailer that's planning to grow to dozens of millions of customers, big data seems to get more relevant to understand your customer behaviour and include it in your forecast.

But where big data really starts to play a role is *beyond* the point of purchase, after the customer has bought a product or service. Once we enter the customer's daily life in real time and start connecting different products and services across multiple industries, the available data explodes.

BEYOND THE POINT OF PURCHASE

With over a billion customers, online services such as Google and Facebook are tracking their customers' every move to forecast the content the customers want to see or places they want to go. Facebook uses AI to curate your content based on your historic behaviour. Google's Moves mobile-phone app tracks your daily movements and makes suggestions on where you might go next. In a similar way, the retailer Amazon has entered the customer's living room with its popular voice-controlled "smart speaker" Echo. With Echo, Amazon will create an understanding of your grocery shopping list, the music and radio stations you listen to, the time you come home and switch on your lights, and your voice-directed Internet searches, among many other things. Amazon can combine all this information with online purchase history of their products and services and it has patented *anticipatory shipping*, a system that forecasts and delivers products before the customer places an order. Applying anticipatory shipping to a 300-million-and-still-growing customer base sounds like big data territory.

Through the creation of partnerships, traditional manufacturers and retailers can also go beyond the point of purchase to gather consumer information. Besides selling running shoes, Nike partners with Apple to sell sport watches that measure all types of real-time consumer health data. If Nike has access to this data, it can now connect online shoe-purchase behaviour with an understanding of workout regimens, sleeping patterns, heart rate, and kilometres run for their customers.

Nike also partners to sell watches with TomTom, a Dutch map provider and consumer-product manufacturer. Besides producing sport watches, TomTom provides the maps for Apple's 600 million iPhone users and for many major car producers. If these three companies, who are already in partnership, were to share all their customer data, they could in fact know their customers' every move – or very nearly – and use this to predict their behaviour. Although privacy and data ownership play a significant role, when manufacturers and retailers across industries team up to gather information beyond the point of purchase across multiple products and services, data availability to forecast customer behaviour explodes.

THE BIG-DATA DECISION

Big data seems to be most relevant for demand-driven businesses with a significant customer base, and even more for businesses that can gather customer information beyond the point of purchase and enter the daily lives of the customer. Even then, the investment in big data seems more a holistic, strategic business decision, rather than a supply-chain or narrow forecasting decision. The analysts and researchers that push big data should provide more context in what industry and supply-chain situation big data will most likely function and should describe the risks and benefits.

Before adopting a new concept in their value chain, it's the supply-chain executives' responsibility to ask themselves several questions, including:

1. Does big data create efficiency in our operation?
2. Does it deliver value to our customer?
3. Does it give us a competitive advantage?
4. What is the risk of implementation versus the return on investment?

Investing in big data is a major decision that should *not* be taken lightly – especially on the advice of analysts and researchers who have an interest in selling big-data solutions.

COMMENTARY: BIG DATA AND THE INTERNET OF THINGS

Peter Catt

Shaun Snapp's review of the Blue Ridge white paper "How to Supercharge Product Availability without Inflating Inventory" centres on its claim that big data will facilitate a shift from product-level forecasting to customer-level supply-chain forecasting. My commentary will briefly address the main concerns raised by Shaun, but I will also explore some areas where I believe big data has the potential to improve supply-chain planning and execution with a focus on supporting demand forecasting.

DETERMINING CUSTOMER INTENT

By way of introduction, *big data* is defined in Wikipedia (2017) this way.

Big data is a term for data sets that are so large or complex that traditional data processing applications are inadequate to deal with them. Challenges include analysis, capture, data curation, search, sharing, storage, transfer, visualization, querying, updating and information privacy. The term "big data" often refers simply to the use of predictive analytics, user-behavior analytics, or certain other advanced data-analytics methods that extract value from data, and seldom to a particular size of data set.

The first area of contention is what to forecast, the product or the customer. Shaun takes the position that Blue Ridge is proposing a customer forecast representing *customer* as an attribute. My interpretation of the "high level" Blue Ridge statements is that they are proposing something much more ambitious: determining customer intent through causal forecasting methods. Either way, I am in full agreement with Shaun that at some point such a forecast will need to be represented as a statement of demand at SKU level (by stocking location). Proven supply-chain planning and execution approaches, e.g., APICS and Oliver Wight's MRP/MRPII methodology, are predicated on data at the SKU level, and Blue Ridge has done nothing to convince me otherwise.

That said, our own Data Science team has led very successful projects involving the use of predictive analytics for customer propensity to buy in response to marketing campaigns. Such response rates can very easily be used to augment baseline statistical forecasts to account for planned marketing campaigns. Interestingly, such models actually only require a relatively small subset of representative data and therefore do not fit the criteria of big data. Although not requiring big data, this is an example of successfully predicting customer behaviour to assist demand forecasting.

Shaun raises a further valid point that some industries do favour causal techniques over univariate forecasting approaches such as exponential smoothing. Depending on the size of the customer base and the product offering, that may well be appropriate, particularly where the business model is more "customer intimate" rather than operationally excellent. Nevertheless, for high-volume, large-customer-base supply chains such as FMCG, univariate methods are the demonstrated cost-effective choice for demand forecasting. I also enthusiastically agree with Shaun that the majority of companies could dramatically improve their levels of customer service and reduce inventory cost by adopting proven statistical forecasting approaches.

THE INTERNET OF THINGS

Having reached a point of agreement with Shaun's critique of the situation, I'd like to introduce some possibilities around the use of big data in supply-chain planning. One of the obvious generators of big data will be the proliferation of Internet Protocol field devices, i.e., the Internet of Things (IoT). McKinsey (2015) defines the Internet of Things as "sensors and actuators connected by networks to computing systems. These systems can monitor or manage the health and actions of connected objects and machines. Connected sensors can also monitor the natural world, people, and animals." To clarify, I consider IoT as a generator of big data that will in many cases require interpretation through the use of statistical techniques including forecasting, machine learning, and data mining.

Examples of IoT cited by McKinsey are shown in Table 2.1.

By identifying only existing IoT technology, McKinsey estimates the potential economic impact to be as much as $11.1 trillion per year in 2025 for IoT applications in the nine settings detailed in Table 2.1.

Table 2.1 Nine Settings Where IoT Creates Value (McKinsey 2015)

Human	Devices attached to or inside the human body	Devices (wearables and ingestibles) to monitor and maintain human health and wellness; disease management, increased fitness, higher productivity
Home	Buildings where people live	Home controllers and security systems
Retail Environments	Spaces where consumers engage in commerce	Stores, banks, restaurants, arenas — anywhere consumers consider and buy; self-checkout, in-store offers, inventory optimization
Offices	Spaces where knowledge workers work	Energy management and security in office buildings; improved productivity, including for mobile employees
Factories	Standardized production environments	Places with repetitive work routines, including hospitals and farms; operating efficiencies, optimizing equipment use and inventory
Worksites	Custom production environments	Mining, oil and gas, construction; operating efficiencies, predictive maintenance, health and safety
Vehicles	Systems inside moving vehicles	Vehicles including cars, trucks, ships, aircraft, and trains; condition-based maintenance, usage-based design, pre-sales analytics
Cities	Urban environments	Public spaces and infrastructure in urban settings; adaptive traffic control, smart meters, environmental monitoring, resource management
Outside	Between urban environments (and outside other settings)	Outside uses include railroad tracks, autonomous vehicles (outside urban locations), and flight navigation; real-time routing, connected navigation, shipment tracking

Linking the potential of IoT to advances in supply-chain forecasting, I'd like to explore an example where radio-frequency identification (RFID or similar) devices interact with your domestic refrigerator and can determine your consumption and the remaining quantity of a particular item. For the sake of our example, let's assume that our "smart" fridge is aware of how much milk is left and can trigger a preset reorder with our local supermarket when the said reorder point is reached (and/or provide real-time consumption data). This situation is of course reactive and not predictive, but it does have the advantage of giving a more accurate demand signal at the point-of-consumption, which must be an improvement on point-of-sale.

The reason for this is the well-researched bullwhip effect, which refers to the increasing swings in inventory as one moves farther up the supply chain. The bullwhip effect was named for the way the amplitude of a whip increases down its length. The farther from the originating signal, the greater the distortion of the wave pattern. In a similar manner, forecast accuracy decreases as one moves upstream along the supply chain. For example, many consumer goods have fairly consistent consumption at retail, but this signal becomes more chaotic and unpredictable as you move away from consumer purchasing behavior.

So smoothing the flow of products by reducing batch sizes and/or making smaller and more frequent replenishments has a positive effect on the stability of the entire supply chain. Increased visibility of actual consumption could also prove useful in ensuring that all supply-chain participants can incorporate such data into their respective material requirements planning systems and further minimise the bullwhip effect. For a proper treatment of the bullwhip effect see Lee, Padmanabhan, and Whang's (1997) seminal work, "The Bullwhip Effect in Supply Chains."

To conclude, the example suggests there is real potential in IoT and big data to improve supply chain forecasting. In the spirit of bridging evidence-based research with practice, we should keep an open mind on these technological developments.

REFERENCES

Big Data (n.d.). In Wikipedia. https://en.wikipedia.org/wiki/Big_data

Bullwhip Effect (n.d.). In Wikipedia. https://en.wikipedia.org/wiki/Bullwhip_effect

Lee, H. L., Padmanabhan, V., and Whang, S. (1997). The bullwhip effect in supply chains. *Sloan Management Review* (Spring): 93–102.

McKinsey Global Institute (2015). The internet of things: Mapping the value beyond the hype.

2.2 HOW BIG DATA COULD CHALLENGE PLANNING PROCESSES ACROSS THE SUPPLY CHAIN*

Tonya Boone, Ram Ganeshan, and Nada Sanders

The previous article and commentaries took a decidedly skeptical view of big data hype. Here, Boone, Ganeshan, and Sanders attempt to provide a measured discussion of the potential for big data to improve forecasting. This is possible, they argue, through better understanding of consumer behavior, upgraded demand-forecasting models, and more efficient supply-chain execution.

It is a fact that companies now have considerably more data available to them. But integration of this fine-grained data into traditional S&OP activities is fraught with challenges and therefore requires careful planning. Concerns include vast volumes of data, security and privacy, and unintended bias.

Another issue is the experience and skillset of planners. It is common to apply machine-learning techniques to project trends, to detect fraud (deviation from the trend), to learn association rules (recommendation engines, market-basket analysis, etc.), and to segment customers. But, the authors concede, planners are unfamiliar with these methods and need to learn much more about them. Additionally, S&OP processes typically are not flexible enough to allow such insights to be incorporated into routine system forecasts. This article documents the major challenges posed for Sales and Operations Planning and proposes how these can be anticipated and met head on.

Introduction

The term "big data" has dominated the popular as well as the academic press in recent years. One definition is offered by James Manyika and colleagues (2017) of McKinsey & Company: "Big data refers to data-sets whose size is so large that the quantity can no longer fit into the memory that computers use for processing."

---

*This article originally appeared in *Foresight: The International Journal of Applied Forecasting* (Summer, 2018) and appears here courtesy of the International Institute of Forecasters.

Here, we define big data at its most generic: data sets that are large ("volume"), that are collected in near real time (high "velocity"), that are present in myriad forms ("variety"), and in which there are various levels of trust ("veracity"). Especially as it relates to forecasting, big data brings with it the potential to better understand customer behavior, to more accurately predict demand, and to make supply-chain execution (typically set in motion by product forecasts) more efficient.

The authors are currently editing a special issue of the *International Journal of Forecasting* that explores the impact of big data on forecasting. What we present here are our own ideas on this topic and the implications and challenges it poses for supply chain planning processes. Interested readers are referred to Boone and colleagues (2018) for a more detailed elaboration.

"Big Data" Sources and the Potential They Bring

Firms are making significant investments in big-data storage and applications. The number of RFID tags sold globally is projected to rise from 12 million in 2011 to 209 billion in 2021 (Manyika et al. 2017). Internet of Things (IoT) investment in production is expected to double from $35 billion to $71 billion by 2020 (http://aradinfocenter. com/wp-content/uploads/2017/07/A.T.%20Kearney_Internet%20of%20Things%20 2020%20Presentation_Online.pdf).

Although big data's forecasting applications are fragmented and often idiosyncratic, there are common themes on its potential impact: big data helps us better understand customer behavior, improves forecast quality, and simplifies supply-chain coordination.

True, there's healthy skepticism in the forecasting community over the potentially disruptive impact of big data on forecasting, as revealed in *Foresight*'s special feature section "Is Big Data 'Big Hype' for Supply-Chain Forecasting?" in the Spring 2017 issue.

What we offer here is our view on the potential benefits and the challenges in reaping them.

Insight into Customer Behavior

Copious data become available as customers move through every stage of their decision journey. Customer clickstreams, social-media interactions, and Google searches inform us on how customers discover and evaluate products. In-store technologies such as beacons, tags, virtual rails, and engagement kiosks track buying behavior. Modern transactional systems not only track sales in real time but are connected to inventory and customer databases across multiple channels. Lastly, technologies are enabling the rise of "omnichannel" experiences, allowing consumers to move seamlessly between physical and online stores as they evaluate, purchase, return, or seek help with products and services.

Such fine-grained data can enable *real-time personalization*. Based on customer attributes – which could include demographics, location, and browsing history – a company can personalize products, offers, and prices, and "push" these to the customer

(Ganeshan 2014). At a more aggregate level, *customer microsegmentation* can offer small groups of customers tailored products and incentives. The retailer Neiman Marcus, for example, uses behavioral segmentation matched with a multitier membership-rewards program to identify top-spending customers. It then tailors purchase incentives for them, often resulting in significantly higher-margin purchases.

Pricing decisions can now be made in near real time using a variety of new data sources – competitor pricing that can be "scraped" from the Web or personalized pricing for customers based on shopping profiles. Uber, for example, uses "surge" pricing, based on customer-demand characteristics. Kroger, a large U.S. grocer, is experimenting with electronic shelf edges that can personalize prices for individual customers: https://www.wsj.com/articles/at-kroger-technology-is-changing-the-grocery-store-shopping-experience-1487646362.

Improving the Quality of Demand Forecasts

Modern POS systems now can provide real-time data on transactions across selling channels. These detailed transactional data sets are helping firms estimate *actual* customer demand more accurately. It is common practice for forecasters to use sales, orders, or shipment data as the historical time series to predict future demand; however, in face of stock-outs, promotions, and supply-chain disruptions, these do not give an accurate picture of the underlying customer demand (Gilliland 2010).

For example, when demand exceeds inventory, resulting in a stock-out, it's often difficult to estimate the real demand from sales data, a scenario commonly referred to as *censored demand*. Planners will manually adjust sales upwards to estimate the true demand. Now, with the ability to track granular sales and traffic data, the actual demand can be estimated from the censored sales data. The planner can use the timing of the stock-out and store traffic until the next replenishment to get better estimates of demand.

Second, these new data streams are enabling *multiproduct* forecasts. Firms plan for both the assortment of products to carry and the appropriate inventory to hold for each. These decisions are often done independently. Marketing considerations drive product assortment, and planners subsequently forecast aggregate demands. With disaggregate data, it becomes possible to forecast demands by SKU as a function of the assortment. This is because we'd have an understanding of the demand for each product in the assortment and the probability that customers would substitute between them. It's therefore possible to generate an optimized forecast for a portfolio of SKUs rather than a product family.

Third, these data sets provide new inputs for forecasting models, such as Google searches and social-media data, potentially reducing forecast errors. Schmidt and Vosen (2013) show how Google trends can improve aggregate consumer purchase indices. For individual product SKUs, Boone et al. (2015) in this journal used a case study to show how "in-sample" errors for two SKUs are reduced for a food retailer, later (Boone, Ganeshan, and Hicks 2015) extending the study to show "out-of-sample" error improvements for multiple SKUs over many categories.

Increased Supply-Chain Coordination

On the customer side, connected devices now enable firms (although implementation is at its earliest stages) to evaluate customer usage patterns, thus improving visibility into demand. For example, Amazon's "dash buttons" can now be placed next to the product (for example, a button to repurchase Tide detergent can be placed on the washing machine) and actuate replenishment when needed (see also Catt's 2017 commentary, giving examples from the Internet of Things).

On the supply side, big data has further enabled the connected supply chain. With initiatives such as Collaborative Planning, Forecasting, and Replenishment (CPFR) and Efficient Customer Response (ECR), supply-chain partners can share large amounts of data and make coordinated real-time decisions on product forecasts and associated replenishment. While such initiatives have focused on product and item-level forecasts in recent years, new efforts are under way to understand buying behavior, both to "shape" and more accurately forecast underlying customer demand.

One area that has a special significance for supply-chain management is the *forecasting of disruptions*. As a case in point, forecasting of high-impact, low-probability events – "black swans" – has significantly improved. Historically our focus was on building resiliency into the supply chain so that we could be ready to adapt to rare but inevitable events. However, big-data analytics is slowly changing this notion – the number of events that we used to consider unpredictable and purely random is getting smaller.

An excellent example of improved prediction is in weather forecasting. New radar technologies, improvements to satellite technology, and computer models that run on more powerful supercomputers allow forecasters to better "see" extreme weather. The key is the big data gathered by these technologies and satellites, which can then be processed within minutes, creating warnings of tornadoes, hurricanes, and other extreme weather events.

Big-data tools bring the potential to better manage risk by reacting faster to real-time alerts on routine disruptions such as traffic or disease outbreaks. Traffic can be rerouted, for example, skirting congestion to keep deliveries on time. Knowledge of outbreaks of flu can be used to determine which areas may need more supplies of medications.

The Challenge for Aggregate and Detailed Planning

The traditional demand-planning process begins with historical sales data and identifies potential explanatory variables. Coupled with demand planners' judgment, forecasts are produced typically by product family over a rolling horizon.

The most common way of combining judgment with sales data is through judgmental adjustments or overrides of statistical forecasts. For short-life-cycle products like apparel, for example, which are plagued with long lead times (sometimes of several months), planners commonly use economic optimization algorithms. These algorithms first estimate demand and error distributions from past sales and use these to commit to the season's need. The forecasts are tracked and compared with actual sales, providing a feedback loop for future forecasts.

Once generated, the forecasts are translated into demand requirements and purchase orders. Many firms that do not use detailed master schedules "fence" or lock the most immediate forecast so that its supply-chain requirements, such as material planning, inventory allocation, and purchases, can be set.

For both S&OP and these related planning processes, big data provides some unique challenges: integration of vast volumes of data, security, and privacy, and unintended bias. We address these next.

How to Integrate Big Data

The amount of data generated can be enormous; in some estimates the daily production is 2.5 exabytes of data, equivalent to 2.5 million petabytes and 2.5 billion gigabytes. About 90% of these data is unstructured. Social media produces 500 million tweets (http://www.internetlivestats.com/twitter-statistics/#trend) and 3.5 billion Google daily searches (http://www.internetlivestats.com/google-search-statistics/).

Supply chains are also inundated: Amazon sells 600 items every second! Walmart collects more than 2.5 petabytes of data every hour from 1 million customer transactions. The question for planners is how much and which data to include in the planning process. Often these large data-sets tend to be "sparse" and "transient." As more data sets are included, the complexity of data management and system support also increases.

Second, planners need to address the seeming contradiction between the increased personalization afforded by big data and the aggregate nature of the S&OP process. Traditionally, the aggregate demand plan is disaggregated into SKU variants. But big data supports a more granular approach, one that starts with detailed disaggregate planning. Big data is enabling, for example, the construction of our best customer, the Ideal Customer Profile (ICP), and provides insights into how to lower the Customer Acquisition Cost (CAC) and increase the Customer Lifetime Value (CLTV). There is significant debate on whether the move from product (top-down) to customer (bottom-up) forecasting is even possible (Snapp, 2017). If it can be done this way, however, the process is complex and time consuming. Since both the volume and velocity of data are high, planners also need to address *how often* these plans need updating.

Third, big data sets are typically used to detect patterns and associations that have predictive value. It is common to use machine-learning techniques to project trends, to detect fraud (deviation from the trend), to learn association rules (recommendation engines, market-basket analysis, etc.), and to segment customers.

In our experience, planners are unfamiliar with these methods, which have typically been used for short-term decision making. As a case in point, when Hurricane Frances was due to hit the Florida coast in 2004, Walmart learned that customers prefer to stock up on strawberry Pop-Tarts (sales rates were 7 times the normal) and beer prior to a hurricane. The stores in the area were stocked with these items, which then sold out. Such data-driven insights can translate to better customer service and higher profits.

Additionally, S&OP processes typically are not flexible enough to allow such insights to be incorporated into routine system forecasts.

Lastly, the role of judgment needs to be revisited. Routine adjustments in forecasts for events unplanned and unexpected (like the demand censor example alluded to earlier) are now being quantified by big-data techniques. On one hand, this brings a more data-driven approach to adjustments; on the other, one has to "trust" machine-learning algorithms to make those judgments.

Security and Privacy

With the explosion of connected devices, the amount of personal data collected is substantial, and some of these data are collected without a purpose. The Identity Theft and Resource Center (ITRC 2018) reports that in just the first three months of 2018, there have been 273 breaches with over 5 million customer records exposed.

There are other well-known data breaches, including the 2017 Equifax breach exposing 140 million customers' Social Security numbers; more recently we saw the use of personal information from Facebook by Cambridge Analytica to help the Trump election campaign. Firms that use disaggregate customer data need to be more careful about security and privacy, lest they violate local and federal laws.

Hidden Biases

Another significant issue concerns hidden biases in data collection and analysis.

Much of the data is collected automatically through sensors, connected devices, and social-media channels. Mark Graham and colleagues studied tweets on "flood" or "flooding" to see if they could predict the impact of Hurricane Sandy. See the graphic and their research summary in https://www.theguardian.com/news/datablog/2012/oct/31/twitter-sandy-flooding. It turns out that the vast number of tweets came from Manhattan, giving at least the mistaken impression that it may have been the site of the most damage. It was actually New Jersey.

Another well-known example is that Google trends were overestimating the incidences of flu. It turns out people searched for terms related to the flu *after* they saw the news on TV. The Centers for Disease Control, however, estimates flu incidences via field surveys.

The lesson here is that while a torrent of data may be available, it may not always represent the signal one is trying to measure. Planners using big-data sources must therefore carefully differentiate the "signal from the noise."

Machine-learning algorithms may unintentionally target or omit certain segments of the population. In her best-selling book *Weapons of Math Destruction*, Cathy O'Neil (2016) describes several cases of unintentional bias in education (how teachers are evaluated), financial services (how certain minorities are denied services), and retail (where only certain demographics are targeted).

Bias can affect the most vulnerable segments of the population. Efforts are under way to measure the bias or fairness of machine-based algorithms by constructing a "fraud score" or a "bias score." While much of the work currently resides in research journals, we foresee a wider use as more planners begin to use these large data sets. John Podesta, President Obama's former Chief of Staff, perhaps sums it up best: "The lesson here is that we need to pay careful attention to what unexpected outcomes the use of big data might lead to, and how to remedy any unintended discrimination or inequality that may result."

Conclusions

Our intention in this paper is to point to the potential of big data to better understand the customer, improve forecast accuracy, and better execute supply-chain transactions.

However, big data brings big challenges:

- The scale of the data is large; there seems to be no consensus on what and how best to integrate into the S&OP and other planning processes.
- Second, the methods and techniques needed with these big data sets are relatively new; planners will need to become familiar with them.
- Third, since the new data sets are helping address some of the uncertainties in the planning process, it's unclear if and how planners should adjust forecasts based on judgment.
- These big data sets and associated techniques are open to unintentional biases that planners must be alert to and guard against.

These are exciting times for forecasters – the new large data sets have the potential to transform and improve S&OP and other related detailed forecasting and planning activities. We are optimistic that as planners come to understand the insights it provides, the challenges posed by big data can be eventually overcome.

REFERENCES

Boone, T., Ganeshan, R., and Hicks, R.L. (2015). Incorporating Google trends data into sales forecasting. *Foresight* 38 (Summer): 9–14.

Boone, T., Ganeshan, R., Jain, A., and Sanders, N. (2018). Forecasting in the supply chain: Consumer analytics in the era of big data. Working paper, invited for the Special Issue on Forecasting and Big Data *in International Journal of Forecasting*.

Catt, P. (2017). Commentary: Big data and the Internet of Things. *Foresight* 45 (Spring): 27–28.

Ganeshan, R. (2014). Clickstream analysis for forecasting online behavior. *Foresight* 33, 15–19.

Gilliland, M. (2010). Defining "demand" for demand forecasting. *Foresight* 18 (Summer): 4–8.

ITRC (2017). https://www.idtheftcenter.org/images/breach/2018/DataBreachReport_2018.pdf

Manyika, J., Chui, M., Miremadi, M., et al. (2017). *Harnessing automation for a future that works.* McKinsey.

O'Neil, C. (2016). *Weapons of math destruction: How big data increases inequality and threatens democracy.* New York: Crown Press.

Schmidt, T., and Vosen, S. (2013). Demographic change and the labour share of income. *Journal of Population Economics* 26, 357–378.

Snapp, S. (2017). Is Big Data the silver bullet for supply-chain forecasting? *Foresight* 45 (Spring): 10–14.

CHAPTER 3

Forecasting Methods: Modeling, Selection, and Monitoring

Artificial intelligence and machine learning have dominated the attention of researchers and practitioners the past five years. Yet there has continued to be important new work in the more traditional areas of forecasting methodology. This chapter shares over a dozen compelling articles and commentaries covering advances in these traditional areas.

The chapter begins with a selection on time-series basics from the Kolassa and Siemsen book, *Demand Forecasting for Managers*. Then, a taxonomy of forecasting problems to help focus efforts on the right data and methods is offered for each type of problem.

Judgment plays a well-recognized role in the override of computer-generated forecasts, but this role is less well recognized in the selection of forecasting models. Groundbreaking research by Fotios Petropoulos is shared, showing that automatic model selection can be improved upon by judicious use of judgment. Multiple commentaries explore the implications of these findings.

Paul Goodwin next contributes two pieces on the more familiar role of judgment in forecasting. The first is a selection from his book *Forewarned: A Skeptic's Guide to Prediction*, and the second, a summary of the most recent research on this topic.

The next two articles deal with topics worthy of the forecaster's attention: the concept of probabilistic demand planning, and the use of prediction markets for corporate planning. While neither approach is commonly used in business forecasting, the ideas merit consideration.

Two brief articles discuss the adaptation of coefficient of variation (COV) to indicate a time series' "forecastability." Despite some acknowledged weaknesses in COV as such an indicator, it has popular adoption and a secure role in the practitioner's toolbox. An alternative – the variation of the naïve forecast error – is suggested to address some of COV's flaws.

Monitoring forecast performance typically means crude exception reporting, where all errors above a certain hurdle are flagged for review. This "one size fits all" approach is problematic and inefficient. A well-performing model may be flagged for review when, simply by chance, an error exceeds the criterion. Other models, for stable and easy-to-forecast time series, may never have errors high enough to be flagged, even though the model may be failing to achieve the accuracy of a more appropriate model. Joe Katz shares a patented approach that can automatically monitor forecast errors and determine when models are satisfactory, should be adjusted/refit, or should be discarded and replaced.

Finally, the chapter ends with a deeper look into the future of retail forecasting, where new technologies, social media, and AI/ML are driving dramatic changes.

* * *

3.1 KNOW YOUR TIME SERIES*

Stephan Kolassa and Enno Siemsen

The analysis of time-series data is at the core of business forecasting, and here, in an adaptation from their book *Demand Forecasting for Managers*, Kolassa and Siemsen explore many of the core concepts of time-series data. They raise awareness of important issues that may be overlooked – or purposely ignored – in our eagerness to generate forecasts.

For example, from a technical modeling standpoint, the stationarity of a time series determines what types of models are appropriate. Yet stationarity is infrequently part of the demand planner's conversation or concern, potentially leading to poor model selection.

Likewise, the length of available history can impact the type of models that are appropriate. The authors advocate utilizing all available history rather than arbitrarily truncating it. They also point out the inherent complication of forecasting future "demand" when the historical record is "sales," which, at best, is just an approximation of what customers really wanted.

The topic of forecastability receives much deserved attention, because it fundamentally impacts the accuracy we can achieve. Forecastability should affect management's expectation for accuracy, and force recognition that the quality of a forecast is not reflected just by the MAPE (or other accuracy metric). Relative measures such as FVA are also important, as they let you assess forecasting performance relative to simple benchmarks.

In short, understanding your time-series data is the first step toward a good forecast.

---

*Adapted from the book *Demand Forecasting for Managers* (2016) and appears here courtesy of Scott Isenberg of Business Expert Press.

Data Availability

A time series is a sequence of similar measurements taken at regular time intervals. Time series analysis means examining the history of the time series itself to gather information about the future. An inherent assumption in time series analysis is that the past of a series contains information about the future of the same series. Regression modeling means using the information contained in another data series to make predictions about the future of a focal time series.

One essential aspect of time series forecasting is that time needs to be "bucketed" into time periods. Many demand forecasts are made on a monthly basis ("how much product will our customers demand next month?"), and thus the time series requires aggregating data into monthly buckets. Note that "a month" is not an entirely regular time interval, since some months have more days than others, but for most applications, this nonregularity is inconsequential enough to be ignored. Financial forecasting works on a quarterly or yearly basis, whereas some operational forecasting requires weekly, daily, and sometimes even quarter-hourly time buckets, for example, in the case of call center traffic forecasting (Minnucci 2006). This temporal dimension of aggregation does, as we shall explain, imply different degrees of statistical aggregation as well, making forecasting more or less challenging. It also raises the question of temporal hierarchies, that is, at what level should the organization forecast, and how does the organization aggregate or disaggregate to longer or shorter segments of time?

Another important aspect to understand about your forecast is the availability of relevant historical data. Most methods assume that some demand history for a time series exists. For example, if exponential smoothing is used and the model includes seasonality, then at least nine past quarters are needed for quarterly time series models, and 17 past months are needed for monthly time series models (Hyndman and Kostenko 2007) – and these are *minimum* requirements; if the time series is very noisy, much more data is needed to get reliable estimates for the method's parameters and thus obtain dependable forecasts.[1] This data requirement may be excessive in many business contexts where the lifecycle of products is only 3 years. If lifecycles are short, changes to the product portfolio need to be carefully assessed as to whether they represent true new product introductions, that is, the introduction of a novel good or service that is incomparable to any existing product in the firm's portfolio, or a semi-new product introduction, that is, a modified version of a product the firm has sold before (Tonetti 2006). In the former case, the methods we will discuss here do not hold; forecasts will require modeling the product lifecycle, which requires good market research and extensive conjoint analysis to have a chance of being successful. Interested readers are referred to a different book by the same publisher for further information on new product forecasting (Berry 2010). In the latter case, forecasting can proceed as we discuss here, as long as some existing data can be deemed representative of the semi-new product. For example, if the semi-new product is a simple engineering change of a previous version of the product, the history of the previous version of the product should apply and can be used to initialize the forecasting method for the semi-new product. If the change is a change in packaging or style, the level of the time series may change, but other components of the series, such as the trend, seasonality, and possibly even the uncertainty in demand, may remain constant. Thus, the estimates of these components from the past can be used for the new model as initial estimates, greatly reducing the need for a data history to be available. Similarly, if the semi-new product is simply a new variant within a category, then the trend and seasonality that exists at the category level may apply to the new variant as well; in other words, smart top-down forecasting in a hierarchy can allow forecasters to learn about these time series components by looking at the collection of other, similar variants within the same category.

A first step in time series analysis is to understand what data underlies the series. Demand forecasting means making statements about future demand; the data that is stored in company databases often only shows actual sales. The difference between demand and sales comes into play during stock-outs. If inventory runs out, customers may still demand a product, so sales may be lower than the actual demand. In such a case, customers may turn to a competitor, delay their purchase, or buy a substitute product. In the latter case, the substitute's sales are actually higher than the raw demand for it. If sales are used as an input for demand forecasting, both point forecasts and their associated prediction intervals will be wrong. Modern forecasting software can adjust sales data accordingly if stock-out information is recorded. The mathematics of such adjustments are beyond the scope of this book. Interested readers are referred to Nahmias (1994) for further details.

Adjusting sales to estimate demand requires clearly understanding whether data represents sales or demand. Demand can be very difficult to observe in business–consumer contexts. If a product is not on the shelf, it is hard to tell whether a customer walking through the store demanded the product or not. In online retail contexts, demand can be clearly observed if inventory availability is not shown to the customers before they place an item into their shopping basket. However, if this information is presented to customers before they click on purchase, demand is again difficult to observe. Demand is generally easier to observe in business–business settings, since customer requests are usually recorded. In modern ERP software, salespeople usually work with an "available-to-promise" number. Running out of "available-to-promise" means that some customer requests are not converted into orders; if these requests are not recorded by the salespeople, databases again only show sales and not demand.

Stationarity

One key attribute of a time series is referred to as stationarity. Stationarity means that the mean of demand is constant over time, that the variance of demand remains constant, and that the correlation between current and most recent demand observations (and other parameters of the demand distribution) remains constant. Stationarity in essence requires that the time series has constant properties when looked at over time. Many time series violate these criteria; for example, a time series with a trend is not stationary, since the mean demand is persistently increasing or decreasing. Similarly, a simple random walk is not stationary since mean demand randomly increases or decreases in every time period. In essence, nonstationary series imply that demand conditions for a product change over time, whereas stationary series imply that demand conditions are very stable. Some forecasting methods, such as the ARIMA methods, work only well if the underlying time series is stationary.

Time series are often transformed to become stationary before they are analyzed. Typical data transformations include first differencing, that is, examining only the changes of demand between time periods; calculating growth rates, that is, examining the normalized first difference; or taking the natural logarithm of the data. Suppose, for example, one observes the following four observations of time series: 100, 120, 160, and 150. The corresponding three observations of the first difference series become 20, 40, and −10. Expressed as growth rates, this series of first differences becomes 20, 33, and −6%.

Essential to these transformations is that they are reversible. While estimations are made on the transformed data, the resulting forecasts can be easily transformed back to apply to the untransformed time series. The benefit of such transformations usually lies in the reduction of variability and in filtering out the unstable portions of the data. There are several statistical tests for stationarity that will usually be reported in statistical software, such as the Dickey–Fuller test. It is useful to apply these tests to examine whether a first-differenced time series has achieved stationarity or not.

A common mistake in managerial thinking is to assume that using "old" data (i.e., 4–5 years ago) for forecasting is bad, since obviously so much has changed since then. Modern forecasting techniques will deal with this change without excluding the data; in fact, they need data that shows how much has changed over time, otherwise the methods may underestimate how much the future can change from the present. Excluding data is rarely a good practice in forecasting. A long history of data allows the forecaster and his/her methods to more clearly assess market volatility and change.

Forecastability and Scale

Another aspect to understand about a time series is the forecastability of the series. Some time series contain more noise than others, making the task of predicting their future realizations more challenging. The less forecastable a time series is, the wider the prediction interval associated with the forecast will be. Understanding the forecastability of a series not only helps in terms of setting expectations among decision makers, but is also important when examining appropriate benchmarks for forecasting performance. A competitor may be more accurate at forecasting if they have a better forecasting process or if their time series are more forecastable. The latter may simply be a fact of them operating at a larger scale, with less variety, or their products being less influenced by current fashion and changing consumer trends.

One metric that is used to measure the forecastability of a time series is to calculate the ratio of the standard deviation of the time series data itself to the standard deviation of forecast errors using a benchmark method (Hill, Zhang, and Burch 2015). The logic behind this ratio is that the standard deviation of demand is in some sense a lower bound on performance since it generally corresponds to using a simple, long-run average as your forecasting method for the future. Any useful forecasting method should not lead to more uncertainty than the uncertainty inherent in demand. Thus, if this ratio is >1, forecasting in a time series can benefit from more complex methods than using a long-run average. If this ratio is close to 1 (or even <1), the time series currently cannot be forecast any better than using a long-run average.

This conceptualization is very similar to what some researchers call "Forecast Value Added" (Gilliland 2013). In this concept, one defines a base accuracy for a time series by calculating the forecast accuracy achieved by the best simple method – either using a long-run average or the most recent demand – to predict the future. Every step in the forecasting process, whether it is the output of a statistical forecasting model, the consensus forecast from a group, or the judgmental adjustment to a forecast by a higher level executive, is then benchmarked in terms of their long-run error against this base accuracy; if a method requires effort from the organization but does not lead to better forecast accuracy compared to a method that requires less effort, it can be eliminated from future forecasting processes. Results from such comparisons are often sobering – some estimates suggest that in almost 50% of time series, the existing toolset available for forecasting does not improve upon simple forecasting methods (Morlidge 2014). In other words, demand averaging or simple demand chasing may sometimes be the best a forecaster can do to create predictions.

Some studies examine what drives the forecastability of a series (Schubert 2012). Key factors here include the overall volume of sales (larger volume means more aggregation of demand, thus less observed noise), the coefficient of variation of the series (more variability relative to mean demand), and the intermittency of data (data with only few customers that place large orders is more difficult to predict than data with many customers that place small orders). In a nutshell, the forecastability of a time series can be explained by characteristics of the product as well as characteristics of the firm within its industry. There are economies of scale in forecasting, with forecasting at higher volumes being generally easier than forecasting for very low volumes.

The source of these economies of scale lies in the principle of statistical aggregation. Imagine trying to forecast who among all the people living in your street will buy a sweater this week. You would end up with a forecast for each person living in the street that is highly uncertain for each individual. However, if you just want to forecast how many people living in your street buy a sweater in total, the task becomes much easier. At the individual level, you can make many errors, but at the aggregate level, these errors cancel out. This effect will increase the more you aggregate – that is, predicting at the neighborhood, city, county, state, region, or country level. Thus, the forecastability of a series is often a question of the level of aggregation that a time series is focused on. Very disaggregate series can become intermittent and thus very challenging to forecast. Very aggregate series are easier to forecast, but if the level of aggregation is too high, these forecasts become less useful for planning purposes as the information they contain is not detailed enough.

It is important in this context to highlight the difference between relative and absolute comparisons in forecast accuracy. In absolute terms, a higher level of aggregation will have more uncertainty than each individual series, but in relative terms, the uncertainty at the aggregate level will be less than the sum of the uncertainties at the lower level. If you predict whether a person buys a sweater or not, your absolute error is at most 1, whereas the maximum error of predicting how many people in your street buy a sweater or not depends on how many people live in your street; nevertheless, the sum of the errors you make at the individual level will be less than the error you make in the sum. For example, suppose five people live in your street, and we can order them by how far into the street (i.e., first house, second house, etc.) they live. You predict that the first two residents buy a sweater, whereas the last three do not. Your aggregate prediction is just that two residents buy a sweater. Suppose now, actually only the last two residents buy a sweater. Your forecast is 100% accurate in the aggregate level, but only 20% accurate at the disaggregate level. In general, the standard deviation of forecast errors at the aggregate level will be less than the sum of the standard deviations of forecast errors made at the disaggregate level.

The ability to use more aggregate forecasts in planning can also be achieved through product and supply chain design, and the benefits of aggregation here are not limited to better forecasting performance but also include reduced inventory costs. For example, the concept of postponement in supply chain design favors postponing the differentiation of products until later in the process. This enables forecasting and planning at higher levels of aggregation for longer within the supply chain. Paint companies were early adopters of this idea by producing generic colors that are then mixed into the final product at the retail level. This allows forecasting (and stocking) at much higher levels of aggregation. Similarly, Hewlett-Packard demonstrated how to use distribution centers for the localization of their products in order to produce and ship generic printers into the distribution centers. A product design strategy that aims for better aggregation is component commonality, or so-called platform strategies. Here, components across stock-keeping units are kept in common, enabling production and procurement to operate with forecasts and plans at a higher level of aggregation. Volkswagen is famous for pushing the boundaries of this approach with its MQB platform, which allows component sharing and final assembly on the same line across such diverse cars as the Audi A3 and the Volkswagen Touareg. Additive manufacturing may become a technology that allows planning at very aggregate levels (e.g., printing raw materials and flexible printing capacity), thereby allowing companies to deliver a variety of products without losing economies of scale in forecasting and inventory planning.

Key Takeaways

- ▧ Understanding your data is the first step to a good forecast.

- ▧ The objective of most forecasts is to predict demand, yet the data available to prepare these forecasts often reflects sales; if stock-outs occur, sales are less than demand.

- ▧ Many forecasting methods require time series to be stationary, that is, to have constant parameters over time. Stationarity can often be achieved by suitable transformations of the original time series such as differencing the series.

- ▧ A key attribute of a time series is its forecastability. Your competitors may have more accurate forecasts because their forecasting process is better or because their time series are more forecastable.

- ▧ There are economies of scale in forecasting; predicting at a larger scale tends to be easier due to statistical aggregation effects.

Note

1. If too little data is available, the risk of detecting seasonality where none exists is much higher than the risk of failing to detect seasonality if it exists. Shrinkage methods to better deal with seasonality in such settings are available (Miller and Williams 2003).

References

Berry, T. (2010). *Sales and market forecasting for entrepreneurs*. New York, NY: Business Expert Press.

Gilliland, M. (2013). FVA: A reality check on forecasting practices. *Foresight* 29, 14–18.

Hill, A., Zhang, W., and Burch, G. (2015). Forecasting the forecastability quotient for inventory management. *International Journal of Forecasting* 31 (3): 651–663.

Hyndman, R., and Kostenko, A. (2007). Minimum sample size requirements for seasonal forecasting models. *Foresight* 6, 12–15.

Miller, D., and Williams, D. (2003). Shrinkage estimators of time series seasonal factors and their effect on forecasting accuracy. *International Journal of Forecasting* 19 (4): 669–684.

Minnucci, J. (2006). Nano forecasting: Forecasting techniques for short-time intervals. *Foresight* 4, 6–10.

Morlidge, St. (2014). Do forecasting methods reduce avoidable error: Evidence from forecasting competitions. *Foresight* 32, 34–39.

Nahmias, St. (1994). Demand estimation in lost sales inventory systems. *Naval Research Logistics* 41 (6): 739–757.

Schubert, S. (2012). Forecastability: A new method for benchmarking and driving improvement." *Foresight* 26, 5–13.

Tonetti, B. (2006). Tips for forecasting semi-new products. *Foresight* 4, 53–56.

3.2 A CLASSIFICATION OF BUSINESS FORECASTING PROBLEMS*

Tim Januschowski and Stephan Kolassa

While we have many taxonomies of forecasting methods, Januschowski and Kolassa present a taxonomy of forecasting problems in modern industrial settings. They classify forecasting problems into three categories: operational, tactical, and strategic. This taxonomy aligns with the typical spectrum of corporate activities, where the strategic level is concerned with long-lasting effects, tactical decisions are roughly quarterly to once per year, and the operational level refers to day-to-day decisions.

To understand the distinctions among the three categories, they define a number of dimensions of a forecasting problem. These include the forecast horizon, time, and product/location granularity, scale, latency requirements, users of the forecasts, the form of the forecast, and data characteristics and drivers of the variable to be forecast.

The authors also identify a number of publicly available data sets with the potential to assist in benchmarking performance in strategic, tactical, and operational forecasting.

Even though different teams and systems may deal with the different forecasting problems, the problems are connected. Interactions between operational, tactical, and strategic forecasting are complex and difficult to understand, and most organizations erroneously assume independence between these problems, ignoring the interactions. Such a classification can help decision makers understand what resources to draw upon when facing a particular problem and may lead to more scientific discourse about the relevant data sets for benchmarking forecasting performance.

Introduction

The field of business forecasting enjoys a rich set of applications. In this article, we discuss the range of applications and offer criteria for deciding whether to work on a problem yourself or to suggest it to other people with a better skill set. Of course, many of you won't have the luxury of turning a problem down or referring it to someone else; we still think you'll find our discussion of required skill sets pertinent. Ultimately, our classification assists in determining which methods to choose. Our criteria are those we've found useful in our daily work as forecasting researchers and consultants.

Let's start by clarifying terminology and defining the scope of this discussion.

The term "forecasting" is an ambiguous, overloaded word that evokes rich and differing mental images. Outside the *Foresight* audience, the word can be used synonymously with "predicting" or "predicting the future." In this article, we restrict ourselves to the case where forecasting means predicting the future values of a time series, be it an input time series to a model or the outputs of the forecast model.

---

*This article originally appeared in *Foresight: The International Journal of Applied Forecasting* (Winter 2019) and appears here courtesy of the International Institute of Forecasters.

We approach forecasting problems with a focus on algorithmic, quantifiable solutions. This means that we do not consider forecasting problems that call for psychological and judgmental approaches or mixtures of judgmental and algorithmic approaches. One example where judgment is important is in forecasting for events that occur for the first time. But algorithmic approaches may still be useful if similar events have occurred in the past.

We consider only forecasting problems that occur in business and industrial contexts. Demand forecasting is a subset of such forecasting problems, as are large-scale supply forecasting or electricity price or load forecasting. We exclude weather forecasting, stock price predictions, and election predictions.

In a business setting, forecasting is usually just a means to an end. For example, for demand forecasting in a retail grocery context, the forecast may be used to make inventory management decisions and is therefore typically an input to a decision problem, which in turn may be modeled as an optimization problem. The close relationship between a forecasting and a decision problem may be one aspect where business forecasting differs from weather and election forecasting. Other business forecasting problems include capacity forecasting of servers or forecasting demand for raw materials in a manufacturing context. These forecasts may be used as inputs for other processes, either for decision problems as above, or for scenario simulations, which are then used for planning without explicit models. However, there are exceptions to the rule that forecasting is not an end in itself: in financial forecasting, for example, the forecast is used directly to build up financial reserves or is presented to investors.

We propose to classify forecasting problems into three categories: operational, tactical, and strategic. The difference between operational and strategic will be immediately clear, and we use the tactical category to cover the area in between these two. Our taxonomy aligns with the typical spectrum of corporate activities, where the strategic level is concerned with long-lasting effects, tactical decisions are roughly quarterly to once per year, and the operational level refers to day-to-day decisions (Simchi-Levi, Kaminsky, and Simchi-Levi 2007).

We use our classification to derive conclusions regarding the forecasters and their skills, as well as the methods and the software needed to address their problems. This should help decision makers narrow down their search for experts and software and enable them to ask the right questions about their forecasting problem.

Dimensions of the Classification

We see a number of useful dimensions for the classification (Syntetos et al. 2016). After listing the dimensions, we'll use them to distinguish the characteristics of strategic, tactical, and operational forecasting. We'll also describe the typical decision-making problems associated with each level.

Forecast Horizon, ranging from short term to long term. These, of course, are relative to the frequency of the data: in a daily time series, a forecast for more than a few weeks into the future may be considered long term.

Time and Product/Location Granularity. While raw data on retail sales typically come in the form of time-stamped transaction-log data (e.g., a single line on a supermarket sales slip), these are usually too fine-grained and thus sales are aggregated to hourly, daily, weekly, monthly, quarterly, or yearly time buckets. Product granularity can vary from SKU/location all the way up to overall brand or product family. In general, the longer the forecast horizon, the more sense it makes to aggregate up.

Scale, the number of time series, from very few (e.g., overall revenue, or revenue split geographically) in strategic applications to numerous SKUs in product-demand forecasting. Large-scale forecasting typically requires more automation.

Latency Requirements. We can differentiate between on-demand and batch forecasting. The former can be useful for pull processes such as promotion planning in which different price points and tactics will be considered. Here the analyst needs to run multiple forecasts and cannot be expected to wait longer than a few seconds for forecasting results, so the latency (delay in receiving) of the forecast computation must be low. On the other hand, batch forecasting for replenishment can involve thousands of SKUs at hundreds or even thousands of stores, and it may be acceptable for a single batch-forecasting run to take hours. As a consequence, batch forecasting is run typically on schedules of relatively low frequency (e.g., daily or weekly), whereas on-demand forecasting can be run reactively and frequently.

Consumers of Forecasts. There are a number of typical consumers of forecasts. They may be systems in highly automated settings (e.g., automated buying or replenishment systems), or they may be people, such as executive decision makers, who need to make long-term investment decisions or who are interested in what-if scenarios. When there is a high degree of automation, we can expect the usage of forecasts to be well defined and stable over time, whereas a high degree of human interaction typically leads to changing requirements and usage of the forecast.

Characteristics of the Time Series. Time series can come in a wide variety. In typical industrial applications, they are non-negative valued (in some rare cases, e.g., for product returns or returns of deposit bottles, negative values may make sense – but here, we can usually just flip the signs, since *positive* values don't make sense), counts (e.g., product demand), or rates (values between zero and one). The characteristics range from short, bursty/lumpy, and sparse/intermittent to regular.

Drivers. Different time series have different drivers that need to be included in models as explanatory variables or time-series components, such as promotions, seasonality, calendar events, and weather.

Form of Forecast. That is, point forecast, prediction interval, or density forecast. Some planning processes require a single-number forecast, typically the conditional expectation. Others need a prediction interval or a quantile forecast. If our goal is a specific service level, we are less interested in a mean forecast and far more interested in the probability of demand exceeding the level that will cause service problems. Yet other consumers, such as sophisticated stochastic optimization algorithms, may require a full predictive density.

Notable Omissions. Note that we do not consider certain aspects that are *consequences* of the taxonomy rather than *dimensions* of it. Examples include the methods to be used for the forecasting problem, the software components, architectures, systems or services that could be deployed, or the skill set of the forecasting team – different forecasting problems require different combinations of statistics or econometrical expertise, business knowledge, programming skill (where "programming" is shorthand for many operations performed on IT equipment, from R hacking over efficient SQL querying up to setting up and running distributed computing environments such as Spark), and, often as important, skill in presentation to and working with colleagues whose talents and abilities are more nontechnical. We see all these as consequences of the taxonomy and will discuss them below.

Strategic Forecasting

A quintessential forecasting problem in most large enterprises is that of *revenue forecasting*. Such forecasts are used to assess questions around cash flow, topology planning (e.g., location of store branches), and market/segment entrance/exit decisions. They are also used to communicate with investors. Other strategic forecasting problems include the trends in long-term energy consumption.

Forecast horizon: Long term, possibly many years into the future.

Granularity: The time series for these forecasts are typically highly aggregated with respect to time, product, and location. For example, in Figure 3.1, we see weekly shipments aggregated over many products and locations. While the time dimension is not highly aggregated in this example, the other dimensions are.

Scale: A handful of time series at most.

Latency: Long. Entire strategic-planning departments may labor for weeks over such a forecast.

Consumers of forecast: Strategic forecasts are directed mainly at people who do ad hoc business calculations and modeling. They may be executives or middle management with limited executive power but who are supported by teams of analysts.

Drivers: Trend, seasonality, calendar events, macroeconomic variables.

Characteristics of time series: Due to the high degree of aggregation, these are normally regular time series. The units may be counts (e.g., number of product sales), but typically such high counts that we do not need to model counts explicitly but can use methods for continuous data.

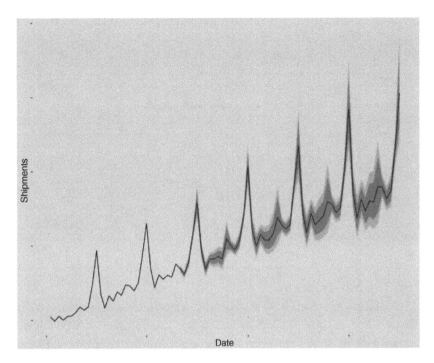

Figure 3.1 Revenue from Product Shipments
The black line denotes the actuals and the shaded regions denote prediction intervals. Data are weekly and the forecasts are for multiple years into the future.

Form of forecast: Point forecasts. Prediction intervals may be resisted because some executives are uncomfortable with the uncertainty implied by prediction intervals and prefer the illusion of certainty implied by point forecasts.

Tactical Forecasting

Our definition of tactical forecasting encompasses promotion planning, which we discuss in detail below. Forecasting for labor and computer-hardware requirements fall into this bucket as well.

Retailers and CPG manufacturers regularly run promotions, during which specific SKUs or entire brands are marketed. Prices are often reduced as well. Promotions cost money: on the one hand, reduced prices eat into margins, and even if prices stay at their regular level, the increase in demand will disrupt the supply chain. Retailers and suppliers typically share the costs of a promotion. In order to budget, we need forecasts for promotional demand.

Figure 3.2 shows daily SKU × store sales with promotional tactics. You can see there are widely varying promotion uplifts. (What is your forecast for the promotion at the end of 2017?)

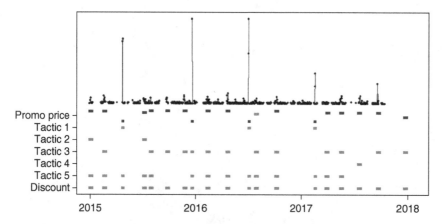

Figure 3.2 Sales for a Promoted Product

Forecast horizon: Three to six months.

Granularity: Prices and promotions are typically identical at all stores within a region, so it makes sense to model and forecast price and promotion sensitivity for this regional aggregate of stores. In terms of product granularity, forecasts are typically calculated for entire brands, since marketing campaigns are mostly conducted on brand level. Retail store layouts may be planned on a (sub-)category level, and supplier negotiations may encompass multiple brands and/or (sub-)categories. (An example of a category might be "dairy products," while a subcategory might be "yogurt.")

Note that promotional forecasts will again need to be broken down to SKU × store level to actually plan the promotional stocks per store. In terms of time, promotional forecasts would normally be calculated in weekly buckets.

Scale: A few brands.

Latency: Each plan may require multiple forecast runs with different scenarios in terms of price points or promotional tactics: should the promotion be communicated via app vs. newspaper ads, via endcaps vs. shelf tags, should it be a simple temporary price reduction or credit additional frequent shopper points, etc. Analysts cannot be kept waiting while their scenarios are being forecasted, so predictions must be calculated at the press of a button.

Consumer of forecast: People such as category managers who negotiate terms with suppliers based on promotion plans and forecasts. Sometimes (semi)automatic electronic data interchange (EDI) systems will translate forecasts into orders to suppliers.

Drivers: Historical promotions and prices, cannibalization, trend and seasonality.

Characteristics of time series: Due to the high degree of aggregation, the time series may be regular with high numbers, perhaps counts (e.g., number of product sales) though with step changes during promotions. Typically, counts are high enough that we do not need to model counts explicitly but can use methods for continuous data. However, series may also be zero during part of the year in the case of seasonal products.

Form of forecast: As with strategic, point forecasts with some reliance on prediction intervals: some planners do understand the uncertainty involved and wish to portray and plan for it.

Operational Forecasting

Operational forecasting problems encompass demand forecasting in the retail sector as well as short-term energy consumption (and production) forecasting.

The most prominent problem at Amazon is product-demand forecasting, illustrated in Figure 3.3, in which metadata such as product descriptions and images as well as past sales are used to estimate the future demand. A good forecast enables automated buying decisions (how many units to order when, or when to liquidate stock – and if so, at what price point).

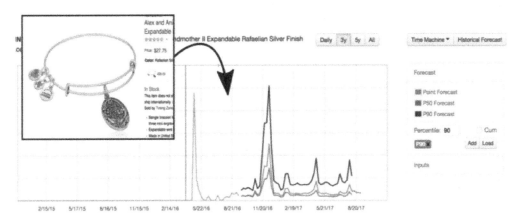

Figure 3.3 Product Demand Forecast for Amazon Retail Offerings

Forecast horizon: Depending on the product, this could be days (for grocery) to weeks.

Granularity: SKU at distribution center (DC), daily and weekly. Sales occur on the SKU level, which is also the granularity upon which we need to make distribution and replenishment decisions. This also applies to, say, fashion retailers who may need to cross-ship product near the end of the season to consolidate stocks in specific stores at minimal cost. Conversely, replenishment in the DC needs forecasts of total demands across all stores served by this DC.

Scale: Thousands, even millions, of time series – truly a big data problem.

Latency: Forecasts are generated every day for all SKUs for which we need to make a replenishment decision. Assuming one order day per week, this means that one-seventh of the entire assortment should be forecast every day. For a retailer like Amazon with millions of SKUs, this means that hundreds of thousands of forecasts need to be calculated – so each one can take only a strictly limited amount of time.

Consumer of forecast: Forecasts feed automatic replenishment systems, with limited degree of human interaction (exception based, on aggregate level or on flagship SKUs).

Characteristics of time series: Can be some of the most difficult time series to forecast because of lumpiness, life cycles, and obsolescence.

Drivers: Prices, competitor actions that may be matched, seasonality, promotional activities, markdowns. Intraweekly seasonality is important for fast-moving products in brick-and-mortar stores, with typically higher sales on Friday/Saturday than during the rest of the week, and similarly for aggregated store-level data. It is less important for slow movers. Intrayearly seasonality, calendar events, and weather are important for certain categories, e.g., fresh items or ice cream.

Form of forecast: The entire forecast distribution. Replenishment needs to cover multiple days, so we need high quantiles of sums of forecasts, for which the entire distribution is required.

Publicly Available Data Sets

Publicly available example data sets for forecasting are hard to come by. This is because the underlying data are among the most sensitive available to a company.

Arguably, the best-known public data sets for forecasting come from the Makridakis (or M) competitions, especially the M3 and the M4 competitions (Makridakis and Hibon 2000; Makridakis et al. 2018). These data sets might appear to be useful for benchmarking forecasting methods, but we find they are not representative of many problems we have seen in practice. They lack metadata, accompanying data, environmental information, absolute time stamps (corrected in an addendum to the M4 competition), and practical complications such as missing values.

For strategic forecasting problems, variations of financial or macroeconomic time series can be used, and a popular time series is the Australia beer production (Hyndman and Athanasopoulos 2018).

For tactical forecasting problems, one interesting publicly available data set is a subset of the tourism data set (https://robjhyndman.com/publications/the-tourism-forecasting-competition/) because it contains a number of related time series together with exogenous variables in various degrees of aggregation by time.

On the nexus of tactical and operational forecasting problems are some of the Kaggle data sets, such as Rossmann's, Walmart, and Favorita's store sales (https://www.kaggle.com/datasets).

For operational forecasting problems, there's the Dominick's data set, although more for marketing research (https://www.chicagobooth.edu/research/kilts/datasets/dominicks); an IRI data set (https://www.iriworldwide.com/en-US/solutions/Academic-Data-Set); and electricity (http://archive.ics.uci.edu/ml/index.php). It is also possible to use Wikipedia page traffic. They all contain a number of related (target) time series and many practical complications such as missing values and metadata. All the aforementioned data sets come with licensing issues, in particular for commercial uses.

Consequences: People, Skills, Methods, and Software

Our problem-oriented taxonomy seeks to allow decision makers to gain an intuitive understanding of the forecasting space with which they are faced and to narrow down the search for people, skills, methods, and systems.

Strategic forecasting problems are long-term forecasts with few time series. Because of the long-term nature of the forecasts, purely data-driven methods (such as deep neural networks) may not suffice; there may not be sufficient data to train them or to conduct back tests, and it may be hard to enforce assumptions about the nature of trends (e.g., that exponential trends will not go on forever).

If purely data-driven methods are inadequate, a model-based approach is necessary. Here we can be transparent about the assumptions made and can deal with critical questions about causality and significance of the model effects (in-data fits). Interpretability is often a key requirement for strategic forecasts, which is a research challenge in purely data-driven models such as neural networks (and hard in general even for simple models).

Model-based forecasting requires econometric and statistical skills, but less so software engineering and machine-learning skills. Also, the exact nature of the forecasting problem may change over time, which demands a highly flexible approach to modeling and to systems, at the expense of potentially less rigor in reproducibility and code quality.

Econometricians and statisticians are typically well qualified from the modeling perspective, as may be machine-learning scientists who have a strong expertise in statistics and/or probabilistic modeling. However, data scientists are typically less so, given their usual emphasis on pragmatic solutions with less regard for theory. (We distinguish machine-learning scientists from data scientists here, where the former invent new methods and the latter use existing methods.) Since the system constraints are minimal due to the size and nature of the data, conventional prototyping tools are often sufficient.

Operational forecasting problems are short term and must deal with lots of time series without much human interaction. Often, adequate historical data are available, so data-driven methods can be used and are present in all forecasting solutions. Since there is little human interaction, interpretability is not quite as important, so black-box models such as Deep Learning (Januschowski et al. 2018) models can be used, assuming these are accepted by the user. However, if black-box methods are used, it is crucial to be able to give insights upon human inspection as to why something went wrong and about how to address any problems. Furthermore, for black-box models, it is necessary to replace careful human monitoring by machine monitoring. For example, it may be advisable to define dynamic thresholds such that if forecasts exceed a certain limit, a system could automatically send it for human inspection.

Given the scale of operational forecasting, software development skills and expertise in data-driven methods are required. Such skills are often associated with machine learning, but this is a loose term. Certainly, software engineering skills are necessary if the amount of data exceeds the storage capacity of a single server and if a high degree of automation is involved. In addition, data scientists or analysts may be needed to help scale the operations of the forecasting system by supporting the business functions. Depending on the scale, companies may opt to outsource this problem to professional vendors – like SAP or BlueYonder/JDA – and long-term consulting, or build in-house solutions, e.g., Uber or Amazon (Böse et al. 2017).

Tactical forecasting problems – for promotion, hardware, and labor planning – fall in between the two buckets. Depending on the concrete problem or family of problems, a careful evaluation is needed to understand how much customization will be required over time and how volatile the data and problem specifically is. This will determine the skill and system mix drawing from the family of people, systems, and methods useful for strategic and operational forecasting problems.

Apart from these hard facts, it is important to note that soft skills are of varying importance for strategic, tactical, and operational forecasting problems. If the consumers of the forecasts are human decision makers and not computer systems, the ability to communicate the forecasts effectively becomes more important. Also, it requires communication skills to understand and model the forecasting problem and to incorporate human judgment into the algorithmic solutions.

Is there a natural ordering in which the four consequences discussed – people, skills, methods, and software – should be addressed? For instance, would it make sense to first decide on the methods to be used to address a forecasting problem, then select software as informed by the methods chosen, derive the necessary skills to implement the methods and operate the software, and finally hire the people possessing these skills?

While such a sequence makes intuitive sense, following it will usually not be practical. To actually understand which methods to use, we already need a basic understanding of forecasting, so we need skills "before" methods. And to analyze which forecasting/ML/data-science skills we need, we already need people who have the basic skills to hold this conversation. Also, any existing business already has software in place, and how well a proposed new forecasting solution integrates with the existing Enterprise Resource Planning (ERP) system is as much a factor in the selection as which methods it supports. We thus have a forecasting chicken-and-egg problem that will in practice be addressed iteratively.

As a closing remark, we want to alert our readers that even though different teams and systems may deal with the different forecasting problems, the problems are connected. The operational forecasting problem for product demand is connected to the tactical problem of promotion planning and to the strategic problem of revenue forecasting. Interaction between the operational, tactical, and strategic forecasting is so complex and difficult to understand that most organizations assume independence between these problems and ignore the interaction.

References

Böse, J.-H., Flunkert, V., Gasthaus, J., et al. (2017). Probabilistic demand forecasting at scale. *Proceedings of VLDB* 2017.

Januschowski, T., Gasthaus, J., Wang, Y., Rangapuram, S. S., and Callot, L. (2018). *Deep learning for forecasting: Parts 1 and 2, Foresight 50 and 51 (Summer and Fall).*

Makridakis, S., Spiliotis, E., and Assimakopoulos, V. (2018). The M4 Competition: Results, findings, conclusion and way forward. *International Journal of Forecasting* 34, 802–808.

Makridakis, S., and Hibon, M. (2000). The M3-competition: Results, conclusions and implications. *International Journal of Forecasting* 16, 451–476.

Simchi-Levi, D., Kaminsky, P., and Simchi-Levi, E. (2007). *Designing and managing the supply chain: Concepts, strategies and case Studies* (3rd ed.). McGraw Hill.

Syntetos, A. A., Babai, Z., Boylan, J. E., et al. (2016). Supply chain forecasting: Theory, practice, their gap and the future. *European Journal of Operational Research* 252, 1–26.

3.3 JUDGMENTAL MODEL SELECTION[*]

Fotios Petropoulos

Despite the rich literature on forecasting with judgment, one area that has attracted little attention is that of using judgment to choose between different statistical models. This is surprising, since modern forecasting support systems allow the user to either select a model manually or press the automatic button for the system to choose. Now, Fotios Petropoulos addresses this gap in the literature. He demonstrates that the application of judgment to the selection of a forecasting model can improve forecast accuracy, and presents the conditions where this is most likely to be the case.

The application of judgment to the model selection process has intrinsic appeal: it allows forecasters to make a mental extrapolation of what a reasonable forecast should look like and hence reject models that produce unreasonable forecasts. Additionally, by participating in the model selection process, forecasters are better able to "own" the forecasts, thus limiting unnecessary judgmental adjustments.

In order to see how effectively judgment can be applied to the selection of forecasting models, a sample of 700 users was presented with a pair of user interfaces: one in which users were shown a list of model options and told to go through these options and select one model, and another in which the users were asked whether or not trend and/or seasonal patterns exist in the data. Results based on the MAPE suggest that both groups of participants perform much better on average than the automatic statistical algorithm.

Petropoulos found that a 50-50 combination of judgmental selection with the statistical algorithm and judgmental aggregation of the selections of multiple users are both strategies that result in superior performance to statistical and judgmental selection. These findings are then expanded up by four commentaries.

[*]This article originally appeared in *Foresight: The International Journal of Applied Forecasting* (Summer 2019) and appears here courtesy of the International Institute of Forecasters.

Forecasting with Judgment

In his featured talk "Forecasting without Forecasters" during ISF2013 in Seoul, Rob Hyndman was demonstrating how significant the progress has been in statistical forecasting algorithms. These algorithms can automatically identify, through information criteria, the best model within the exponential smoothing or ARIMA families. Even if I agree that advancements in automatic statistical forecasting are significant and allow for batch production of a large number of forecasts, I disagree with the statement that we should now forecast without forecasters.

As the oft-cited review paper from Lawrence and colleagues (2006) has shown, judgment plays a very important role in forecasting and is integrated into numerous stages of the forecasting process. Judgment may be used directly to produce point forecasts or prediction intervals or to adjust a statistical baseline forecast in the light of information that is not captured in the model (see, for example, the *Foresight* article by Fildes and Goodwin 2007). When judgment is used, there is evidence that its performance can be improved by timely and salient feedback as well as by aggregation (combining the judgments of different forecasters). In some cases, decomposition of a complex task into smaller, manageable subtasks can also help.

But despite the rich literature on forecasting with judgment, one area that has attracted little attention is that of using judgment to choose between different statistical models. This is surprising, since modern forecasting support systems allow the user to either press the magic button for the system to choose the model or to select a model manually. For instance, the commercial software ForecastPro offers an automatic model selection option called "expert selection," but also provides a user interface for selecting a specific model, such as single exponential smoothing or Holt-Winters. Additionally, SAP's ERP offers a manual model selection feature in its Advanced Planning and Optimization functionalities. Until recently, however, the empirical performance of judgmental model selection had not been investigated.

So to better grasp the difference in the mechanics between judgmental point forecasting, judgmental adjustment of a statistical baseline, and judgmental model selection, we can use a standard IQ question as an analogy (see Figure 3.4) in which the requirement is to logically define how the last of the four objects in a sequence should look. In the first instance (judgmental forecasting), we would be given a sequence of three boxes showing different patterns of dots and asked to fill in the blank fourth box. In the second instance (judgmental adjustment), we would be given the same sequence of three boxes together with a pre-filled fourth box and asked to make changes on the fourth box (if we felt they were needed) so that it better fits the sequence. In the third instance (judgmental model selection), we would be given four distinct options (a, b, c, and d), and asked which one of these should be the fourth box in the sequence.

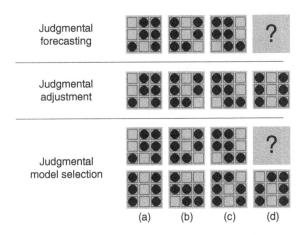

Figure 3.4 Forecasting with Judgment: An IQ Test Analogy

There are two reasons we would expect that judgmental selection of statistical models will work well. The first – and most important – is that forecasters, when visually exploring the forecasts from a pool of candidate models, can assess the quality of these forecasts by comparing them against a mental extrapolation of what a reasonable forecast should look like. This makes it possible for forecasters to reject models that produce unreasonable forecasts. In contrast, automatic statistical model-selection approaches can only assess the performance of the candidate models on historical data, by either measuring the penalized-for-overfitting goodness-of-fit or by evaluating the performance on a validation set.

Secondly, by allowing forecasters to participate in the model-selection phase of the forecasting process, such participation might fulfil their wishes of "owning" the forecasts, thus limiting unnecessary judgmental adjustments to the statistical forecasts (Fildes and Goodwin 2007).

Of course, biases associated with judgment, such as over-optimism and inconsistency, may still be present, but we expect their negative effect will decrease, as human input will be limited to a discrete number of (statistical) choices.

Exploring the Performance of Judgmental Model Selection

Along with three colleagues (Petropoulos et al. 2018) I ran an experiment to explore the performance of judgmental model selection. Our objectives were threefold:

- First, we wished to compare the performance of algorithmic/automatic versus human judgment selection of forecasting models and to determine if humans and algorithms select models differently.

- Second, we sought to understand when judgmental selection performs better.

- Third, we explored the performance of models that combine statistical and judgmentally selected models. Previous research has shown that both simple combinations of forecasts (50% statistics + 50% judgment) and judgmental aggregation (wisdom of crowds) have worked well in many situations. We felt it would be interesting to see if these strategies also work well for model selection.

Statistical Algorithm versus Human Judgment in Model Selection

We assumed that automatic statistical selection is done on the basis of information criteria, metrics such as Akaike's Information Criterion (AIC) or the Bayesian Information Criterion (BIC), that measure goodness of fit to past data adjusted to penalize model complexity. Overly complex models can see patterns in what are really random movements in data histories and then mistakenly extrapolate these patterns when producing forecasts. Use of information criteria is implemented in the very popular forecast package for R statistical software as well as in some commercial programs.

However, you could instead make an automatic model selection based on the out-of-sample performance of different models. Here, the available data are divided into fit and validation sets. Models are fitted using the first set, and their performance is evaluated in the second set. The model with the best performance in the validation set is put forward to generate forecasts for the future. The decision maker can choose the appropriate accuracy metric. The preferred metric can reflect the costs of any errors associated with the forecasts.

Model selection on out-of-sample performance has two advantages over selection based on information criteria. First, the performance of multiple step-ahead forecasts can be used to inform selection. Second, the validation approach is able to evaluate forecasts derived from any process (including combinations of forecasts from various models). The disadvantage of this approach is that it requires setting aside a validation set, which may not always be feasible, especially for short time series. Given that product life cycles are shortening, having a validation sample available can be a real luxury for forecasters.

Under What Conditions Does Judgmental Selection Perform Better?

To this end, we compared two user interfaces that presented users with a graph of a monthly time series over five years and the forecasts of a particular model for the following 12 months. The first, which we call *model selection*, simply provided candidate models as a list of options, and users could go through these options and select one. This is very similar to the default interface in the majority of modern forecasting support systems.

The second interface prompted the user to decide if the graphically displayed series exhibited a trend and/or seasonality, and on the basis of this decision a model was selected in the background. This interface we called *model-build* and is based on the principles of decomposition. The model-build interface also provides a trend and a seasonal plot of the in-sample data and supports the user in choosing the appropriate form of these components.

In both interfaces, a change in the selected model (directly in the case of the model-selection interface by clicking another radio button, indirectly in the case of the model-build interface by choosing the form of trend and seasonality) will automatically refresh the graph and the forecasts of the new model are displayed.

Figure 3.5 illustrates the two user interfaces. Both encompass the same four exponential smoothing models (level only, trended only, seasonal only, trended and seasonal) to allow for a direct comparison.

The Behavioral Experiment

We designed a behavioral experiment that was distributed via the Web and completed by almost 700 participants (students studying operations and/or forecasting, forecasting researchers, and forecasting practitioners) around the globe. Each of the participants was randomly assigned to one user interface, model selection or model-build, and was asked to apply judgment to select a model for each of 32 time series that exhibited a variety of characteristics (trend and seasonality). Subsequently, their judgments were compared against the automatic statistical selections.

Algorithms versus Judgment

To rate the performance of individuals in judgmentally selecting forecasting models, we assigned a score of 3, 2, 1, or 0 points each time they respectively selected the best, second-best, third-best, or worst of the four models. The rank of each model was decided after comparing their forecasts to the actual future data. The points for each participant were summed to get a total for the 32 time series and then were standardized into a 0–100% scale. The results are shown in Figure 3.6.

The standardized performance score for each participant is represented by a point in the left panel of Figure 3.6. Scores for forecasting practitioners are depicted with black dots and all other participants with grey dots. The horizontal dashed line is the comparable score of the automatic statistical selection (based on the AIC). The middle and right panels show the percentage of times the best, second-best, third-best, and worst models were selected for each user interface. In each case, we summarize the results using boxplots, where the horizontal boundaries of the boxes are the quartiles and the horizontal bold line within the boxes is the median.

We offer these key conclusions:

▪ The performance of different participants significantly varies, even within the same user interface. The range for the model-build scores spans between 32% and 83%. This means that some participants significantly outperform the automatic statistical selection (which scored 65%), while others fall far short.

▪ On average, participants using the *model-build interface* are as good as the automatic model selection. The performance of participants using the *model selection interface* was inferior.

▪ If we compare the black dots (practitioners) with the grey dots (all other participants), we cannot observe any significant difference in performance. This is supported by formal statistical tests. This result is supportive of the recruitment of students for behavioural experiments on time-series forecasting.

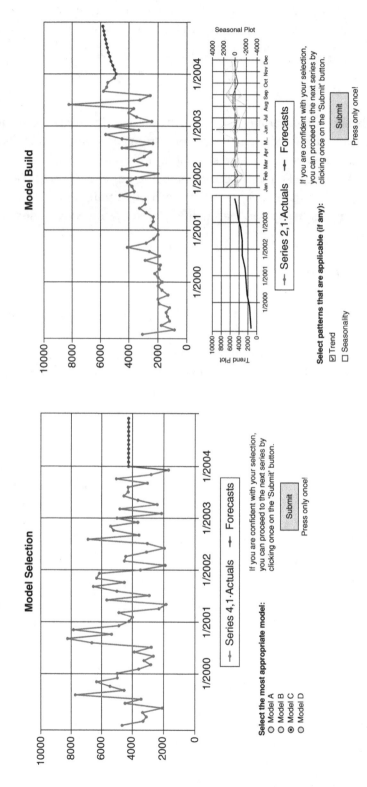

Figure 3.5 Two Interfaces Source: Adopted from Petropoulos and colleagues, 2018.

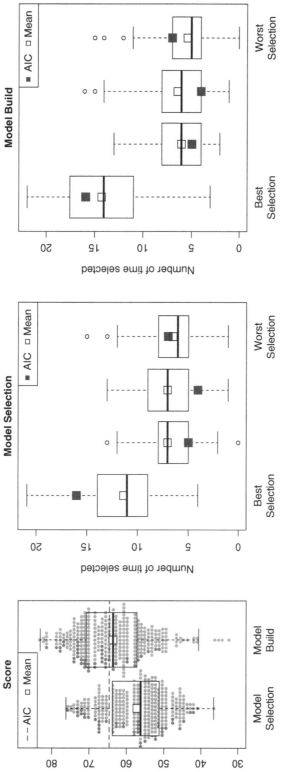

Figure 3.6 Performance of Individual Judgmental Model Selection Source: Adopted from Petropoulos and colleagues, 2018.

▪ From the middle and left panel of Figure 3.6, we see that humans select the best model less frequently than the algorithm does. This is particularly true for participants assigned to the model-selection interface. At the same time, however, humans succeed in avoiding the worst model more often than the algorithm did. Apparently, when humans visually explore the forecasts from different models, they are able to reject the most unreasonable models, performing the mental evaluation of what constitutes a reasonable extrapolation. This is an exciting result and should stimulate more research into how automatic model selection can incorporate mental extrapolations.

▪ We also compared the forecast accuracy of the judgmental model selections versus that from the automatic model selection. The accuracy metrics used were the mean absolute percentage error (MAPE) and the mean absolute scaled error (MASE). Results based on the MAPE suggest that participants using either interface, model selection or model-build, perform much better than the automatic statistical selection on the average. Results based on the MASE match the observations of the percentage score presented above (for a description of the MASE, see Hyndman, 2006). Even if humans are not always able to pick the best model, the avoidance of bad models is crucial with regards to average forecast accuracy.

Combined Judgment and Statistical Models

We tested the *combined performance* of automatic model selection and judgmental model selection in this way:

> If a participant selected a model that differed from that based on the automatic selection, then the forecasts of the two models were combined with equal weights.

This 50%-50% combination resulted in forecasting performance superior to both automatic statistical selection and individual judgmental selection. In fact, when the judgmental selection of each individual is combined with the statistical selection, the performance for 90% of the participants is better (in terms of MASE) than simply using the automatic statistical selection. Additionally, a 50%-50% combination brings robustness in the sense that the variance in the performance between subjects is halved.

The Wisdom of Crowds

We also examined the performance of groups of participants (wisdom of crowds) by aggregating participants' model selections. For example, assume that we randomly select 5 participants from our sample of almost 700. As these 5 might have selected different models for each series, we calculated the weighted forecast combinations of their chosen models by assigning linear weights to the forecasting models: the more often a particular model was selected, the higher the weight. Consequently, we can calculate the MASE across series. We repeated this for 1,000 groups of 5 participants each, with re-sampling. We also assessed the sensitivity of the results to the size of the groups, considering groups from 1 to 50 participants.

The results for the model-build interface are presented in Figure 3.7 in the form of "boxplots." The horizontal axis shows the size of the group (number of experts). For a given group size, the curved black line represents the median performance, the dark-gray area represents the box of the boxplot (with its limits being the upper and lower quartiles), and the limits of the light-gray area show the maximum and minimum values of the MASE. The curved gray line presents the average performance for the wisdom of crowds using the model-selection interface.

In the same plot, we also present the statistical benchmark (straight black) and the average performance of the 50%-50% combination (straight light gray), as well as two additional simple benchmarks: random selection (black dashed line) and simple combination of all candidate models (straight dark gray). The results suggest that:

- Two experts are enough to outperform the statistical selection in 75% of the cases.

- Five experts will suffice to almost always outperform the statistical selection.

- The average performance and the variance in the performance across randomly sampled groups of experts are not noticeably improved when the selections of more than 20 experts are aggregated.

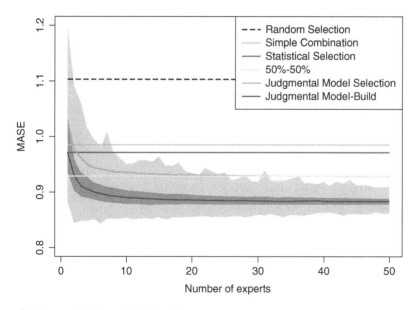

Figure 3.7 Summary of the Results

Why Model-Build Works Better

I participated in another research project (Han et al. 2018) that investigated the reasons behind the good performance of *model-build* compared to *model selection*.

We designed a process in which users were exposed to trended or nontrended series and then were asked to perform:

- Model selection: Select the forecasts from a nontrended (single exponential smoothing) or a trended (Holt's linear trend) exponential-smoothing model.
- Model-build: Decide if the presented series has a trend or not.

An innovative aspect of this experiment is that we managed to measure the cognitive effort that was required to perform each of the above tasks. This was achieved by applying a psychophysiological process – an electroencephalogram (EEG) – to capture the brain activity. The EEG records the changes in the electric potential in different regions of the scalp through a number of electrodes (small metal discs attached on wires). We focused on three particular changes in the electrical potential that the neuroscience literature has connected with attention and cognitive load and working memory.

The results from this research confirmed the empirical superiority of model-build and additionally showed that:

- Users require more time to submit their choices under the model-selection interface compared to the model-build.
- Model-build requires significantly less mental effort.
- Model selection is associated with increased working memory storage and retrieval.

Moreover, we found that, regardless of the user interface utilised, the superiority of judgmental model selection grows as the noisiness in the series decreases, the strength of trend increases, or the trend has a positive direction.

Implications for Software

New avenues are opening for the designers of forecasting software:

- Forecasting software should not only allow judgmentally selecting models but also encourage and support its application.
- Judgmental selections could be used independently, but we suggest that these should be combined with the automatic selections of the forecasting software.
- The superior performance of the model-build interface over the simpler model selection suggests that some changes need to be made in the way software guides users to manually select models. The adoption of the new model-build interface will also lead to a substantial decrease in the cognitive load of the users.

A big question is whether such an approach can be scaled, especially given that modern inventory settings may involve hundreds of thousands of stockkeeping units (SKUs). The simple answer is that we may not need to scale it if we simply focus on what matters: the most important and hard-to-forecast items. These would be the

AZ items in a standard ABC/XYZ classification, where ABC is the Pareto classification for importance (20% of the SKUs are classified as the most important, A; 50% as the least important, C) and XYZ the respective classification for forecastability (50% of the SKUs are classified as the most forecastable, X; 20% as the least forecastable, Z).

Final Comments

Judgmental model selection is a concept that has been insufficiently explored, despite the imposing fact that it is explicitly offered by major forecasting providers and widely exercised. This paper provided a summary of the results of the two published papers investigating this area. On balance, we can say that there is much potential for a model selection process informed by judgment, either in terms of combining judgmental and statistical selections or even by aggregating multiple judgmental selections.

And there are other unexplored opportunities for injecting judgment into the model selection, as summarized in Figure 3.8. Apart from selecting models, producing forecasts, and finalizing forecasts through adjustments, judgment could be potentially used to define a set of contender models (from the long list to the short list) and – why not? – to select the parameter values of the models, such as the smoothing parameters in the exponential-smoothing models.

The forecasting process

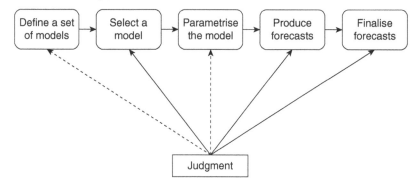

Figure 3.8 Judgment within the Forecasting Process

References

Fildes, R., and Goodwin, P. (2007). Good and bad judgment in forecasting: Lessons from four companies. *Foresight* 8 (Fall): 5–10.

Han, W., Wang, X., Petropoulos, F., and Wang J. (2018). *Brain imaging and forecasting: Insights from judgmental model selection. Omega: The International Journal of Management Science.* https://doi.org/10.1016/j.omega.2018.11.015.

Hyndman, R. J. (2006). Another look at forecast-accuracy metrics for intermittent demand. *Foresight* 4 (June): 43–46.

Lawrence, M., Goodwin, P., O'Connor, M., and Onkal, D. (2006). Judgmental forecasting: A review of progress over the last 25 Years. *International Journal of Forecasting* 22 (3): 493–518.

Petropoulos, F., Kourentzes, N., Nikolopoulos, K., and Siemsen, E. (2018). Judgmental selection of forecasting models. *Journal of Operations Management* 60, 34–46.

COMMENTARY: A SURPRISINGLY USEFUL ROLE FOR JUDGMENT

Paul Goodwin

Fotios Petropoulos and his research colleagues are to be congratulated on their innovative study. They have produced some exciting – and to me, surprising – findings about an important but neglected area of forecasting, namely the effectiveness of using judgment to choose between forecasting models. In an age when algorithms are playing an increasing role in our lives, it is interesting to see that judgment can still play a beneficial part in this crucial aspect of the forecasting process.

As Fotios's article mentions, we know that judgment can yield valuable inputs when point forecasts or prediction intervals are being estimated, especially when historic patterns are disrupted by special or changing conditions or there is a paucity of past data. In these tasks, however, judgment tends to be overused in practice and is frequently applied even when stable conditions and long data histories favor forecasts based on statistical methods.

The research literature in forecasting is brimming with examples of cognitive biases that can afflict judgmental forecasters. They have a tendency to place too much emphasis on the latest observation, are deceived by random patterns, underestimate trends, and tend to be too confident about their forecasts when considering the level of uncertainty they face in the future. When provided with statistical forecasts, judgment overrules them all too often or imposes unnecessary adjustments that damage accuracy (Fildes et al. 2009). So why should judgment typically perform so well when the task involves choosing between statistical models, rather than making the forecasts themselves?

One possibility is that the task draws the forecaster's attention to the big picture of how the data series has behaved over its entire history. This would seem to be particularly likely in the model-building task that Fotios describes where forecasters had to assess whether the history exhibited trends and/or seasonality. When making a forecast – as opposed to a choice between models – research suggests that a forecaster's focus tends to be directed predominantly to the most recent observations (e.g., Bolger and Harvey 1993). Like Henry Ford, who reputedly said that history "is more or less bunk," earlier observations are often discounted as irrelevant. Thus, in the model-choice task, forecasters may be availing themselves of all the useful information that lies in the full data history, while those making judgmental forecasts may be largely ignoring this information.

Despite the differences between judgmental forecasting and judgmental model choice, the results reported in Fotios's article have much in common with the findings of research in judgmental forecasting when it comes to improving the quality of judgments. These show that decomposing the judgmental task into a series of sub-tasks, such as identifying trends and seasonality, can lead to better choices. In judgmental forecasting, similar types of decomposition have been shown to lead to more accurate forecasts (e.g., Edmundson 1990). The human brain is limited in the amount of information it can process at any one time, so there are often gains to be made by focusing in turn on a series of simpler tasks, each dealing with a different aspect of the problem.

The results also show the benefits of combining the output of statistical algorithms with those of human judges. The finding that combining forecasts from diverse sources improves accuracy has been reported in a wide range of contexts (Blattberg and Hoch 1990; Goodwin 2009). Improved accuracy is thought to result partly because the different forecasting methods included in the combination draw on a wider range of information than a single method, or they draw on different aspects of the information. The same advantage appears to apply in model selection.

Averaging the judgments of different people can also lead to large accuracy gains, as James Surowiecki showed in his bestseller *The Wisdom of Crowds*; the results presented in Fotios's article reflect this. But, in common with judgmental forecasting research, these results indicate that you don't need large groups of people to make these big gains. Even if the forecasts of the people in the group are made independently, the gains tend to diminish by successively adding individuals to the group. If their forecasts are correlated, perhaps because they have access to the same information sources or have shared their views beforehand, the gains are likely to lessen even more quickly. In a classic study involving the forecasting of annual sales of advertising pages at *Time* magazine, it was found that there was little to be gained by averaging the forecasts of more than five executives (Ashton and Ashton 1985).

Overall, Fotios's article should provide reassurance to forecasters who choose which models to use rather than relying on the automatic selection of their software. But it also raises some interesting questions for future research:

- Is judgmental model selection beneficial when prediction intervals, as opposed to point forecasts, are being estimated?
- When people have selected the model themselves, are they less likely to tinker with, or even overrule, the model's forecast?
- Why are some people better at choosing the correct model than others? And can people learn to improve their model choice even further over time by learning through feedback?

References

Ashton, A. H., and Ashton, R. H. (1985). Aggregating subjective forecasts: Some empirical results. *Management Science* 31, 1499–1508.

Blattberg, R. C., and Hoch, S. J. (1990). Database models and managerial intuition: 50% model+ 50% manager. *Management Science* 36, 887–899.

Bolger, F., and Harvey, N. (1993). Context-sensitive heuristics in statistical reasoning. *The Quarterly Journal of Experimental Psychology Section A* 46, 779–811.

Edmundson, R. H. (1990). Decomposition: A strategy for judgemental forecasting. *Journal of Forecasting* 9, 305–314.

Fildes, R., Goodwin, P., Lawrence, M., and Nikolopoulos, K. (2009). Effective forecasting and judgmental adjustments: An empirical evaluation and strategies for improvement in supply-chain planning. *International Journal of Forecasting* 25, 3–23.

Goodwin, P. (2009). New evidence on the value of combining forecasts. *Foresight* (Winter): 33–35.

COMMENTARY: ALGORITHMIC AVERSION AND JUDGMENTAL WISDOM

Nigel Harvey

Fotios Petropoulos's article on judgment in model selection provides food for thought for researchers as well as potential new applications for practitioners. It has long been recognized that judgment is involved at every stage of the forecasting process, but Fotios is right to say that until very recently research has been restricted to pure judgmental forecasting and judgmental adjustment of statistical forecasts. Extending the scope of this work to the role of judgment in model selection is clearly worthwhile. For me, it raises a number of interesting questions.

What is it that makes forecasters choose manual model selection over automatic model selection in ForecastPro and other forecasting support systems? A number of papers have shown that people exhibit a degree of algorithm aversion (e.g., Dietvorst, Simmons, and Massey 2015). This reaction can be reduced by giving people some control over the outcome produced by the algorithm – for example, by allowing users to make judgmental adjustments to the algorithmically produced forecasts.

But why does this aversion exist in the first place? In a landmark article, Bainbridge (1983) argued that there are a number of "ironies of automation." People, for example, who are fully reliant on algorithms eventually forget the skills that enabled them to perform tasks without algorithms. New trainees may not even be taught those skills in the first place. And yet possessing those skills may be crucial when dealing with unusual versions of the task not covered by the algorithms: for example, the Airbus A320 fly-by-wire system was not sufficient to enable US Airways flight 1549 to ditch in the Hudson River – but fortunately, Captain Chesley "Sully" Sullenberger's well-maintained piloting skills were. People may be cautious about relying fully on algorithms because they have some intuition that such reliance can have disadvantages.

The research that Fotios describes shows that people select the best model less often than the algorithm but that their forecast accuracy is still superior to that of the algorithm. Most practitioners are primarily interested in their forecast accuracy rather than in whether they are able to discriminate the best from the second-best model. So does this mean that they should always choose manual model selection over algorithmic model selection?

In the experiments reported, judges selected between four exponential-smoothing models that are able to capture different data patterns (level, trend, seasonality, trend plus seasonality). The data series were selected so that each of the four models was identified as best for some of the series. Thus there appears to have been a reasonably good match between characteristics of the models that were available for selection and the characteristics of the data series for which they were selected.

If the models had been more heterogeneous (e.g., exponential smoothing, ARIMA, frequency domain approaches, etc.) and the data series more varied (e.g., containing trends, autoregressive and moving average components, fractal patterns with different Hurst exponents, etc.), selecting the best model may have been much more difficult, and accuracy of judgmental selection may have been reduced below that of algorithmic selection.

In combining judgment and statistical models, Fotios reports that performance of a 50%-50% combination was superior to performance of both judgmental model selection and algorithmic model selection. Previous work in other domains has also shown an advantage of equally weighing output of judgment and statistical models.

But we could also allow judges to select the weights. Would their selection of weights outperform the 50%-50% combination? I suspect not. If we put the judge in charge of deciding on the weights, we can think of the statistical output as advice to the judge that can be ignored (0% weight), totally adopted (100% weight), or allowed some influence. When people combine external advice with their own judgment, they tend to underweight it. Typically, they give the advice a weight of around 20–30% when performance would be improved by giving it a higher weight.

Fotios provides us with a powerful example of the "wisdom of crowds" effect. As he points out, it does not require aggregation of many experts' judgments to produce an impressive improvement in forecast accuracy. How useful is this information for practitioners? When forecasting is the responsibility of a group, it would be relatively straightforward to obtain a model selection from each group member and then to aggregate the resulting forecasts.

However, when forecasting is the responsibility of an individual, there may be all sorts of reasons why that individual might find it difficult or undesirable to recruit additional forecasters. In such a case, the application of the "wisdom of crowds" approach might appear to be out of the question. However, it would still be possible to use the "wisdom of the inner crowd" (van Dolder and van den Assem 2018).

Similar advantages to aggregating estimates from different people can be obtained by aggregating repeated estimates from a single person. Thus if someone has to produce a set of, say, 50 forecasts by selecting an appropriate statistical model from each one, an accuracy improvement would be expected from doing the task twice and aggregating the results. Obviously, it would be sensible to minimize the chances that the model chosen in the second round of forecasting was simply the one that the forecaster remembered using for that series in the first round. This could be achieved by randomizing the order of the series before each round and leaving a reasonable interval between the two rounds.

References

Bainbridge, L. (1983). Ironies of automation. *Automatica 19*, 775–779.

Dietvorst, B. J., Simmons, J. P., and Massey, C. (2015). Algorithm aversion: People erroneously avoid algorithms after seeing them err. *Journal of Experimental Psychology: General* 144, 114–126.

van Dolder, D., and van den Assem, M. J. (2018). The wisdom of the inner crowd in three large natural experiments. *Nature Human Behaviour* 2, 21–26.

COMMENTARY: MODEL SELECTION IN FORECASTING SOFTWARE

Eric Stellwagen

Many thanks to Fotios Petropoulos for sharing his research on judgmental model selection. Having spent the last 35 years creating business-oriented forecasting software, I would like to offer a few thoughts on the implementation of model-selection algorithms in software.

Your Interface Matters

One of the author's primary findings is that users of the *Model Build interface* outperform users of the *Model Selection interface*, while at the same time expending less mental energy. Both interfaces provide the same four model choices, so why are the Model Build interface users consistently more successful?

The answer is simple – interface matters! The Model Build interface is superior to the Model Selection interface in three important regards:

1. It identifies how the models differ.
2. It provides more diagnostic information.
3. It simplifies the model-selection process.

When selecting a forecasting model, understanding the differences among the available models is essential. The four underlying exponential-smoothing models used in the study differ by whether or not they incorporate trend and/or seasonal components. The Model Build interface emphasizes the differences by explicitly labeling these components, while the Model Selection interface hides the differences by labeling the models generically as A, B, C, D. In addition, the Model Build interface provides graphs of the underlying trend and seasonal pattern and simplifies the model-selection process to answering two yes or no questions: "Is it trended?" and "Is it seasonal?"

Domain Knowledge Matters

Domain knowledge decreases uncertainty in the model-selection process. In a business setting, corporate forecasters often know a priori if the time series they are trying to forecast are trended, seasonal, promoted, price driven, etc., and this knowledge can (and should) factor heavily into the model-selection process.

In the absence of domain knowledge, combining forecasts is often a useful technique to mitigate risk and uncertainty. Petropoulos found combining forecasts to be a successful strategy, and this approach has also been found to be successful in other academic studies where domain knowledge was lacking (most notably the M competitions).

The Model Universe Matters

The model selection in the study is limited to choosing among four exponential-smoothing models, each unique in its treatment of the trend and seasonal pattern. This is an extremely limited model universe for business forecasters. Commercial forecasting software typically offers a much broader number of models from which to choose, many of them differing from one another in less distinct ways.

For example, the automatic expert selection algorithm in Forecast Pro selects from a model universe consisting of 13 exponential-smoothing models, hundreds of ARIMA models, three low-volume models, and six other forms of extrapolation. (Multivariate methods such as dynamic-regression models, event-index models, and others are also available but not considered by the expert selection algorithm.) Using a Model Build interface for a model universe this large would be impracticable because it would require forecasters to select among hundreds of models with subtly different treatments of components such as trend and seasonality.

The Statistical Algorithm Matters

The statistical algorithm in the study consists of selecting the model that minimizes the AIC. This is an extremely simplistic approach and would not work well with a larger and less homogeneous model universe. It's also what I refer to as a *stream-of-numbers* approach, wherein the statistical algorithm knows nothing about the data to be forecasted beyond the values in the time series.

State-of-the-art automatic model selection algorithms do more than minimize an information criterion or crown the winner of an out-of-sample tournament. Some allow forecasters to incorporate domain knowledge up front, in the form of business rules, or to specify known data characteristics (seasonality, promotions, etc.)

that help guide the automatic selection process. Others utilize expert systems or other AI concepts to recognize, respond to, and learn from specific situations.

At times these approaches will substantially outperform stream-of-number algorithms. When appropriate, they also allow two different forecasters *with identical time series* to generate substantially different forecasts. For example, let's say a time series exhibits a very substantial dip at the end of the historical data. If the automatic algorithm is trained to recognize this type of dip as the introduction of a competing product (say, a generic drug coming on the market), then the forecast will be much lower than if the algorithm was trained to recognize this type of dip as a temporary stockout.

Conclusions

Model selection is a critical step in the forecast-generation process and, as Fotios's research has illustrated, how the process is implemented by software designers has a direct impact on the quality of the forecasts that are created. Ideally, business forecasting software should offer the following functionality:

1. A carefully thought-out model universe that addresses all mainstream business needs.
2. A state-of-the-art automatic model-selection algorithm that provides solid baseline forecasts.
3. A well-designed interface for manually selecting models that organizes the available models by usage scenario (e.g., basic extrapolation, intermittent demand, promoted, new products, etc.), and that provides interactive diagnostic displays to aid the model-selection process.

EXPLOIT INFORMATION FROM THE M4 COMPETITION

Spyros Makridakis

More than 13 years have passed since Lawrence, Goodwin, and Onkal (2006) wrote their seminal paper on this subject, so the time has ripened for another influential publication on the role of judgment in forecasting. With his follow-up, Fotios Petropoulos has nicely filled the gap.

The author states that the purpose of the paper is to "use judgment to select the most appropriate statistical model." However, the article does much more than that, showing the critical importance of judgment in forecasting in that accuracy deteriorates with automatic forecasting selections – or, as he puts it, when "forecasting without forecasters" – and by demonstrating the value of combining more than one of the selected time-series models.

The author's main idea is that forecasting accuracy can be improved by aiding the decision maker in the task of selecting an appropriate model. He starts with the old notion of *decision support systems* – now more eloquently named *intelligence augmentation* – which is used in what he calls a *model build* interface. Here a user is shown information about the trend and/or seasonality in a time series, allowing the user to judgmentally select an appropriate model.

Subsequently, his major innovation is a survey of almost 700 participants from around the world to test his hypotheses empirically. His findings are significant and are bound to influence the practice of model selection when forecasting. More specifically, the survey found the following:

- The equally combined performance of automatic and judgmental model selection resulted in superior performance in both the automatic statistical selection and in the individual judgmental selection.

■ The "wisdom of the crowd" (averaging the performance of groups of participants) provided more accurate results than single participants did:
  ■ Two experts are enough to outperform the statistical selection in 75% of the cases.
  ■ Five experts will suffice to outperform, almost always, the statistical selection.
  ■ The average performance and the variance in such performance across randomly sampled groups of experts is not noticeably improved when the selections of more than 20 experts are aggregated.

Fotios's paper ends by providing the following suggestions to the designers of professional software packages:

■ Software designers should not only allow selecting models judgmentally, but should also encourage and support their application in order to improve forecasting accuracy.

■ Judgmental selections could be used independently. However, they should be also combined with the automatic selections allowed by forecasting software.

■ Software should guide users to select models manually, providing a model-build interface that would increase accuracy and lead to a substantial decrease in the cognitive effort of users to select appropriate forecasting models.

Finally, having been heavily involved with forecasting competitions, I would suggest to Fotios that he investigate the possibility that his model selection could be improved by exploiting information about the most accurate models for each category (domain and frequency) of data provided – for instance, using the 100,000 time series of the M4 Competition. Let's see if such information may further improve forecast accuracy.

Reference

Lawrence, M., Goodwin, P., and Onkal, D. (2006). Judgmental forecasting: A review of progress over the last 25 years. *International Journal of Forecasting* 22, 493–518.

3.4 A JUDGMENT ON JUDGMENT[*]

Paul Goodwin

Through his books, articles, and entertaining conference presentations, Paul Goodwin has kept practitioners informed about the critical research findings in forecasting. In this selection from his book *Forewarned: A Sceptic's Guide to Prediction,* Goodwin explores a variety of psychological issues relating to judgment, such as our innate vulnerability to find patterns in everything – even in randomness. Such vulnerability has direct negative impact on our abilities in time-series forecasting.

Goodwin covers other recognized issues, including selective memory, confirmation bias, anchoring, and our desire for tidy explanations – preferring a neatly packaged story to a more realistic account expressing all the requisite ambiguity. Throughout, it becomes apparent that business forecasting is much more than just an exercise in statistical modeling. Knowledge of the underlying psychological issues is one key to improving forecasting practice.

---

[*]Adapted from the book *Forewarned: A Sceptic's Guide to Prediction* (2017), Biteback Publishing, and appears courtesy of Paul Goodwin.

Patterns That Aren't There

Obesity is a major problem in many countries. In the United States more than two thirds of adults are considered to be overweight and obese. In the UK, between 1993 and 2013, there was almost a doubling of the proportion of men who were obese, and more than a 7 percent increase in the proportion of women (hscic.gov.uk, 2015). One explanation is that we have evolved to cope with a world where periods of abundance were followed by periods of famine. We needed to gorge ourselves when there was a surplus of food in order to survive the lean periods. But the problem begins when a good supply of food is constantly available, as we continue to stuff ourselves and grow fatter because food is never scarce. Our bodies aren't designed for this modern environment. Some people argue that the same applies to our minds.

Those sharp intuitive skills, which we honed in order to predict when we might be in danger from wild animals or where a harvest of luscious fruit might be found, don't always equip us for making accurate predictions in the modern world. Given the right circumstances these skills can still be astonishingly effective. However, there are also occasions when they can be seriously misleading.

One way we learned to survive was by searching for patterns in the world (Shermer 2011). A flock of birds suddenly taking flight with a cacophony of distress calls could be perceived as a sign that lions were around. Eating the leaf of a particular plant might be associated with stomachache. Performing a ritual before hunting might appear to increase the success of the hunt. While many of these apparent patterns might be illusory, disbelieving them usually carried more risk than choosing to believe them. Ignore the distressed birds and you risked being killed by a lion. Getting away quickly when there was no threat simply burned a few more calories. Thus our brains evolved to see patterns everywhere and to believe in these patterns whether they truly existed or not.

In the modern world our need to find patterns, and believe in them, has a cost – we can be seriously misled by randomness. Look closely at the graph below, which shows the monthly demand for a product. After studying the graph, I eventually began to see three underlying cycles in the demand, each lasting about six months – one from months 2 to 7, the second from months 8 to 13, and the third from about months 14 to 19. Within each of these cycles the demand rises to a peak and then declines. I began thinking about why this might be. Perhaps the product sells well in the summer and is sold in both Europe and Australia, so the six-month peaks coincide with summers in the northern and southern hemispheres. Perhaps the product is an alcoholic drink that sells well in the summer and also around the festive season. If you asked me to use my judgment to forecast the future demand, I'd probably try to extend the pattern I see in the graph by forecasting another six-month cycle that I would expect to end in the 25th month.

There's just one problem – the apparent 'demand figures' on the graph are actually random numbers generated by a computer. Rather like rolling a 100-sided die, the computer has produced a series of numbers between 1 and 100 where each number is independent of the others. There is no systematic pattern underlying the numbers at all so my forecasts based on the perceived cycle are likely to be well off target.

Not only are we adept at finding patterns where there are none, but we are also brilliant at inventing theories to explain these patterns. Stock market indices often follow random patterns, but watch any business programme on television and you'll find the commentators offer ready explanations for every small twist and turn in a graph – poorer than expected growth figures from China, the resignation of a leading CEO or good weather in California.

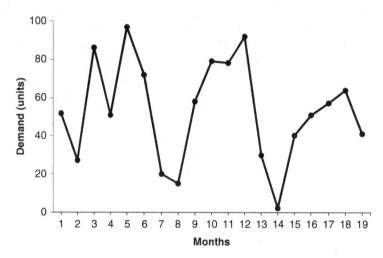

When our theories are challenged we are just as clever at embellishing them. I once sat in a forecasting meeting at a pharmaceutical company. The sales of a drug were slightly up on the previous month, but this was probably just one of those random twitches that we see in all sales graphs. 'I think,' said one of the managers, 'our customers are stocking up in anticipation of the forthcoming price increase.' 'But they didn't stock up last time they knew there was a price increase on the way,' retorted the accountant. 'Yes, but interest rates were high then so holding large stocks was expensive. Now they're lower there is an incentive to stock up,' replied the manager. Often, the very last thing we are prepared to do is admit that we don't know why a graph has gone up or down, or to admit to ourselves that it's just the effect of randomness. The Latin phrase *felix, qui potuit rerum cognoscere causas* – happy is he who understands the causes of things – is apt.

Our compulsion to find patterns means that even animals can outperform us when we encounter randomness. In one experiment, a rat was placed in a maze shaped like the letter T. At intervals, food was placed at the end of either the left 'arm' of the T or the right 'arm'. The sequence between left and right was random, but on 60 percent of occasions food appeared at the left side. The rat soon learned that the left side was more likely to deliver food and always went to that side, so its prediction was correct 60 percent of the time. When the sequence of left and right placements was shown to Yale University students, their large brains started searching for patterns. Perhaps after two right placements a left placement was more likely or perhaps after three lefts a right would nearly always follow. Of course, these perceived patterns were false. As a result the students only predicted the correct side 52 percent of the time. The rats were the more accurate forecasters (Tetlock 2005).

Admitting we don't know what's going on may be anathema, but so is contemplating the possibility we might be wrong. Once we've established a belief that a particular pattern exists we tend only to recall events which support that belief – a phenomenon known as illusory correlation. If some years ago I bought an unreliable car made by 'The Speedy Company', I might develop an inkling that all cars built by Speedy are unreliable. Every time I see a Speedy car broken down by the side of the road I sigh knowingly, and my belief is reinforced. But I have no recollection of all the other manufacturers' cars that I pass with their bonnets open, or of the hundreds of Speedy cars that zoom down the road taking their happy owners on yet another trouble-free journey. 'Don't buy a Speedy car', I tell my neighbour, 'I predict you'll have problems.' In fact, if I looked at the data, Speedy might be near the top of the league table for reliability. If we believe that Friday the 13th is unlucky, that the phone tends to ring more often when we're in the shower, that redheads are hot-tempered, or that Geminis are socially outgoing, then our experiences will probably only reinforce our beliefs.

Selectively recalling events is a passive process – events simply register with us more often when they conform to the pattern we believe in. But we also have a tendency to actively search for information that confirms our beliefs and downplay any disconfirming evidence. Psychologists refer to this as confirmation bias. Tony Blair and George W. Bush exhibited confirmation bias when they believed that Iraq had weapons of mass destruction (WMDs) in 2003 and decided to invade the country. Huge weight was placed on the evidence of Rafid Ahmed Alwan al-Janabi, an Iraqi defector codenamed 'Curveball', who claimed he had worked as a chemical engineer in a factory manufacturing biological weapons that were a part of Iraq's WMD programme. This was despite earlier misgivings that many intelligence agents had had about Curveball's claims. One suspected he was 'a lying alcoholic . . . trying to get his green card . . . and playing the system for what it was worth' (howtogetyourownway.com). The fact that United Nations weapons inspectors could find no WMDs was also discounted, and there was a rush to gather evidence to support the case for an invasion. Any information would do. This even included an American student's PhD thesis that was plagiarised in documents arguing the case for invasion. Even its typographical errors were transcribed and included in what became known as the 'dodgy dossier.' Of course, no WMDs were found.

Confirmation bias has also been found amongst executives who favour a merger between two firms (Bogan and Just 2009). They actively seek evidence of synergies between the two companies and highlight the forecasts of savings that will result. In contrast, little attention is paid to the costs the merger might incur – such as the costs of getting rid of excess production capacity. Information that provides strong indications the merger will be a failure is also discounted.

Most forecasts don't have the disastrous consequences of the Iraq War or even a failed merger when people get them wrong, but we should still be wary of confirmation bias. For the forecaster who believes they have found reasons for patterns in their data, confirmation bias serves only to intensify these beliefs. And if we've written down explanations for our thoughts then we're even more likely to stand by them, even as evidence that we're wrong mounts up. Michael Cipriano, now based at James Madison University in Virginia, and Thomas Gruca of the University of Iowa observed students who were engaged in prediction markets set up to forecast the success of movies. Those who were asked to write down the rationale for their initial forecasts tended to stick with them even when the latest box office information indicated they should rethink their initial prediction. Students who had not recorded their arguments were less resistant to the new information (Cipriano and Gruca 2015).

Stories Trump Numbers

Our skill at inventing theories to explain what are really random movements in graphs is symptomatic of our close relationship with stories. Stories have been used throughout history to hand down wisdom from one generation to another or to bring colour and meaning to advice about how we should live our lives. We often make sense of the world through stories. One study (Wagenaar 1994) found that when jurors had to decide on whether a defendant was innocent or guilty, they rehearsed stories of what might have happened to explain why the person was, or wasn't, involved in the crime and how it might have been committed. Our natural inclination toward narrative explanations means that when they clash with indications from numerical data, the story usually wins.

Imagine you are in a company forecasting meeting and the sales graph is showing a 10 percent increase in sales over the last month. You are told by the forecasting manager, who has a 'first' in Maths, that: 'a computer-based exponential-smoothing forecast indicates that the underlying trend in sales will remain flat, despite last month's high sales. The computer forecast is discounting the recent rise as a random blip.'

The marketing manager jumps in: 'last month we appointed a dynamic new young sales manager who has an MBA from the Harvard Business School. His energies seem to be endless. These results show that he is already working miracles with our sales. We can now expect a significant upward trend.'

Which account would you go with: the flat trend or the significant upward trend? There's evidence that, to most of us, the dull technical statistical forecast would offer no competition to the colourful inspiring story about the new manager. We would opt for the forecast of an upward trend. And this would be despite the evidence of only one month's sales.

The Perils of Imagination and Memory

Earlier we saw that we have a tendency to selectively recall events that support our belief that two things are correlated and forget about events that would disconfirm this belief. When we need to judge the probability of future events, such as a terrorist attack, being a victim of robbery or winning a lottery, we are likely to rely again on our memories. A few years ago neighbours of mine won a fortune on the national lottery. Soon there were shiny, new expensive cars in their driveway. Then fleets of vans arrived to fit their new kitchen, install a hot tub and build an ornamental fishpond. When I recall this, the chances that I'll win one day don't seem quite so slim. In cases like this, the ease with which we can recall similar events occurring in the past acts as our guide to the likelihood that they'll occur in the future. This is not necessarily a bad strategy. More frequent events are more easily recalled and also generally more likely to happen in the future. Most people would correctly give themselves a relatively high probability of suffering from a cold at least once in the next five years. Colds are common; we easily recall instances of ourselves or others having colds and they are likely to continue to be common in the future.

Problems arise when ease of recall is not related to the chances of an event occurring in the future. Some relatively rare events are easily recollected precisely because they were unusual. Or we do so because they were vivid or simply as they had occurred recently. As a result people tend to overestimate the probability of these events occurring again. One source of this bias is the media. Events are newsworthy because they are unusual or dramatic. An ordinary person dying as a result of a fall will not usually make the national news on television, but if they are savaged by a dog and die, the news cameras will soon be heading for the scene of the tragedy. As a result, the probability of being killed by a dog might seem to be higher than the probability of dying as a result of a fall. Yet in the United States in 2009, for example, the probabilities were one in 9 million and one in 15,000, respectively (National Safety Council). One study in the United States found that people thought deaths through homicide were more frequent than deaths from diabetes, and that tornados killed more people than asthma (Lichtenstein et al. 1978). In both cases the second cause of death was more common. Many people fear shark attacks, but in September 2015 the Huffington Post revealed that so far in that year more people had died worldwide trying to take selfies than from shark attacks. Attempts to take selfies had led to people falling down flights of stairs at the Taj Mahal, being gored by a bison in the Yellowstone National Park, and being hit by moving vehicles. News about an airline crash might make us fearful of flying. But spending time in our kitchens is much more dangerous.

Terrorists, in particular, exploit our tendency to overestimate the risk of dramatic or media-highlighted events occurring. Their terrible crimes are inevitably headline news and many people live in fear of being a future victim. Yet the probability of being physically harmed is extremely small. Despite this, predictions that they might be victims of terrorism can have a negative effect on people's enjoyment of their lives, such as their willingness to travel. In a 1993 study, people were asked how much they were willing to pay for life insurance to cover a flight to London. On average, they were willing to pay $14.12 for insurance that solely covered death resulting from a terrorist attack, but only $12.03 for insurance covering death for any reason (Johnson et al. 1993).

Chained to an Anchor

People can be too eager to spot trends that aren't there, but when there really is a trend, are we likely to be better at extrapolating it than a mathematical forecasting method? About 40 years ago, the psychologists Amos Tversky and Daniel Kahneman conducted a simple and now famous experiment, involving a group of individuals (Tversky and Kahneman 1974). The participants were asked to estimate the percentage of African countries that were members of the United Nations. But before they made their estimate, the experimenters spun a wheel of fortune, containing the numbers 0 to 100, to generate a random figure. Let's say the number 10 appeared. The participant was then asked whether the required percentage was higher or lower than the generated number. Next, they were asked to make their estimate by moving upwards or downwards from this number. Remarkably, the random number had a significant influence on the estimate. For example, those who saw the number 10 generated typically estimated that the percentage of African countries in the UN was 25 percent. Those who drew the number 65 typically estimated a figure of 45 percent. Once we have a number in our head it becomes what is known as an 'anchor.' Like the planet Jupiter, anchors have a large gravitational pull, which mean it's difficult to get away from them so the participants' estimates stayed close to the random number, even though it was irrelevant to the task. When I told my students about anchoring, some of them thought they'd spotted an opportunity. They wrote '99 per cent' in large characters at the front of their coursework in the hope that I'd anchor on this when deciding their mark.

Anchoring has been found in a huge variety of situations and it also appears to affect people when they make forecasts by eyeballing graphs that contain trends. It seems that they anchor on the most recent observation in the graph and then adjust from this to try and take into account the upward or downward trend. The problem is that the adjustment is usually insufficient so the effect of the trend tends to be underestimated. Study after study (Lawrence et al. 2006) has shown that, when graphs exhibit upwards trends, people's forecasts underestimate the rate of growth so the forecasts they make are too low. For downward trends, the problem is even worse and forecasts tend to be far too high.

A Pleasant Pension Surprise?

Most spectacular is our inability to use our judgment accurately to forecast things that are growing at exponential rates, such as populations, energy use or pollution. Many people have the same problem forecasting the growth in their savings when they are receiving compound interest. As a result, they tend to grossly under-forecast the amount of money they will have in their pension pot when they retire (McKenzie and Liersch 2011). In this case our inability to handle non-linear relationships may be the source of the bias. We are happier making predictions when numbers appear as a straight line if plotted from left to right on a graph, such as 2, 4, 6, 8, 10, 12 and so on. When numbers grow in a non-linear way, such as 2, 4, 8, 16, 32, 64 . . ., our predictions are usually much too low.

To illustrate this, assume that you have a sheet of A4 paper that is 0.193 mm (0.0076 inches) thick – dimensions that are fairly standard – and you can fold it 40 times. How thick do you think the folded sheet would be? Most people give answers such as one centimetre, or possibly, two. In fact, if we do the calculations we'll get 0.193mm × 2^{40} = 212,206 kilometres or 131,859 miles. That's more than half the distance to the moon. You might have argued that the sheet was impossible to fold 40 times in the first place because it would become too thick after about six folds. The answer shows that it would also be impossible without a ladder into outer space.

In a series of experiments Dutch psychologist William A. Wagenaar and his research colleagues found that intuitive judgment is hopeless when it comes to forecasting phenomena that are growing exponentially (Wagenaar and Sagaria 1975). The majority of people produced forecasts that were less than 10 percent of the actual value. Even people whose jobs involved dealing with exponential growth processes (members of the Joint Conservation Committee of the Senate and House of Representatives of the Commonwealth of Pennsylvania) did not do any better. When it comes to predicting exponential growth, stick with the computer.

Judging Lots of Possibilities

Suppose you are asked to estimate the probability that each of this year's short-listed movies will win an Oscar for best picture. For the 2017 award I estimated that *La La Land* had a 65 percent chance of winning, *Manchester by the Sea* had a 15 percent chance, *Hacksaw Ridge* a 10 percent chance, and so on. Or imagine you've been asked to estimate the probability that each Olympic finalist in the men's 100 metres will win the gold medal. Typically our judged probabilities in these situations don't add up to 100 percent. Either they amount to more than 100 percent, suggesting it's more than certain that one of the outcomes will occur. Or they add up to less than 100 percent, suggesting their forecast hasn't exhausted all the possibilities. In one experiment (Wright and Whalley 1983) people were given a record of the previous performances of horses in a race and then asked to estimate probabilities that each horse would win. The more horses that were in the race, the more the sum of the probabilities exceeded 100 percent. This was also true when more information was given about each horse. By focusing separately on each horse's chance of winning it seems that people lost the big picture of the race as a whole.

Another problem comes when people are asked to estimate probabilities for quantities like sales, costs, or time. One approach is to ask them for the most likely value and then for a smaller and larger value, so the range (called a prediction interval) has a 90 percent chance of capturing the actual outcome. For example, I might be asked to forecast how long it will take to build an extension to my house. I estimate that it will most likely take 10 weeks. But, if everything goes well, I might complete the work in 7 weeks. If I hit snags, the job might take 12 weeks. Overall I reckon there's a 90 percent chance I'll get the job done in between 7 and 12 weeks. All the evidence from research suggests that my range will be too narrow to give it a 90 percent chance of including the actual building time. If I regularly estimate ranges like this I'm likely to be surprised how often the actual time falls outside them. When Itzhak Ben-David and his co-researchers asked a large sample of U.S. financial executives to produce 80 percent prediction intervals of one-year-ahead stock market returns, the ranges they estimated should have captured the actual returns 80 percent of the time (Ben-David, Graham, and Harvey 2013). In the event, they were so narrow that they only included the true values on 36.3 percent of occasions.

There are many situations like this where we tend to underestimate the scale of uncertainty we face (Soll and Klayman 2004). One potential cause of overly narrow ranges arises when we estimate the most likely value first. In my building time example this was 10 weeks. Once the 10 weeks was in my head it became an anchor and my subsequent estimates of the high and low values were likely to be too close to it, leading to a range that was too narrow. But the excessive narrowness might also result from a failure of imagination – I just couldn't contemplate circumstances where the building work would take more than 12 weeks. Or perhaps I just had a problem thinking in terms of probabilities. After all, I took '90 percent chance' to mean I'd be right 90 percent of the time – but I'm only building my extension once. So it's likely that I'd have difficulty relating the concept of probability to my one-off project.

Forecasts based on split-second intuitive judgments can be astonishingly accurate in areas where we have plenty of experience and practice. In other circumstances our judgment can also lead to awful forecasts. If the forecasting problem is unfamiliar, or there are mountains of data to process, or there are complex relationships between what we want to forecast and the factors that influence it and if we need to memorise what happened in the past, then we probably would be better off turning to the computer.

References

Ben-David, I., Graham, J. R., and Harvey, C. R. (2013). Managerial miscalibration. *Quarterly Journal of Economics* 128, 1547–1584.

Bogan, V., and Just, D. (2009). What drives merger decision making behavior? Don't seek, don't find, and don't change your mind. *Journal of Economic Behavior & Organization* 72 (3): 930–943.

Cipriano, M., and Gruca, T. S. (2015). The power of priors: How confirmation bias impacts market prices. *The Journal of Prediction Markets* 8, 34–56.

How to get your own way. www.howtogetyourownway.com https://digital.nhs.uk/data-and-information/publications/statistical/statistics-on-obesity-physical-activity-and-diet/statistics-on-obesity-physical-activity-and-diet-england-2015

Johnson, E. J., Hershey, J., Meszaros, J., and Kunreuther, H. (1993). Framing, probability distortions, and insurance decisions. *Journal of Risk and Uncertainty* 7, 35–51.

Lawrence, M., Goodwin, P., O'Connor, M., and Önkal, D. (2006). Judgmental forecasting: A review of progress over the last 25 years. *International Journal of Forecasting* 22 (3): 493–518.

Lichtenstein, S., Slovic, P., Fischhoff, B., Layman, M., and Combs, B. (1978). Judged frequency of lethal events. *Journal of Experimental Psychology: Human Learning and Memory* 4, 551.

McKenzie, C. R., and Liersch, M. J. (2011). Misunderstanding savings growth: Implications for retirement savings behavior. *Journal of Marketing Research* 48 (SPL): S1–S13.

National Safety Council (USA). https://injuryfacts.nsc.org/all-injuries/preventable-death-overview/odds-of-dying/

Shermer, M. (2011). *The believing brain*. Dutton.

Soll, J. B., and Klayman, J. (2004). Overconfidence in interval estimates. *Journal of Experimental Psychology: Learning, Memory, and Cognition* 30 (2): 299.

Tetlock, P. (2005). *Expert political judgment: How good is it? How can we know?* Princeton University Press.

Tversky, A., and Kahneman, D. (1974). Judgment under uncertainty: Heuristics and biases. *Science* 185 (4157): 1124–1131.

Wagenaar, W. A. (1994). The subjective probability of guilt. In G. Wright and P. Ayton (Eds.), *Subjective probability*. Wiley.

Wagenaar, W. A., and Sagaria, S. D. (1975). Misperception of exponential growth. *Perception & Psychophysics* 18 (6): 416–422.

Wright, G., and Whalley, P. (1983). The super-additivity of subjective probability. In B. P. Stigum and F. Wenstop (Eds.), *Foundation of utility and risk theory with applications*. Reidel.

3.5 COULD THESE RECENT FINDINGS IMPROVE YOUR JUDGMENTAL FORECASTS?*

Paul Goodwin

Paul Goodwin looks at several fascinating new research studies examining the role of judgment in complementing the statistical forecast. For example, common sense suggests that our forecasts will become more accurate the nearer we are to the period being forecast. But this is often not the case, especially when large positive adjustments are made to keep the forecast matching the sales target or operating plan. (The "stagger chart" is a nice tool for exposing this kind of "hold-and-roll" behaviour. See articles by Ramosaj and Widmer and Gilliland in the Summer 2020 issue of *Foresight*.)

We also commonly assume that the more data we have, the more accurate our judgmental forecasts will be. But one study finds a U-shaped relationship between accuracy and length of history: either have very little data (such as just one point) or much data. When there are just two to five data points, people tend to see patterns that aren't really there. These and other findings challenge many of our accepted beliefs, and suggest creative new ways to improve judgmental forecasts.

---

*This article originally appeared in *Foresight: The International Journal of Applied Forecasting* (Winter 2020) and appears here courtesy of the International Institute of Forecasters.

Surprises

The pros and cons of judgmental forecasting have been widely documented over the last 40 years or so. A wealth of research papers has shown how judgment can act as a valuable complement to statistical models as long as organizational politics and psychological biases don't lead the forecasts astray. Nevertheless, researchers continue to produce interesting and potentially useful findings – and some of these are surprising.

More Recent, More Accurate?

Common sense would suggest that the less far ahead we forecast the more accurate our forecasts will be. Not necessarily so, say Maud Van den Broeke and her coauthors (2019), who analysed over a quarter of a million judgmentally adjusted statistical forecasts in four businesses. Adjustments made close to the sales period did not always improve accuracy, even though the forecasters would have had access to the very latest information about their markets. This was especially the case when the statistical forecast had itself recently been updated so that it may already have incorporated recent information.

Worse still, these late adjustments tended to be large and positive, potentially causing a twofold problem for operations managers: a last-minute rush to increase production followed by sizable stocks of products that failed to sell. The authors recommend that companies should track the performance of judgmental adjustments made at different forecast horizons, and not simply assume that those made closest to the sales period will be the most accurate.

More Data, More Accurate

Common sense might also suggest that the more past sales data we have, the better judgmental forecasters will be at detecting patterns and extrapolating these into the future. Again, the latest research findings don't bear this out. Zoe Theocharis and Nigel Harvey (2019) of University College London found there was a U-shaped relationship between accuracy of forecasts and the length of history to which a forecaster had access. When forecasters were presented with graphs of time series, they tended to perform best when the series were either very short (even as short as one observation) or relatively long (20 or 40 past observations). Five observations were associated with the largest average errors. It makes sense that 20 or 40 observations will be sufficient to allow forecasters to discern underlying patterns in series with some accuracy. But why should having access to just one observation lead to better forecasts than having access to five?

When only one past observation is available, forecasters making extrapolations have no option but to offer a naïve forecast (where the forecast is simply equal to the latest observation). Naive forecasts have been shown to outperform more sophisticated methods in a wide range of contexts. However, as the number of available past observations increases to, say, two or five, forecasters are tempted to see patterns in the data that may not exist. For example, two points on a graph might suggest an upward trend, if the latest observation is higher than its predecessor. But if the increase is simply a random twitch, that would be akin to claiming there's a trend in numbers generated by a roulette wheel if it produced successive scores of two and three. Five observations are likely to lead to even worse forecasts because they increase forecasters' inclinations to see false patterns. These findings led the authors to make the counter-intuitive suggestion that when only about five observations can be obtained, the series should be shortened to include only the most recent observation before a judgmental extrapolation is made.

Competition

"Competition makes us all better and better," claimed the South Korean soccer star Son Heun-min. No doubt true enough where sport is concerned, but does this work for judgmental forecasting? To investigate, Hyo Young Kim, Lee, and Jun (2018) at KAIST College of Business designed a laboratory experiment where people made one-step-ahead judgmental forecasts from past data displayed on graphs. All the judgmental forecasters received feedback on their accuracy. Those in one treatment, however, were also informed how their accuracy ranked compared to other fore-casters in their group. In other treatments, the participants were just told that they were either the best or worst forecaster in their group – irrespective of how they had actually performed.

Competition seemed to work. People who were told their rank – real *or* fake – went on to make more accurate forecasts than those who only received accuracy feedback. But interestingly, the effect was more pronounced for those told that they lagged behind other participants. Forecasters who received indications that they topped the rankings appeared to rest on their laurels, while people at the bottom strove to improve their standing. The researchers attributed this to our natural aversion to losses. The forecasters who were told their rank was low perceived this to be a loss and did all they could to avoid it when making their later forecasts.

Combination

When it comes to groups of forecasters, it's well known that combining their fore-casts (e.g., by taking a simple average) can often lead to high levels of accuracy. Even averaging judgmental adjustments made to a statistical forecast by different experts can be beneficial, according to a recent study by Dick van Dijk and Philips Hans Franses (2019) of Erasmus University in Rotterdam. In this case, combining led to more accu-rate forecasts even though the individual adjustments would have been damaging to accuracy. This was because there was disagreement among the experts, so their errors tended to cancel each other out.

Diversity like this is an asset when forecasts are drawn from groups of people. However, in many situations different forecasters have access to the same information, so their forecasts tend to be subject to similar biases and turn out to be correlated. To deal with this, Mary Thomson and her colleagues (2019) at Northumbria University have devised a series of measures based on forecasters' past performances that enable lack of diversity to be detected. This allows groups of forecasters to be assembled so that diversity can be maximised. The measures have the advantage that they can also be broken down to reflect specific aspects of an individual forecaster's performance. For example, they can reveal a tendency a forecaster might have to forecast too high or too low, or their ability to discriminate between small and large future changes in time series. They can even reflect a forecaster's propensity to see false patterns in the series. By examining these characteristics, forecasters can be selected for a group based on what is considered to be most critical for the forecasts. Let's say that avoiding persistent overforecasting is crucial; in this case, the forecasts of those with the greatest tendency to exhibit this bias could be excluded from the combination.

Some biases in judgmental forecasts are intentional, rather than psychological. Organizational politics is a common source of such biases. When different departments have different interests, their demand forecasts may be intentionally biased in opposite directions. A sales manager might deliberately overestimate future demand to ensure that customers are never disappointed by stock-outs. A production manager, on the other hand, may be motivated to underestimate demand to avoid the danger of funding excessive inventories. This suggests that the average of the two forecasts might eliminate these biases.

In an experiment that simulated forecasting and production-level decisions in an interdepartmental decision-making context, Pennings, van Dalen, and Rook (2019) at Erasmus University and Delft University of Technology investigated whether averaging such forecasts would remove these intentional biases from forecasts. They found that a simple average was far less effective in reducing the biases than a weighted average, where the weights are based on the past performance of the forecasts, though neither method completely eliminated the biases. A scheme that involved "de-biasing" the forecasts before they were combined led to the greatest improvements in forecast accuracy.

Conclusions

It might be difficult to persuade people not to adjust forecasts for next week's demand, despite their belief that they have the very latest information about their market. It's likely to be even more challenging to get them to throw away four of their last five data points before they make a forecast. Telling people that their forecasts are the worst of the bunch is unlikely to motivate them for long. Nor is knowing that their forecast is going to be averaged with someone else's. It might even lead to game playing: make your forecast more extreme to pull the average in the direction you want.

Nevertheless, all of these studies contain pointers on how judgmental forecasts can be improved. They alert us to dangers we may have been unaware of up to now. And in many cases, the careful and imaginative application of their findings might work. For example, people might be convinced not to tamper with near-term forecasts when clear evidence is provided that this is damaging. When you only have around five observations, it might be advisable simply to use their average as the forecast or at least treat any judgmental forecast with extreme caution. And making competition fun, or rewarding people if their forecast turns out to be the best of those that were averaged, might keep them motivated.

Hopefully, future researchers will tell us if these suggestions are helpful.

References

Kim, H. Y., Lee, Y. S., and Jun, D. B. (2018). The effect of relative performance feedback on judgmental forecasting accuracy, *Management Decision* 57, 1695–1711.

Pennings, C. L., van Dalen, J., and Rook, L. (2019). Coordinating judgmental forecasting: Coping with intentional biases, *Omega* 87, 46–56.

Theocharis, Z., and Harvey, N. (2019). When does more mean worse? Accuracy of judgmental forecasting is nonlinearly related to length of data series, *Omega* 87, 10–19.

Thomson, M. E., Pollock, A. C., Önkal, D., and Gönül, M. S. (2019). Combining forecasts: Performance and coherence, *International Journal of Forecasting* 35, 474–484.

Van den Broeke, M., De Baets, S., Vereecke, A., Baecke, P., and Vanderheyden, K. (2019). Judgmental forecast adjustments over different time horizons. *Omega* 87, 34–45.

van Dijk, D., and Franses, P. H. (2019). Combining expert-adjusted forecasts. *Journal of Forecasting* 38, 415–421.

3.6 A PRIMER ON PROBABILISTIC DEMAND PLANNING[*]

Stefan de Kok

Using means and standard deviations of statistical forecasts has been the default method for demand planners for decades, but there is a key shortcoming with this approach, namely that it assumes that demand is normally distributed, which it rarely is. This incorrect assumption severely impacts forecast accuracy and accuracy of all dependent plans. The solution, and an increasingly adopted method, is probabilistic forecasting.

In this article, Stefan de Kok discusses how probability distributions allow planners to work with the real uncertainty in demand and enjoy more accurate demand plans as a result. He also explores other benefits of this approach and the differences between deterministic and probabilistic forecasting.

---

[*]This article originally appeared in *Journal of Business Forecasting* (Winter 2019–2020) and appears here courtesy of Dr. Chaman Jain, editor in chief.

If you have ever heard expressions like "a forecast is always wrong" or "plans are useless by the time they are published because things changed" it is because forecasts and plans traditionally approximate uncertain values with exact numbers. The problem with using exact numbers when uncertainty is present is that it is impossible to find one number that works for all its uses. If the number is too low, there will be cases where the actual value is larger, leading to shortages in quantity or time and disruption of plans. If the number is too high you are adding bloat, creating waste and inefficiency. Common examples are lead times where often a safe near-maximum value is picked, leading to inefficiency, and inventory or production quantities where often some average value is picked leading to instability. The dilemma is that there is conflict. To reduce one problem, you need to accept an increase in the other. Reducing lead times or increasing inventory and production quantities in plans just replaces one problem for another one.

Moving to a Probabilistic Perspective of the Future

The solution is to change the paradigm. One logical way to do so is to replace all numbers in our plans and forecasts that represent uncertain values with probability distributions. Instead of stating that next month we will sell exactly 100 units, which will never occur except by chance, we could state that we will sell anywhere between 50 and 200 units and each value within that range has a stated probability of occurring. We would trade precision for accuracy. Or in the terminology of John Maynard Keynes, instead of being precisely wrong, we would now be roughly right. But if all we did was use that extra information and accuracy to set better safety stock levels, we still have not changed the paradigm and would still suffer all the same problems, only slightly lessened them. The real breakthrough occurs when we replace all traditional, so-called deterministic math with probabilistic math throughout all our plans. Every single number that represents something uncertain or random in every single plan would be replaced by a full distribution. All time series of numbers would become time series of distributions. All lead times, durations, quantities, yields, grades, and so forth would become distributions, until they happened, at which time they become regular numbers.

Whilst this may seem logical, even common sense, it raises lots of new questions to be answered. A key one is that probabilistic math is a lot more complex than deterministic math. You can add and multiply regular numbers with expected results. You cannot do the same with probability distributions. You need probabilistic arithmetic. Another commonly encountered response is that determining the correct probability distribution and parameters cannot be done accurately and requires a lot more data, even Big Data. This however is a myth. A number of companies have solved this problem and successfully deployed probabilistic solutions to companies of all sizes as far back as the 1970s. And they do this with all the same data used by traditional systems. There is a lot more information present in historical transaction data than most people realize. It just requires a different way of looking at that data. Whilst these solutions prove that it is not only possible to create probabilistic forecasts and plans, and that these dramatically increase accuracy, efficiency, and stability over their deterministic equivalents, they do not explain clearly how humans fit into this paradigm. That is what this article is about, in the context of demand planning.

The Differences between Statistical and Probabilistic Forecasts

A traditional demand planning cycle typically starts with an automated statistical forecast, to which people then make adjustments, often in multiple rounds at various levels of aggregation. The statistical forecast is expressed as series of numbers. It is intuitive for a human to increase or decrease a number when they know or expect some event that will increase or decrease demand in some time period. In case they only know this at an aggregate level, maybe across a certain region, for a product family or account, the detail numbers can be tallied up and the change made at the aggregate level directly by the person. The system can then split that aggregate change back down into the detail using the before-change detail values to determine the proportion of change to assign down. But how does this work if the forecast were probabilistic instead of statistical? Let's first see how these forecasts are different.

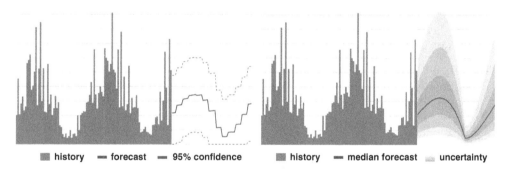

Figure 3.9 A Statistical Forecast with Confidence Limits and a Probabilistic Forecast

Note the similarities and the differences between two graphs in Figure 3.9. Both show time along the horizontal axis with historical demand on the left and future forecast on the right. The difference is that the statistical forecast on the left could provide confidence limits (the dash lines), whilst the probabilistic forecast on the right gives the whole spectrum of uncertainty (the shaded area). In this case, the graph simplifies the richness of the full distribution by only switching shades at quantities that have cumulative probability values equivalent to one, two, or three standard deviations of a normal distribution. In other words, they equate to approximately 68.3%, 95.4%, and 99.7% confidence levels. That is just to make the graph more insightful, and any other confidence levels may be chosen if desired. In the background all math uses the full distribution, not just the levels shown for convenience in the graph. The key takeaway here is that a probabilistic forecast (and any probabilistic plan for that matter) provides all information a statistical forecast does. It adds more information but removes nothing.

Planning with Probabilistic Forecasts

Whilst interpreting a probabilistic forecast is not any harder than a statistical forecast, making adjustments requires some stricter rules. Both "how" and "when" change. In terms of frequency, the number of changes required are dramatically lower. A common scenario is a sales organization that makes hundreds of adjustments to statistical forecasts every month, may go down to just a handful of changes after switching to a probabilistic forecast. There are two reasons for this. First, probabilistic forecasts are more accurate, reducing the need to intercede. Second, they express uncertainty, and any would-be adjustments that fall within reasonable uncertainty are simply not needed. If a somewhat large adjustment would be at the 2-sigma level, then why make it at all? It is already taken into account. What is left are the very large and truly impactful adjustments. When adjustments are made, this generally takes one of three forms. Either it is a simple numeric adjustment overriding the calculated value or it is adding causal information allowing the system to recalculate a new forecast, or a combination of both. The first option, which is the most commonly used one, is bad practice, regardless of statistical or probabilistic environment. It deprives the system of information, making it anemic, and consistent use will deteriorate the quality of the calculated forecast. This leads to a vicious cycle where the need to override becomes ever greater and the quality keeps deteriorating. In a probabilistic environment the impact is worse, because, whilst the mean of the forecast adjusts as expected, there is no accurate way of determining how uncertainty changes. Providing causal information on the other hand will allow the system to learn and improve. This is true for both statistical and probabilistic forecasts. Every adjustment should mandatorily provide such information, whilst providing a best estimate of the impact on quantity is optional.

The type of causal information provided could be as basic as a manually entered reason code or as complete as heaps of detailed event information retrieved from a dedicated system, such as a trade promotion management system. Probabilistic systems usually isolate signal from noise, both of which are expressed as distributions. The signal is time-variable based on trends, seasonalities, and events. The noise is static, pardon the pun. The detail of causal information provided is determined by availability, effort, and the ability of the specific system to process it. The system then uses any information to isolate more signal from the noise, reducing overall uncertainty, increasing both precision and accuracy.

If a planner does want to provide a numeric override, it is very similar to a traditional forecast. The mean of the distribution will adjust as dictated, whilst the rest of the distribution accommodates. So, the resulting adjusted forecast is again a probabilistic forecast, allowing multiple successive overrides by people in various roles. Just like a traditional forecast, adjustments can be made at any level of aggregation, and then summed up or split down to ensure all levels provide the same version of truth. As probabilistic arithmetic goes, summing and subtracting is relatively straightforward. Whilst the math may be too complex for a human to validate on the back of a napkin, the important characteristics such as mean and variance are simple to verify. What planners and executives gain with probabilistic demand planning is greater accuracy and valuable information when upside potential and downside risk are lopsided.

3.7 BENEFITS AND CHALLENGES OF CORPORATE PREDICTION MARKETS*

Thomas Wolfram

While prediction markets have become common platforms for political forecasts, they have received limited interest in the business world. Here, Thomas Wolfram discusses recent research on the benefits and challenges of implementing corporate PMs.

At the foundation of a successful prediction market are the anonymity and diversity of participants. But within a corporation, information sharing and herding behavior can bias PM forecasts and undermine their acceptability. Another major challenge lies in the hierarchical structure of management in most companies.

Big data and its various incarnations can be viewed as a competitor to PMs, but also suffers similar flaws: improperly curated data and algorithms entrench bias and crimp accuracy and acceptance. Prediction markets can succeed as a forecasting methodology in companies – but only with appropriate management support, employees committing to engage on a regular basis, and management acknowledging that it does not have all the answers and can benefit from employee input.

Introduction: Corporate Prediction Markets

In its first issue of 2019, the *International Journal of Forecasting* (IJF) dedicated a special section to prediction markets serving as a business tool for forecasting event outcomes but also regarding their value for socioeconomic forecasting. Companies can implement a prediction market as an in-house tool as well as utilize publicly available (political) prediction markets, such as PredictIt (https://www.predictit.org/).

The Betfair prediction market proved useful in gauging the impact of a no-deal Brexit on Sterling's exchange rate (*The Economist* 2019c), important for companies with exposure to the British currency. Betfair's predictions were based robustly on a £3.9m ($5.1m) trading volume in the two months prior to March 21, 2019 when the EU extended the original Brexit deadline, making a no-deal more unlikely.

Limited Diffusion

The editors of the special issue believe there is significant interest in prediction markets in the business community, but this is questionable. Some of the corporate applications

---

*This article originally appeared in *Foresight: The International Journal of Applied Forecasting* (Summer 2019) and appears here courtesy of the International Institute of Forecasting.

cited in the articles have either been abandoned or were never really implemented. As I learned through personal interviews, the latter is the case for Siemens, France Telecom (Orange), and Hewlett-Packard.

Furthermore, a study that requested participation from hundreds of companies found very few successful corporate prediction markets (Rieg and Schoder 2011), and another study of 130 German companies (three quarters of which were large enterprises) reported that prediction markets were unknown to more than a fifth of the recipients, while nearly half had heard the term but weren't sure of its precise definition (Wagner 2013).

Nor were corporate prediction markets included in business press publications that seek to bring new tools to the attention of management (Andler 2015). Professor Emeritus Donald Thompson from York University, Canada, calls prediction markets one of the least understood ideas in business (Thompson, 2012), even though they would overcome the inability of many companies to aggregate the views and insights of their employees on critical issues.

Still, examples of PM use in corporate settings do exist: Eli Lilly, a pharmaceutical company, used a PM to predict whether or not new drugs would gain regulatory approval by the U.S. Food and Drug Administration. Deutsche Telekom used an internal PM setup by Crowdworx, a prediction-market provider, to supplement its market research into future trends in sales and product development.

The Hierarchical Challenge

Jim Lavoie, CEO of Rite-Solutions, an information technology company (https://www.rite-solutions.com/), argued that management hierarchies (or pyramid structures) create the perception that individuals at each level must try to be smarter than those below them. This has the unintended result of inhibiting input from those lower in the pyramid (Lavoie 2009).

Prediction markets do threaten the privileges of the dominant management hierarchy – such as restrictions on information flow or on concentrated decision making – and there remains an "ingrained suspicion of the idea that lower-level employees might have input to management decisions. Senior managers . . . when in doubt hire consultants" (Thompson 2012).

Executives seem to favour the viewpoints of their management consultants: at least you can talk to the consultants, you can't "talk to the market." In an interview I conducted, the CIO of Jaguar Land Rover ranked his internal employees third behind his fellow CIOs and behind consultants in providing trustworthy predictions.

The hierarchy puts particular pressure on those at the top to always be right. Thompson asserts that by treating all participants equally and anonymously, prediction markets can circumvent the pyramid and its restrictions on information flow.

Thompson also argues that by entrusting employees with the future direction of the company, PMs might overcome dissatisfaction with their own use. According to a survey by McKinsey & Company (Bughin, Manyika, and Miller 2008), only 21% of corporations were satisfied with their PM while 22% voiced clear dissatisfaction with the tool. In a later survey of major corporations, 43% of respondents said they have not considered investing in prediction markets (Bughin, Chui, and Harrysson 2015), a strikingly negative finding.

Thus, prediction markets underscore that "an employee's value must not be measured by the hierarchical rank," as Manny Maceda, Bain & Company's worldwide head, pointed out, helping to lead to a more meritocratic company environment.

Revealingly, a PM at Best Buy met with initial hostility from the sales forecasting team as they were humiliated by being outperformed by a PM: the crowd's forecast error at 0.5% was compared to the official forecast, which was off by 5.0%. However, the company learned an important lesson: "Never allow market results to be interpreted as reflecting negatively on existing managers" (Thompson 2012, p. 100).

Prediction markets may also facilitate decision making more directly than traditional forecasting methods. Luckner et al. (2012) argues that

> Continuous scanning of ongoing developments as an input to strategic planning . . . may be difficult to implement with traditional forecasting methods such as brainstorming techniques, expert groups, Delphi studies, and scenario workshops. The results of such approaches usually have to be . . . analyzed, evaluated and summarized . . . [before becoming useful, whereas] . . . prediction markets are set up with the explicit purpose of soliciting information. Engineered carefully . . . [they] can directly guide decision making.

Forecast Accuracy

Of course, forecast accuracy is an important consideration in adopting a forecasting method or system, and there is some empirical evidence on the performance of PMs.

Factors influencing the exactness of PM predictions were a major theme in the 11 papers in the special issue of the IJF and beyond. Here are the important takeaways:

- PM accuracy varies considerably with the setup of the market (Strijbis and Arnesen 2019).
- "Many of the models of prediction markets lack robust empirical validation" (Restocchi, McGroarty, and Gerding 2019).
- Systemic biases plague prediction markets and harm the quality of their results.
- It is less straightforward to "detect and correct . . . erroneous forecasts" of a PM than with common statistical methods (Sung et al. 2019, p. 389). Where interpretation of a market's results ex post is needed, this simply renders results less useful.

▪ Tetlock found that so-called superforecasters "beat by 40% a prediction market . . . of the same questions" (Tetlock and Gardner 2015, p. 93). One reason is that superforecasters were more successful in spotting trends (Bradley, Hirt, and Smit 2018).

▪ But prediction markets can provide superior forecasts of future events (Gruca and Berg 2007) by aggregating information from public and private sources, from facts that can be widely scattered at various levels of a company.

▪ Nevertheless, prediction markets can fail spectacularly. A PM seesawed between good and bad results in predicting German federal elections, providing the least accurate forecasts in 2013 but the most accurate component method in 2017 (Graefe 2019). PMs for the 2016 Brexit vote and the 2016 U.S. presidential election are also considered high-profile forecasting failures (Vaughan Williams, Sung, and Johnson 2019).

▪ Still, evidence supports that prediction markets were better than opinion polling and got to the right answer more quickly than most political analysts (Arnesen and Bergfjord 2014).

Attaining exactness in predicting is considered essential and worthy of improvement, and prediction markets are still considered to be among the most accurate forecasting methods. For prediction markets to therefore play out their advantages in an enterprise, proper implementation is important. There is empirical evidence (Costa Sperb et al 2019) that *"significantly better forecasts can be derived from prediction markets,"* at least when the PM implementation properly accounts for key factors such as the biases of the participants (Krause et al. 2018).

Factors Influencing Accuracy

Scale

PM accuracy depends on its scale. In businesses they are inevitably implemented on a small scale. According to Rieg and Schoder (2011), small groups of participants can provide very accurate predictions. One study notes that PM results become slightly less accurate if there are 15 or fewer traders in a market, and even less reliable if there are 10 or fewer participating, and that 16 or more traders should be sufficient to obtain quality predictions (Christiansen 2012).

Other researchers see 12–20 people as a good number for initial pilots, so a better idea is to include more people (Bingham and Nagar 2013). And PMs are highly scalable in terms of the number of possible participants. With active participation of 30–50 players, quite good results can be achieved. To succeed though, the operative implementation needs to be supported by clear support from top management (Riekhof, Riekhof, and Brinkhoff 2012).

Information Sharing

A second factor concerns information sharing among traders, through online interaction, service on an expert panel, or even face-to-face meetings – the result being an exchange of beliefs and the rationales behind them.

Some studies have found that information sharing diminishes PM accuracy (Lorenz et al. 2011; Graefe 2011) while others note improvements (Farrell 2011; Gürçay, Mellers, and Baron 2015; Vaughan Williams and Reade 2016).

The way the exchange happens may be important, for example whether it's continual or intermittent. If the information exchange is intermittent it may improve PM accuracy, according to a new study that found collaborators got a better average solution than groups acting individually and independently (Bernstein, Shore, and Lazer 2018).

Social influence – receiving information on the responses of other traders – can undermine the wisdom-of-crowds effect in a prediction market (Lorenz et al. 2011). But social interactions can also eliminate some of the bias that exists in these crowd approaches (Madirolas and De Polavieja 2014), as people on their own may be prey to a subconscious bias when relying on intuition rather than facts.

Carol Gebert (2008), former CEO of Incentive Markets, sees an advantage in personal contact among traders, through nurturing the competitive aspect of prediction markets. Gebert also points out that the number of traders needn't be large, but they must be active.

Viewpoints of traders become much more similar as a result of direct contact via social-networking links (Takac, Hinz, and Spann 2011), eliminating diversity – one of the tenets of a successful prediction market – where diversity is seen as having a clear benefit and hence why companies should cultivate it (Mau 2018).

Aggregation of individual estimates by a PM when there is information exchange and the possible revisions of estimates during market trading is a Catch-22. On the one hand, traders have a strong incentive to obtain useful information and make accurate forecasts (Brown, Reade, and Vaughan Williams 2019), but it must be good information: there is danger when only one information source is available (Mason, Conrey, and Smith 2007).

Herding

Because the aim of a prediction market is to elicit the average of the crowd's estimates, knowledge about that target would drive – "herd" – trader behaviour toward the current, potentially incorrect, value. Such convergence suppresses an individual's real information. In other words, herding arises when traders decide to imitate the observed decisions of others rather than follow their own beliefs and information. And people who are aware of the viewpoints of others are "reluctant to look foolish by deviating from the majority view" (*The Economist* 2018a). Herding diminishes the wisdom-of-crowds effect in cases where accuracy relies on the guesses being independent.

Mispricing

Herding can also cause mispricing, in that "final prices can fail to reflect all relevant information appropriately . . . [due to] pricing anomalies" (Costa Sperb et al. 2019, p. 321).

Mispricing that stems from herding is visible in the so-called *favourite-longshot bias*, i.e., outcomes deemed more likely are underpriced and "long shots" overvalued.

And when important events attract more traders, the extent of mispricing increases, diminishing the predictive power of a market. To alleviate this, market structure – e.g., the underlying rules for pricing and payoff – becomes more important than the composition of the traders.

Inefficiency in a PM might be further aggravated by active deception: traders not revealing their true beliefs in order to maximise their individual payoff, leading to incorrect pricing and game playing in which the trader intends to correct the prediction probability later and benefit in the market as a result.

Expert Weighting

Researchers from the Karlsruhe Institute of Technology suggest that PM forecasts could improve when distinguishing informed from uninformed experts and giving more weight to the former (Kloker et al. 2018). Algorithms based on identified attributes of the participants can be used to objectify the selection of experts without sacrificing anonymity.

An important tenet of a successful market, *anonymity*, runs contrary to the fact that in decision making a lot of reasoning is devoted to affirming the identity of the group one belongs to and an individual's position within it. People are "using their skills to reinforce the opinions of their group, rather than to establish facts" (*The Economist* 2018b). Prediction markets do not allow "tying" oneself to a group, potentially making users feel uncomfortable.

Big Data – A Competitive Approach

Like PMs, big data aggregates individual preferences through anonymity and diversity and may even be considered a competitive forecasting approach (LaRiviere et al. 2016).

In a study based on retail time series, big data improved predictive accuracy, spotting trends impossible for humans to detect, feeding off information often hidden in unstructured data repositories, and identifying patterns that can improve demand forecasts (Boone et al. 2019). Big data applications using machine learning had good forecast accuracy (Seeger 2006).

Big-data analytics can evolve into an ersatz prediction market or even a full successor, with the advantage of such tools stemming from their unprecedented ability to see around corners, helping to anticipate disruptive new technologies or tracking possible warning signs (MacArthur and Rainey 2019).

All the same, big data acts passively by extracting conclusions from the data, whereas prediction markets behave actively: through trading and the underlying price mechanism, findings and conclusions are immediately put to the test of other traders' views.

Both approaches suffer from trust issues, but even proponents of prediction markets recognise that alternative forecasting approaches can make for easier bedfellows because users "are uncomfortable with the 'black box' nature of prediction markets" (Green, Armstrong, and Graefe 2007).

Scenarios

Big data supports a new focus in the strategy and planning literatures, which has moved away from "the mental picture of a *singular* or unique future to the paradigm of *alternative* futures, or scenarios" (Tiberius and Rasche 2011). Companies must take account of several plausible futures and no longer plan on the basis of individual projections alone.

Big data creates scenarios by automatically analysing vast amounts of information, thus encapsulating a range of possibilities. In contrast, prediction markets only aggregate results into the likeliest future, with alternative developments being overlooked. That said, new technologies, including Web 2.0 applications that encompass prediction markets, allow companies to use the crowd or collective intelligence to a greater extent than ever before (O'Reilly 2013).

Advanced Analytics

Extracting information from vast amounts of data is one of big data's key tenets, for which it may be better than prediction markets. The nascent Web 3.0 – envisioned as the machine-readable Web – represents a move away from Web 2.0's more participatory approaches (connecting people and crowd sourcing) toward big-data analytics. As the consulting firm Bain & Company avers, allowing machines to identify patterns hidden in massive data flows or documents can help firms derive the kind of proprietary insights that give them an essential edge against rivals. Decisions that rely on (large) data sets are useful when experiences of individuals are limited: big data can unearth neglected facts beyond what intuitive understanding recognises (Muller 2018).

However, Boone et al. (2019) argue that, in the context of supply-chain forecasting, "the forecasting community thus far has taken a rather myopic view of big data."

Biases Again

For systems like machine learning that use large data inputs to perform well, humans still must train the systems. But human choices can be biased, such as in the selection of the examples used for training (Standage 2019). Human expertise is still needed for systems to have human judgment, because even well-automated evaluation and selection algorithms in big-data analytics may lead to false conclusions (O'Neil 2016).

But each execution of an algorithm further embeds the human biases, and the underlying technical procedures – which create these representations of reality – are not often questioned; neither are concerns raised about the individuals who choose the inputs. The processing steps carried out by computers and software are considered neutral, authoritative, and always accurate, so they are hardly scrutinised (Mau 2018).

And this points to the risk that "neural networks used in machine learning are intrinsically vulnerable to spoofing" (*The Economist* 2019a), meaning that someone actively interferes with them. With vast amounts of "unsupervised" data being processed, data of inferior quality can lead to misleading outcomes. AI systems can make bad decisions and do so much faster than other technologies.

This risk has been recognised, and the threat that an individual loses control over their own data and who has access to it has found its way into new regulations (*The Economist* 2019b) – in Europe, chiefly among them the General Data Protection Regulation (GDPR) – reining in the exploding demand for information in shaping automated decision making.

The potential of losing easy access to data as a valuable resource can hinder big data and AI systems. Unintended consequences can occur if the quantitative systems emphasise what can be measured over the motives of choosing certain data in the first place (Mau 2018). This personal touch, however – the motives – is also present in prediction markets.

Concluding Thought

As often as not, enthusiasm about social technologies belies their actual measurable benefits. More data do not automatically create value. The organisational structure of a company is decisive in making the most of big data, and the same is true for corporate prediction markets.

As laid out in this article, implementation aspects are important to harness these new technologies, and this requires internal change first and foremost:

> The good news is much of the technology a company might leverage to create an internal feedback loop, like prediction markets . . . and other collective intelligence / crowdsourcing capabilities already exist. *But ultimately solving this problem* [of identifying and removing potential roadblocks] *will be about a willingness to change culturally. A leader must be humble enough to acknowledge they are biased, don't have all the answers, and need the input.* And employees must commit to giving [such input] on a regular basis (Siegel 2016, emphasis added).

Prediction markets can succeed as a forecasting methodology for companies, but only with clearly mandated goodwill from the top.

References

Andler, N. (2015). *Tools für Projektmanagement, Workshops und Consulting: Kompendium der wichtigsten Techniken und Methoden* (6th ed.). Erlangen: Publicis Publishing.

Arnesen, S. and Bergfjord, O. (2014). Prediction markets vs. polls – An examination of accuracy for the 2008 and 2012 elections. *Journal of Prediction Markets* 8 (3).

Bernstein, E., Shore, J., and Lazer, D. (2018). How intermittent breaks in interaction improve collective intelligence. *Proceedings of the National Academy of Sciences.* https://doi.org/10.1073/pnas.1802407115

Bingham, A., and Nagar, Y. (2013). *Prediction markets – A practitioner's guide. Expert Series.* www.consensuspoint.com/wp-content/uploads/2017/01/Practitioners_Guide-1.pdf

Boone, T., Boylan, J. E., Fildes, R., Ganeshan, R., and Sanders, N. (2019). Perspectives on supply chain forecasting, special section: Supply chain forecasting. *International Journal of Forecasting* 35 (1): 121–127.

Bradley, C., Hirt, M., & Smit, S. (2018). *Strategy beyond the hockey stick.* Hoboken, NJ: Wiley.

Brown, A., Reade, J. J., and Vaughan Williams, L. (2019). When are prediction market prices most informative? *International Journal of Forecasting* 35 (1): 420–428.

Bughin, J., Chui, M., and Harrysson, M. (2015). *McKinsey global survey on social tools and technologies in the business world, 2014.* [Data file]. McKinsey & Company. Unpublished dataset, cited with permission.

Bughin, J., Manyika, J., and Miller, A. (2008). McKinsey global survey results: Building the web 2.0 enterprise. *McKinsey on Business Technology (Fall)*, 38–47.

Christiansen, J. D. (2012). Prediction markets: Practical experiments in small markets and behaviours observed. *The Journal of Prediction Markets* 1 (1): 17–41.

Costa Sperb, L. F., Sung, M. C., Ma, T., and Johnson, J. (2019). Keeping a weather eye on prediction markets: Improving forecasts by accounting for environmental conditions. *International Journal of Forecasting* 35 (1): 321–335.

The Economist (2018a). Bartleby – the pros and cons of collaboration (2018a). 8 September: 51.

The Economist (2018b). Political thinking – The partisan brain. 8 December: 39.

The Economist (2019a). Briefing – Autonomous weapons. 19 *January*: 23–26.

The Economist (2019b). Leaders – Europe takes on the tech giants. 23 March: 11.

The Economist (2019c). Graphic detail – Brexit and the markets. 30 March: 85.

Farrell, S. (2011). Social influence benefits the wisdom of individuals in the crowd. *Proceedings of the National Academy of Sciences* 108(36), E625–E625.

Gebert, C. (2008). Prediction markets: A guide to practical adoption in the pharmaceutical industry. *Foresight* 9 (Spring): 25–29.

Graefe, A. (2011). Prediction market accuracy for business forecasting. In W. L. Vaughan, *Prediction Markets* (pp. 87–95). Routledge.

Graefe, A. (2019). Accuracy of German federal election forecasts, 2013 & 2017. *International Journal of Forecasting* 35(3): 868–877.

Green, K. C., Armstrong, J. S., and Graefe, A. (2007). Methods to elicit forecasts from groups: Delphi and prediction markets compared. *Foresight* 8 (Fall): 17–21.

Gruca, T. S., and Berg, J. E. (2007). Public information bias and prediction market accuracy. *The Journal of Prediction Markets* 1 (3): 219–231.

Gürçay, B., Mellers, B. A., and Baron, J. (2015). The power of social influence on estimation accuracy. *Journal of Behavioral Decision Making* 28 (3): 250–261.

Kloker, S., Klatt, F., Höffer, J., and Weinhardt, C. (2018). Analyzing prediction market trading behaviour to select delphi-experts, *Foresight* 20 (4): 364–374. https://doi.org/10.1108/FS-01-2018-0009

Krause, R. W., Huisman, M., Steglich, C., and Snijders, T. A. (2018). Missing network data – A comparison of different imputation methods. *Italian Journal of Applied Statistics* 30, 33–56, Forthcoming.

LaRiviere, J., McAfee, P., Rao, J., Narayanan, V. K., and Sun, W. (2016). Where predictive analytics is having the biggest impact, *Harvard Business Review* 25 (May). https://hbr.org/2016/05/where-predictive-analytics-is-having-the-biggest-impact

Lavoie, J. (2009). The innovation engine at Rite-Solutions: Lessons from the CEO. *The Journal of Prediction Markets* 3 (1): 1–11.

Lorenz, J., Rauhut, H., Schweitzer, F., and Helbing, D. (2011). How social influence can undermine the wisdom of crowd effect. *Proceedings of the National Academy of Sciences* 108 (22): 9020–9025.

Luckner, S., Schröder, J., Slamka, C., et al. (2012). *Prediction markets – Fundamentals, designs, and applications*. Wiesbaden: Gabler Verlag.

MacArthur, H., and Rainey, B. (2019). *Global private equity report 2019*. Bain & Company, Boston.

Madirolas, G., and De Polavieja, G. G. (2014). *Wisdom of the confident: Using social interactions to eliminate the bias in wisdom of the crowds. arXiv preprint arXiv*: 1406.7578.

Mason, W. A., Conrey, F. R., and Smith, E. R. (2007). Situating social influence processes: Dynamic, multidirectional flows of influence within social networks. *Personality and Social Psychology Review* 11(3): 279–300.

Mau, S. (2018). *Das metrische Wir – Über die Quantifizierung des Sozialen* (3rd ed.). Berlin: Suhrkamp Verlag.

Muller, J. Z. (2018). *The tyranny of metrics*. Princeton University Press.

O'Neil, C. (2016). *Weapons of math destruction: How big data increases inequality and threatens democracy*. New York: Allen Lane.

O'Reilly, T. (2013). What is Web 2.0? In H. Donelan, K. Kear, and M. Ramage, (Eds.), *Online Communication and collaboration: A reader* (pp. 225–235). London and New York: Routledge, 225–235.

Restocchi, V., McGroarty, F., and Gerding, E. (2019). The stylized facts of prediction markets: Analysis of price changes. *Physica A: Statistical Mechanics and Its Applications* 515 (1): 159–170.

Rieg, R., and Schoder, R. (2011). Corporate prediction markets: Pitfalls and barriers. *Foresight* 21 (Spring): 35–40.

Riekhof, H. C., Riekhof, M. C., and Brinkhoff, S. (2012). *Predictive markets: Ein vielversprechender Weg zur Verbesserung der Prognosequalität im Unternehmen?* (No. 2012/07). PFH Forschungspapiere/Research Papers, PFH Private Hochschule Göttingen.

Seeger, M. (2006). *Bayesian modelling in machine learning: A tutorial review, Report at Saarland University*. https://infoscience.epfl.ch/record/161462?ln=en

Siegel, A. (2016). *Uber's costly fail in Germany is symptomatic of an age-old problem in big companies.* Blog at *Cultivate Labs.* www.cultivatelabs.com/posts/uber-s-costly-fail-in-germany-is-symptomatic-of-an-age-old-problem-in-big-companies

Standage, T. (2019). Rewind – The human inside the machine. *The Economist – 1843 Magazine* (December 2018/January 2019): 95.

Strijbis, O., and Arnesen, S. (2019). Explaining variance in the accuracy of prediction markets. *International Journal of Forecasting* 35 (1): 408–419.

Sung, M. C., McDonald, D. C., Johnson, J. E., Tai, C. C., and Cheah, E. T. (2019). Improving prediction market forecasts by detecting and correcting possible over-reaction to price movements. *European Journal of Operational Research* 272 (1): 389–405.

Takac, C., Hinz, O., and Spann, M. (2011). The social embeddedness of decision making: Opportunities and challenges. *Electronic Markets* 21 (3): 185.

Tetlock, P. E., and Gardner, D. (2015). *Superforecasting: The art and science of prediction.* New York: Crown.

Thompson, D. N. (2012). *Oracles: How prediction markets turn employees into visionaries.* Boston: Harvard Business Review Press.

Tiberius, V., and Rasche, C. (2011). Prognosemärkte, *Zeitschrift für Planung & Unternehmenssteuerung* 21 (4): 467–472.

Vaughan Williams, L., and Reade, J. J. (2016). Prediction markets, social media and information efficiency. *Kyklos* 69 (3): 518–556.

Vaughan Williams, L., Sung, M., and Johnson, J. (2019). Prediction markets: Theory, evidence and applications. *International Journal of Forecasting* 35 (1): 226–270.

Wagner, B. (2013). *Crowdsourcing – Eine Welt voller Ideen!* Master of Science, Hochschule Esslingen, unpublished.

3.8 GET YOUR CoV ON . . .*

Lora Cecere

The Coefficient of Variation (CoV) is frequently used as a measure of the volatility of a time series, and is often a good indicator of a time series' forecastability. Here, Lora Cecere shows a broader use of CoV to understand the rhythm and flow of an organization's supply chains. She uses CoV along with sales volume as part of a classification matrix to help set an organization's tactics for sales, delivery, production, and sourcing.

Citing data from a 2015 survey, demand volatility is seen as an increasing risk, with companies making little progress to mitigate this risk. Cecere points to many flaws she observes, such as 9 out of 10 demand planning solutions not improving FVA, and the improper measurement of demand accuracy. All too often, she finds, the focus is on technological implementation rather than getting better answers.

---

*This article is adapted from SupplyChainShaman.com (February 13, 2020) and appears here courtesy of Lora Cecere.

My friends would tell me to relax and get my groove on; but, today, I find myself deep into a presentation for a client's design thinking session next week. I am delving into CoV (coefficient of variation) analysis. So, as I tap my foot to the music, I am substituting CoV for groove. I think that more companies would benefit by getting *their CoV on*. . . . Let me explain.

Getting Your CoV On . . .

The Coefficient of Variation (CoV) is the ratio of the standard deviation to the mean. It is useful to analyze demand data to understand "forecastability" and randomness. Not all data is forecastable, and not all demand optimization engines are equal. The more forecastable the data set, the easier it is to find an optimizer. With a lower CoV, the process is easier and the required skill level not as high.

It is for this reason that I use CoV analysis to type logical supply chain flows. Using demand classification logic, you can understand the rhythm and flows of demand. . . . and hopefully get your groove on.

Companies do not have one supply chain, they have many. There are usually three to seven supply chains. The tactics need to align with the flows based on volume and variability. Most supply chain leaders cannot get their groove on because they generalize the use of the same metric targets and tactics for the supply chain without paying attention to the flows. Typically, the focus is volume-based segmentation with a bias to build supply chains for predictable and high-volume products. This is problematic because sometimes the low-volume products are mission dependent. This is the case for samples.

Let me give you an example of a client where a low-volume product was critical to brand positioning. The client manufactured baby formula. The goal was to build brand loyalty by giving a new mother the formula product in the hospital. The concept was simple, but the execution was flawed. The concept was to build brand loyalty at birth. The problem? The company focused only on high-volume product to retail. The product was losing market share to competitors because the company was shorting the shipments to hospitals of the samples for new mothers.

Here is how I build the demand classification logic. Start with high volume and predictable demand. Most companies have a high volume and predictable supply chain (CoV of less than .5), an intermittent supply chain (CoV of .5–1.5), and a supply chain that is less predictable (greater than 1.5). In addition, there is often a seasonal group of products, new product launch streams, and a service supply chain logical model. To be successful, each logical supply chain model needs different tactics. In Table 3.1, I share an example of assignment of tactics from a customer session. While the table was quickly generated in group discussion and is not perfect, it is designed to help the reader understand the logic.

Table 3.1 Sample Use of Tactics Per Supply Chain

Classification			Tactic	
	Sell	Deliver	Make	Source
High Volume/ Predictable	Forecasts based on orders	Full truck load movement Container/ rail/ocean	Lean	Just in Time Procurement DDMRP
Low Volume/ Predictable	Forecasts based on orders	Transportation optimization for routing and pooling	Constraint-based planning/Finite scheduling (reduce cycle stock through campaigns)	Source in market. Platform rationalization. DDMRP
High Volume/ Not Predictable	Use of sales data/market information Demand sensing	Postponement Shorten cycles	Production in market Strong what-if Capabilities	Source in market/short lead times Demand orchestration of alternate bill of materials
Low Volume/ Not Predictable	Demand sensing	Air freight Late stage postponement	Make to order/ Configure to order capabilities	Platform rationalization
Seasonal	Product profile planning	Seasonal builds based on market data		
New Product Launch	Attribute-based planning	Translation of market data to inventory strategies	Flexible work stations	Scaling partners

Discussion on Demand

When companies tell me that their demand variability increased over the last decade, I ask why. I want to know the drivers. Most cannot answer the simple questions. Organizations have a better understanding of supply than demand.

In Figure 3.10, I share data from the risk management study of 2015. Note that at this time, demand volatility risk was larger than economic uncertainty. However, as an industry, little progress has been made to mitigate demand variability as a supply chain risk. The answer is more than simple demand planning techniques. Making the shift is a change management opportunity for companies to move from a supply-centric thinking to think about demand as a river that flows through the supply chain. The CoV helps business leaders to understand the rhythm of the river flows. To make this journey requires the building of outside-in processes from the market and orchestrating the signal seamlessly across make, source and deliver. This is a radical shift from the functional orientation of traditional supply chain thinking.

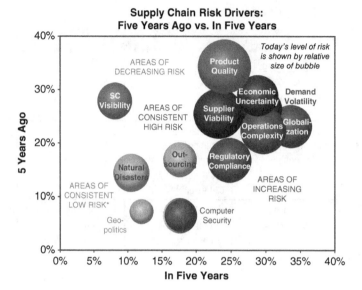

Figure 3.10 The Role of Demand Variability in Risk Mitigation from the 2015 Study
Source: Supply Chain Insights LLC, Supply Chain Risk Management Study (July 2015).

Base: Manufacturers, Retailers, Wholesalers/Distributors/Co-operatives Familiar with Risk Management at Company – Total (n = 125).
Q8: What do you see as the top 3 drivers of supply chain risk at your company today? Please select no more than three.
Q9: What were the top 3 drivers of supply chain risk at your company five years ago? Please select no more than three.
Q10: What do you expect will be the top 3 drivers of supply chain risk at your company in five years? Please select no more than three.
*Others with low risk not shown: Corruption, Intellectual Property Right, Energy and Water Scarcity and Increasing Consumer Power.

When I delve into the data, I find:

- **Forecasting Solution Signal Efficacy.** Nine out of 10 demand planning solutions I test are not improving the forecast (using Forecast Value Added analysis with the definition of a naive forecast as a three-month average of shipments.) Most initial deployments will lift or improve the forecast error by 7–12%. Over time there is degradation. It is usually not one issue, it is the combination of data cleanliness, optimization tuning, and employee understanding/training.

- **Elongation of the Supply Chain Tail.** Product proliferation results in lower volume per item. Supply chain design is normally focused on high-volume products, and traditional techniques are unable to adapt to shorter cycles.

- **Measurement.** Companies struggle to measure demand accuracy. Many companies mistakenly measure demand error at a "national" or a "customer level" at a "product family" level. This is insufficient for supply chain planning. Supply chain processes require accurate data at an item/shipment level. In addition, bias is an issue. In growth companies, the forecast is usually under-forecasted while in a down market there is usually a positive bias, or the tendency to over-forecast.

- **Supply-Centric Thinking.** One of the largest issues is supply-centric thinking. This includes:
  - **A,B,C Analysis by Volume.** This analysis is blind to demand variability.
  - **Generalization of Tactics.** Supply chain leaders love shiny objects – new technologies and processes. They tend to jump from one fad to another. As a result, tactics are applied across the supply chain without alignment to volume/variability analysis.
  - **Wrong Metrics.** In a supply-centric model, weighted MAPE is sufficient (WMAPE), but as the long tail increases, companies need to focus on MPE and MAPE. Weighting error hides the issues of intermittent demand.

A Side Discussion on MAPE and WMAPE

In the discussion of MAPE versus WMAPE, to make the point, I use the example of premature babies in the hospital. (At this client, they are shorting one out of two orders due to short shipments of intermittent demand. They feel over-confident in supply chain performance because WMAPE hides the issues of demand variability with lower volume shipments. [In this client example, WMAPE of high-volume predictable products is 26% versus 76% when measured at a MAPE level.]) On average in the United States, 11.5% of children are born premature. Premature children require extra precautions (a different supply chain of sorts). I then ask the group a question, *"Would it be acceptable to drop one out of every two premature babies from their neonatal units? You are what you measure . . ."*

Back to my client case study. In Figure 3.11, I share their current state of FVA analysis across the tail. The client analysis supports that at no point in the product tail is the forecast generated by their current technology and processes better than the naive forecast; yet, all the client wants to talk about is the roll-out of the current technology globally. In this discussion, I scratch my head.

Why are they not more focused on using decision support to get a better answer? And, why is there not a focus on fine-tuning the engines and applying different demand planning techniques? The answer lies in the truism, *"You manage what you understand."* All too often the focus is on implementation, not getting better answers.

Demand planning is all about attention to detail at an item/location level. As the CoV increases, the engine sophistication needs to change, and the organization must always answer the question, *"Are my processes and technologies improving forecast error and bias? And, how does the supply chain variability affect process flows? Then based on volume and variability, what are the right techniques to apply to each supply chain?"*

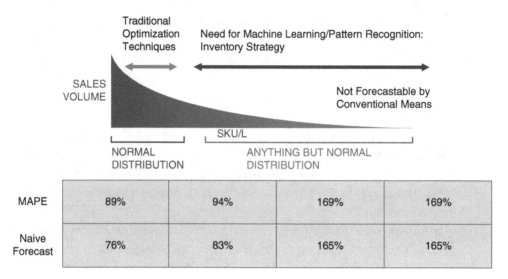

	NORMAL DISTRIBUTION		ANYTHING BUT NORMAL DISTRIBUTION	
MAPE	89%	94%	169%	169%
Naive Forecast	76%	83%	165%	165%

Figure 3.11 A Client Case Study

Yes, I strongly believe CoV helps companies get their groove on. . . . It helps companies understand the rhythm and flows of the supply chain dance.

3.9 STANDARD DEVIATION IS NOT THE WAY TO MEASURE VOLATILITY*

Steve Morlidge

In this brief excerpt from his book, Steve Morlidge offers an alternative to the commonly used Coefficient of Variation as a proxy for forecastability. While CoV indicates time-series volatility (and is often a good indicator of forecastability), it does not take into consideration the sequence of data points. When there is some pattern in the data such as trend or seasonality, the sequence can be very important.

As Morlidge illustrates with a simple example, two time series with equal CoV may have very different levels of forecastability. He shows that variation in the one-period-ahead naïve forecast (i.e., "no change" model) will more accurately represent forecastability. Thus, while CoV is useful as a "quick and dirty" rough indicator of forecastability, the Morlidge computation takes more effort, but gives more generally correct results.

Often traditional standard deviation (SD) metrics – or variants on it like the Coefficient of Variation (CoV) – are used to measure the volatility of demand series, and by implication the difficulty of forecasting them.

*This excerpt originally appeared in *The Little (Illustrated) Book of Operational Forecasting* (2018) and appears here courtesy of Steve Morlidge.

SD measures variation around the mean of a data series. In other words, it looks at the characteristics of the population of data points. The sequence in which the data arrives is irrelevant.

This means that data series that look very different can have the same SD.

But forecasters are more interested in the volatility of a data series from one period to the next because it is this that determines how difficult or easy it is to forecast the next data point(s). Forecasters are interested in the *sequence* of data.

Instead, use the variation of the (one-period-ahead) naïve forecast error to measure volatility for analyzing the characteristics of data series. This is mathematically related to SD but in some circumstances will give very different results.

Takeout

Never use standard deviation to measure the volatility of demand series for forecasting purposes. Use the variation of the naïve forecast error instead.

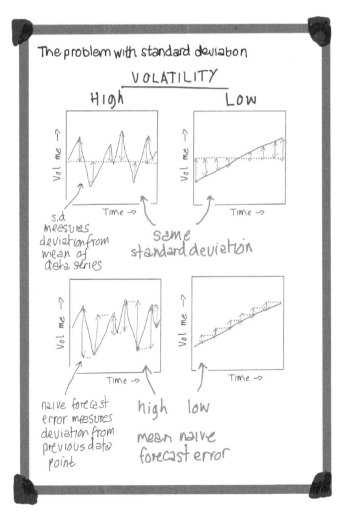

3.10 MONITORING FORECAST MODELS USING CONTROL CHARTS*

Joseph H. Katz

While automatic forecasting algorithms are adept at simplifying the model-selection process and generating forecasts without manual input, the monitoring of model performance – determining when a model must be adjusted or discarded – has not reached a similar level of sophistication. Joe Katz addresses this issue, presenting a new application of control charts for monitoring model performance.

Once forecast models are selected and forecasts are generated, the resultant models need to be monitored for quality and continued suitability as time passes and new data points are added to the history. Katz's method applies the traditional rules of statistical process control along with custom rules, and flags residuals for classification into severity zones. User rules then determine the action to be taken, whether a forecasting model should be maintained, adjusted/refit, or discarded and replaced. Automating this process is a valuable advance, and one even more critical when the number of time series is very large.

Introduction

When should a forecasting model be adjusted or replaced? This is an important consideration, because an inappropriate model results in avoidable forecast bias and error and can consume management resources making manual forecast adjustments.

Until now, there has not been an automated capability for monitoring forecast-model fitness for each time series to determine when models need to be discarded, adjusted, or left unchanged. Automating this process becomes even more critical when the number of time series is very large. The two main questions that need to be answered are

- Is it possible to evaluate forecast-model suitability and viability for each individual time series as time passes, and as new data points are added to the historical data?
- Can this forecast monitoring methodology be automated?

The answer to both questions is yes! The approach described in this article demonstrates that it is possible to evaluate and automate the monitoring of forecast-model fitness using control charts. Please note that this methodology is patented and owned by SAS Institute (Katz 2015).

---

*This article originally appeared in *Foresight: The International Journal of Applied Forecasting* (Winter 2020) and appears here courtesy of the International Institute of Forecasters.

Background

Today automatic forecasting software is available. These software tools will develop candidate models, incorporate events and independent variables, select the "best" model with optimized parameters, and generate forecasts – all without the need for human intervention. Yet the monitoring of model performance – determining when a model must be adjusted or discarded – has not reached a similar level of sophistication.

There are two common practices for monitoring model performance:

- Assess all time series based on a common criterion, such as "MAPE > 50%." In this approach, every time a forecast error exceeds the criterion, the time series is flagged for review.

- Replace models for all time series at fixed intervals (e.g., weekly, monthly, quarterly, biannually, or annually).

Note that both methodologies use a "one size fits all" approach, where *all time series* are treated in the same manner. This is problematic and inefficient. Regarding the first approach, a single forecast may exceed the error criterion just by chance, with nothing fundamentally wrong with the model. Such a model would not need to be reviewed. Or for a stable, easy-to-forecast time series, the error may always fall below the criterion, yet still be much higher than should be achievable with a more appropriate model. In this case, such a model should be replaced even though it may never be flagged for review.

Regarding the second approach, a suitably performing model does not need to be replaced on a routine basis. Doing so is just a waste of time and computational resources. Also, frequent model replacement is neither practical nor advisable as it can result in a lack of forecast-model stability and cause forecasts to fluctuate, in some cases dramatically.

Once forecast models are selected and forecasts are generated, the resultant models need to be monitored for quality and continued suitability, as time passes and new data points are added to the historical data. This ability to automatically evaluate each individual time series would represent a paradigm shift from the "one size fits all" approach that currently exists in many forecasting tools. The approach described below demonstrates that it is possible to automate the monitoring of forecast-model fitness using control charts.

Residual Analysis Methodology

For each individual time series, the new approach begins with an examination of model *residuals* – the difference between the forecast value and the actual value. The focus on residuals makes it different from the discussion of process behavior charts in forecasting (Joseph and Finney 2013), which is based on time series of *product sales*. For a more general discussion on statistical process control and control charts, refer to Wheeler and Chambers (1992) and Montgomery (2009).

When the forecast model is well specified, the residuals will be centered on a mean of zero, appear random with no specific patterns evident, and thus represent a process that is *in control*. Since the method uses only model residuals, it is model agnostic. The models used could be traditional time-series based, machine-learning based, ensemble models, or hybrid models.

The method analyzes residuals using Shewhart Control Charts for individual measurements, since the data is time-series based and there is one observation for each time period. The control chart, as shown in Figure 3.12, is constructed around the mean, $\bar{X}$, of the residuals, with UCL/LCL representing the Upper/Lower Control Limits. Zone C represents the 1-sigma range above and below the mean. Zone B represents the 1-sigma to 2-sigma range above and below the mean. Zone A represents the 2-sigma to 3-sigma range above and below the mean.

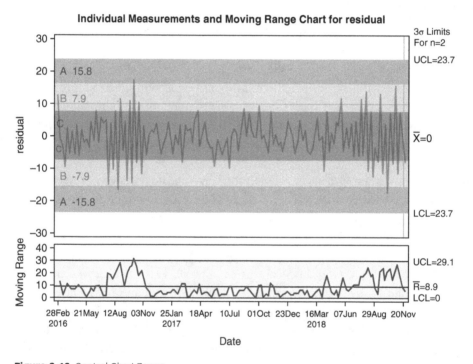

Figure 3.12 Control Chart Zones

Once the control limits and zones have been specified, exceptions are identified in the residual patterns using a combination of standard Western Electric rules and additional rules that are customizable by the user to best suit their business needs. As such, these rules can be made to be very sensitive to changes in residual patterns or structured to take a more conservative approach. The rules below try to strike a balance and are provided as guidelines.

Table 3.2 Western Electric Rules or Tests (Source: SAS®/QC Documentation)

Rule/Test	Pattern Description
1	One point beyond Zone A (outside the control limits)
2	Nine points in a row in Zone C or beyond on one side of the central line (The number of points can be specified as 7, 8, 9, 11, 14, or 20)
3	Six points in a row steadily increasing or steadily decreasing (The number of points can be specified as 6, 7, or 8)
4	Fourteen points in a row alternating up and down
5	Two out of three points in a row in Zone A or beyond
6	Four out of five points in a row in Zone B or beyond
7	Fifteen points in a row in Zone C on either or both sides of the central line
8	Eight points in a row on either or both sides of the central line with no points in Zone C

The standard Western Electric Rules or Tests are shown in Table 3.2.

The custom rules/tests that we have employed in this example are shown in Table 3.3.

These custom rules/tests provide an example of how a user might set the trigger conditions for when to discard and redevelop a model, when to adjust and refit a model, or otherwise when to just leave the current model alone. They represent a judgment call on how sensitive or conservative the user wishes the method to be.

We use the term *model vintage* to represent the date of the last model update or adjustment. You can think of it as the date of the most recent actual value included in the latest model update.

Once the exceptions are identified for dates greater than or equal to the model vintage date, residual process anomalies are classified by applying additional logic/business rules to the exceptions flagged from the Shewhart Control Charts. The anomalies are then sorted by level of severity and appropriate action is taken:

- Low severity – No model changes required
- Medium severity – Adjust/refit existing model parameters
- High severity – Discard current model and develop new model

Table 3.3 Shewhart Residual Analysis Custom Control Chart Rules/Tests

Rule/Test	Pattern Description
Discard/Redevelop	2 out of 2 points beyond 3-sigma limits
Discard/Redevelop	7 out of 7 points between 1-sigma and 3-sigma limits
Adjust/Refit	3 out of 3 points beyond 2-sigma limit
Adjust/Refit	5 points in a row increasing
Adjust/Refit	5 points in a row decreasing

Illustrative Examples

For illustrative purposes, we'll execute the method for the two time series shown for an item sold from Distribution Centers DC1 in Figure 3.13 and DC5 in Figure 3.14. The data are weekly, spanning February 28, 2016, through December 30, 2018.

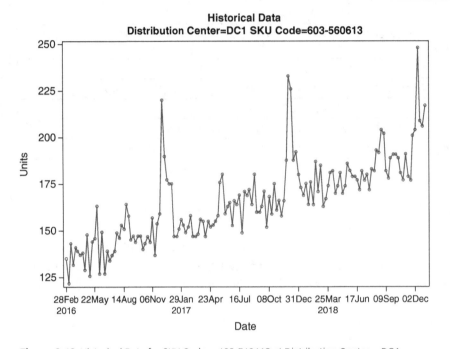

Figure 3.13 Historical Data for SKU Code = 603-560613 at Distribution Center = DC1

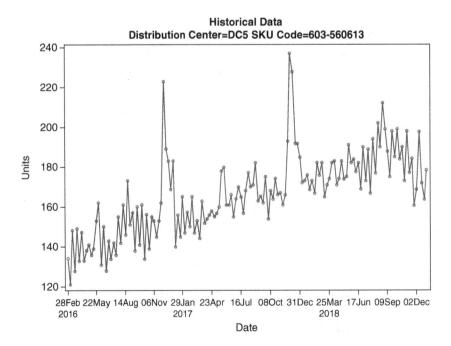

Figure 3.14 Historical Data for SKU Code = 603-560613 at Distribution Center = DC5

Table 3.4 Initial Models by Location

Location	Model Type	Model Specification
DC1	Winters Method (Additive)	A = 0.0327137184, β = 0.0265873762, and γ = 0.001
DC5	ARIMA	P = ((1)(52)) D = (1) Q = (1,2,3)

The patterns for these time series look somewhat similar except near the end of the series. The difference in their behaviors becomes apparent, however, when analyzing the residuals over time.

Shown in Table 3.4 are the initial models created via automated model selection, using actuals posted through November 18, 2018 (which becomes the model vintage date).

Using a forecast horizon of six periods, the plot of the initial model for DC1 is shown in Figure 3.15 with a fit MAPE = 2.63%. The model for DC1 is a traditional exponential-smoothing model with linear trend and additive seasonality. For DC5, a seasonal ARIMA model was chosen. (For *Foresight* tutorials on exponential smoothing and ARIMA models, see Stellwagen 2012; Stellwagen and Tashman 2013.)

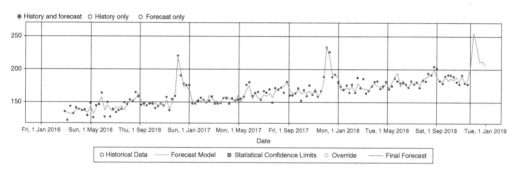

Figure 3.15 Winters Model Fit and Forecast SKU Code = 603-560613 at Distribution Center = DC1

Using a forecast horizon of six periods, the plot of the initial model for DC5 is shown in Figure 3.16 with a fit MAPE = 4.46%.

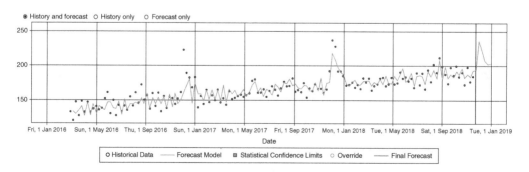

Figure 3.16 ARIMA Model Fit and Forecast SKU Code = 603-560613 at Distribution Center = DC5

As noted, our monitoring methodology begins with the calculation of the residuals from a forecasting model. Control limits are then determined based on the residuals. Residuals are, in effect, the "fit error" of the model over history.

Once the control chart has been created, we begin evaluating each new observation starting on the model vintage date. How the current model has fit in the past is no longer relevant since it isn't actionable: the model developed on November 18, 2018 can't be used to assess what happened in history – even though there may be several historical points outside the control limits or patterns detected. We react only to new observations and associated patterns that are actionable.

Example for DC1

Figure 3.17 illustrates the Shewhart Control Plot when the next week of data (November 25) becomes available.

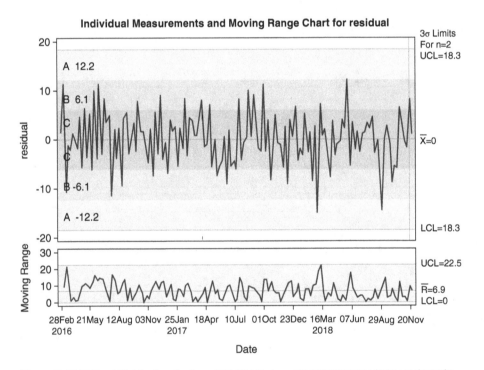

Figure 3.17 IR Chart Distribution Center = DC1 SKU Code = 603-560613 Posted History through: 25NOV18 Model Vintage: 18NOV18

The residual of 1.34 for November 25, highlighted above, is within the control limits with no patterns detected so no additional action is taken. This residual evaluation process is conducted each week as the new actual is observed and posted. Fast-forwarding four weeks, with actuals posted through December 23, 2018, the updated control chart is shown in Figure 3.18.

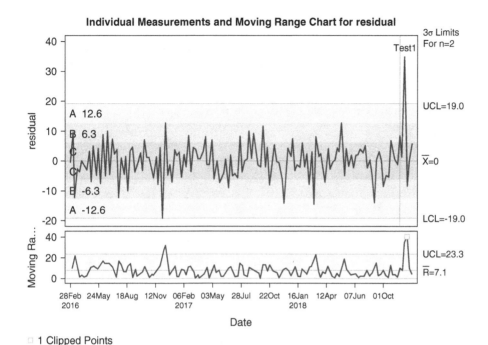

Figure 3.18 IR Chart Distribution Center = DC1 SKU Code = 603-560613 Posted History through: 23DEC18 Model Vintage: 18NOV18

Except for December 2, where the residual is outside the 3-sigma limit, we see that the residuals posted each week from November 25 to December 23 all fell within the control limits, so no action was required. We do not want to overreact to a single point being outside the 3-sigma limits. The original model developed on November 18 has remained in place without the need for any updates. (Note: A "Clipped Point" indicates an extreme value beyond the scale of the axis to make the chart more readable.)

Using an out-of-sample range of six periods, the plots of the Winters model with a November 18 vintage date and data through December 30 is shown in Figure 3.19 with a fit MAPE = 2.63% and an out-of-sample MAPE = 6.57%.

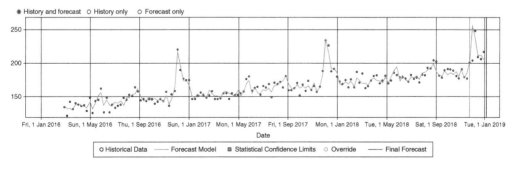

Figure 3.19 Winters Model Fit and Out-of-Sample Forecast SKU Code = 603-560613 at Distribution Center = DC1

Example for DC5

Figure 3.20 shows the Shewhart control chart plots with actuals posted through December 2, two weeks following the vintage.

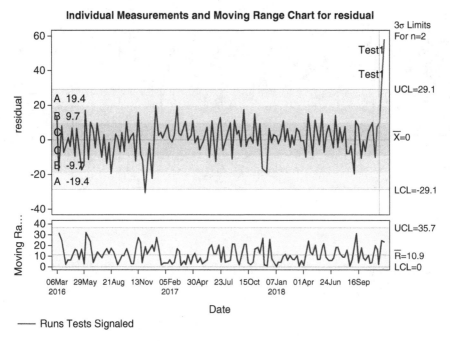

Figure 3.20 IR Chart Distribution Center = DC5 SKU Code = 603-560613 Posted History through: 02DEC18 Model Vintage: 18NOV18

We now see five consecutive points increasing in value, which indicates (per Table 3.3) that the model needs an adjustment/refit. In this case, the pattern started prior to the model vintage date but continued after it. Since the test is not signaled for these five points until after the model vintage date, it is a legitimate pattern that has been flagged. But we also observe that a Test 1 exception is thrown for both November 25 and December 2 – two consecutive points beyond the 3-sigma limits indicates (per Table 3.3) that the model should be discarded.

Since the discard flag is of higher priority than the refit flag, the model will be discarded and redeveloped with a new model vintage date of December 2, 2018. The new model is as follows:

$$\text{ARIMA}: P = 1 D = (1) Q = \big((1,,,2,,,3)(52)\big) + \text{AO02DEC2018D} + \text{AO25NOV2018D}$$

The plot of the new model is shown in Figure 3.21 with a fit MAPE = 4.38%.

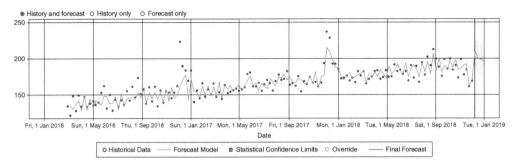

Figure 3.21 Updated ARIMA Model Fit and Forecast SKU Code = 603-560613 at Distribution Center = DC5

This residual evaluation process is conducted each week when the new actual is observed and posted. Fast-forwarding four weeks, with actuals posted through December 23, 2018, the updated control chart is shown in Figure 3.22.

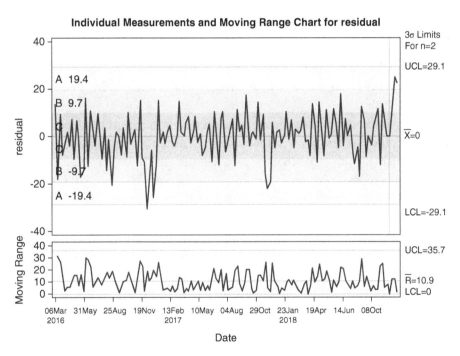

Figure 3.22 IR Chart Distribution Center = DC5 SKU Code = 603-560613 Posted History through: 23DEC18 Model Vintage: 02DEC18

The residuals posted each week from December 9 to December 23 all fell within the control limits with no patterns detected, so no action was required.

The plot of the new ARIMA model with a December 2 vintage date and data through December 30 is shown in Figure 3.23 with a fit MAPE = 4.38% and an Out-of-Sample MAPE = 13.51%.

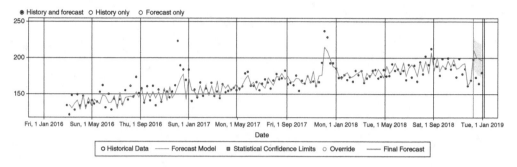

Figure 3.23 Updated ARIMA Model Fit and Out-of-Sample Forecast SKU Code = 603-560613 at Distribution Center = DC5

For DC5, the original model developed on November 18, 2018 was discarded and redeveloped on December 2.

Summary

The methodology demonstrates an innovative use of control charts for monitoring forecasts and determining forecast-model suitability. Each time series is managed and modeled (i.e., discard/redevelop, adjust/refit, or reforecast) based on its individual residual pattern and characteristics.

The methodology can be extended for use with each level in hierarchical forecasting and other modeling techniques. The methodology is efficient, robust, customizable/extendable, and scalable. It also avoids the "one size fits all" limitation that exists in many forecasting tools today.

References

Joseph, M., and Finney, A. (2013). Using process behavior charts to improve forecasting and decision making, *Foresight* 31 (Fall): 41–48.

Katz, J. H. (2015). *United States of America Patent No. 9,208,209.*

Montgomery, D. C. (2009). *Introduction to statistical quality control* (6th ed.). Hoboken, NJ: Wiley.

SAS®/QC 15.1 User's Guide (2019). https://go.documentation.sas.com/?cdcId=pgmsascdc&cdcVersion=9.4_3.4&docsetId=qcug&docsetTarget=titlepage.htm&locale=en

Stellwagen, E. (2012). Exponential smoothing: The workhorse of business forecasting. *Foresight* 27 (Fall): 23–28.

Stellwagen, E., and Tashman, L. (2013). ARIMA: The models of Box and Jenkins. *Foresight* 29 (Spring): 28–33.

Wheeler, D. J., and Chambers, D. S. (1992). *Understanding statistical process control* (2nd ed.). Knoxville: SPC Press.

3.11 FORECASTING THE FUTURE OF RETAIL FORECASTING[*]

Stephan Kolassa

The retail industry has been changing with breathtaking speed. New digital technologies such as the Internet of Things (IoT) are altering the expectations of retail customers – who overwhelmingly say they are willing to pay more for a better customer experience. Consequently, new competitors and innovative business models are emerging. In this article, Stephan Kolassa examines the implications of these retail trends on the shopping experience and the retail industry and details the challenging new requirements that will be imposed on retail forecasters.

As one example, the IoT allows improved optimization of inventories because its sensors can react immediately to unanticipated demands. Innovations like these will have wide-ranging impacts on how retail forecasting is done. Retailer data-science teams will have to utilize increasingly sophisticated forecasting and ML algorithms. Product variants will proliferate so that the demand data we need to forecast will have lower and lower volumes on increasingly granular levels, possibly invalidating standard statistical assumptions and methods. Furthermore, personalized offers and pricing, based on location, context (e.g., your cart's contents), situation (e.g., an overstock on fish), or emphasis (suppliers may be paying the retailer to have their brands recommended more prominently) will require instantaneous decision tools.

These retail trends will affect shopper centricity (focus on the shopper rather than category management), service to the "segment of one" (personalization of the individual shopper experience), smart retail technology (an expansive view of the "shopper" and inventory management), and the digital consumer supply chain (end-to-end tracking from supplier to consumer). Since consumer-packaged-goods (CPG) businesses depend heavily on retailers and many consumer-focusing businesses are vertically integrating, the changes are also very pertinent for nonretailers.

This article is followed by a commentary from Brian Seaman.

Introduction

One business we all come into contact with is retail sales. Whether we shop at a brick-and-mortar supermarket or order something online, each of us is a retail customer. And like any other industry, the retail sector needs and uses forecasts. These range from strategic forecasts to help decide where to build a new store or distribution center (DC), over tactical forecasts about what kind of promotion to run next month, to operational forecasts on SKU × day × location granularity for replenishing shelves *before* shoppers demand a product.

In recent years, the retail industry has been changing with breathtaking speed. In this article, I'll chronicle some of these changes and discuss their implications for

---

[*]This article originally appeared in *Foresight: The International Journal of Applied Forecasting* (Winter 2019) and appears here courtesy of the International Institute of Forecasters.

retail forecasting. Since many of these changes also apply in other industries, and since consumer-packaged-goods (CPG) businesses heavily depend on retailers and many consumer-focusing businesses are vertically integrating, I believe that the insights here are also interesting for nonretailers.

Your Next Shopping Trip

As an example of what is already – or mostly – possible, picture yourself entering your favorite supermarket. As you cross the threshold, the retailer's app on your mobile phone notices that you have entered the store. It automatically pulls up your shopping list, which is ordered according to the layout of this particular market's floor plan. As you walk past the shelves, you see the smart price tags adapt the prices – the store's forecasting algorithms have determined that there is a chance there may be a surplus of minced meat by evening, so prices are slashed in real time to draw shoppers. As you stop to inspect the meat counter, a camera tracks your eye movements. When it notices that you linger on a particularly appetizing cut of meat, your phone chirps and informs you that, as a valued Gold Star loyalty customer, you will get an additional 25% off this particular cut. Incidentally, did you know of this wine that goes really well with it? And we just happen to have a recipe that would work beautifully with both – especially considering that your cart just told the system what you had already put into it.

When you arrive at the dairy counter and admire the projection of happy Swiss cows chewing their cud at a distance on the back wall, your mobile phone pipes up once more. Your spouse just took the last carton of milk out of your smart fridge and, before she can message you to ask you to buy more, the fridge has already talked the matter over with the app on your phone. You notice a new brand of organic milk on the shelf and wonder whether to try it. Scanning the QR code gives you more information on the provenance, which looks promising, but you remember a friend of yours posting on social media that this particular brand of milk spoils extremely quickly. You put the carton back – not even the 30%-off coupon that just arrived on your phone will entice you to buy it.

At the wine section, you would really like to try the app's recommendation. Unfortunately, the range of selections seems daunting at first, but your phone comes to the rescue, telling you exactly where to look. There it is! No – there it *should* be. It seems to be out of stock. You scan the QR code on the shelf. The app tells you that two bottles should still be there, but they aren't. They're probably already in some other shopper's cart. Rather than try to find that cart and pilfer them, you decide to order a bottle for same-day delivery. What you don't see is that a machine-learning algorithm notices your scan of the QR code and your immediate order, assumes that the wine is out of stock, and notifies a store associate. By the time the associate arrives to restock the shelf from the back room five minutes later, you are long gone – and your wine is on its way to your doorstep.

Finally, you have everything. Your app knows not to bother you overmuch and does not send superfluous information your way – it noticed almost immediately how you recently changed your diet and you haven't seen an ad or a coupon for Pepsi since. No more nagging you anymore with "great deals" from that source. As you wheel your cart past the checkout directly to the parking lot, you not-so-fondly recall lines at the cashiers' stations, and having to load everything from the cart on the conveyor belt only to repack it in your bags afterwards – nowadays, your cart's contents are automatically tallied and charged against your credit card.

Digital Technologies and Trends

New digital technologies are disrupting business models. Examples include:

- Mobile solutions
- Hyperconnectivity
- The Internet of Things (IoT)
- Big data
- In-memory databases
- Cloud computation
- Social media
- Artificial intelligence (AI) and machine learning (ML)

The expectations of modern retail customers change accordingly. Customers have gotten used to the convenience of checking the weather across the country on their smartphones, and they have come to expect similar convenience when shopping for books, clothes, or groceries. In one survey, 86% of customers say they will pay more for a better customer experience, which corresponds well to the 80% of online shoppers who want same-day shipping – though less well with the fact that few online customers are willing to pay for delivery at all. New competitors and innovative business models emerge continually – like Amazon Fresh, estimated to be a $9 billion business – and they have started taking over traditional businesses, as when Amazon recently acquired Whole Foods.

Of course, the technologies discussed above interact. Mobile solutions and the IoT work only because we and the things around us are hyperconnected. The incredible amounts of big data generated can only be handled with new computing paradigms like in-memory databases and the cloud, and we need advances in ML to actually derive value from the data generated by traditional sources and social media.

Much of the above is not quite as new as it seems, although only recently have these technologies taken hold (Inman and Nikolova 2017). "Smart carts" with displays showing offers have been around for over 30 years! The patent for "videocarts" was filed in 1988 (back then, carts communicated with shelves using infrared signals), and by 1992 there were 46,000 carts. Sadly, Videocart, Inc., filed for bankruptcy in 1993.

Its displays were humongous, shoppers could not see their toddlers in the toddler seat, batteries ran down quickly, and customers did not appreciate having to push a heavy, nonfunctional display around.

Similarly, the ubiquitous self-checkout is already quite established; in 1992, both a patent for "an automatic point-of-sale machine" was granted and the first system installed. And ML – back then quaintly called "statistics," "time-series analysis," and "forecasting" – has predicted retail sales for automatic replenishment at least since 1996.

Some technologies really are new, though, or at least are now applied on an unprecedented scale. The Internet of Things connects more and more objects, starting with your car, your air-conditioning and heating, and the shades in your living room. Industrial machinery is already equipped with millions of sensors that notify users of impending breakdowns so they can be taken offline in a controlled way ("predictive maintenance"). It won't be long before your fridge not only suggests you need more milk but also calls the repairperson, advises which tools and spare parts to bring, and automatically schedules their visit after consulting with your calendar! Possible applications are incredibly diverse, really constrained only by the limits of interconnectivity.

Why is the Internet of Things important? For one, knowing exactly where every box of goods is at all times allows for optimizing our inventories – we can react immediately to unanticipated demands. Since not only products but also trucks and trailers are connected, we can analyze and optimize flows of product and of our fleet. When we consider connections not between objects but between people (and objects), the implications on improved workplace safety, health care, and home life become obvious. In addition, predictive maintenance will improve asset use and operational productivity. Finally, when we add ML to the mix, the resulting data streams and insights can be monetized.

Implications for the Retail Industry

The implications of the retail trends described above can best be explored through four channels:

- Shopper engagement
- Retail processes
- Retail work
- Monetization of new customer offerings

We can examine each of these on the basis of these characteristics:

- Shopper centricity – the focus on the shopper rather than category management
- Service to the "segment of one" – personalization of the individual shopper

- ▨ Smart retail technology – expansive view of the "shopper" and inventory management
- ▨ The digital consumer supply chain – end-to-end tracking from supply to consumer

Shopper Engagement

In terms of shopper centricity, as forecasters we are most concerned with improved prediction of demand. Note that we hope to predict *demand*, not *sales* – there is a difference; when product A is out of stock so that sales of A are zero, demand is nonzero, while sales of a substitute B are higher than demand would have been had A been available. As described above, new technologies allow retailers to influence customer navigation and decisions in many ways, from personalized ads based on shopper history, location, or eye tracking to improving customers' convenience through reordered shopping lists, smart carts, or mobile/self-checkout and paying. Social media and digital feedback loops, reviews, and product ratings are replacing traditional marketing surveys and directly influence forecasting, sourcing, assortments, and pricing.

In terms of service to the segment of one, this quote from the U.S. Census Bureau sums things up nicely: "Millennials are more diverse than the generations that preceded them." Personalization to each and every one of us is expected, even from discount retailers. However, internationally active retailers need to take cultural and legal norms of privacy into account (Maxwell, Dahlhoff, and Moore 2018). For delivery, this implies faster and faster – possibly proactive – fulfilment, subscriptions (Amazon Dash) and one-click service. The increasing diversity means that the "long tail" (Anderson 2008) is expanding, driven by online retailers that can offer much larger assortments than brick-and-mortar competitors, and by make-to-order, which in turn feeds back into the ever-higher expectations on fast fulfilment.

In terms of smart retail technology, shopper engagement means that retailers need to expand their definition of what a "customer" is to the technology that surrounds us: while the customer still has to push a button on his Amazon Dash, your supermarket will soon start to market milk directly to your smart fridge, which will hopefully be smart enough to take advantage of offers and stock up on milk (keeping your wishes on fat content, organic vs. conventional, glass vs. plastic vs. carton container, and price sensitivity in mind), while noting that you will go on vacation tomorrow, so better not to buy too much. Digital households (you, your spouse, your kids, fridge, car, mobile phone, and many others you may not think of as members of your household) are increasingly integrated in an omnichannel supply network, so connecting the dots allows the retailer to spot changes and trends quickly.

Retail Processes

Modern technologies will of course also have an impact on retail processes. Service to the segment of one means that many marketing processes will need to change. No longer can retailers simply insert coupons in the Sunday newspaper. Modern marketing needs to be personalized and location and context dependent. What to recommend and market to you needs to depend on your shopping history, on where you are in your supermarket (or, heaven forbid, whether you are actually in a competitor's store – best to immediately lure you back with a 10%-off coupon on your next purchase, a coupon that expires in 60 minutes so you had better hurry), and on context, by cross-selling according to the contents of your cart.

Smart retail technology will also change other retail processes, such as planograms – the exact specification of where on the shelf a given product is to be. Planograms are supremely important in determining maximal stocks (does a given product have one, two, or more "facings"?), and cheaper and cheaper cameras with image recognition software allow better monitoring of planogram execution. Heat maps tell us where customers are at a given time and where more store associates should be on hand to help them. Smart shelves track their own inventories and automatically trigger replenishment orders.

In terms of the digital consumer supply chain, end-to-end tracking (IoT again) will improve on-shelf availability and replenishment, as will demand-driven operations in planning and replenishment. Extending this digital supply chain back to digitally engaged suppliers and vendors will allow faster reactions.

Retail Work

Retailers also employ colossal numbers of people, from store associates to DC pickers to forecasters at central HQ. For store associates in particular, customer centricity and service to the segment of one mean leveraging real-time shopper and consumer insights from many channels and sources as well as social media. The retail associate will have to know *exactly* who the shopper is, what they bought last week, and what they said about it on Facebook. All this can and will inform their interactions. (How to make this non-creepy is a fine line.) And, like shoppers, retail employees are millennials, too, and they also have preferences older generations may not fully share. How about gamifying their everyday processes on their mobile devices to increase associate retention?

Smart retail technology will improve employee productivity. Prescriptive data science can turn scheduled activities into on-demand ones: no need to walk *all* the shelves to look for stockouts if your tools can tell you where a stockout might be, based on recent transactions and camera feeds. Store associates can be directed to offer help to specific high-value customers, where "high value" can either be someone who spends a lot of money at your chain, or someone who is vocal on social media about their retail experiences.

Alternatively, some client-based activities can be directly handed over to systems. No need to go looking for a store associate to help you if you can talk directly to the virtual assistant on your app, who is unfailingly polite and knows exactly where your favorite brand of chips is. In the backroom, HR processes can profit from the same productivity enhancements as other industry sectors through mobile apps and self-service functions, and workforce planning and scheduling can be improved through better store-traffic forecasts.

Monetization of New Customer Offerings

As any retailer who competes with Amazon can attest, the business model can have the greatest long-term transformational impact. The core idea is to monetize new customer offerings. Retailers can move beyond selling products to delivering *outcomes*. Subscription services offer more than just groceries – they offer convenience paired with healthy outcomes (which earlier business models emphasizing convenience did not necessarily focus on).

One example is HelloFresh.com. Retailers boast truly massive customer data: who bought what, where, and when. As described above, this treasure trove of data will only grow and it can be linked to external data sources like social media or your fitness tracker. These data can be leveraged and monetized as long as data protection regulations are observed, but retailers can also use them in-house to build brand loyalty and generate even more data.

Implications for Retail Forecasting

Having explored the future retailing landscape, what does all this imply for forecasting in retail, and what trends do we see?

Forecasting Expertise

The first trend in retail forecasting is that retailers are getting better and better positioned in terms of expertise for addressing imminent changes. More and more common are field data-science teams that consider increasingly sophisticated forecasting and ML algorithms. At the start of my retail forecasting career, 13 years ago, statistical know-how was scarce. This has changed. Big players like Amazon or Walmart show up in force at the annual International Symposium on Forecasting, recruit new data scientists there, give talks – including keynotes and featured talks – and write academic papers (e.g., Seaman 2018). Academic journals like the *International Journal of Forecasting* invite reviews of forecasting in retail – our contribution is in the Working Paper stage (Fildes, Ma, and Kolassa 2018). Other retailers recruit data scientists and experiment with Bayesian neural networks, Poisson regression and regression trees, and are capable of discussing predictive densities – all unheard of a decade ago.

Retailers will need to understand the changing capabilities of their competitors. They will have to invest in forecasting and data-science competence or be left behind. The potential payoffs from improved forecast accuracy and competitor understanding are lucrative. The same applies to individual forecasters at retailers.

Figure 3.24 encapsulates my thinking of the dimensions that the modern Renaissance Man (or Woman), the Data Scientist, needs to cover. Suppliers, vendors, and wholesalers will need to upgrade their skills, too, if they want to hold their own in discussions and negotiations with retailers, who typically have a very strong position in such relationships. The same applies to software vendors and consultants who work

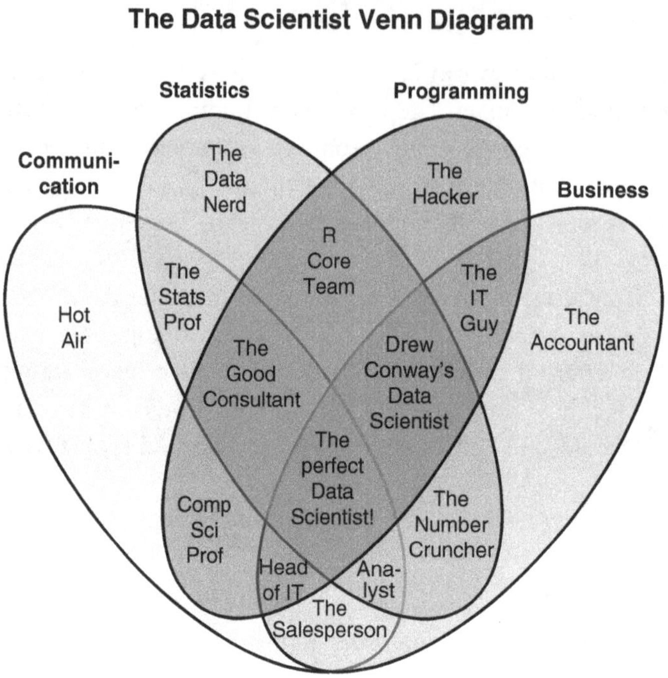

The Data Scientist Venn Diagram

Figure 3.24 A Data Scientist Venn Diagram Taken from https://datascience.stackexchange.com/a/2406/2853

with retailers. For these specifically, it is important not only to build up statistical and IT knowledge, but also domain knowledge about forecasting and the specific challenges this industry offers. You can become a laughingstock quite as easily by not knowing about neural networks and random forests as by not understanding the problems with data quality, delisting, stockout bias, and more.

Experimentation

Nobody really knows what's going to happen. Grocery is moving online just as books and durable goods did, but the speed differs markedly between countries, and it's anyone's guess where the saturation point is. Everyone is experimenting with fulfilment: home delivery by truck or by drone, click-and-collect in stores vs. "dark stores" (i.e., locations that only serve for click-and-collect fulfilment, with no customers walking the aisles), digital natives like Amazon entering the market vs. established players leveraging their supply networks and decades of experience, and so forth. I love this quote from Nielsen: "Across all of these models there is no evidence that any are fulfilling ongoing digital transactions profitably." The first retailers are already scaling back some of their more ambitious experiments, and no one has yet figured out how to stop burning money.

In terms of forecasting, this means you should be taking everything I am writing here – well, almost everything – with a grain of salt. One thing I have learned in my years of forecasting is humility. Another thing I've learned is that it's good to be prepared, even if you don't know what's coming. Collect all your data *now*. We don't know yet what will be useful in five years. There are many retailers who wanted to implement a forecast-driven replenishment system and actually had three years of past sales for the model to learn from – but did *not* have three years of historical promotion information, so the model could learn "regular" sales but not promotional sales, for lack of data. Don't be that retailer in five years.

Figure 3.25 A Google Trends Search for "Fidget Spinner"

Web and Social Media Amplify Feedback Loops

Remember fidget spinners, which were a huge craze at the beginning of 2017? The trend was propagated through social media like an epidemic, and many retailers (and suppliers) were caught by surprise. The scarcity may have driven demand even higher (Mello, Philhours, and Hill 2018), and supply chains scrambled to procure spinners – only to see demand collapse a few weeks later with excess stock purged by giving the spinners away for free. I imagine many forecasters were chewed out for not forecasting the explosion of demand – only to be raked over the coals later for not forecasting its collapse! In general, life cycles are shortening (see the recent trend toward so-called "fast fashion"), variances are increasing, and dynamics are getting faster and faster.

Do I have a recipe for how to deal with this? No. Forecasts may need to be more adaptive – but higher adaptivity means that we will also amplify spurious signals. Forecasters will have to work hard to explain these relationships to nontechnical colleagues, and it will be necessary to emphasize scenario and contingency planning to mitigate the effects of misforecasting.

New Kinds of Data Will Need to Be Forecast

Retailers are becoming increasingly data-driven and may even be able to monetize new data streams – if they understand them and can forecast them correctly. The proliferation of sales channels ("omnichannel") means that a single stockkeeping unit (SKU) may not only need to be forecast at each store and DC, but also in the Web store, separately for home delivery (out of which DC?), and for click-and-collect in a store, etc.

Life cycles are shorter and assortments change faster and faster – more SKUs to forecast in a year. Variants proliferate: remember the "most diverse" comment about millennials earlier? If you still doubt this, check the variants available at your yogurt shelf. But having 20 flavors instead of five doesn't mean that people eat four times as much yogurt as they used to; instead, it means that pretty much unchanged total demand now has to be forecast across four times as many SKUs. We will need to predict which personalized offers have a high conversion rate so we can only send the most promising ones to the shopper's app. Same for cross-selling product recommendations. We will need to forecast stranger and stranger things: footfalls in the store, the demand for services, and the stock in my smart fridge, and when I will likely replenish it.

As forecasters, this means that we will need to understand the main drivers for each time series or other prediction task – and also which drivers *not* to include (Kolassa 2016). In addition, the difference between (numerical) forecasting and (categorical) classification is blurring: it's not all that useful to classify customers into those who will take up an offer vs. those who won't; rather, we may need to forecast *how many* units a given customer might buy if we send them an offer. Thus, beyond classical time-series algorithms and ML, we may need new tools in our toolbox.

So the demand data we need to forecast have lower and lower volumes on more and more granular levels. This is a consequence of variant proliferation, long tail effects, and make-to-order already mentioned above. A similar driver is channel proliferation – each sales channel will need to be forecast separately for budgeting and target setting. Each fulfilment channel will also need to be forecast separately for physical fulfilment, and the two dimensions will need to be crossed in forecasting.

Another driver is personalization, which necessitates what-if forecasting on the consumer or household level. Connected homes and smart fridges contribute their shares of time series to be forecast. Fortunately or not, modern databases are capable of storing and munging all these data. Unfortunately, the expectations on forecasters increase at least as quickly as our capabilities of addressing them – some expectations certainly being driven by ML hype.

We as forecasters mainly need to note that lower volumes of so-called *count data* have a couple of statistical consequences. One is that standard normal distribution assumptions that underlie the fitting routine of most exponential smoothing, ARIMA, and other models (yes, also ML models!) are not applicable. Sadly, the theory of count-data modeling is far less advanced. Another point to keep in mind is that standard forecast accuracy or error measures may become less and less informative – or even actively misleading! – for low-volume-count data (Kolassa 2016b; Morlidge 2015).

Proliferation of Inputs

To differentiate themselves, retailers perform wilder and wilder gyrations. Their promotions become ever more complicated. They collaborate across sectors and cross-market, such as between supermarket and gas station chains. At the same time, they collect more and more data via loyalty cards and other schemes. Social media, fitness tracker, location, and other personal data are available, as are more and more nonpersonal data such as weather.

These inputs can be used to improve forecasts. And most nonforecasters believe that any additional input *will* improve forecast accuracy or at least not harm it. Well, that simply ain't so: sometimes it's better to be simple than correct in modeling (Kolassa 2016a). Adding inputs that are weakly correlated with demand quickly runs into overfitting and actually harms accuracy. *Regularization* https://en.wikipedia.org/wiki/Regularization_(mathematics) offers a way forward in this situation, and forecasters are acquiring the expertise to actually include this. However, we will still need to explain to our forecast consumers why including social-media information does not improve the forecasts in line with their expectations.

Instantaneous Decision Tools

These proliferating inputs can be fed back into *instantaneous decision tools*. We have personalized offers and pricing, based on location (e.g., a competitor's store), context (e.g., your cart's contents), situation (e.g., an overstock on fish), or emphasis (suppliers may be paying the retailer to have their brands recommended more prominently).

The consequences for forecasting are twofold. On the one hand, we'll have a say in optimizing these decision tools and their input (which information should be fed into a "recommender" system to maximize margin?). On the other, we may need to take these into account when forecasting demand. If a retailer implements a new recommendation engine that suggests products based on your shopping history, this will likely have a differential impact on different products – we'll see feedback effects. Do we at some point need to forecast who enters our store and what they put into their cart, in order to predict what other products they will be recommended to buy, so we can improve forecasts for *those* products?

Data Quality May Improve – Or Not

We know that the IoT and hyperconnectivity will give us more data, and of course the hope is that the data will also get better. But will proliferating data rot faster than we clean it? It is well known, for example, that most system inventories are wrong, an effect known as IRI or inventory-record inaccuracy (DeHoratius and Raman 2008).

One might think that this may improve as more and more products and systems go online. However, there are countervailing trends. One instance is the move toward mobile checkout and pay. There are indications that having people "do the retailer's work" by allowing them to self-scan with their mobile device lowers the psychological barriers to shoplifting (Taylor 2016). Of course, this will make IRI worse.

For us as forecasters, this means that even in this brave new world of new technologies, the old truisms remain: data quality is always an issue, and we will always have to think about what systematic (and systemic) problems may be present in our data, and how to clean it before modeling. There are no silver bullets.

Conclusion

The retail industry is in an exciting place, and it is difficult to be certain about where we'll stand in five years. We will see new challenges. However, much hard-won experience in retail forecasting will stay relevant and, in spite of vendors' hyperbole, new technologies and emerging trends are not assured to usher in a wonderful new world of permanently higher forecast accuracy.

References

Anderson, C. (2008). *The long tail: Why the future of business is selling less of more*. Hachette.

DeHoratius, N., and Raman, A. (2008). Inventory record inaccuracy: An empirical analysis. *Management Science* 54, 627–641.

Fildes, R., Ma, S., and Kolassa, S. (2018). Retail forecasting: Research and practice. https://www.researchgate.net/publication/328095900_Retail_forecasting_research and practice

Inman, J. J., and Nikolova, H. (2017). Shopper-facing retail technology: A retailer adoption decision framework incorporating shopper attitudes and privacy concerns. *Journal of Retailing* 93, 7–28.

Kolassa, S. (2016a). Sometimes it's better to be simple than correct. *Foresight* 40 (Winter): 20–26.

Kolassa, S. (2016b). Evaluating predictive count data distributions in retail sales forecasting. *International Journal of Forecasting* 32(3): 788–803.

Maxwell, J., Dahlhoff, D., and Moore, C.-L. (2018). Competing for shoppers' habits. *Strategy+Business* (Summer): 74–93.

Mello, J., Philhours, M., and Hill, K. (2018). Warning signs for forecasting consumer-induced shortages. *Foresight* (Fall): 17–23.

Morlidge, S. (2015). Measuring the quality of intermittent demand forecasts: It's worse than we've thought! *Foresight* (Spring): 37–42.

Seaman, B. (2018). Considerations of a retail forecasting practitioner. *International Journal of Forecasting* 34, 822–829.

Taylor, E. (2016). Supermarket self-checkouts and retail theft: The curious case of the SWIPERS. *Criminology & Criminal Justice* 16, 552–567.

COMMENTARY

Brian Seaman

The retail industry is in the middle of an enormous transition, moving from single-channel businesses to a hyper-connected "omni-channel" ecosystem that continually elevates customer experiences. Stephan Kolassa's article in this issue does an excellent job of explaining how traditional retailing is evolving, and projects many of the possible future adaptations. It's an environment that well-prepared forecasters can guide and inform.

Kolassa highlights the role of customer-centric retailing, which focuses on improving customer experiences. This manifests in various ways, including the convergence of physical stores and e-commerce, interactions via the Internet of Things (IoT), and revamping internal processes to support these changes. Retailers are continuously experimenting with new offerings to gauge customers' reactions, and it's crucial that forecasters stay ahead of the data to reinforce these services. However, I would like to expand on two areas in particular: the effects of omni-channel retailing on forecasting requirements and the impact of data science on retail forecasting.

Omni-Channel Retailing

One key issue is the impact of innovation in digital technologies on brick-and-mortar retail. Companies are adapting to this new environment by putting customer-centric and omni-channel experiences front and center, with e-commerce not an afterthought but a driving force.

Customers' expectations are constantly increasing, and retailers must lead the way. Some businesses can do so by integrating stores and online shopping experiences in a seamless way. Consumers understand that they can go to a store or go online, and these choices clearly align with off-line and online commerce. Distinctions become muddled, however, when you order your groceries online and have them delivered to your car, or when a store associate places an order for an extended assortment to be delivered to your home later that day, or when you have a shirt delivered to your home but you return it to the seller's brick-and-mortar location. The convergence of online and physical retailing opens up new opportunities. In this environment, customers are enabled to shop how and when they want.

The intermingling of omni-channel commerce creates complications for retailers though. Sales and profitability will always be critical, but there are other financial breakouts that drive business strategy. For instance, the supply chain may primarily track sales based on the origin of inventory, but the front-end website team considers the customer's order placement method (online or off-line) more important, since they need to scale resources to support online traffic patterns. The marketing team may care most about the detailed transaction from placement of order to customer pickup, to provide timely and relevant advertisements and promotions.

In this situation, there is no single hierarchy that encompasses all the business's needs, since you can group by order placement method and inventory location independently. There have been several advances in hierarchical forecasting (e.g., Villegas and Pedregal 2018) that I'd like to see extended into *multi-membership hierarchy forecasting models*. These models would make it easier to leverage a single forecasting framework into support for multiple uses. Doing so becomes more important as advances in technology enable improvements in integrated S&OP tools. Wickramasuriya, Athanasopoulos, and Hyndman (2018) have come up with a promising candidate to support these forecasting requirements. Future assessment with large-scale multi-membership hierarchies will help to validate this approach.

Retail Forecasting

Kolassa describes the increasing amounts of data available to forecasters from social media, devices like fitness trackers, and the multiplicity of sales channels. Each of these data sources gives retailers additional avenues for customer connection.

Data science in all of its varieties – statistics, forecasting, machine learning, et al. – will play a larger role in decision making, linking goals and forecasts more immediately. Suppose a retailer has set a growth goal for a particular product category. Traditionally, you might adjust your promotion and marketing strategies. With an automated marketing system that seeks to minimize costs while achieving growth goals, marketing expenses can fluctuate hourly, on the fly. In this situation, sales forecasts will be actively influencing the marketing spend – which in turn influences sales.

This isn't necessarily a new forecasting phenomenon or challenge, but the real-time levers of action can make the impact more profound. Here, we need two kinds of forecasts: one that's internal to the real-time decision-making systems, that guides decision making from moment to moment, and another that is external to the system, that projects a longer-term horizon for strategic planning.

Imagine a marketing team is attempting to hit a specific sales goal for the month and is leveraging an automated marketing system that minimizes advertising spend for a particular sales target. Their judgmental forecast of aggregate sales would likely be very close to the sales goal, even if they were not trending there currently, since they know that the data-science systems can raise or lower marketing spend to change sales. Due to the feedback loop, this externally derived forecast would be ineffective as part of the internal automated marketing system. The automated system would need an internal forecast based on the current ad spend to determine whether or not to change that ad spend. Here, a human-created forecast might well be better than one that is algorithmically derived for long-term aggregate sales but ineffective dealing with disaggregated short-term sales.

There is interesting work now being done to compare algorithmic forecasts with human experts in the context of promotions (Trapero, Kourentzes, and Fildes 2014). Extensions of work such as Petropoulos, Kourentzes, Nikolopoulos and Siemsen (2018) will be valuable if they can continue to determine the situations in which human experts perform better than models – and why.

Judgmental forecasts are affected by individual incentives: the importance, say, of having enough inventory to meet promotional demand. Lower sales can be handled by simply extending the promotional window; but if the inventory-management system is not able to satisfy a sales spike, the sales forecaster may hedge by producing a higher forecast to achieve adequate stock. In this situation, measuring the relative accuracy of the forecasts via metrics like MAPE or MASE doesn't appropriately measure the *asymmetric* impacts of forecast errors. As the new retail ecosystem becomes more complicated, it is imperative that forecasters keep pace and continually examine the context in which forecasts are being used.

Conclusion

Retail is going through extraordinary changes that greatly benefit consumers and also cause us to rethink how we can best serve them. It is good to see the focus on the future of forecasting in this industry; hopefully Stephan Kolassa's article will stimulate many fruitful discussions and new research.

Acknowledgment

I would like to thank Quoc Tran for many useful forecasting discussions, as he has continually helped me to stretch my thinking and provides invaluable feedback.

References

Petropoulos, F., Kourentzes, N., Nikolopoulos, K., and Siemsen, E. (2018). Judgmental selection of forecasting models. *Journal of Operations Management* 60, 34–46.

Trapero, J. R., Kourentzes, N., and Fildes, R. (2014). On the identification of sales forecasting models in the presence of promotions. *Journal of the Operational Research Society* 66, 299–307.

Villegas, M. A., and Pedregal, D. J. (2018). Supply chain decision support systems based on a novel hierarchical forecasting approach. *Decision Support Systems* 114, 29–36.

Wickramasuriya, S. L., Athanasopoulos, G., and Hyndman, R. J. (2018). Optimal forecast reconciliation for hierarchical and grouped time series through trace minimization. *Journal of the American Statistical Association.* doi:10.1080/01621459.2018.1448825

CHAPTER **4**

Forecasting Performance

The evaluation of forecasting performance is a perennial topic for discussion. Dozens of metrics have been developed, with some (such as Mean Absolute Percent Error) gaining wide adoption despite being unsuited for some common situations. While no single metric has gained universal acceptance, we covered many of the options in our 2015 collection, *Business Forecasting: Practical Problems and Solutions*. This brief chapter provides four new perspectives on issues relating to forecasting performance.

In the first article, Steve Morlidge attempts to move beyond the arcane debate between experts, where little attention is paid to how an error metric can be used to improve the process of forecasting. He describes a control system that provides timely, actionable feedback, intended to promote the right behavior to effect forecast improvement.

Next, Patrick Bower argues from a similar starting point, rejecting the "exercises in intellectual preening that offer little in terms of practical guidance." Bower then provides 10 practical guidelines for selecting and implementing a forecast performance measure.

In the third article, Stefan de Kok introduces us to an entirely new metric, Total Percentage Error (TPE). TPE measures the full range of uncertainty in our forecasts, providing a tool for better decision making. He further extends the concept to provide an enhanced version of Forecase Value Added (FVA), which he dubs Stochastic Value Add (SVA).

Finally, Len Tashman explores the performance of prediction intervals. Calculated PIs are known to be too narrow to reflect the confidence we should have in the forecast, and this article shows the reasons why.

* * *

4.1 USING ERROR ANALYSIS TO IMPROVE FORECAST PERFORMANCE*

Steve Morlidge

In a series of ground-breaking articles published in *Foresight* (and listed below in the references), Steve Morlidge exposed glaring deficiencies in the practice of business forecasting. His research showed that the quality of business forecasts is generally poor, and companies lack the proper tools and methods to address the problem.

In this article, Morlidge focuses on ways to improve forecasting performance by improving the ways we measure forecast error. He shows how the right measures, analyzed and presented appropriately, can provide insights and promote the right behavior.

Preview and Key Points from the Author

Over the last two years I have written a number of pieces for *Foresight* with proposals about how to improve the measurement of forecast error. In this article, I show how these and related ideas can be used to manage the performance of the forecast process.

Drawing upon my own experience, I will show how to

- Measure and track trends in forecast performance.
- Compare and benchmark forecasts.
- Identify the drivers of forecast performance.
- Routinely track down the root causes of performance failures.
- Conduct periodic reviews of the performance of a portfolio of forecasts.
- Measure the impact of avoidable forecast error on the company.

Such analyses can be embedded in a control system to provide speedy, actionable feedback to forecasters and to their internal customers. They could also form the basis of an approach for consultants or internal experts to audit the quality of the forecasting process.

This article furnishes examples of the practical application of this approach in the demand-forecasting process of a typical consumer-goods business, selling product from stock.

---

*This article originally appeared in *Foresight: The International Journal of Applied Forecasting* (Spring 2016) and appears here courtesy of the International Institute of Forecasters.

Key Concepts

In my earlier articles, I proposed using two "new" metrics:

Relative Absolute Error (RAE)

The RAE (Morlidge 2013) is the ratio of the mean absolute forecast error to the equivalent error for a naïve (or no-change) model in which the current actual value is the forecast for the subsequent period. The naïve forecasts represent the period-to-period volatility in the data.

An RAE =1 indicates that, on average, the forecast errors for your chosen method are equal to those from a naïve method; in other words, you've not improved on the naïve forecasts. An RAE >1 is a red flag that your forecasts on average are not as accurate as the naïve forecasts.

Your hope is that your chosen method will improve on the naïve, yielding an RAE < 1.

I have amassed considerable evidence that, in practice, short-horizon, very granular forecasts (of the kind used in planning supply) very rarely achieve an RAE as low as 0.5, a level that suggests that this represents the best forecast performance achievable.

Since the period-to-period volatility of a data series is arguably the most important determinant of how easy or difficult it is to forecast accurately, the use of the RAE metric corrects for *forecastability* and so makes it possible to compare the results of disparate forecasts.

It is also a reliable measure of the value added to a business by its forecasting function, since the alternative to forecasting is to replenish stock based upon what has been sold in the previous period, which is equivalent to using the naïve forecast.

The Bias-Adjusted Mean Absolute Error (BAMAE)

The BAMAE is calculated (Morlidge 2015a,b) by decomposing error into two components: net systematic error (bias) and unsystematic error, which is the average error variation around the net error. Adding together the two elements (expressed in absolute terms) results in the BAMAE.

The BAMAE is an improved version of the conventional mean absolute error (MAE or MAD) statistic.

a. It corrects for inconsistencies in the way that MAE accounts for the impact of bias. As I've shown, the MAE can give misleading results when used to measure forecast accuracy when the distribution of demand is skewed, such as for items with intermittent demands.

b. It enables us to reflect more clearly the impact of forecast error on the business. This is because the two components affect the business in different ways: bias leads to too much or too little *cycle stock* being held, while any avoidable variation requires more *safety stock* to meet any given customer-service target than is strictly necessary.

Bias-Adjusted Relative Absolute Error

Combining these two measures produces *a bias-adjusted RAE*. While the RAE is calculated as MAE/naiveMAE, the Bias-Adjusted RAE is BAMAE/naiveBAMAE. This metric offers the prospect of creating a powerful system of measurement that allows for forecastability, is insensitive to extreme patterns of demand, and captures how much value the process adds to the business. Translating these insights into practice, though, is not without challenges.

Operational Hurdles to Using New Metrics

Like many other aspects of forecasting, the major challenge in transferring concepts to the workplace lies less in the mathematics per se than in building an infrastructure capable of deploying the concepts at scale while also communicating the results in a simple and intuitive way. We want to maximise their impact while minimising the need for expert knowledge and training.

For my particular metrics to deliver the actionable insights they promise, they need to be calculated "bottom up"; this is because, when used in supply planning, it is the quality of the demand forecast made at the lowest level in the product hierarchy that is most important. While we will still need to be able to measure the quality of an entire portfolio, analysing high-level errors always underestimates the negative impact of forecast errors on the business. Also, since it is not possible to draw sensible conclusions from a single data point, any robust analysis requires a reasonably long series of forecasts, ideally a dozen or more.

The results also need to be analysed across multiple dimensions, which brings fresh challenges. The examples shown below are based on data for a fictional company, ABC Inc., which forecasts demand at SKU level to plan production for the following month. In total, the business has about 2,000 products, which are forecast for up to 300 different customers based in any of three regions of the world; this means that, over the 24 periods analysed, up to 25 million data points need to be captured, analysed, and reviewed. And adding different dimensions will increase the size of the database exponentially.

While the data-management challenges are significant, the potential to deliver powerful, usable insights is limited only by the ability to communicate the results in a manner that makes it easy for a wide range of nontechnical users to understand and interpret the results quickly and easily. The examples shown below illustrate the range of the insights that such an approach is capable of delivering, how they can be enacted in the firm's systems, and a spectrum of data visualisation techniques to aid analysis and communication.

Error Analysis

The Level and Trend of Forecasting Performance

Table 4.1 shows the level of performance for the total portfolio over the last 18 months. The Value Added Score (VAS) is calculated by converting the Bias-Adjusted RAE to a scale of minus-to-plus 100, making it more palatable for nonexperts.

Table 4.1 Level of Forecast Performance

Level of Performance	VAS	Bias-Adjusted RAE
Excellent	60–100	0.50–0.70
Good	30–60	0.70–0.85
Adequate	0–30	0.85–1.00
Poor (value destructive)	<0	>1.00

I've colour-coded the VAS to emphasize the quality of the forecasting results. So, for example, a negative VAS score would be shown in dark gray, and a VAS greater than 60 is coded light gray to represent an excellent performance.

Figure 4.1 reveals the trend in the VAS over time and compares it to a benchmark VAS shown in gray.

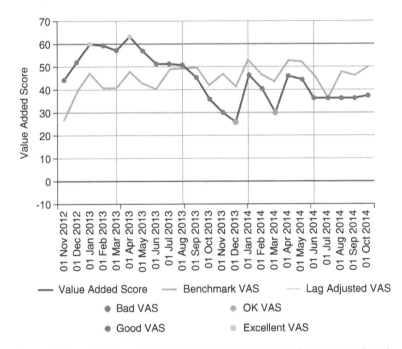

VAS by Period

Figure 4.1 Trend in Forecast Performance, Including a Comparison to a Benchmark

In this case, you can see that the performance of the total portfolio has deteriorated over time from generally excellent early on, then to good, and dipping to adequate in the latter half.

Tellingly, forecast performance has dipped below that of a benchmark method. For the benchmark, I have chosen Simple Exponential Smoothing (SES), which forecasts each future period as a weighted average of the historical data up to that point, where more weight is given to the recent rather than distant past. It is the simplest credible extrapolation technique, ignoring possible trend and seasonal patterns.

The VAS of our chosen methods cross the benchmark VAS in August 2013, confirming that the deterioration in forecast quality is real.

Demand managers in charge of forecasting for a portfolio would typically use a chart like this to identify when action needs to be taken.

Portfolio Performance Comparisons

The VAS rating can be applied to each part of a portfolio, permitting comparisons of forecasting performance across business segments. Table 4.2 shows the relative performance of five business areas, ranked from best to worst in order of the VAS score in the second column.

Table 4.2 A Value-Added League Table

VAS Period League Table

Class	VAS	bVAS	Ranking	Status	Impact Alarmed		Value Added
Business Area 1	39	51	1		4,682k		3,827k
Business Area 4	38	48	2		1,169k		879k
Business Area 5	6	-45	3		30k		3k
Business Area 2	-6	56	4		127k		-14k
Business Area 3	-35	31	5		42k		-13k
	37	50			£6,050k		£4,683k

The column 3 table – labelled bVAS – shows the VAS for the benchmark method (SES). It is interesting that the forecasting performance for the best-performing business area is below that from applying the benchmark method to the items in this area. So there is still significant scope for improvement there.

Column 5 contains a status symbol whose colour represents the VAS – the same colour scheme as in Table 4.1 – and whose performance relative to the benchmark method is shown as a plus (+) or a minus (–). So Business Area 5, for example, is coloured medium gray for *adequate* forecasting performance but given a plus for its improvement on the benchmark.

In column 6, we show the "Impact Alarmed," defined as the value of all those low-level forecasts within this part of the portfolio that have statistically significant levels of bias. The size of the "Impact Alarmed" is a good measure of the scale of the improvement opportunity. For example, for Business Area 1, 4682k units of error are associated with SKUs that are in an alarmed state, which is an indication of the scope for improvement: reducing this by 50% would increase the value added by around 60% (2341/3827).

The far-right column – labelled "Value Added" by forecasting – shows how much better in aggregate the forecasts are than simple replenishment (in error units).

This table provides practitioners with the ability to benchmark forecast performance within their organisation, since using the naïve forecast as a comparator provides a level playing field between disparate products. In principle, provided that care is taken to ensure data was captured and analysed in a consistent manner, the same approach could be used to benchmark forecasts between organisations, too, since this method assumes that both the ease of forecasting and the value it adds are entirely the product of the volatility of the data series rather than any specific or unique characteristic of a business or industry.

Benchmarking in this way enables management to determine the need and scope for improvement, and, perhaps more important, helps to identify forecasting good practice that can be spread.

Drivers of Forecast Quality

The quality of a forecast has two components: how successfully low-level forecasts have captured the *level* of demand and the *pattern* of demand. Net error (bias) measures the level of forecast error, and this determines whether the business has too much or too little cycle stock. Variation around the net error measures how well the pattern has been captured and determines how much safety stock is need to meet customer-service targets.

The panels in Figure 4.2 show the level of bias and variation, and (in the left panel) their relative contribution to the VAS (using the BAMAE methodology). This chart shows the negative impact of bias (−14 VAS points) on value added, indicating that the VAS would have been 14 points higher if the forecasts had no greater bias than the naïve forecasts.

Figure 4.2 Showing the Relative Contribution of Bias and Variation to Total Value Added

In addition to the net bias number for the total portfolio, the middle panel also quantifies what is driving it: the relative contribution made by over- or under-forecasting at the lowest level in the portfolio. Aggregate bias is critically high at 15.7%, as is the contribution made by those low-level forecasts that are over-forecast (22.5%). Despite the high aggregate level of over-forecasting, there are some low-level forecasts that are under-forecast, albeit their contribution of −7.6% is not at a significant level in total.

Lastly, the right panel shows the variation component of the BAMAE, which is the product of the variation in demand (as measured by the naïve forecast error) and the variation of the forecast, both of which are also shown in the right-hand panel.

This chart provides management with a high-level summary of overall forecast quality, and the nature of the changes that need to be made to improve it.

Root-Cause Analysis

To be actionable, any measure of forecast quality needs to help forecasting practitioners identify the drivers of performance and allow them to trace these back to the relevant low-level forecasts. This can be achieved by separately analysing bias and variation measures. We'd look for evidence of critically high values, ideally using statistical significance tests (Table 4.3). By drilling down through the product hierarchy to find the low-level forecasts responsible for generating these alarms (Table 4.4), practitioners can use their contextual knowledge to determine the root cause of the problems and take appropriate remedial action.

Table 4.3 Showing High-Level Organisation Units (Business Areas) with High Bias Levels

Bias Snapshots

Class	Alarm	Time	Alarmed Impact		Total Impact	Bias
Business Area 1		●	£1,289k		£1,715k	21%
Business Area 4		●	£361k		£436k	33%
Business Area 2		◕	£48k		£89k	111%
			£1,698k		£2,240k	

Figure 4.3 is a graph of forecast error, showing the high level of net error driving the bias alarms in the worst-performing channel: persistent over-forecasting for more than a year, excepting March 2014.

In a company like ABC Inc., forecasters often have difficulty finding the needle in the haystack. They will therefore use tables like this as part of their normal routine to quickly identify and root out problems before they have an opportunity to significantly degrade overall forecast quality.

Table 4.4 "Drill-Down" Showing Subunits of Business Area 1 with High Levels of Bias

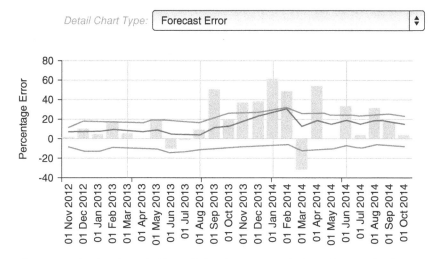

Bias Alarms

Class	Alarm	Time	Impact of Bias Alarmed		Impact of Bias	Bias
BA1-BC82411			£736k		£947k	22%
BA1-BC82410			£264k		£325k	27%
BA1-BC82409			£139k		£220k	21%
BA1-BC82412			£112k		£159k	17%
BA1-BC82409			£17k		£20k	-14%
BA1-BC82413			£33k		£40k	54%
			£1,301k		£1,712k	

Detail Chart Type: Forecast Error

Figure 4.3 Showing the Period-by-Period and Average Level of Error in One Subunit

Portfolio Analysis

ABC Inc. has a large number of forecasts that need to be managed, and periodically there may be a requirement for a snapshot of the entire portfolio.

Figure 4.4 is a scatter chart of the performance of all low-level forecasts in part of the portfolio. Movement from left to right on the horizontal axis indicates a reduction in bias, and movement up the vertical scale represents a reduction in forecast error variation. Thus the northeast quadrant – lower bias and variation – contains the best value-added scores (VAS).

Value Added Matrix

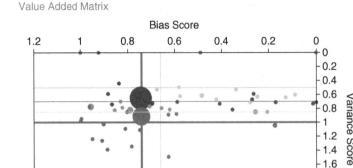

Figure 4.4 Forecasting Performance Characteristics of a Portfolio

The diagram represents not only the level of bias and variation and forecast quality category (colour), but the scale of the avoidable error (size of bubble). I define avoidable error as that error in excess of 0.5 RAE. In this chart, there are a number of products in the "bad" bottom-left quadrant with significantly high levels of both bias and variation; but the biggest problems – or, better: improvement opportunities – are the big light gray and dark gray bubbles that you see near the intersection of the thick lines that demarcate the quadrant. The light gray bubble is perhaps the more troublesome: since the colour represents the quality of forecasts, logically it should be easier to improve poor accuracy results than those that are good. The reason we don't start with the bigger (dark gray) blob is that while the potential prize is greater, it is more difficult to access, so the likely quantum of any improvement will be smaller.

This chart could be used by managers to get a quick overview of a large portfolio with a view to allocating forecasting resources to where there is most scope for improvement. Forecasting experts might use it as part of a periodic review of forecasting methods in the portfolio (Morlidge 2014b).

Costing

In his insightful article for *Foresight*, Peter Catt (2007) argued that the cost of forecast error was an important and badly neglected metric and demonstrated how it might be calculated. Building on the approach and the fact that bias and variation can be measured independently, it is possible to estimate the financial impact of avoidable error on inventory and the costs associated with having too much of it (financing, warehousing costs, and obsolescence) or not having enough (lost sales and the expense of expediting supply).

Figure 4.5 shows that avoidable error adds £7.8m cost – nearly 2% to the cost of production – and inflates stock levels by the equivalent of nearly 15 days of sales.

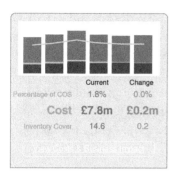

Figure 4.5 Impact of Avoidable Forecast Error on Cost and Inventory

By comparing this to the cost of error from the simplest naïve forecast, we can also quantify and track the financial value added by forecasting. Comparing the results between different forecast versions (e.g., before and after judgment is applied) enables us to identify the value added by different steps in the process (i.e., the financial Forecast Value Added).

Being able to estimate the financial impact of forecasting helps forecasters in companies like ABC Inc. raise the profile and importance of the process and creates a language to engage colleagues at all levels. It also helps to justify and measure the impact of investment in the forecast process. In all the examples shown above, the avoidable cost is used as the "unit of error."

Lessons Learned

I have been using these techniques for some years in a range of different companies. While every business is unique, there are some consistent themes that serve to illustrate their value.

1. As measured by the VAS, I've found there is little correlation between how good companies *think* they are at forecasting and how good they *actually are*. This is due in part to the failings of traditional metrics, in particular their inability to allow for forecastability and so give a true measure of forecasting performance. It is also because people often assume that the more sophisticated the process the better the outcome will be, whereas additional process steps often destroy value (Gilliland 2013) and simple methods can outperform more complex ones (Kolassa 2016).

2. Performance levels can change significantly without a conscious change being made to the process. Few companies consistently sustain "good" performance (VAS in the range of 30–60), and many struggle to beat a simple benchmark method (SES); but I have come across some that are excellent (70 or above), which suggests that there is scope for considerable improvement in most businesses.

3. In all cases, between 30% and 50% of low-level forecasts destroy value (where VAS <0) (Morlidge 2014a). Since it is harder to beat the naïve forecast when demand patterns are relatively stable, particularly if too many judgmental interventions are made, it is not unusual to see value destruction associated with forecasts where error, as measured by MAPE, is relatively low (Gilliland 2013; Morlidge 2014b). These examples are testament to the fact that forecast performance can be quickly improved if you know where to look – and how conventional metrics like MAPE shed little light on the issue.

4. Forecast improvement comes from a mix of constant vigilance, using exception-driven "alarms" as illustrated above, and intelligent choices of forecasting methods guided by analysis rather than hunches or blind faith in technology. Most businesses start the journey by focusing on eradicating bias because it is easier to understand and remedy, particularly where it is caused by inappropriate judgmental interventions in the process.

5. Avoidable error is typically in the range of 1–3% of the cost of production, or perhaps $5–15 million per $1 billion of revenue. Reducing it by a fraction will generate significant savings.

Conclusion

The selection of error measures has too often been the subject of arcane debate between experts, with little attention being paid to how they can be used to improve the process of forecasting in practice. The examples presented here demonstrate how the right measures, analysed and presented in a way that is relevant and appealing to a broader community of users, can be used to provide insights, guide actions, and promote behaviour that will improve the contribution of forecasting to all businesses.

References

Catt, P. (2007). Assessing the cost of forecast error: A practical example. *Foresight* 7 (Summer): 5–10.

Gilliland, M. (2013). FVA: A reality check on forecasting practices. *Foresight* 29 (Spring): 14–18.

Kolassa, S. (2016). Sometimes it's better to be simple than correct. *Foresight* 40 (Winter): 20–26.

Morlidge, S. (2013). How good is a "good" forecast? Forecast errors and their avoidability. *Foresight* 30 (Summer): 5–11.

Morlidge, S. (2014a). Forecastability and forecast quality in the supply chain. *Foresight* 33 (Spring): 26–31.

Morlidge, S. (2014b). Using relative error metrics to improve forecast quality in the supply chain. *Foresight* 34 (Summer): 39–46.

Morlidge, S. (2015a). A better way to assess the quality of forecasts. *Foresight* 38 (Summer): 15–20.

Morlidge, S. (2015b). Measuring the quality of intermittent demand forecasts: It's worse than we've thought! *Foresight* 37 (Spring): 37–42.

4.2 GUIDELINES FOR SELECTING A FORECAST METRIC*

Patrick Bower

There has long been debate about the best metric to represent forecasting performance. Some software, such as SAS, gives you dozens of metrics to choose from. Many of the metrics have well-recognized issues and limitations, such as MAPE being inappropriate for intermittent demand patterns (because of zeroes in the denominator). And it has been observed that ranking performance (such as for a forecasting competition) can be somewhat impacted by which metric is used.

Relative performance metrics, such as the RAE described above by Morlidge, Theil's U, or FVA, view performance with respect to some baseline, such as a naïve model. In short, all metrics have a place – there is just not a universal perfect fit measure of forecast performance. In this article, Patrick Bower explores his journey through the metric debate and arrives at 10 guidelines that should be used when considering the most appropriate metric for your organization.

The one sad truth that each and every demand planner should agree upon, regardless of pay grade, education, or experience on the job, is that demand forecasts are almost always and without exception, wrong. Alan Greenspan has correctly stated:

> We really can't forecast that entirely well, and yet we pretend that we can, but we really can't.

What's not so clear, however, is the best way to measure this wrongness or forecast error, which is a question that often leads to discussion and sometimes debate about the most appropriate forecast error calculation. The most commonly used measure of forecast error is APE, otherwise known as absolute percent error, which is calculated as:

$$\text{Absolute Percent Error}(\text{APE}) = [\,|\text{Actual} - \text{Forecast}|\,/\,\text{Actual}\,] \times 100$$

Seems pretty straight forward, right? Well, not so fast. Considering this simplest of forecast error calculations, there are actually those who advocate many different forms of the APE calculation. For example, some propose that one should divide by the forecast (sometimes called APEf). Others combine both forecast and actual in the denominator and then divide by two, resulting in symmetrical or sAPE. Furthermore, some practitioners even suggest using actual or forecast – whichever is greater – as the denominator (maxAPE). Finally, there are also those who completely ignore APE in all its variations, and instead focus on RMSE (Root Mean Square Error) – a completely

---

*This article originally appeared in *Journal of Business Forecasting* (Spring 2015) and appears here courtesy of Dr. Chaman Jain, editor in chief.

different calculation. The debate even extends to the best way to present aggregate forecast error. Is MAPE (mean of APEs) or WMAPE (weighted mean of APEs) more correct? And of course, there are countless ways to calculate forecast bias.

Idiosyncracies about the Measurement of Forecast Error

Is your head spinning yet? I know mine is. I often attend conferences on forecasting and planning where debates over the correct equation for calculating the measure of forecast error are first formally presented, and then informally argued at luncheons and throughout the cocktail hour. These debates are standard fare, and those of us with many years in the profession have heard them countless times.

Every so often, someone will even present a new equation for calculating forecast error that proposes to address all of the other idiosyncrasies and flaws associated with all the aforementioned older equations (i.e., divide-by-zero error, and so on). Eventually, all of these new calculations are proven to be equally flawed.

Finding the perfect calculation (and thereby the resulting perfect measure of forecast error) sometimes seems like the search for the Theory of Everything – a quest for mathematical nirvana, at least as it pertains to forecast error. Frankly, I'm not sure whether Einstein or Dr. Sheldon Cooper (from CBSTV's *The Big Bang Theory*) could even solve this one.

Many years ago, I too was drawn into the various debates on this topic. Maybe I've matured as a demand planner or have a better understanding of forecast error and its role within the S&OP process and the supply chain in general, but I no longer quest for the "eureka" formula. Instead, I seek out a calculation that makes sense for my organization, and then I spend time educating my key stakeholders so that everyone understands it.

In retrospect, intense debates over minor mathematical differences are nothing more than exercises in intellectual preening that offer little in terms of practical guidance. I understand all the mathematical nuances being debated, but a more useful application of my knowledge as a demand planning silverback is to encourage the use of situationally correct measures – data that make the most sense for a specific business in a specific industry – rather than debating minor mathematical tweaks.

Indeed, the calculation debate often does more harm than good, bordering on absurd wonkiness, with its arcane formulas. Worse yet, it ignores the reality that even the simplest algebraic discussions often make the average corporate executive's eyes glaze over.

While debating mathematical denominators among ourselves, we miss the golden opportunity to educate our user base on how these measures should be selected and used. We are, in most cases, business people, and our value – that is, the way we demonstrate our relevance to the business – should affirm the process of our measurement, its root cause, and potential for improvement, and not merely center on the math used.

As I previously noted, I was once one of those math nerds asserting that actual should always be used in the denominator. Then, as a consultant, I came across a chemical distributor that sold one barrel of a specific type of product every four months.

Over 40% of the 2,500 SKUs in the company's portfolio exhibited this lumpy demand behavior. All of my "actual in the denominator" rationale went out the window as I encountered a significant percentage of them had a divide-by-zero error. I was forced to use the forecast as a denominator.

Similarly, I also came across a company that did 80% of its business based on demand for just 20 of its 120 total SKUs. And this top 80% reflected highly predictable demand with low COV (coefficient of variance) and error. Based on this demand anomaly, my forecast statistics were artificially fantastic – and improbably accurate – relative to any actual performance benchmark, but they hid significant forecast errors across the other 100 SKUs that accounted for the "remaining 20%" of the company's business.

As it turned out, this last 20% of the volume was where most of the challenging supply chain problems existed. In this case, the weighted measure, while providing a realistic portrayal of aggregate demand planning performance, masked the problems in the other 20%. In the real world, there are countless stories like this in which the predetermined notion of a proper measure was violated by actual data or the supply chain/business model itself. That's why understanding the business model – not just the math – is so essential to nailing down the right measure.

Forecast Error Is a Funny Thing

Forecast error is a measure of actual performance, but it can also be part of an analytical toolset used to improve forecast error rates in the future. To consider this, it helps me to draw a mental line between forecast error rates used for presentation – a summary of the net performance of the forecasting process – versus the measure of error that helps me understand what is happening in the demand curve (even though the calculation used to determine these rates may at times have been the same).

For example, I don't look at absolute values when doing analysis since one of my forecast review steps is to look for a preponderance of directional forecasts (i.e., persistent over-forecasting or under-forecasting). I also calculate CoV, which – while not a forecast error measure *per se* – is nonetheless an analytical tool that helps me understand the volatile nature of the item in question. If there is a high CoV, the item will be harder to forecast accurately – and knowing this I might set a lower forecast exception target in my periodic ABC encoding exercise. I give myself permission to use any measure – picking and choosing the ones that make the most sense when analyzing the results.

Over the years, my journeys into the world of forecast error have helped me arrive at 10 best practices relative to forecast error measurement and usage – none of which pertains to any specific mathematical calculation. The 10 guidelines are presented here in no specific order.

1. **Pick just one measure.** You may routinely calculate multiple demand measures that you use behind the scenes during your statistical analysis or even during the demand consensus process, but there should be only one single measure used to present forecast accuracy within the S&OP process. Portraying multiple

measures of demand planning quality to an S&OP executive team will create cognitive dissonance. I typically calculate multiple measures and test them against some of the following criteria; then I pick and present the most appropriate single measure. You need to pick only one measure to present forecast performance.

2. **The measure must be easy to understand.** The more complex the measure, the more difficult it will be for non-experts and new team members to understand. Use simple examples when explaining the measure (for example, forecast = 100; actual = 90) and be prepared to educate S&OP stakeholders over and over again. This process of periodically revisiting the means by which S&OP practitioners measure forecast error is essential because staff turnover at most organizations is significant enough to reset the knowledge base at least once a year. This will ensure that all key decision makers understand how and why we determine performance metrics, and how and why these metrics are important and relevant to their own job functions.

3. **The measure needs to be smart for the business.** If you have a business with a huge number of zero instances, you may want to consider using the forecast in the denominator. If you have huge forecast bias – demand hockey sticks, or a history of year-end "roll the miss" behaviors – then a measure of bias is in order. With heavily skewed data (be it SKU volume or customer sales), use weighting. The point is this: one should pick a measure that works best for the business (with an eye toward Guidelines 1 and 2 above) to serve as your presentation measure.

4. **The measure should be lagged to typical supply lead times.** Yes, Virginia. Discussing a lagged forecast might put a few people to sleep, but a lagged measure is the most realistic view of how the forecast will be used by the supply chain planning organization, which is a key stakeholder in the process. A lagged forecast is the forecast at the supply lead time. If supply lead time is two months, then the most important measure of, as an example, January's forecast performance is the forecast for January in November, not in January. At the very least, the supply chain planning organization will appreciate you for measuring "the lagged forecast." And while it is a touch that is more difficult to explain to the business leaders, this measure will begin to stretch the forward view of the plan, and is likely to lead supply chain to reduced schedule cuts, lower inventory, and better fill performance. These benefits will be realized as you improve the forecast beyond the supply chain lead time. If you do not measure error based on supply lead time, you will spend most of your effort evaluating and tuning forecasts that have only the briefest of forward-looking horizons, and thus add very little value to the supply chain. The "most correct" lag period for presentation to management is that of the typical supply lead time, but I have also lagged

multiple periods to see the earliest point at which forecast improvements could be visualized.

5. **Run the history.** Once you pick the measure (or as a means to determine the best measure), do a year of *ex post* analysis, applying your proposed equation(s) to actual historical data, to back-check calculations and thereby errors, and then present the (graphed) measures in the next S&OP meeting. Sometimes a picture is worth a thousand words, and a simple graph can be a powerful tool, especially when the *ex post* analysis will provide a year of history to begin the process of tracking error over time. The ex post process will help the group understand the current range of forecast errors and also answer the important question, "Are we getting better?"

6. **Establish control limits.** Whether you are just starting your measurement process or it's already well under way, you may be on the worst-case error performance and average error. Set these bounds – upper and lower limits – 25%± of what you would think is appropriate for your company. Use the *ex post* analysis described in Guideline 5 to understand the bounds of the measure. From there, focus on the average error, and then examine each instance of error outside these bounds. As your forecast accuracy improves over time, continue to tweak these bands gradually to reduce the size of error tolerance.

7. **Perform a root-cause analysis of any error that exceeds your control limits.** This practice is not commonplace in most S&OP processes, but it is very illustrative of problems related to forecasting. You may find you are regularly missing a promotional activity at a retailer, or substitutions in order management, or stock fill issues for a particular product line in supply. If you are not tracking the reasons for the forecast error, then you cannot resolve the problem. Not all large variances have a clear root cause, but many do, and simple tally sheets of possible reasons can be powerful to identify the cause and, consequently, help to improve forecasts.

8. **Use other measures to help with analysis.** The presentation measure you choose in guideline 1 may not provide enough information to help you understand demand. A Lag 2 MAPE of a sales region may be of interest in S&OP, but not meaningful enough to analyze underlying demand issues. You may need to look at more granular levels. The forecast error might be caused by fill allocation issues at a SKU level or a bad adjustment to the baseline. Or, the demand may be volatile. As I mentioned earlier, I use simple percent error (PE) for SKU-level exception processing in my demand planning review process. We also use COV to understand the variability of demand, and to set ABC levels, while using a blended measure to report problem items at the S&OP meetings. Only one measure is used for presentation, but many measures are used during the pre-consensus analysis of the demand.

9. **Someone needs to own the measure.** Regardless of which measure is chosen, it must have an owner – a champion. In fact, part of the process of selecting the

right measure is determining whether a group or a person should be accountable for it. By the same token, however, simply stating that "the demand consensus team owns the forecast accuracy measure" is a bit wishy-washy since no one is specifically accountable. If you measure forecast error by brand, then the brand manager owns the quality of the forecast. If you forecast by sales region, then the salesperson in that region owns that sub-segment of the demand plan. Find an owner of the measure(s).

10. **Communicate expectations.** I always provide S&OP participants with my expectations for forecast error. It's not very hard. If you expect cannibalization of an old product line with a new product, you can expect some amount of "mix-related" error. Tell the group that you expect this, and will be looking for it. If you lose distribution for a product, and are unsure whether the customers in other outlets and regions will pick up the slack, suggest to the consensus group that there may be region-to-region demand mismatches that will show up in error. Similarly, if you correct some glaring forecast errors, but note that it may take some time for the lagged error measure to disappear, you should tell the stakeholders that while the no-lag error has been corrected, the lagged error may be sticky for a couple of months. The key is to communicate your expectations.

Using most or all of these tips will help your organization see an improvement in both performance and understanding. You will note I have left out topics like "segmentation" and "exception processing" and other ways to analyze a forecast, which – while important – are part of the analytical exercise roughly outlined in Guideline 8, and thus are outside of the broader scope of this discussion.

Lies, Damn Lies, and Statistics

After so many years of listening to debates about forecast calculations, my opinion is that specific metrics don't really matter all that much. Feel free to use any, all, or merely select a set of measures. What really matters is that your measurement is widely understood and aligned with an organizational desire to improve upon that measure.

I've paid close attention to what the social sciences have to say about performance measurement, and I find myself drawn to the often (mis)paraphrased quote people use when discussing metrics of any type: "What gets measured/observed will change or improve," usually attributed to the "Hawthorne Effect." I have witnessed countless examples of forecast improvement that come from nothing more than the simple observation of forecast error – regardless of the math used. This experience enables me to be agnostic about the math used. Whatever you measure will improve, if you give it the proper organizational focus.

If you still feel compelled to debate metrics, consider this cautionary quote from former *60 Minutes* commentator Andy Rooney about the 50-50-90 rule: "Anytime you have a 50-50 chance of getting something right, there's a 90% probability you'll get it wrong."

4.3 THE QUEST FOR A BETTER FORECAST ERROR METRIC: MEASURING MORE THAN THE AVERAGE ERROR*

Stefan de Kok

In an article in the Summer 2006 issue of **Foresight**, Tom Willemain presented the argument that:

> While most forecast-error metrics are averages of forecast errors, for intermittent-demand series, we should focus on the demand distribution and assess forecast error at each distinct level of demand. Accordingly, the appropriate accuracy metric will assess the difference between the actual and forecasted distributions of demand.

There has not been much adoption of this approach – except perhaps in energy studies – and we do not find error metrics based on full distributions present in forecasting support systems. Now Stefan de Kok picks up the argument and extends it to develop an error metric – Total Percentage Error – that measures the full range of uncertainty in our forecasts. In doing so, TPE both enables better inventory-planning and provides a more comprehensive way to gauge the quality of the forecast.

The way we traditionally measure forecast error prevents us from knowing how to drive improvement in forecast performance. Having an accurate understanding of the uncertainty drives greater efficiencies, leading to reductions in obsolescence and other waste, fewer stock-outs, and increased customer-service levels. It also enables better business decisions: rather than plan for the middle of the road, the company can protect itself against selected risks or can position itself to grab even the most fortuitous opportunities.

The TPE is more complex than currently used error metrics and requires storing more data for historical accuracy analysis. Yet its virtues are considerable, in terms of measuring the complete value of a forecast, not just the average value per item/period.

Introduction

How good is the forecast? How much damage does my business suffer due to forecast error? If we could improve accuracy by X%, what impact would it have on the business? Which metric is the right one to measure these things? If these questions keep you awake at night, you're very much like me. My personal quest over the years has taken me from accepting the status quo to seeking a better way to forecast and finally to measure forecast accuracy in a way that drives business value.

There were a few epiphanies along the way. First, that just because it's the way we've always done it doesn't mean it's necessarily the best way – sometimes not even remotely close. Second, that the traditional approach of statistical forecasting, often supplemented with human input, is fundamentally flawed. Third, that the way we measure error is preventing us from making any meaningful improvement.

*This article originally appeared in *Foresight: The International Journal of Applied Forecasting* (Summer 2017) and appears here courtesy of the International Institute of Forecasters.

Along the way, one realization I had is that a single metric is not sufficient. Depending on the purpose of the forecast, we need at least three: *direction* of error, *size* of error, and *value* of error reduction.

- ▪ For the direction – or central tendency – of the forecast error, *bias* is an elegant metric: it is simple and powerful. Like a precision tool, when used correctly it does what it is supposed to do very well.

- ▪ For forecast value-added, some reasonable metrics exist (for example, see Gilliland [2013] although there is room for improvement).

- ▪ For size of error, commonly referred to as forecast error – or its converse, forecast accuracy – there is no silver bullet.

The fiery discussion over which metric is best has raged for decades and is ongoing. In this article, I will add fuel to that fire and present a new forecast error metric – the Total Percentile Error (TPE) – which aims to overcome the last hurdle of not merely measuring error, but actually driving improvement where it matters. As a bonus, in its standard form it can serve as a basis for an improved forecast value-add metric, one which I have dubbed Stochastic Value Add (SVA).

Point Forecasts vs. Probabilistic Forecasts

In the days when computing power was low, one would create a forecast at high aggregate levels (such as item totals by month) where historical demand is smooth and through which it is easy to fit a curve. At those same high levels of aggregation, the errors tend to be normally distributed, and any error metric that assumes symmetry, such as standard deviation, MAD, or RMSE, worked as expected.

Intermittency

Even then, we knew that both forecasts and error metrics were inadequate for intermittent demand: i.e., demand patterns where some periods have zero demand. The most popular error metric to date, MAPE, completely breaks down under intermittent conditions, because even one period with zero demand causes a division by zero.

Since most value used to reside in the higher-volume items, it was easy to dismiss the shortcomings of the metrics with regard to intermittency. But times change. Many companies have realized there is little value in forecast accuracy by item by month when shipments occur weekly, by item, and by warehouse.

Unfortunately, at those less-aggregated levels, demand patterns that are smooth at higher levels of aggregation become unstable and frequently intermittent. Add market trends of globalization, product proliferation, and increased agility of supply chains, and intermittency is suddenly everywhere. Even the fastest-moving goods in fast-moving industries show intermittency in some regions. Benchmarks show that against the tough demands of modern customers, global fast-moving consumer goods (FMCG) companies today have anywhere between 90% and 95% of their item-locations by count, upwards of 80% of inventory by cost, and 60% of total revenue that behaves intermittently. For other industries, this is typically worse. In short, intermittency can no longer be ignored.

Limits of Traditional Metrics

Under these changed conditions, most traditional forecasting approaches, as well as traditional forecasting error metrics, fail for the same pair of reasons. First, they both assume a symmetry that simply does not exist for intermittent demand, which instead is characterized by a fat head and a long tail. More damaging, however, is that they focus solely on the central value of demands instead of the full range of possible values. Most traditional forecasting approaches predict the future with so-called point forecasts. For any given item in any given month, the forecast would be a single value. In reality, future demand is anything but certain, and neither should a forecast be.

To illustrate, consider repeatedly rolling two dice, as shown in Figure 4.6, and being asked to predict the total number of pips of each roll. The equivalent of a traditional forecast is to predict that the answer is 7 pips each time, since that is the average you can expect. If we then roll the dice, any difference from 7 is a forecast error and, with enough rolls, the average absolute error will approach 70/36 or 1.944.

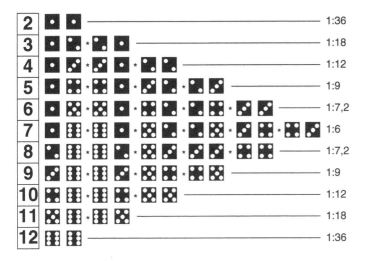

Figure 4.6 Pips, Combinations, and Odds When Throwing Two Dice

However, you could instead have predicted that "7 would only occur with a probability of 1/6, and similarly 2 with probability 1/36, 3 with probability 1/18, and so forth for all possible outcomes." This alternative approach is a *probabilistic forecast*, also called a *stochastic* or *density forecast*. The "error" – the difference between the observed actual and the unbiased point forecast of 7 – is not really an error at all. It is fully predictable variability and, in the traditional perspective, would be considered the limit of the dice roll's forecastability. This predictability, however, is something we can and should plan for, just as we would do when playing games of chance.

An improvement on single-point forecasts are *multipoint forecasts*. Examples are interval forecasts, forecast plus confidence limits, or forecasts expressed in terms of scenarios – for example, pessimistic, realistic, and optimistic. The problem with these is that you do not know a priori what interval or confidence level you need, and you may need many. Moreover, judgmental pessimistic/optimistic scenarios are typically as heavily biased as the central forecast. In the example of rolling two dice, an interval forecast is equivalent to stating the forecast is with 95% confidence between 3 and 11 pips. This is obviously better than the single-point forecast of 7 pips but still leaves out important information – the frequencies of the individual pip counts – that would allow us to know whether or not any bet would be profitable over the long term.

The only correct way to address the uncertainty in future demand is to model and predict uncertainty as a time series of probability distributions across possible future demand values, rather than a time series of single values: one distribution for each item, in each location, for each time period. These probabilistic forecasts are especially suited for (but not limited to) intermittent demand patterns. Rather than state some average level, which will never occur as an actual (if you sell, on average, one unit every five periods, your average demand is 0.2 – but you will never actually sell 0.2 units), they state the probability of occurrence for each demand level.

These probabilities will be a key input to determine inventory levels and other buffers. It should then come as no surprise that a useful forecast error metric must measure *the accuracy of entire probability distributions*, rather than of just their average values.

Uncertainty and Inventory

If you had unlimited capacity, negligible lead times, and no intermittency, or did not care about customer-service levels, the above distinction would not matter. You could plan for average demand and accommodate departures whenever necessary. In modern supply chains, however, an accurate understanding of the amount of uncertainty around the average is essential information. How much inventory is needed to buffer and how far ahead to build to satisfy demand are more dependent on the uncertainty than they are on the average expected level. Very roughly speaking, your cycle stock will depend on the average predicted demand, whilst your safety buffers will depend on the uncertainty. For smooth, fast-moving demand patterns, safety buffers are insignificant compared to cycle stock, whilst for slow-moving or intermittent patterns, the safety buffers are more significant than the cycle stock.

Traditional metrics measure only the error of the predicted average level versus actual demand, ignoring the uncertainty. As a consequence, any forecast-accuracy-improvement efforts target only those averages. As for the prediction of the uncertainty: may the chips fall where they may. By not explicitly targeting improvement in the prediction of uncertainty, we cannot improve the accuracy of our safety buffers, except by sheer coincidence. Thus, a forecast-error metric that not only measures the error of the expected value but also of the uncertainty is a primary driver of improvement.

Having an accurate understanding of uncertainty drives greater efficiencies, leading to reductions of obsolescence and other waste, fewer stock-outs, and increased customer-service levels. It also allows making better business decisions: rather than plan for the middle of the road, the company can protect itself against selected risks or position itself to grab even the most fortuitous opportunities. The right metric will tell how good or bad the forecast is in this regard, and how much improvement is attainable.

Forecast Value Added

One other benefit of having a metric that captures the complete distribution of a forecast is that it allows one to better answer the question, "What is the business value of X% forecast accuracy improvement?" All metrics that capture only half the value, and notably miss most of the value for the difficult items to forecast, will fundamentally not be able to provide much, if any, correlation to business value. It is exactly those difficult items where our business value feels the most impact. It is those items that suffer most from obsolescence, stock-outs, discounting, and poor service levels – exactly the ones where traditional metrics such as MAPE fail.

Percentile Error Metrics

Measuring the accuracy of probabilistic forecasts requires a different type of metric from that needed to assess the accuracy of single-point predictions. Nassim Nicholas Taleb describes the difference in his book, *The Black Swan* (2010). He explains that if you predict that something will happen with 20% probability, over many occurrences it should happen 20% of the time to be accurate. Obviously, this needs to apply not just for the 20% probability value, but for all predicted probability values. This is where percentiles come in.

Percentile metrics should not be confused with *percentage* metrics. The latter are relative versions of distance metrics, whilst percentiles are a means of ranking values. Just as students are ranked by their percentile within a distribution of test results across a whole population of students, demand values can be ranked by their percentile according to their location within the distribution that was predicted for them.

The following fictitious example is of an item, which for now we will assume has a stationary (non-trended, non-seasonal, essentially unchanging) demand pattern, and we record daily values (not shown here) across consecutive workdays. We use these to forecast the entire distribution of future values. The gray line in the left frame of Figure 4.7 shows the forecast distribution which is output from a forecast engine. It could be the result of fitting a Poisson or Negative Binomial Distribution to the historical data.

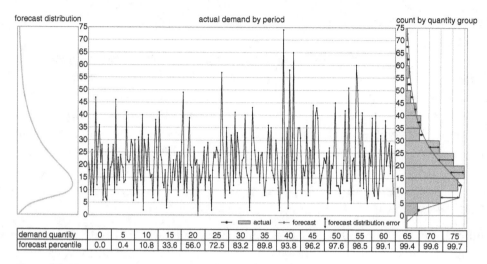

demand quantity	0	5	10	15	20	25	30	35	40	45	50	55	60	65	70	75
forecast percentile	0.0	0.4	10.8	33.6	56.0	72.5	83.2	89.8	93.8	96.2	97.6	98.5	99.1	99.4	99.6	99.7

Figure 4.7 Actual Demand Accounted by Forecasted Quantity

Future actual demands across 250 days are shown in the middle frame, and a histogram counting these demands in groups of 5 units are shown in the right frame overlaid with the forecast distribution. The black arrows spanning the distance between actual and forecast distribution measure the error for each quantity group.

The table at bottom shows which percentile each quantity represents according to the forecast.

We can see that any quantity greater than 35 is in the 90th percentile, any quantity greater than or equal to 60 is in the 99th percentile, and the median (i.e., 50th percentile) is somewhere between 15 and 20. So the forecast distribution can be used to determine the percentile for each future demand value. Technically, the percentiles above equate to cumulative density function (CDF) values of 0.9, 0.99, and 0.5. For probabilistic forecasts, the CDFs are given as output of the forecast engine, whilst for traditional forecasts they are usually derived from a normal distribution based on the standard deviation of error residuals.

Percentile Bins

One limitation of this approach is that demand patterns are not generally stationary – there are trends, seasonal shifts, and so forth – so that demand values would have different probability distributions in different time periods. For example, a value of 35 may fall on the 85th percentile one period and on the 95th percentile the next. And if we compare forecasts of different items, they will all have different distributions. To overcome this limitation, we can group the demand values not by predefined ranges of demand quantities as above, but by predefined *groups of percentile ranges*, commonly known as *percentile bins*.

Imagine grouping the distribution on the left of Figure 4.7 differently. Let us create a different histogram, where each bar represents an equal-sized *percentile* range, not an equal sized *realization* range as before. For instance, our probability forecast (the left-hand panel in Figure 4.7) implies that 10% of future actuals will be less than 9.8. So the first bar of our new histogram, corresponding to percentiles 0–10%, would count how many of these are actually below 9.8. Further, the probability distribution says that 20% of actuals should be below 12.2, so the second bar, corresponding to percentiles 10–20%, would count actuals between 9.8 and 12.2. If we do likewise for the rest of the 250 future demand values, the right-hand graph in Figure 4.7 will transform to Figure 4.8.

Notice that the forecast distribution has transformed into a level line – because *by construction*, each bin should contain exactly 10% of our future actuals. If this distribution were 100% accurate to a precision of 10 percentiles, every one of these 10 bins would hold exactly 25 of the 250 total demand values. This holds in general: if the forecast distribution is accurate, then each percentile bin will contain an equal number of actual demand values. Thus, the differences between the red line and the gray bars are again measures of forecast error.

Total Percentile Error – Basics

To calculate the total percentile error (TPE), we determine the absolute difference between the actual and forecasted counts for each bin (the black arrows in Figure 4.8) and take the sum of those absolute values. In this fashion, we obtain a single error value that judges the accuracy of the predicted distribution. This error increases as the sample size increases. To make it a relative metric, we scale it by the maximum possible error, which occurs if all actual demand falls in one percentile bin, leaving all other bins empty.

The calculation is shown in Table 4.5. The absolute values of the differences sum to 46. The maximum possible error – where nine bins contain zero instead of the expected 25 actuals, and one bin contains all 250 instead of the expected 25 actuals, is calculated as $9 \times |0 - 25| + 1 \times |250 - 25| = 450$. And so the TPE= 46/450 = 10.2%.

Looking at the differences in Table 4.5, we get more useful information. They show that we are under-forecasting both tails (−13, −8) and generally over-forecasting the lower-mid portion (+5, +6) of the distribution. This knowledge can help us determine *how* to improve forecast accuracy. In particular, since we are underestimating the frequency of high actuals, we are likely underachieving our service-level targets.

A key characteristic of this percentile perspective of error is that it holds for every combination of forecasted distributions. Since each distribution individually transforms into a uniform distribution (a level line as in Figure 4.8) it is now possible to apply this error calculation without limitations or assumptions. We can count each actual in its own predicted percentile group and evaluate the sum over all samples for an overall error.

I have prepared an Excel worksheet showing the full steps in the calculation of the basic TPE on data similar to those in our illustrative example – including the original historical data, the forecast model, forecast distribution and TPE calculation on future values: https://foresight.forecasters.org/issue46_forecast-error-metric/.

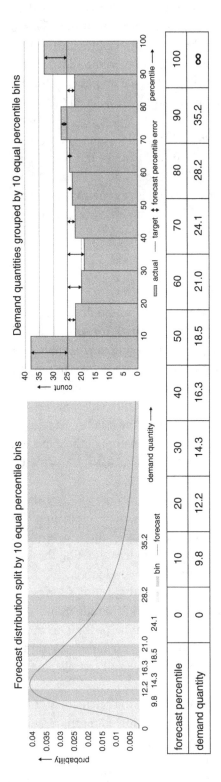

forecast percentile	0	0	10	20	30	40	50	60	70	80	90	100
demand quantity	0	9.8	12.2	14.3	16.3	18.5	21.0	24.1	28.2	35.2	∞	

Figure 4.8 Actual Demand by Forecasted Percentile Bin

Table 4.5 Calculating the TPE for the Example Data of Figures 4.2 and 4.3

Bin	0–10	10–20	20–30	30–40	40–50	50–60	60–70	70–80	80–90	90–100	SUM
Forecast	25	25	25	25	25	25	25	25	25	25	
Actual	38	22	20	19	22	23	24	27	22	33	
Difference	–13	3	5	6	3	2	1	–2	3	–8	
ABS (diff)	13	3	5	6	3	2	1	2	3	8	46
										TPE	10.2%

Total Percentile Error – Complete

The total percentile error utilizes this uniform behavior but adds some flexibility over the simplified scenario above and addresses some corner cases, which were not present in the example data. In general, we may want more control over the calculation, and the TPE allows customizations to set:

1. The number of percentile bins. In the above example, there are 10. This number may be lesser or greater as needed.

2. Varying sizes (or widths) of percentile bins. In the example, they are all the same size for clarity, but this is not required in general.

3. Different weights per percentile bin. In the example, they were all assumed equal, but we may want to emphasize errors on the upper tail of the distribution (where service feels the most impact) more than the average or the lower tail (where obsolescence is the focus).

4. Different weights per time series. The example was assumed to apply to a single item and location, but in general we may want to measure errors across groups of items and regions. Some may be more important than others, for example, because they represent a greater portion of revenue than others.

5. Different weights over time. Some time periods may be more important than others, e.g., Black Friday or the run-up to Christmas, or promotional time periods.

6. Different time granularity. Like other metrics, they could be applied to daily, weekly, monthly, or any other time granularity.

The Appendix below presents the standard formula for the TPE and describes how it could be customized to fit the forecast context in a more general formula. It also provides formulas to determine the maximum error and the minimum error (due to rounding when the number of samples or bin sizes does not allow a perfect accounting). These minimum and maximum errors are used to make the TPE scale from 0% to 100%.

The standard form is also used as the basis of a forecast value-added metric (stochastic value added, SVA) as an alternative to the traditional FVA (Gilliland, 2013). But while the FVA measures improvement in the *average* error from a forecast method, the SVA measures improvement in the difference between actual and forecasted *distributions*, giving a more complete picture of the value of a forecast.

Conclusions

Even in its simplified standard form, the TPE is more complex than most error metrics. Its calculation requires a sufficient number of recorded forecasts, at least as many as the number of percentile bins, and possibly more if varying bin sizes or weights are used. It also requires storing more data for evaluations of forecast accuracy: where simpler metrics require only a history of forecast values and actual demand values, TPE requires storing uncertainty values, such as standard deviations, distribution parameters, or percentile bin factors. For traditional statistical forecasts, these may need to be determined retroactively by applying the same algorithm used at the time on the stored demand and forecast data, since not all companies store this data.

In return, TPE offers a more complete and more intuitive metric in its use (although not in computation).

With the goal of avoiding shortcomings of existing metrics and preserving their merits while adding the uncertainty requirement, here is a list of properties the TPE seeks to establish:

1. **Completeness.** Measure the complete value of a forecast, not just the average expected value per item/period.

2. **Impartiality.** Be oblivious to the forecasting method that created the forecast, and specifically the type of forecast. The forecast values should speak for themselves.

3. **Robustness.** Be impervious to intermittency, to outliers, trends, seasonality, level shifts, impacts of demand shaping such as promotions, or whatever else a real supply chain may throw at it.

4. **Fairness.** Allow fair comparison across items, accounts, portfolios, and even industries, regardless of scale or complexity of demand patterns.

5. **Symmetry.** Do not favor either over-forecasting or under-forecasting.

6. **Usefulness.** Be flexible to allow weighting different items, different time periods, and different ranges of the probability distributions differently. For example, it may weigh high-revenue errors more than low-revenue errors, if that makes sense to the business.

7. **Relevance.** Rather than being merely an academic exercise, it is implementable in real supply chains, and does not require constraining assumptions or excluding certain demand patterns.

8. **Intuition.** Ensure that the results make sense to business people, not just statisticians.

On the last point, values range between 0% for a perfect forecast and 100% for the worst possible forecast. Most importantly, it is theoretically possible to actually achieve the very intuitive 0% error using this metric, since forecastability becomes much less of an issue. An error in the forecast is not the difference between actual value and forecasted value, but between the actual distribution and the forecasted distribution. What would traditionally be considered a difficult-to-forecast item would simply have a longer tail in its distribution, which we can predict just as easily as its counterparts with normal tails. The TPE does not penalize for perfectly common variability as traditional metrics do; instead, it penalizes when we do not forecast that variability accurately.

Appendixes

A: Scaling from 0% to 100%

To make TPE range from 0% to 100% we adjust the unscaled percentile error (ε) with a minimum (ε_{min}) and a maximum (ε_{max}) error. In this way, TPE takes the following form:

$$TPE = \frac{\varepsilon - \varepsilon_{min}}{\varepsilon_{max} - \varepsilon_{min}}$$

The formulas for ε_{max} and ε_{min} are provided in Appendixes E and F. The error ε is provided in both a general form ($\varepsilon_{general}$) in Appendix C and standard form ($\varepsilon_{standard}$) in Appendix D.

B: Spreading Ambiguous Quantities

There are circumstances in which one demand value could possibly fall in multiple percentile bins. To address this, TPE spreads the count of such quantities proportionally across all bins that could contain it. In the formulas below, $\lambda_{b,I}$ is the spreading factor that gives the portion of measurement i that is counted in bin b. It is 1 when the measurement falls completely inside a bin, 0 when completely outside, and some value in between when partially inside.

It is equal to the probability that a demand quantity x_i for sample i falls in the bin b, divided by the probability that the demand quantity x_i would occur at all.

> Note that only these $\lambda_{b,I}$ need to be determined after actuals are known. Every other part of the TPE formula is known when the forecast is generated.

An example where one measurement has no unique bin to be assigned to is a slow-moving item with only a third of the time periods having demand. This means a zero-demand quantity in any period has a 0.66666 probability. If again we split the distribution into 10 equal bins, the lowest 7 bins all represent the zero-demand quantity. TPE spreads such ambiguous values proportionally across bins they fully or partially fall into. In this example, the first 6 bins get 0.15 (= 0.1/0.66666) accounted for each zero actual, and the 7th bin gets 0.1 (= 0.066666/0.66666) accounted, for a total of exactly 1.

C: General Form of TPE

The TPE can be highly customized. The formula provided here provides the definition of its most complete, general form. Links below the article provide working examples in MS Excel and more detailed technical documentation. The *general form* is defined as:

$$\varepsilon_{general} = \frac{\sum_{b=1}^{B} w_b \left| \sum_{i=1}^{n} \mu_i \left(l_b - \lambda_{b,i} \right) \right|}{\sum_{b=1}^{B} w_b \sum_{i=1}^{n} \mu_i}$$

Where n is the number of measurements, B is the number of percentile bins, w_b is the weight for percentile bin b, and l_b is the size of the percentile bin. In case the bins are of equal size, all l_b would equal $1/B$. Each μ_i is a weight assigned to the ith actual. For instance, this could be higher for promotional forecasts, or it could simply be the mean of the i-th forecasted distribution, in order to weigh larger forecasts more heavily; or, if we weigh by revenue, then μ_i is the average revenue predicted for measurement i. The $\lambda_{b,I}$ is the spreading factor (see Appendix B).

D: Standard Form of TPE

The *standard form TPE* is a simplified version that would ideally be used unless there is good reason not to:

$$\varepsilon_{standard} = \frac{\sum_{b=1}^{8} \left| \sum_{i=1}^{n} c_i \left(l_b - \lambda_{b,i} \right) \right|}{\sum_{i=1}^{n} c_i}$$

Where c_i is the average predicted cost of goods sold per week for the item of measurement i, and the percentile bin partition is set to the following 8 bins based on the CDF values of 6 standard deviations around the mean of a normal distribution, plus the two tails on each end of the range:

Table 4.6 A 6-Sigma Partition of Bins

Bin	Normal	Percentile Range	l_b
1	0	0–0.135	0.00135
2	$\mu - 3\sigma$	0.135–2.275	0.02140
3	$\mu - 2\sigma$	2.275–15.866	0.13591
4	$\mu - \sigma$	15.866–50	0.34134
5	μ	50–84.134	0.34134
6	$\mu + \sigma$	84.134–97.725	0.13591
7	$\mu + 2\sigma$	97.725–99.865	0.02140
8	$\mu + 3\sigma$	99.865–100	0.00135

The standard TPE has equal weight for each percentile bin but weighs items by their cost, which is more generally applicable than other weight factors. Note that the percentile bins decrease in size as we move away from the average toward the tails. In effect, this means tail bins tend to be weighted more, even though there is no weight factor.

E: Maximum Error

The choice of percentile bins and bin-weight factors dictate the complexity of calculating the maximum error. When all bins are equal size and all bin weights are equal, the maximum error is given by $2n\ (1 - 1/B)$. When different bin weights or different bin sizes are used, it becomes a little more involved:

$$\varepsilon_{max} = n\left(\sum_{b=1}^{B}l_b w_b + \max_b\left((1 - 2l_b)w_b\right)\right)$$

This calculation needs to be performed only once for each sample size over which TPE is determined.

F: Minimum Error

The minimum error is the most complex to determine, but like the maximum error only needs to be determined once for each sample size. So, to determine TPE over 1,000 samples we need to account 1,000 values to their respective percentile bins, but only need 1 calculation for minimum error. The minimum error behaves as a series of hops. For the example of 10 equal-size bins, it looks like this:

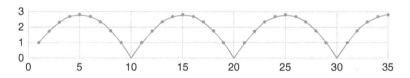

Each cycle has a periodicity of exactly 10 since each bin size is exactly 1/10. For the standard-form TPE, the minimum error will be 4 different length cycles superimposed onto each other with periodicities 740.8 (= 1/0.00135), 46.73 (= 1/0.0214), 7.36 (= 1/0.1359), and 2.930 (= 1/0.3413) because there are 4 different bin sizes, and the amount of each is proportional to the bin sizes.

In general, the minimum error has the following definition:

$$\varepsilon_{min} = \sum_{r=1}^{R}w_r\left(\lceil l_r n\rceil - l_r n\right) + \sum_{r=R+1}^{B}w_r\left(l_r n - \lfloor l_r n\rfloor\right)$$

Here the bins are reordered with index r, ranked by descending $w_b\left(2\left(l_b n - \lfloor l_b n\rfloor\right) - 1\right)$, where $\lfloor . \rfloor$ is the round-down operator. The number $R = n\ mod\ B$ is the remainder after dividing the number of samples n by the number of bins B, and $\lceil . \rceil$ is the round-up operator.

You may download an Excel Worksheet for calculating the standard TPE by item and product family, including calculation of the Maximum and Minimum error value, at: https://foresight.forecasters.org/issue46_forecast-error-metric/.

References

Gilliland, M. (2013). FVA: A reality check on forecasting practices. *Foresight* 29 (Spring): 14–18.

Taleb, N. N. (2010). *The black swan: The impact of the highly improbable* (2nd ed.). Random House.

Willemain, T. (2006). Forecast-accuracy metrics for intermittent demands: Look at the entire distribution of demand. *Foresight* 4 (June): 36–38.

4.4 BEWARE OF STANDARD PREDICTION INTERVALS FROM CAUSAL MODELS*

Len Tashman

We're all aware that point forecasts are subject to a degree of error, and so we frequently report the forecast with a margin for error around it – referred to as a prediction interval (PI). It is well recognized that our prediction intervals are often too narrow to reflect the true uncertainty in the forecast. This happens for several reasons – and is especially so when we forecast from regression and other causal models.

For these models – those that forecast future values based on drivers (the explanatory variables) – the prediction intervals are calculated under the assumption that future values of the drivers are known or can be controlled. When this assumption is unjustified, these prediction intervals will be erroneously narrow. In this article, Len Tashman explains why, and provides a case study on just how serious the problem can be.

The case study shows how errors in forecasting the drivers of a regression model can double or triple the width of prediction intervals. While various analytical and simulation capabilities are available to generate more realistic prediction intervals for regression forecasts, these are rarely used in practice.

Introduction: Standard Prediction Intervals for a Regression Model Forecast

Figure 4.9 shows the forecasts and 95% prediction interval (PI) for an annual sales forecast. The company, which we're calling Alpha Concrete, created a straightforward regression model to predict annual revenue from sales of its concrete products, largely used in home construction.

$$\text{Sales} = B_0 + B_1 * \text{Population} + B_2 * \text{Building Permits} + \text{Error Term}$$

or

$$\text{Sales} = B_0 + B_1 * \text{Pop} + B_2 * \text{Perms} + \epsilon$$

---

*This article originally appeared in *Foresight: The International Journal of Applied Forecasting* (Winter 2018) and appears here courtesy of the International Institute of Forecasters.

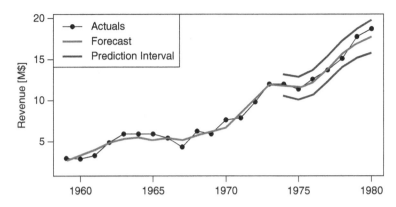

Figure 4.9 Standard Prediction Interval for Regression Forecasts from the R Program

(Sales revenue plotted on the vertical axis)
Width of the 95% PI in $000

1974	1975	1976	1977	1978	1979	1980
2,522	2,723	2,998	3,086	3,256	3,545	3,958

Using the data through 1973, the model generated forecasts for 1974–1980. You can see that the model does a reasonable job tracking the annual sales history up to 1973, and there was a 40% reduction in the MAPE compared to a (Holt) exponential-smoothing procedure. The forecasts extend the long-term trend in which population was slowly rising but permits were cyclical, declining through 1976 before resuming growth. To make its sales forecasts for 1973–1980, the actual values of the drivers – Pop (population) and Perms (building permits) – over this out-of-sample period were fed into the model.

Sources of Error in the Standard Prediction Interval

The standard PI depicted here, described in textbooks and implemented in software, takes into account several sources of error in predicting the future:

- **Random Error** (the variance of the error term ε): This is an estimate of the variance in sales revenue from year to year that is unexplained by the predictors Pop and Perms but presumably due to factors not represented in the model.

- **Estimation Error** (also called sampling error or coefficient error): The estimated B coefficients will vary about the true regression coefficients. The implicit assumption here is that the data used to estimate the model represent a single realization (i.e., a sample) from the true data-generating process that transforms Pop and Perms into sales revenue. As is commonly the case, estimation error decreases as sample size increases.

- **Divergence of future values of the drivers from their historical means,** in relation to the overall historical variation in the drivers.

Most statistics and forecasting textbooks show you the formula to calculate the traditional PI in the simplest case of a single driver. A typical version is shown in Table 4.7.

Table 4.7 The Standard Prediction Interval

PI = Point Forecast of Revenue +/- (Confidence Coefficient * Standard Error for a Forecast)

$$StdErrorforaForecast = SD_{Errors} \cdot \sqrt{1 + \frac{1}{n} + \left(\frac{\left(X_{value} - \bar{X} \right)}{\sqrt{n} \cdot SD_x} \right)^2}$$

Where X denotes a driver, either Pop or Perms, with its mean X-bar
n is the number of time periods (here, years) used to fit the model
SD_{Errors} – often called the standard error of estimate – is the standard deviation of the historical errors in tracking sales: it is our estimate of Random Error
Here $SD_{Errors}/\sqrt{n}$ is our estimate of Estimation Error
The Confidence Coefficient is normally derived from a t distribution to represent the desired level of confidence; for example, for a 95% PI, a t value approximately equal to 2 is used to multiply the Standard Error for a forecast

The first two sources of error – Random Error and Estimation Error – are constant over the forecast period. The third – the divergence of future values of the drivers from their historical means – is the only source of error that can cause the PI to change width as we move further into the future. If the set of explanatory variables does not trend away from its historically normal levels, the PI will be bounded by parallel lines.

For the most part, however, the standard prediction interval presents a deceptive picture of forecast accuracy. How is this so?

Sources of Error Not Accounted For

The problem is that standard PI does not account for several other likely sources of error, such as:

> **Error in forecasting future values of the drivers.** The standard assumption is that the drivers are known with certainty, are controllable, or can be forecast without error.

Organizational revenues typically change in response to both internal and external drivers. The former can be controlled (e.g., price schedules, promotion budgets), but the latter cannot (weather, movements in the economy, demographics). Some of the external drivers (e.g., population growth) vary slowly over time and can be projected very accurately for a few years ahead. Others, though, can be quite volatile, especially over a business cycle (e.g., building permits).

Accounting for errors in forecasting the drivers, particularly the volatile ones, must increase the width of a prediction interval. And since forecast errors tend to increase as we project farther ahead, the prediction interval should become increasingly wide.

The bottom line? Ignoring this source of error may well lead to *erroneously narrow prediction intervals*, making it seem like your model can be expected to forecast more accurately than the reality of its performance.

How serious can the problem be? How much wider should the prediction interval be to account for errors that the standard PI does not?

Note that the standard PI fails to account for several other sources of error, such as model misspecification and data errors. The standard PI is calculated based on the assumption that the model itself is a "correctly specified" representation of the true data-generating process. In our case, this means that sales respond linearly and additively to changes in Pop and Perm. The software has no way of knowing how far from the truth this is; neither can it know how reliable are the data fed into it.

A comprehensive list of the sources of error is offered in Ord, Fildes, and Kourentzes (2017).

A Case Study

In a case study reported in the *Journal of Forecasting* (Tashman, Bakken, and Buzas 2000), the Alpha Concrete data were used to determine the proper width of the prediction interval if the drivers had to be forecast. First, the results, which are summarized in Table 4.8.

Table 4.8 Relative Forecast Error: Alpha Concrete Case

Large-sample approximations of the $\sqrt{rfev}$ in the Alpha Concrete Products case (base of 1.00 is the *Standard*)					
Forecast	Forecast Horizon				
	1	2	3	4	5
Sales(Pop, Perms!)	1.38	2.09	2.32	2.56	2.02
Sales(Pop!, Perms)	1.05	1.31	1.87	2.34	3.22
Sales(Pop!, Perms!)	1.42	2.26	2.87	3.32	3.67

On average, the standard error for calculating the PI is TWICE OR MORE the standard error used in the software calculation. Effectively, when the **X** variables have to be forecast, the PI should be twice as wide.

Each entry in the body of the table can be thought of as an "inflation factor": how many times larger the standard error of the forecast should be if it is to account for forecast error in predicting the drivers. For a given level of confidence, the figure serves as the inflation factor for the width of the standard PI.

An exclamation mark after the variable name denotes that that variable was forecast. So the term Sales(Pop, Perms!) means that, for the figures in this row of the table, building permits were forecast but population was assumed to be known. In the bottom row, both population and permits were forecast. Some notable conclusions:

- The inflation factor was always greater than 1, even for a one-year-ahead sales forecast when only population had to be forecast.

- The inflation factors in the first row are much larger than those in the second, a reflection of the reality that permits are less forecastable than population.

- The inflation factors tend to increase with the forecast horizon, indicating ever widening prediction intervals.

- More than half the inflation factors are above 2, a figure suggesting that the prediction intervals can be at least twice as wide as the standard PI.

The Derivation of the Inflation Factors

The Alpha Concrete case study attempted to clarify the relationship between (a) the amount of error in forecasting a driver, and (b) the standard error of the forecast (and hence width of the prediction interval). They made the traditional assumptions that underpin the standard single-equation regression model and, in addition, they assumed that errors in forecasting the drivers are independent of each other as well as of random error. They also assumed that sample size (number of time periods) was large enough to ignore the *estimation error* component of the prediction interval (which tends to be its smallest component anyway).

So there were some simplifying assumptions, but none that would be liable to invalidate the main conclusions.

Their analytical results showed that the size of the inflation factor for any one driver depends upon two key factors:

- The improvement in explanatory power from including that driver in the model (as was measured by a *partial correlation* coefficient)

- The degree of error in forecasting future values of that driver

The factors were found to interact so that a given degree of error in forecasting a driver has a more powerful effect on the inflation factor, the greater the benefit from adding that driver to the model. The worst combination of events for the validity of the standard prediction interval is serious forecast error in an important driver. On the other hand, if a driver has but a weak effect, error in forecasting that variable will be less serious.

Simulation

Another approach to account for error in forecasting the drivers is the use of computer simulations. We'd start by considering a range of possible future values for each driver at each period in the future. Then, for each value within the range, we generate forecasts for the dependent variable (Sales). A successful simulation will reveal the variability of our Sales forecasts after allowing for error in forecasting the drivers.

An excellent tutorial on Monte Carlo simulation (MCS) with an illustration of its use to assess the impact of driver forecast error on prediction intervals is provided by Sam Sugiyama in a 2007 *Foresight* article, "Forecast Uncertainty and Monte Carlo Simulation." His case study revealed that while "[t]he theoretical standard error for the one-period-ahead forecast was 187," the simulated standard error was 350. The result is that the standard error for the period-1 forecast is now nearly double the theoretical standard error. Sugiyama's conclusion:

> When you incorporate explanatory-variable uncertainty, the standard error of a forecast can increase significantly, and hence the prediction interval can widen significantly. Excluding explanatory variable uncertainty can result in a significant understatement of forecast uncertainty. (p. 36)

It's regrettable that commercial software packages do not embed this simulation functionality.

Another type of simulation capability, based on resampling procedures, is offered in the EViews econometric program (www.eviews.com).

Conclusions

In the Alpha Concrete study, my colleagues and I noted that many textbooks take care to distinguish between conditional (or *ex post*) and unconditional (*ex ante*) forecasts from a regression model. The PI for a conditional forecast assumes that the true values of the drivers are known. In this case, the standard PI formulation is reasonable, although contingent on the assumption that the model is correctly specified.

When the drivers must be forecast, however, the standard PI is no longer appropriate but must be adjusted by suitable inflation factors. Drivers that are particularly difficult to forecast include the weather, many economic and financial factors, and political events. For those whose impact on the dependent variable is substantial, the inflation factors will be large. Even for variables such as population, which are easy to forecast but have a large impact, the inflation factor will be significant.

No admonitions about the need for inflation factors are to be found in the manuals of most forecasting programs. This assertion is all the more surprising because the adverse impacts of forecast error in a driver have been reported going back many decades. Articles by Richard Ashley and William Bassin in the 1980s showed that the errors in forecasting a driver can dramatically increase the forecast errors for the dependent variable, and may make the very inclusion of that driver in the regression model questionable. Subsequent articles in *Foresight* by Bassin (2005) and Peter Kennedy (2006) clarify the trade-off in deciding whether to include a new driver in the regression model.

In a 1991 article in the *International Journal of Forecasting*, Pamela Geriner and Keith Ord performed *ex ante* versus *ex post* evaluations to compare bivariate (one explanatory variable) against univariate (pure time series) forecasting models. The *ex post* forecasts were made using the known, post-sample values of the explanatory variables. The *ex ante* forecasts were based on univariate ARIMA projections of the explanatory variable. For their four annual data series, they found *ex ante* forecasting accuracy to be "substantially worse than *ex post*, at both short and long horizons. For the average of 1 to 6 periods ahead, the *ex ante* measure is 2–5 times as large."

Our case study, the Monte Carlo simulation reported above, and the prior published research are in close agreement: realistic prediction intervals for regression-model forecasts would be considerably wider.

Extensions

The very same issues apply to other causal forecasting models such as ARIMAX (Box-Jenkins models that include explanatory variables). In his forecasting routines for R, Rob Hyndman creates prediction intervals conditional upon the known values of the explanatory variables (https://robjhyndman.com/hyndsight/arimax/). As such, errors in forecasting the explanatory variables are not propagated to the prediction intervals.

This is not to say all ARIMAX programs are open to the same critique. AUTOBOX creates point forecasts in the dependent (or output) series based on forecasted values of the X drivers and offers options to employ simulation and judgmental techniques to produce prediction intervals around these forecasts.

The bottom line for any program, however, is this: the forecaster should not assume that the prediction intervals provided for causal models represent an accurate portrayal of the bounds of the errors to be expected in the future. Rather, they should assume that these prediction intervals are too narrow, since they fail to account for potentially important sources of error. A simple if painful rule of thumb could be "double the width of the prediction interval."

References

Bassin, W. (2005). To include or not to include an explanatory variable: That is the question. *Foresight* 2 (October 2005): 33–36.

Geriner, P. T., and Ord, K. (1991). Automatic forecasting using explanatory variables: A comparative study. *International Journal of Forecasting* 7 (2) (August): 127–140.

Kennedy, P. (2006). To include or exclude an explanatory variable: Beware of rules of thumb. *Foresight* 5 (Fall): 16–21.

Ord, K., Fildes, R., and Kourentzes, N. (2017). *Principles of business forecasting* (2nd ed.). Southwestern/Cengage Learning.

Sugiyama, S. (2007). Forecast uncertainty and Monte Carlo simulation. *Foresight* 6 (Spring): 29–37.

Tashman, L., Bakken, T., and Buzas, J. (2000). Effect of regressor forecast error on the variance of regression forecasts. *Journal of Forecasting* 19, 587–600.

CHAPTER 5

Forecasting Process: Communication, Accountability, and S&OP

A focus on modeling alone does not solve the business forecasting problem. In fact, the quality of the "statistical forecast" (i.e., the forecast generated by the computer model) can play a relatively unimportant role when it is subject to management overrides. Even the best state of the art modeling is of little consequence if management ultimately adjusts the forecast to whatever they please.

This chapter explores many of the issues and considerations relating to the forecasting process. It begins with guidance from Steve Morlidge's book *Present Sense*, where he implores forecasters to communicate like reporters, providing the facts and uncertainties, rather than try to wrap inherently uncertain forecasts into tidy unambiguous stories.

Further issues with communication and accountability are covered in the next several articles, including ways to explain the forecast to executives and provide insights from the data, and how to share the bad news of a downturn in the forecast. Sales and Operations Planning (S&OP) remains an important topic, and Patrick Bower warns of change management pitfalls when trying to implement the S&OP process.

The chapter ends with two articles calling for a rethinking of the business forecasting process. John Hellriegel shows how principles from lean manufacturing can be applied to help streamline a forecasting process. And Michael Gilliland argues for a change in the paradigm – dropping focus from the statistical modeling aspects of forecasting, to instead focus on avoiding the bad practices that just make the forecast worse.

* * *

5.1 NOT STORYTELLERS BUT REPORTERS*

Steve Morlidge

Steve Morlidge has contributed work of fundamental importance to our understanding of the practice of business forecasting. His studies of forecast quality exposed the abysmal nature of the practice, including the startling statistic that perhaps 30–50% of real-life forecasts – that businesses are using to make decisions – are less accurate than a no-change forecast. Morlidge introduced the concept of avoidable error, and through his consulting and software development, has created ways for organizations to pinpoint opportunities for improvement, and make that improvement happen.

In this article, adapted from his new book *Present Sense*, Morlidge returns to his roots in performance reporting. Drawing on theories of data visualization and the latest insights from cognitive science, he lays out an approach to reporting that exploits the physiological strengths of our brains and compensates for its weaknesses.

Present Sense is about how to present data in a way that makes sense – that communicates meaning effectively to decision makers. While the book covers the broad topic of performance reporting, this section is particularly apt for the professional who must communicate forecasts to organizational management. The orthodox recommendation has long been to communicate by storytelling – to wrap complex information in a conveniently understandable and unambiguous narrative that neatly explains everything. But Morlidge rejects the storyteller approach. Instead, the forecaster must communicate like a reporter – fairly spelling out the facts as known at the time, expressing them simply, but with all their requisite ambiguity. Forecasting is, after all, an exercise in uncertainty. Disguising – or ignoring – that uncertainty does a disservice to those relying on the forecast for their decision making.

Human beings have the desire for things to 'make sense' – even when we don't have the information to do more than make a guess. This is the reason we like stories. It has been proven that the less we know the more confident we are of our opinions (the Dunning-Kruger effect), probably because it gives us more latitude to bend the 'facts' to fit our prejudices.

Stories neatly explain what happened and why, with simple cause and effect relationships, populated by 'goodies' and 'baddies' with simple motivations. We (or at least part of us) are uncomfortable with ambiguity and dislike suspending judgement or giving multiple competing interpretations equal weight. This is why intelligent people construct stories about 'why the market moved today' even when they and their audience know that they are just making things up. Understanding the motivation of even one person is difficult. How can anyone read the mind of thousands of market agents whom they have never met, particularly since many of them are machines. We want

---

* This article is adapted from Steve Morlidge's book *Present Sense: A Practical Guide to the Science of Measuring Performance and the Art of Communicating It, with the Brain in Mind* (2019) and appears here courtesy of the author.

something that isn't possible in real life: absolute certainty. Even better if the story we create confirms our pre-existing opinions and prejudices.

Imposing order on and attributing meaning to a complex and fast-moving reality is the primary goal of information professionals. But it is at least as important – at the same time – to find ways to help your audience appreciate the highly provisional and contingent nature of any attempt to impose a simple explanation on a complex, dynamic and fundamentally unknowable world where ambiguity is rife.

All the traditional tools of the trade, like variance analysis, are already biased toward simple binary judgements that provide no scope for argument. Instead of finding new ways to drive out uncertainty, we should be encouraging people to perceive the world in a more holistic way and become more open to ambiguity. In particular, both learning and assessing risk – highly desirable traits in business – require us to take much more notice of things that *don't make sense* in the context of our current mental models.

This is why I flinch whenever I hear people describing that they want information professionals to 'tell stories.' Granted, stories are powerful. They are clear and compelling. Too much so. They have a beginning and an end and a simple clear narrative that can only be interpreted in one way. Stories *tell* you what and why. There is no scope for alternative explanations or for doubt. And I think that is dangerous.

News and Evidence

If we ever doubted the importance of having a capability to assimilate mountains of detail, synthesize it and present it in an accessible and balanced way, the storm around the recent reporting of political events has brought it home.

Despots have always exploited the ability to control news media in a world where facts are at a premium. So many tech entrepreneurs naively assumed that the instant availability of news and the proliferation of communications channels would provide us with a plurality of voices and views that would enable us to make up our own minds in a considered way, and help bring about a more tolerant, inclusive society.

Unfortunately, recent events have demonstrated how easy it is for the opposite to happen. Faced with an overabundance of data and opinion, we simplify matters by choosing a limited range of news sources; and in the process can too easily become trapped in a world of self-reinforcing views only loosely anchored in fact, where fake news is undistinguishable from reality.

On the unregulated news frontiers of our highly interconnected world we need the voices of trusted and reasoned judgement to be heard louder than ever before if we are not to revert to a tribal world where everyone retreats behind the palisades of their own prejudices.

In a different context, and on a smaller scale, this applies to organizations just as much as it does to societies. Information professionals have a key role in making sense of the world and communicating it in such a way that organizations come together around a measured and balanced view of the world. The alternative is a 'free' market where dominant dogma swamps all other voices and competing interpretations.

Not Storytellers But Reporters

It is possible to tell a coherent, simple story from the vantage point of a historian. After the event, all the facts are known and a balanced judgement can be made with the full benefit of hindsight. But it is rarely possible to do this 'in the moment.'

This is the reason I think information professionals should not aspire to be 'storytellers.' But as Phil Rosenzweig (2007) observes: 'management is about taking action, about doing things. So what can be done?' He argues that as a first step we should 'set aside the delusions that color so much of our thinking about business performance. To recognize that stories of inspiration may give us comfort but have little . . . predictive power.'

I would argue that information professionals should think of themselves not as storytellers but as reporters. A good model for what they do is the war correspondent attempting to make sense of what is happening on the ground in a conflict situation. Their job is to present a balanced report, recognizing we don't have access to all the facts and the events that are being reported on can be interpreted in different ways. A reporter's role is to communicate the relevant facts in order to help us form *our own opinions*. A good reporter doesn't promote a particular version of the truth. That is called propaganda. History can only be told after the event; it cannot be observed in real time.

Even though the performance reporter doesn't have the job of 'telling the story,' the role still carries great responsibility. While any report can be interpreted in a number of different ways, what a reporter chooses to include and exclude and how information is communicated has a big influence on the psyche of the audience and how they respond to what they learn. And with power comes responsibility, so it is important that performance reporters have a sense of their duty to the 'truth,' in so far as it is possible, guided by a clear set of principles to steer their activities.

This is not the place to explore the role and ethics of performance reporting in detail, but I think there are at least four key duties.

The Duty of Clarity

Performance reports should be clear. The intended meaning must be communicated in a way that can be quickly assimilated by the intended audience. Data that confuses or distorts the message needs to be excluded where possible. Significant data that would otherwise be hidden or obscured should be emphasized.

The Duty of Balance

A reporter has to make choices about what is, and what is not, 'said.' These choices must be made in a way that does not favour the interests of any constituency in the business.

The message should neither reinforce received wisdom nor challenge it merely to be provocative. Communication should, as far as possible, be balanced and free from bias.

The Duty of Requisite Ambiguity

Communication needs to be clear, balanced, and nuanced – simple but not simplistic. The collective knowledge and experience of the audience is always greater than that of an individual performance reporter. So, it is important that he or she provides sufficient contextual information to allow the audience to validate or challenge the message, or to come up with an alternative interpretation of the facts, particularly if they have contextual knowledge that can be brought to bear. Reports therefore have to contain a degree of redundancy (slightly more information than is needed to support the intended message), even to the point of ambiguity, since the 'truth,' if such things exist at all, is only obvious in hindsight.

The Duty of Integrity

Finally, reports should not mislead, intentionally or otherwise. In particular, reporters need to ensure that:

- Trends are not presented in a way that magnifies or suppresses them (Figure 5.1).
- Information is presented in a way that does not invite false correlations to be made. This involves careful consideration of the scales used, particularly when a single chart has a secondary scale (Figure 5.2).
- Anything that is presented that could easily be misinterpreted is highlighted. For example, a reporter might add a comment to a data point if it is known to be unrepresentative of the series – perhaps because of an exceptional event or a data collection issue (Figure 5.3).

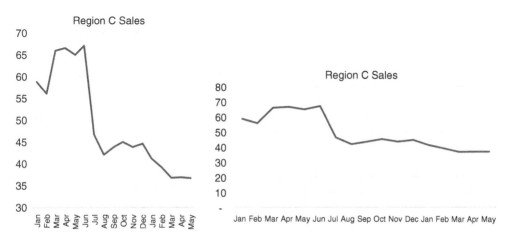

Figure 5.1 Left Chart Overstates Magnitude of the Change by Tampering with the Aspect Ratio as Well as Origin of the Y \Axis

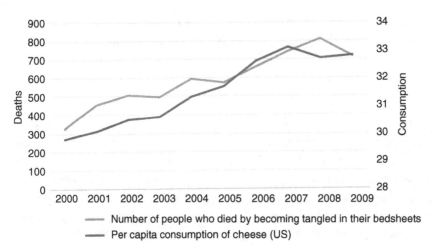

Figure 5.2 Dishonestly Juxtaposing Two Unrelated Data Series and Tampering with the Scale of the Secondary Axis Creates a Misleading Impression of Correlation

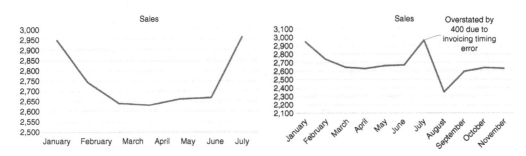

Figure 5.3 Selective Presentation of Historical Context on Left Creates False Impression. On Right the Rapid Decline and 'Bounce Back' Is Better Interpreted as a Steady Decline with a False 'Spike.'

Although being 'right' all the time is a noble aspiration, it is unattainable. Instead, what reporters should strive for is to be respected – for their skills – and trusted – for their judgement and impartiality.

Sometimes the best, and perhaps the only, thing that you can achieve in the limited time available to you is to direct the attention of the right people in the business to the right things, and help them ask the right questions.

Reference

Rosenzweig, P. M. (2007). *The halo effect . . . and the eight other business delusions that deceive managers.* Free Press.

5.2 WHY IS IT SO HARD TO HOLD ANYONE ACCOUNTABLE FOR THE SALES FORECAST?*

Chris Gray

Who holds responsibility and accountability for the forecasts and demand plans? This is a critical question, and it exposes the all-too-common problem of "everyone is responsible, no one is accountable" which appears in many multistep processes like demand planning. In this final contribution to *Foresight* before his untimely passing in October 2019, Chris Gray presents an indispensable checklist of issues that every organization must address to clarify individual responsibilities as well as overall accountability for results.

Gray observes that most companies have multiple people from multiple departments responsible for forecast-related activities, but only one department (typically marketing or sales & marketing) that is accountable for achieving the demand plan. This creates the danger that individual responsibilities interact, overlap, and potentially conflict. And it raises many questions of what's needed to create clear lines of accountability.

Assigning all sales-planning tasks to people in the sales & marketing department is not always optimal. Other departments – customer service, master scheduling, planning – can be responsible for the number crunching and reconciliation tasks. But the ultimate measurements, performance, and accountability must remain with the marketing or sales & marketing department. They must own the forecasting and sales planning process and ultimately accept overall accountability for results.

Gray provides guidance for achieving the ultimate goal of clear and unambiguous accountability for each step throughout the process, as well as establishing ownership and accountability for the process in its entirety.

"Who's on First?," a famous comedy routine between the duo of Bud Abbott and Lou Costello, has Abbott identifying players on a baseball team for Costello. But because the players' names and nicknames are somewhat strange (Who, What, Why, I-don't-know, Because, Tomorrow, Today, I-don't-give-a-darn, etc.), Abbott's apparently ambiguous answers to Costello's questions seem hilariously nonresponsive. For example, the first baseman is named Who; so the question "Who's on first?" is ambiguous between the question ("Which person is the first baseman?") and the answer ("The name of the first baseman is 'Who.'").

Here's an excerpt:

Costello: I'm only asking you, who's the guy on first base?
Abbott: That's right.
Costello: Okay.
Abbott: All right.
pause
Costello: What's the guy's name on first base?

---

* This article originally appeared in *Foresight: The International Journal of Applied Forecasting* (Summer 2019) and appears here courtesy of the International Institute of Forecasters.

Abbott: No. What is on second.
Costello: I'm not asking you who's on second.
Abbott: Who's on first.
Costello: I don't know.
Abbott: He's on third, you're not talking about him.

(See http://abbott-and-costello-whos-on-first.info/whos-on-first-script/ for the full text of "Who's on First?")

Responsibility versus Accountability

In manufacturing enterprises, we sometimes have the same kind of problem as Bud and Lou – the answer to "Who's responsible for the forecast?" is too often ambiguous. And sometimes it's worse – it's a dodge, and often a dodge with an implied "Don't blame me," something you may have heard in your own company:

- Everyone knows the forecast will be wrong . . .
- The computer produces the numbers . . .
- We no more than produce a forecast than something changes . . .
- Our metrics tell us when we missed the forecast and we constantly chase individual errors . . .
- Nearly everyone has their own forecasting models . . .
- Corporate sales and marketing produce a forecast for revenue planning and don't share it . . .

Is it possible you're asking the wrong questions or thinking about forecasting in the wrong way? Have you confused forecasting with sales planning? Are you confusing "responsibility" for one or more of the demand-planning activities with "accountability" for the entire multistep planning process? Are your metrics appropriate for assessing the effectiveness of your external demand planning, or are they really achievement metrics against a company target? Where can you make changes, consistent with so-called best practice, that will improve your own demand-planning processes and/or clarify accountability for results?

The ultimate goal in any kind of demand planning is clear and unambiguous responsibility for each step throughout the process and established and accepted accountability for the process in total.

Are You Forecasting or Sales Planning?

Forecasting is foremost a prerequisite to planning, just as planning is prerequisite to control. In the current context, forecasting is prerequisite to *sales planning* – which in turn is prerequisite to supply and resource planning processes like S&OP, master scheduling, lean leveling, and more.

Forecasting

Forecasts are typically produced from historical data with inputs of judgment concerning the changes to be expected for the future. The forecasts may be calculated from simple averaging techniques (naïve forecasts), statistical methods like exponential smoothing or ARIMA, or more complex methods that include explanatory variables. Each statistical-baseline forecast has its own assumptions – like "the future can be modeled from the past" for some kinds of products, or "this new product will have demand similar to that of this other product during the same place in its life cycle" – and these should be documented for postmortem reviews.

Baseline forecasts will often be adjusted based on management overrides, new-product adjustments and anticipated knock-on effects (cannibalization), known future promotions, pricing adjustments in future periods, and more. Each of these is, in some sense, a forecast in its own right, and all have their own assumptions that must be documented.

Because aggregated demand drives S&OP while detailed demand drives material and capacity plans, forecasts may be generated by product family over an extended horizon (12–18 months in the future) and then broken down to individual items over a much shorter horizon. They may be generated by product family over an extended horizon as well as by item over a shorter horizon, or some similar variant. In almost all variants, the aggregate family forecast must be reconciled over the appropriate horizon with the sum of the individual item forecasts – otherwise the numbers driving S&OP's capacity plans and financial projections will be different from the detailed planning numbers that people are working toward.

Documenting assumptions and reconciliation or validation of aggregated-detail forecasts to family forecasts are often two of the earliest steps in the transformation of forecasts to sales plans.

Sales Planning

Sales plans imply the existence of a baseline forecast, along with defined actions needed to achieve the demand plan, and a degree of commitment from the sales and marketing organization to realize the agreed plan. Defined actions in sales planning typically include reconciliation of aggregated-detail forecasts to family forecasts, documenting assumptions, adjustments to advertising plans and anticipated lift, promotional planning, developing social-media campaigns, sales-force training, different focus by territory, market segmentation, opening new markets and closing old ones, monitoring performance, conducting postmortem reviews and adjustments, and more. When done properly, sales planning involves multiple steps, and often provides a division of labor for specific tasks needed to arrive at the final number.

Sales planning may also be the driver of improvement activities that spill into production and supply-chain redesign: product and process rationalization, waste reduction to improve flow, lead-time reduction and implementation of fulfilment strategies like "mass customization." These improvement activities, frequently outside the domain of sales and marketing, spill into sales planning in significant ways.

If you think of forecasting as "c'mere," then sales planning is "sic 'em."

Are Responsibilities and Overall Accountability Well Defined?

It seems clear, based on decades of industrial experience, that the road to effective sales planning depends on a clear vision of the process steps as well as of the individual responsibility for each step, with properly defined accountability for overall results.

Baseline forecasting can be done in multiple ways and in any of several places in the organization. In some companies, the "demand manager" or "demand planner" or "forecast coordinator" works for the production department. This would be typical of enterprises with well-established products whose baseline demand can be predicted from historical sales. In other companies, customer service does this job or it is given to someone who works directly for the marketing organization. Many times, the person who developed the original baseline forecast continues to coordinate most of the downstream forecast-related activities down to the sales plan, sales plan achievement, and the postmortem on results.

But subcontracting responsibility for individual steps within the sales planning process does not change accountability for the overall process and results. Assigning all the tasks associated with sales planning to people in the sales and marketing department is not always optimal. Customer service, master scheduling, planning, or other departments may be responsible for some of the number crunching and reconciliation tasks. A forecast coordinator or demand manager may report to almost any department – yet he or she does not, alone and in isolation, do all the activities that make up sales planning. A product or process engineer in conjunction with production may be working on lead-time reduction or product designs that allow for "finish to order" fulfillment strategies. All of these tasks are clearly part of overall sales planning and have individual owners who will be responsible for them. And in my judgment, it is impossible to prescribe how an individual company might choose to, appropriately, subcontract the tasks that are part of sales planning.

However, it is clear that accountability for the overall sales planning process and its results must remain with the business's *demand function*. The marketing department owns the sales planning process and all the steps leading up to it, and must accept overall accountability for results. The only exceptions – mostly having to do with semantics – are in companies where the sales function and marketing function have been combined (the sales and marketing department is accountable), or in wholly captive subsidiary plants where there are no outside sales (here "customer service" is typically accountable).

I know of no "best practice" companies where production (or finance, or quality, or human resources) is accountable for sales planning performance, and I suspect this has nothing to do with my personal sample size. To be effective at sales planning, the marketing department must be accountable.

Appropriate Metrics for Sales Planning Process Monitoring

Metrics for sales planning are needed to *drive process improvements* as well as improved "performance."

Too often, the typical forecast "accuracy" metrics simply set off a wild-goose chase trying to explain deviations that are not really changes in demand but reflections of the larger process. When results are less than forecast, it's a mad scramble to find out why; but when results are greater than forecast, it's "attaboys" all around. Clearly these kinds of "point in time" metrics based on achievement against a target are misplaced, as is any metric whose improvement depends upon telling people to "work harder."

A major step in the right direction has been the use of process monitoring tools like SPC's X-bar and R charts to measure and monitor whether the forecasting process is in control or whether changes to the process are required to achieve targeted results. While process monitoring is not universally done, it ranks high among simple improvements that many companies should do.

Monitoring tools such as Forecast Value Added (FVA) can also be applied to the individual elements of the sales planning process, including the baseline forecast and adjustments to it. Is the baseline forecast more accurate than the final forecast, considering all the adjustments? Which planning steps (management overrides, promotion planning, social-media planning, etc.) actually add value against an ultimate goal of an accurate sales plan, and which should be eliminated?

Changes to the Game

Companies that are doing a superior job managing demand have achieved the greatest strides in forecasting by creating improvements such as these:

- Attitudes toward what the forecast can achieve are more realistic, regarding both forecast accuracy and how much variability will exist in the forecast.
- There's a better focus on what actually needs to be forecast – including consideration of whether the forecast should be by item, by family, or some combination – and how far in the future the forecast must be generated.
- Appropriate metrics are utilized that focus on measuring real change in demand levels as opposed to solely gauging accuracy or achievement.
- Improved clarity is achieved about *what* is being measured and *who* is responsible for taking action when a real change in demand occurs.
- There's better linkage – where linking is possible – to customer planning systems, so as to eliminate or reduce the need to forecast.

- Improved information systems are developed for forecasting and sales planning – systems that can not only develop initial projections, but also record assumptions and more clearly define responsibilities.

- You establish more responsive downstream planning systems and process flows that can simplify the demand-planning processes. This includes reengineering products and processes in order to reduce the need to forecast and consequently eliminate the need to deal with so much variability–for example, reconfiguring the supply chain so as to reduce or eliminate surges in component demand or capacity that result from the bullwhip effect.

- Streamlined forecasting and sales planning processes arrive at consensus numbers faster and with less effort.

- More clarity exists in the relationship between strategic and financial plans and the agreed sales plan, along with better-defined processes for reconciling all these plans.

- There's clear and unambiguous accountability for each step throughout the process, as well as establishing ownership and accountability for the process in total.

Who's "On First" in Your Company? The Checklist

How can you improve forecasting and sales planning processes, especially if you are struggling with overall performance? In general, improvement will require basic process adjustments and clarification of overall accountability, followed by changes to process steps (both adds, changes, and deletes from the sales planning process), then establishment or adjustment of individual responsibilities for forecasting and sales planning activities, and ultimately reconsideration of the metrics of forecast effectiveness.

You should probably conduct an impartial assessment of your current forecasting and sales planning processes. This can be done as a self-assessment, with your own personnel using one of the many standardized checklists available, or by an independent, impartial observer guiding the assessment. When using a standardized checklist, do some preliminary work to eliminate questions that are clearly not applicable to your own situation.

In evaluating each process step, identify who is responsible and why, as well as what metrics are available to monitor how effectively that step is accomplished.

Make sure that you consider the following:

- How are the aggregate sales planning process (part of S&OP) and the detailed sales planning process that drives the master schedule and material and capacity plans connected, and how are the numbers in each one reconciled to the numbers in the other?

- By what mechanism will baseline family forecasts be validated and reconciled with item forecasts? Who is responsible for this activity?

- Which individuals in the company are best suited to produce the baseline forecast? Is the answer different for existing product groups and individual items? For new products?

- Is the same person or persons who are responsible for developing the baseline forecast also responsible for coordinating the process that transforms the forecast to the sales plan?

- What are the individual steps embedded in the sales planning process, and who is responsible for each one? How do these interact, overlap, and potentially conflict? Is there a way to create clearer lines of accountability?

- Who is responsible for documenting assumptions behind the forecasted volumes? Are the responsible people doing an adequate job in capturing assumptions so that, in the monthly postmortems or retrospectives, bad assumptions can be identified?

- Within that process, who is responsible for overall marketing and advertising plans that will be used to realize specific sales volumes for each product family?

- Have the expected lifts from marketing plans, social-media activities, and advertising campaigns been quantified? Who is responsible for these?

- Who is responsible for promotions, and has the effect from each planned promotion been quantified?

- Are those marketing and sales activities targeted to specific sales regions or major customers planned out and quantified? Who is responsible, and how much of the agreed demand volume is attributable to these activities?

- Are there specific sales training activities needed to achieve the demand volumes? How much of the demand will be affected by these sales training activities, and when? Who is responsible for these?

- What additional changes should be made to production processes to simplify or at least reduce the amount of forecasting that is needed?

- What additional changes should be made to fulfillment methods that simplify or reduce the amount of forecasting that is needed?

- What are the best metrics for each step in the sales planning process?

- What mechanisms are in place for evaluating the quality of the baseline forecasts? Are there metrics that truly reveal when demand has changed or is changing, so that "chasing ghosts" – blips in demand that are within statistically expected limits – never happens again?

- Who is responsible for monitoring sales planning process behavior, and for taking corrective actions when corrective actions are required?

- What are the postmortem processes for evaluating the effectiveness of assumptions – of marketing, social media, and advertising campaigns; of promotions, territory – and customer-specific targeting activities, etc? What is being learned from recent results that will help with future achievement?

▪ What systems are in place to test which potential actions are most likely to produce the best results in step-change improvements in demand?

▪ Who is responsible and will be accountable for this entire process – from forecast through sales plan through postmortem and back to forecast? When sales plans fall short of targets, is this person also responsible for authorizing the process improvements needed to break free of the constraints of the existing process?

Conclusion

Almost no one denies that some form of forecasting is important. Even so, have you created the necessary processes – including assigning responsibilities and clear-cut accountability for results – in a way that truly reflects its importance to your company, marketplace, and overall strategy? Because if you haven't, you may be stuck in an endless "Who's on First" – and it won't be for laughs.

5.3 COMMUNICATING THE FORECAST: PROVIDING DECISION MAKERS WITH INSIGHTS*

Alec Finney

Forecasts are necessary, but not in themselves sufficient for effective decision making. Here, Alec Finney describes his takeaways from asking decision makers to reveal what's missing from the numerical outputs they receive from forecasters. Key themes that emerge are the need to agree on assumptions, manage risk, and sell "a story – not a spreadsheet." His analysis led to the development of a new sharing platform to improve communication and decision making.

Finney describes a storyboard structure to communicate the forecast in an intuitive and transparent way, providing the contextual information asked for by decision makers. Uncertainty and risk management are handled through a Monte Carlo approach, enabling development of functional plans based on the most likely future.

Asking Decision Makers What They Need

I remember a senior VP in the pharmaceutical industry telling me that "forecasting is more than just the numbers – much more." He is, of course, absolutely correct. But how so? In what ways?

Over the last three years I've been listening to many development/portfolio directors in pharma to find out just what "much more" is. I did this by taking a deep dive

---

* This article originally appeared in *Foresight: The International Journal of Applied Forecasting* (Summer 2019) and appears here courtesy of the International Institute of Forecasters.

into interviews with creators, users, and approvers of forecasts in the field. My questions were designed to cut to the core of the forecasting experience, such as "What are the attributes of a quality forecast?" and "If you had a magic wand, what aspect of forecasting would you fix?"

Several themes emerged about *communicating the forecast*. Decision makers need outputs that:

- Measure uncertainty and manage the associated risk;
- Make the assumptions more visible;
- Differentiate between a forecast that describes the most likely future and one that serves the needs of functional planners;
- Are delivered by an "alive and kicking" support system that keeps the numbers and the assumptions up to date; and
- Use a "storyboard" approach to the structure and evolution of the forecast.

From these discussions we needed to develop the *storyboard structure*, *risk management*, and *functional plans* requested.

Storyboard Structure

Make the way the forecast is communicated more like a story rather than a spreadsheet.

A spreadsheet model is lost on me – tell me the story of the forecast as it evolves.

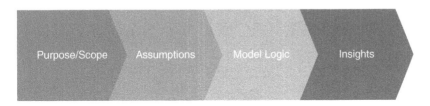

Figure 5.4 Composition of the Storyboard

Purpose and Scope

- First, what is the business process the forecast supports? Is it a decision emerging from the result of clinical trials, a budgeting/target-setting exercise, or a collection of information to support long-term strategy?
- What are the contributing markets, the time horizon, granularity, and units of measure of the forecast?
- Are the *Forecast Owner* and *Forecast Creator* for the specific forecast included? The Owner is accountable for the forecast – "the buck stops here." The Creator is responsible for the forecast – creating and populating the model.

Assumptions

What are the challenges and opportunities presented by the competitive, regulatory, and market-access environments? What resources will be invested to support the launch of a new product and its subsequent growth? What is the assumed size of the potential market, and what market share will our asset achieve? What future events will significantly impact product performance?

A *Forecast Evolution* document should be prepared to describe the ways in which the drug classes and associated brands, including generics, evolve during the forecast timeline.

Changes in assumptions since their last submission – and their impact on forecast values – must be documented. This provides a coherent audit trail of changes in the forecast over time, as well as context provided by the change in assumptions.

Model Logic

I need to see the forecast logic structure clearly defined – not hidden in a large, complicated spreadsheet.

Prevalence models are based on a cascade of patient populations, from the number of possible patients through to those who are seeking treatment, diagnosed, and drug treated. Once this total patient pool has been established, then the brand market share can be modeled. Figure 5.5 details the steps involved.

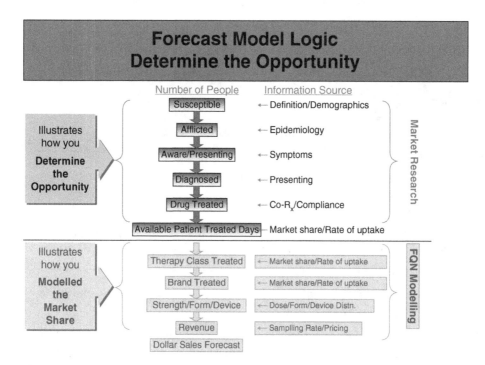

Figure 5.5 Steps in the Forecasting Process

Insight

Can we see the history of how good we are at forecasting, and if we're getting better – or not?

The storyboard structure (scope, assumptions, and model logic) provides the background and context to the forecast. The "Insight" section provides the analytics to make comparisons.

Prevalence-based models contain a vast amount of information. Comparisons and "sense checks" against the supporting assumptions can be made at every level of the cascade – across time, markets, and forecasts created within each business process. Forecasts can be made at each level within the organization (Global, Regional, Country) and for specific business processes (Budgeting, S&OP, Portfolio Prioritization).

The results:

- Audit trails that show how the forecasts change over time;
- Information on how the forecast drivers differ across different markets;
- Recommendations on how the forecasting organizations can present different perspectives of asset value.

In the Insight phase, the decision makers are shown not only the numerical outputs, but also the supporting assumptions. Information on forecast accuracy and other KPIs can be imported from external applications.

Risk Management

In more direct terms, all forecasts have risk associated with them – just tell me when I'm leaning out of the window too far.

Are there any other possible futures of which I should be aware?

Presenting a forecast model, even with a strong link to the assumptions and a transparent description of the model logic, will not satisfy all the contextual needs of the decision makers. We also need to measure uncertainty and manage the associated risk. Doing so requires answers to these three questions:

- What is the Most Likely Future (MLF)?
- How confident am I in the forecast?
- Are there other futures of which I need to be aware?

The Most Likely Future (*MLF*)

This MLF forecast is based upon the agreed assumptions across the business as well as on evidence-based models/algorithms. It is the 50/50 forecast right in the middle of the range of expectations (Finney and Joseph 2009).

How Confident Are We in These Forecasts?

Describing clearly and openly how much uncertainty surrounds the forecasts will require honesty and, very possibly, courage, especially if the margin for error is wide. But it has to be done.

A good way to illustrate the uncertainty around a forecast is to draw a band denoting, say, 80% of all possible outcomes around the MLF, as shown in Figure 5.6.

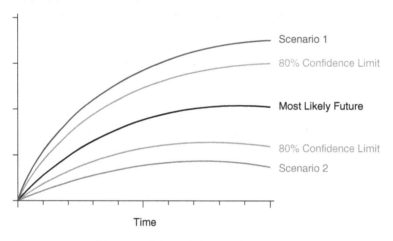

Figure 5.6 MLF with 80% Confidence Limits Including Two Scenarios

This prediction interval can be based on Monte Carlo simulation (MCS). Here, we specify the amount of uncertainty around each *assumption* from "the worst nightmare" on one extreme to "the best dream" on the other. MCS then allows us to create an uncertainty profile covering all assumptions behind the forecasting model.

Other approaches to depicting uncertainty are nicely presented by Paul Goodwin (2014), including fan charts and probability density charts.

Are There Other Futures of Which I Need to Be Aware?

Some of these assumptions may be binary – either "on" or "off." These should be represented as specific scenarios.

Scenario 1 – An upside. The brand is launched into market first-in-class rather than second.

Scenario 2 – A downside. A competitor's new indication is approved and will hurt our market share. The total picture is shown in Figure 5.6.

In MCS, one can select a particular shape distribution of possible outcomes, such as a Normal distribution, which we'll now use as an illustration.

Developing Functional Plans

We can now ask each functional stakeholder what operational plan they will need to manage expectations and risk.

The responses could be as follows:

Supply Chain: I want to manage the uncertainty in the forecast to make sure that we meet 90% of our customer-service levels and minimize inventory (Manufacturing Plan). This is depicted in Figure 5.7 at the right end of the distribution consistent with a high outcome (ca. 1.2 Bn) with a corresponding low-level risk.

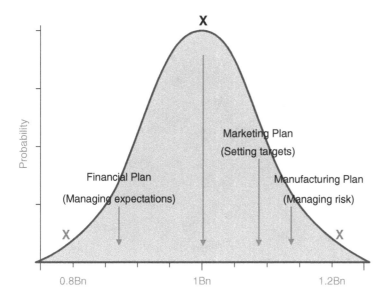

Figure 5.7 Planning End Points Chosen by Each Function

Finance: I want to be able to set a target within the confidence limits (high or low) to manage both risk and stakeholder/investor expectations (Financial Plan). This is indicated in Figure 5.7 toward the left of the distribution consistent with a medium risk and a low level of outcome.

Marketing: I want to set targets with full understanding of the risk involved (Marketing Plan). This is indicated toward the right of the distribution consistent with a medium risk and a midrange level of outcome.

Does this communicate the forecast in an effective way? I believe it does.

The alternative is to create a "Consensus Forecast" – more appropriately, a "Compromise Forecast" – where none of the functional planning requirements are met. Better to afford each function the choice of how to manage expectations and risk; at the least, their plans will be made transparent and can be monitored and amended when necessary.

The Sharing Platform

One common question I hear from decision makers is "Why has the forecast changed since the last update?" Figure 5.8 shows the updates made in the sales forecast of a particular pharmaceutical product.

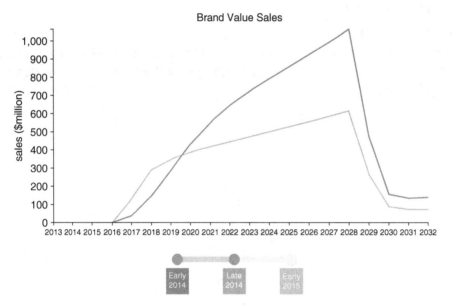

Figure 5.8 Impact of Changes in Assumptions on Peak Year Sales

The original assumptions were made early in 2014. The first updates of these, made later in 2014, were as follows:

1. Price reduction from $10 to $8 per day
2. Price growth reduced from 5% per annum to 3% per annum
3. A reduced comparative advantage in efficacy and safety

Impact: Peak Year Sales down from $1.0 Bn to $600 M

The light gray line in Figure 5.9 shows the further revisions made in 2015 and represents a slightly more positive view of sales prospects based on assumptions of improved compliance from a recent study, and a small increase in patient numbers from a new epidemiology study. Peak year sales now forecast at $700 M.

Conclusion

A key question is how to translate forecasts into actionable plans. A note I received recently from a portfolio director reads, "Nothing is certain; whatever the forecast tells me, I will be taking a risk. Just tell me what I would be leaving on the table."

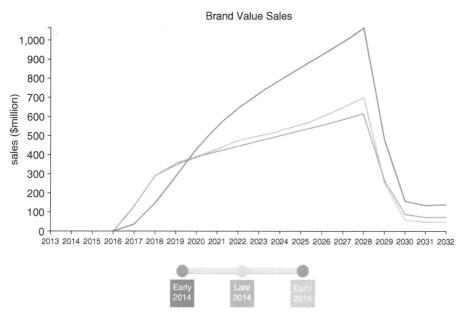

Figure 5.9 Early 2015 Added

By combining the clarity of the storyboard with the power of visual risk profiles and insights, we can give decision makers more than just the numbers. Much more.

References

Finney, A., and Joseph, M. (2009). The forecasting mantra: A holistic approach to forecasting and planning. *Foresight* 12 (Winter): 5–13.

Goodwin, P. (2014). Getting real about uncertainty. *Foresight* 33 (Spring): 4–7.

5.4 AN S&OP COMMUNICATION PLAN: THE FINAL STEP IN SUPPORT OF COMPANY STRATEGY*

Niels van Hove

Sales and Operations Planning has been around for nearly 40 years, and has generally advanced beyond the original goal of balancing supply and demand. More recent discussion has been around the integration of finance and senior leadership into supply chain planning, as well as ways in which S&OP can be broadened to encompass enterprise-wide planning and performance management.

---

* This article originally appeared in *Foresight: The International Journal of Applied Forecasting* (Summer, 2016) and appears here courtesy of the International Institute of Forecasters.

Mature S&OP processes now support rolling forecasts, enterprise resource reallocation, and strategy execution. But to keep employees informed, engaged, and focused on executing strategy, S&OP outcomes must be communicated properly. To do this, Niels van Hove calls for a variety of communication channels, both structured and informal. This includes a corporate communication plan, with S&OP communication structured to bring the appropriate message to different groups. Two-way communication, up and down the organizational hierarchy, is key to not just inform employees, but to align, engage, energize, and refocus them.

Introduction

Most companies have a business "strategy," but many struggle to execute it. According to a study by Kaplan and Norton (2005), the fundamental disconnect between strategy formulation and implementation has resulted in implementation failure rates of 60 to 90 percent. Smith and Ward (2005) found that while 80 percent of executives express satisfaction with their business strategy, only 14 percent are satisfied with the execution of the strategy.

The ultimate goal of S&OP is the generation of a plan to support an organization's efforts to deploy and execute its strategy. In our busy day-to-day schedules, it's easy to forget that communication is a key feature of these efforts. But to support strategy, communication must be an integral part of the S&OP process.

Communications to Support Business Strategy

In our fast-changing and volatile world, effective communication is a necessity for organizational success. In his ground-breaking work on leading organizational change, John Kotter identifies eight steps for successful change, including clear and frequent communication of the vision (Kotter 1995).

A McKinsey report (Jacquemont, Maor, and Reich 2015) considers communication to be one of the top three impact factors on business transformations, resulting in a four- to eightfold greater transformation success rate. Information flow is considered the strongest contributor to good strategy execution (Neilson, Martin, and Powers 2008), and there is statistical evidence that poor communication and misaligned information flow are directly correlated with poor strategy execution and decreased profit (Radomska 2014a).

I believe practitioners do recognize that communication is an important part of S&OP. In my annual online questionnaire, the S&OP Pulse Check, practitioners suggest that the main reason to implement S&OP is to "improve cross-functional communication," and the main cultural change driven by S&OP is "improved understanding and communication between business functions" (Van Hove 2015).

All this makes sense in a classical, operationally focused S&OP environment, one where demand, supply, and inventory are kept in balance, and different functions need to communicate and coordinate to fix issues. To fix an inventory problem, for one example, S&OP participants can agree that a sales promotion or a product introduction will be delayed while operations gears up in capacity and procurement looks for alternative sources.

To effectively support strategy execution, however, S&OP communication needs to do more than fix operational issues. As Kaplan and Norton (2005) argue, *horizontal communication* is not enough. Horizontal communication – information flow across functions – is often at the same hierarchy level, where it is useful to solve business issues and run processes within an existing context. But there is also a need for *vertical communication* to create alignment throughout the organization in support of a strategy.

Vertical communication gives direction and context to the business. A new market or new business reality needs to cascade down to the lowest level of the organization to ensure that a critical mass of employees understands and supports the new direction. Beer and Eisenstate (2000) mention poor vertical communication as one of six strategy killers.

To become more effective in sharing information, executives also need to develop informal modes of communication. The days of top-down, formal, command-and-control communication, where top management simply tells employees what to do, have passed. Employee autonomy – one of the three major intrinsic human motivators (Pink, 2009) – is severely reduced by top-down communication; it's a management style that no longer fits how the millennial workforce expects to be treated. Additionally, it reduces the speed and agility of information sharing, a critical requirement in today's hyper-connected world. With globalization, mobility, flexible work places, and social networks, informal communication has become a significant factor in strategy implementation (Radomska 2014b).

In their article "Leadership Is a Conversation," Groysberg and Slind (2012) argue that traditional corporate communication must give way to a process that is more dynamic and sophisticated. It must be more conversational in tone. As they put it, *"Smart leaders today engage with employees in a way that resembles an ordinary person-to-person conversation more than it does a series of commands from on high."*

In short, to become more effective in supporting strategy execution and more influential in the overall business, S&OP must move beyond the traditional focus on horizontal, operational, issue-focused communication. S&OP has to advance two-way vertical and informal communication in support of a strategy – not just to inform employees, but to align, engage, energize, motivate, and refocus them. S&OP output has to become an integral part of overall corporate communication.

S&OP and Strategy Execution

To add value to strategy execution, the S&OP process needs to encompass at least the following three elements.

An Integrated Strategy Plan

According to Mankins and Steele (2006), strategy planning tends to be done once a year, while strategic decisions are not bound by a calendar. Their research shows that less than 10 percent of companies have any sort of disciplined process for adapting to changes in the external environment. They find that companies with a more dynamic strategic-plan review make twice as many important strategic decisions each year than those that follow the traditional planning model.

Through periodic review of strategic projects within the budget year and beyond, S&OP should promote visibility into the strategic planning progress. Strategic goals, measurements, and targets such as a balanced scorecard (Kaplan and Norton 1992) should be integrated into the S&OP cycle to further support the execution of the strategic plan.

Kaplan and Norton also note (2005) that 95 percent of the typical workforce doesn't understand the firm's strategy. Without proper communication of the strategy to a critical mass of employees, it seems unlikely a company strategy can be well executed. The S&OP communication plan can keep employees periodically informed on the strategy progress and, as a result, increase the strategic knowledge and understanding of the average employee.

A Rolling Forecast

The annual plan or budget is the first phase of the strategic plan and therefore critical to the plan's execution. However, according to Kaplan and Norton (2005), 60 percent of companies do not have strategic initiatives in the budget. To improve strategy alignment and execution, they suggest an Office of Strategy Management (OSM) to focus on the creation, deployment, and execution of the strategic plan. One of the important elements to incorporate is the provision of a periodic rolling forecast, a task that should fit well within the scope of an S&OP process.

Rolling forecasts as part of S&OP are not a new proposition. Dougherty and Gray (2013) describe in detail how S&OP interacts with the development of annual plans and budgets, decisions about capital investments, and the management of cash flow.

A periodic rolling forecast as part of an S&OP process provides the opportunity for leaders to review gaps versus budget. However, without employee understanding of what the *gaps to budget* are and what to do about them, a company will not effectively coordinate progress in returning to budget. With an S&OP communication plan, executives can communicate these gaps to their employees, with a call for action and with guidance on how to close them.

Resource Reallocation

Tangible and intangible resources are one of the five most mentioned *strategy-to-execution* factors (Ivancic 2013), and early resource allocation is mentioned as a key contributor to strategy execution (Mankins and Steele 2005). Unfortunately, business and resource plans are usually updated and aligned only yearly: "Ninety percent of resource allocation doesn't change year on year, but companies that do reallocate resources improve their shareholder value by 30 percent" (Birshan, Engel, and Sibony 2013).

In their recent *Foresight* article, Mark Moon and Pete Alle (2015) correctly observe that, in most companies, S&OP focuses upon production resources but does not address *all* enterprise resources. An advanced S&OP process, with strategy integration and a rolling budget, can deal with resource allocation more holistically. Insights in gaps to budget in any P&L line can trigger resource reallocation.

As S&OP manager, I managed the status of more than 75 new-product-development projects as well as several dozen continuous improvement projects. In these projects, our priorities could change during an S&OP cycle, but resources were not always reallocated and employees not properly informed about the new priorities. I realized that an S&OP communication plan was needed to bring structure to our communications and to refocus our employees as needed to attend to the most important projects.

If these three efforts are embedded, S&OP will play an important role in the execution of the business strategy. S&OP outcomes and decisions can then be communicated to employees in support of the strategy. In the end, S&OP and strategy execution should be all about decision making and follow-up actions.

The S&OP Communication Plan

A corporate communication plan needs to address the right stakeholders with the right information, through the right channels, at the right time. It has a powerful impact on keeping employees informed and engaged. The output of an advanced S&OP process provides an ongoing opportunity to support corporate communication on gaps to budget, status of strategic initiatives, resource reallocation, and a call to action to solve critical business issues.

Communication Structure

An S&OP communication plan helps to structure the messages and conversations across different echelons and groups of employees. The message type and communication channel have to be chosen to reflect those different groups.

Information shared with higher echelons might contain more sensitive information and use different language than communication with lower echelons. Millennials would rather have a short, 140-character news bite than a presentation or newsletter, formats that older employees might prefer.

So we should make use of different types of communication channels to share the messages that emerge from the S&OP meetings. Formal channels like newsletters, roadshows, and presentations can be complemented by more informal channels like blogs, videos, and instant messaging. Senior leaders can provide personalized commentary on business status through blogs or video messages. Further intimacy and inclusion can be created by direct messages or Q&A sessions through internal social-network and collaboration platforms like Yammer – and, of course, direct one-to-one conversations.

As shown in Table 5.1, an S&OP communication plan synthesizes the various channels of communication.

You can quickly see that an S&OP communication plan gives structure to the flow of information across the organization.

An S&OP newsletter, CEO blog, or news bite can inform employees whether the business is on track to meet its budget as well as regarding the status of its strategic initiatives. These communications can also serve to motivate employees by highlighting project success stories, announcing the launch of a new product or celebrating the

Table 5.1 S&OP Communication Plan

Audience	Type	Channel	Objective	Frequency
S&OP Meeting Participants	S&OP feedback	S&OP meeting	An informal roundtable feedback after every S&OP cycle meeting. Opportunity for participants to share thoughts.	Weekly
All S&OP Stakeholders	S&OP minutes	Email	A call to action to follow up on decision being made or actions agreed upon in the execution S&OP meeting.	Monthly
Whole Business	Newsletter	Email, intranet	Information on all decisions taken in the S&OP cycle, gaps to budget, status of strategy plans and business focus.	Monthly
Whole Business Gen Y	News sites	Intranet, messaging system (Yammer)	Headlines, with max 140 characters, summarizing the S&OP output information in the newsletter.	Monthly
Whole Business	CEO blog	Intranet	A thought from the CEO on current business status, the market, progress against budget and strategy.	Quarterly
Whole Business Gen Y	Executive Q&A	Internal messaging system (Yammer)	Information short 30 min, conversation with employees on questions regarding priorities, focus, budget.	Quarterly
Whole Business	Video message	Intranet	An energizing message from the leadership team to celebrate successes during the year.	Quarterly.
Business Unit or Division	Roadshow	Presentation	Formal presentation on H1 results, H2 outlook, market conditional and overall business status.	Half-yearly
Group of Chosen Employees	Roundtable	Face-to-face meeting with leadership	Formal meeting with employees after the roadshow to listen to concerns and understand engagement.	Half-yearly

achievement of a major milestone. S&OP minutes can be more directive and used to refocus S&OP stakeholders when priorities change, or make a call for action to close budget gaps or solve operational problems. More formalized communication on quarterly business results and outlook can be done through a CEO email, presentations at roadshows, and video messages.

Listening to Feedback

The S&OP communication plan should reveal how and when the leadership team is going to listen to employee feedback. To develop a two-way conversation, executives must be open to receive feedback and must respond to it productively.

The communication plan can support feedback and conversation through organized formal roundtables, or more informal online Q&A sessions with a small group of employees. A CEO blog with an option for readers to comment creates another opportunity to listen.

The S&OP cycle itself can support feedback and conversation. After every product review, demand review, and supply review, the leading chair can ask meeting participants for an open round of feedback on meeting effectiveness and displayed behaviours. As S&OP manager and executive S&OP meeting facilitator, at the end of a meeting I made sure some of the following questions got airtime: Were we all listening actively? Did we take the time to understand each other's point of view? Did we follow through on our actions? Did we stay constructive while discussing opposing views? After a while, these questions become common and habitual.

In the end, however, it is up to executives to listen to feedback and act on it. Rather than ignoring others or listening inactively, executives should demonstrate higher forms of listening skills: attentive listening and listening with empathy (Covey 1989). To drive real engagement in a conversation, employees need to feel that what they say has an impact. Therefore, executives need to listen with the *intention of being influenced*: you shouldn't act as if your mind has already been made up.

Listening is a skill that executives can, and indeed must, develop to achieve genuine two-way conversation with employees. And to improve company communication, listening is a valuable skill that should be part of the communication toolbox of every employee.

Summary

Once the strategy plan, a rolling forecast, and enterprise resource reallocation are integrated, the S&OP process can provide valuable input to a corporate communication plan. With an S&OP communication plan in place and through the facilitation of feedback, S&OP will more effectively support the communications – horizontal and vertical, formal and informal, one-way and two-way – that inform, motivate, and refocus employees, all of which are essential to the execution of company strategy.

References

Beer, M., and Eisenstate, R. (2000). The silent killers of strategy implementation and learning. *Sloan Management Review*. http://sloanreview.mit.edu/article/the-silent-killers-of-strategy-implementation-and-learning/

Birshan, M., Engel, M., and Sibony, O. (2013). Avoiding the quicksand: Ten techniques for more agile corporate resource allocation. *McKinsey Quarterly (October)*. http://www.mckinsey.com/insights/strategy/avoiding_the_quicksand

Covey, S. R. (1989). *The seven habits of highly effective people: Powerful lessons in personal change*. http://www.amazon.com/The-Habits-Highly-Effective-People/dp/0743269519

Dougherty, J., and Gray, C. (2013). S&OP and financial planning. *Foresight (Spring)*. https://forecasters.org/pdfs/foresight/SOP_and_Financial_Planning_Gray_Dougherty.pdf

Groysberg, B., and Slind, M. (2012). Leadership is a conversation. *Harvard Business Review (June)*. https://hbr.org/2012/06/leadership-is-a-conversation

Ivancic, I. (2013). *The biggest failures in managing strategy implementation*. University of Rijeka Faculty of Economics. https://ideas.repec.org/a/osi/journl/v9y2013p197-208.html

Jacquemont, D., Maor, D., and Reich, A. (2015). *How to beat the transformation odds*. *McKinsey Insights and Publications*. http://www.mckinsey.com/insights/organization/how_to_beat_the_transformation_odds

Kaplan, R. S., and Norton, D. P. (1992). The balanced scorecard: Measures that drive performance. *Harvard Business Review*. http://www.hbs.edu/faculty/Pages/item.aspx?num=9161

Kaplan, R. S., and Norton, D. P. (2005). Creating the office of strategy management. http://www.hbs.edu/faculty/Publication%20Files/05-071.pdf

Kotter, J. P. (1995). Leading change: Why transformation efforts fail. *Harvard Business Review*. https://hbr.org/2007/01/leading-change-why-transformation-efforts-fail

Mankins, M. C., and Steele, R. (2006). Stop making plans: Start making decisions. *Harvard Business Review*. https://hbr.org/2006/01/stop-making-plans-start-making-decisions

Moon, M., and Alle, P. (2015). From sales & operations planning to business integration. *Foresight* 37 (Spring).

Neilson, G. L., Martin, K. L., and Powers, E. (2008). The secrets to successful strategy execution. *Harvard Business Review (June)*. https://hbr.org/2008/06/the-secrets-to-successful-strategy-execution

Pink, D. H. (2009). *Drive: The surprising truth about what motivates us*. Riverhead Books.

Radomska, J. (2014a). *Linking the main obstacles to the strategy implementation with the company's performance*. *Sciencedirect*. http://www.sciencedirect.com/science/article/pii/S1877042814051039

Radomska, J. (2014b). Model of successful strategy execution: Revising the concept. *Problems of Management in the 21st Century*. http://www.scientiasocialis.lt/pmc/?q=node/120

Smith, S., and Ward, P. (2005). *Strategy execution: Executing your strategy and delivering results*. Quest Worldwide Consulting LTD. http://www.quest-worldwide.com/Downloads/pdfs/Quest%20Strategy%20Execution.pdf

Sorenson, D. (2015). Beyond integrated business planning and sales and operations planning to enterprise planning and performance management. *Foresight* 40 (Winter): 27–37.

Van Hove, N. (2015). The S&OP pulse check 2015.https://supplychaintrends.files.wordpress.com/2015/12/supply-chain-trend-sop-pulse-check-2015.pdf

5.5 COMMUNICATING FORECASTS TO THE C-SUITE: A SIX-STEP SURVIVAL GUIDE*

Todd Tomalak

Most forecasting practitioners have extensive training in technical skills but end up having to "learn the hard way" about discussing forecasts with CEO/CFOs. Above, we've seen two alternative (but still overlapping) approaches to this issue. Finney expanded on the more common paradigm of "telling a story," and described a sharing platform to improve communication and decision making. Morlidge favored the paradigm of a reporter – providing a balanced account of what is known, admitting we don't have access to all the facts, and acknowledging that events being reported on can be interpreted in different ways. Both authors recognize the unavoidable uncertainty inherent in forecasting, and that this uncertainty cannot be packaged up into a tidy explanation with no loose ends.

In this article, writing from the perspective of the real estate industry, Todd Tomalak offers guidance on how to talk forecasts with the C-Suite. He provides six tips for explaining the forecast to executives, complementing the advice of Finney and Morlidge. While these tips were developed for talking about real estate forecasts, they deliver suitable guidance for a wide swath of industries.

SIX TIPS FOR EXPLAINING THE FORECAST TO EXECS

1. Articulate what the CFO needs to believe to use the forecast. Do you face knee-jerk reactions to a surprising forecast? Articulate what the executive needs to believe for your forecast to work. Even better, think through what understandings are necessary to believe other forecasts that have a different outlook.

2. Remember: accountants and statisticians think differently about data. Keep the conversation around totals, not detailed segments. Unlike accounting ledgers, statistical estimates become less reliable as minutiae are scrutinized.

3. Don't talk about complex diagnostic statistics. Statistics are a tool, not the deliverable. The CEO expects you to do your job well, as evidenced by a reliable forecast, which is different from great-looking diagnostic statistics.

4. Know the skewness of consensus forecast participants. Do forecasts of firms that have "skin in the game" cluster differently than forecasts of a broader group of firms? Your CEO will be thinking of those peers.

5. Explain sensitivities in thumb-rules, not coefficients. Thumb-rules are easy to remember and make CFOs look smart in front of investors.

6. Your forecast is wrong. Have an opinion on whether the error is upside or downside. Your model should have equal upside/downside bias, but thinking through possible direction of error will make you more valuable to the executive team. They will have more confidence in you if you can articulate what other factors are on your radar.

---

* This article originally appeared in *Foresight: The International Journal of Applied Forecasting* (Summer 2017) and appears here courtesy of the International Institute of Forecasters.

Introduction

Which is harder: building your forecast, or getting aligned with the CEO/CFO? Developing a reliable forecast is a different skill than communicating the forecast to the C-Suite. And while forecast practitioners typically have extensive training in various technical skills, they only "learn the hard way" about discussing forecasts with the CEO/CFO. So here are some observations and tips on how to bridge the gap when talking forecasts with the C-Suite.

Articulate What the CFO Needs to Believe to Use the Forecast

Clearly explain what needs to happen for your forecast to materialize. Even better, think through what beliefs are necessary to buy into other forecasts. When you share the growth forecast, be sure to concisely explain the "why" behind the number. The underlying logic is more important than the outcome.

Remember, not everyone in the room always has the goal of an unbiased best-estimate forecast (Mello 2009). Game playing happens when the *implication* of the forecast gets more focus than the *accuracy* of the forecast.

Sales execs are typically graded on exceeding their sales goals, not forecasting accurately. Some compensation structures reward execs for exceeding revenue targets, which means the exec has every reason to *sandbag* to a lower forecast. Taken to an extreme, this can lead to problems from insufficient inventories, headaches in production planning, or even more serious consequences.

An insightful working paper from researchers at the Atlanta Federal Reserve (Foote, Gerardi, and Willen 2012) examines the underlying forecasts used by issuers of mortgage-backed securities (MBS) before the 2008 financial crisis. It points to the dangerous role that bad forecasts of home-price appreciation had on the housing crisis. Even if a subprime homeowner defaulted, rising home prices on the underlying home were assumed to offset the default risk. The most expensive, risky MBS could still make sense if the buyer had the "right" assumption on home prices (right in this case meaning *aggressive* rather than *correct*).

This is a clear example of gaming the forecast to achieve the desired outcome. MBS issuers get paid when they issue mortgage-backed securities, not based on the accuracy of their home-price forecasts.

Below are two tables from Lehman Brothers and J.P. Morgan, which candidly show the dangerous forecasts of home-price appreciation (HPA) underwritten into MBS. Lehman assigned very low probabilities to downside scenarios, which made bonds look more appealing to investors. Right before home prices plummeted, J.P. Morgan communicated that home prices were stabilizing and near bottom.

Rosy forecasts made otherwise terrible investments look promising. The consequences were dire: home prices fell even faster than the "least likely" meltdown scenario that Lehman forecasted. Lehman filed for bankruptcy just three years after making this forecast, partially due to losses that could have been avoided if a more balanced forecast scenario had been used. To give credit where it is due, I am showing both tables, including excellent footnotes that point to the poor forecast, exactly as they were presented in the Atlanta Federal Reserve Working Paper.

Table 5.2 Conditional Forecasts of Losses on Subprime Investments from Lehman Brothers

Name	Scenario	Probability	Cum Loss
(1) Aggressive	11% HPA over the life of the pool	15%	1.4%
(2)	8% HPA for life	15%	3.2%
(3) Base	HPA slows to 5% by end-2005	50%	5.6%
(4) Pessimistic	0% HPA for the next 3 years, 5% thereafter	15%	11.1%
(5) Meltdown	−5% for the next 3 years, 5% thereafter	5%	17.1%

This table shows that investors knew that subprime investments would turn sour if housing prices fell. The "meltdown" scenario for housing prices implies cumulative losses of 17.1 percent on subprime-backed bonds; such losses would be large enough to wipe out all but the highest-rated tranches of most subprime deals. The table also shows that investors placed small probabilities on these price scenarios, a fact that explains why they were so willing to buy these bonds.
Source: "HEL Bond Profile Across HPA Scenarios" from Lehman Brothers: "U.S. ABS Weekly Outlook," August 15, 2005.

[Note that prices of bonds on the secondary market would already have traded at a discount, as they've priced in losses due to higher rate of defaults (compared to bonds issued to primary markets). Therefore, the Aggressive scenario still would look profitable to secondary market investors despite the 1.4% cumulative loss from the original bonds. Loss rates refer to defaults of underlying loans within the mortgage backed security.]

Table 5.3 View on House Price Appreciation from JPMorgan Analysts

Date of	Data from	Title
12/8/06	10/06	"More widespread declines with early stabilization signs"
1/10/07	11/06	"Continuing declines with stronger stabilization signs"
2/6/07	12/06	"Tentative stabilization in HPA"
3/12/07	1/07	"Continued stabilization in HPA"
9/20/07	7/07	"Near bottom on HPA"
11/2/07	9/07	"UGLY! Double digit declines in August and September"

Even as housing prices began to fall from their elevated levels, many analysts believed that prices would soon stabilize. The table provides further evidence that investors were optimistic about house prices during the boom.
Source: Flanagan et al. (2006b).

Most organizations run into some form of forecast gaming, albeit less severe than the financial crisis. Discussing what you need to believe changes the tone of the discussion from "Who is right/What number is right" to "What beliefs about demand seem the most plausible?" If you think your forecast is going to be surprising to the C-Suite, communicate early, and focus on the reasons. Spoon-feed executive leadership about the changing outlook before unveiling a big forecast surprise.

Accountants and Statisticians Think Differently about Data

Most CFOs are trained to believe that diving deep into the granular details is always a good thing to do. Accountants are accustomed to working with factual records, which are just as reliable at the individual record-level as when totaled up. In contrast, statisticians are trained to distrust small sample sizes and overly granular estimates. They recognize that each piece of information has some noise. Unlike accounting ledgers, *statistical estimates become less reliable as minutiae are scrutinized.*

This fundamental difference in how to think about detail can make your forecast discussions difficult. One CFO that I worked with exclaimed, "If I can't believe the detailed segment forecast, I can't believe the total!" To keep the conversation from falling into a downward spiral, do the following:

1. Keep the conversation around totals, not overly detailed segments. Don't go into individual subsets unless absolutely necessary.

2. Articulate the limitations of your forecasting procedure (limitations, not "weaknesses," is the operative word).

3. You might remind the executive that other data they trust such as estimates of GDP growth or other Census estimates *all break down into meaningless numbers if looked at under a microscope.* The Census and Bureau of Economic Analysis post abundant warnings about the dangers of relying on the "underlying detail" tables within GDP or other statistical estimates.

It is okay to say that a forecast is only reliable at a high level of aggregation. Show your confidence in the strengths of your forecast process, and be modest and honest about the limitations.

Don't Talk about Complex Diagnostic Statistics

Remember that your forecast model is a tool, and not the deliverable. The CEO cares a lot more about the driving factors than the fit of your model. If you are desperate to prove the credibility of the model, make a simple graph of your forecast and the actual data (the rest of us know this is oversimplified). Keep all those complex diagnostic statistics in your back pocket if you need them (as an appendix). The CEO doesn't care if you've run a stationarity test, and you will lose relevance if you make a showy display of statistics without any serious need to go there.

Inexperienced forecasters focus on selecting and fitting a model, and then act like the forecast is finished. I think this stems from the fact that many econometric programs focus on curve-fitting, but spend less time on other aspects of forecasting. As a result, some forecasters are much better at fitting curves than they are at digging into the independent impelling factors driving demand.

Expect a Skew in Consensus Forecasts

I dislike the term "consensus forecast." The word *consensus* means "general agreement" – however, if you dig under the hood of most consensus forecasts, the first thing you notice is that the forecast is far from a general agreement.

The histogram here illustrates the challenge of using a consensus forecast:

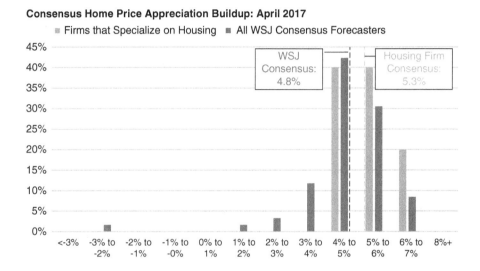

Consensus Home Price Appreciation Buildup: April 2017

Firms that Specialize on Housing ■ All WSJ Consensus Forecasters

WSJ Consensus: 4.8%

Housing Firm Consensus: 5.3%

Shown are forecasts of 2017 home-price appreciation compiled by the *Wall Street Journal* in April 2017. The forecasters come from a diverse group of companies, including housing-focused companies, sell-side equity research from Wall Street, and economists at companies completely unrelated to housing (but asked, nevertheless, to contribute their forecasts across all *WSJ* forecast categories).

The firms that focus on housing skew about *150 basis points higher* than the so-called consensus. It is common for companies that have the most skin in the game to develop a different outlook than the broader consensus of companies. The impact of these differences can be significant, and can change the thrust of the outlook-planning discussion. In this example, the difference between the housing firm consensus and the broader *WSJ* consensus could drive an additional $2 billion dollars of building-material spending at the large home-improvement retailers like Home Depot and Lowe's.

Anytime you talk to your CEO about consensus forecasts, you should know the key players and their respective forecasts. The CEO will especially want to know if other firms in the same industry are guiding higher or lower. Wall Street analysts will question CEOs on the outlook compared to competitors. In the example above, home-improvement retailers who built their forecast using only the *WSJ* consensus would likely be planning for slower growth than their competitors: *a big deal to your CEO/CFO when speaking with investors.*

A word of caution is in order regarding *peer-group consensus* forecasts. Peer-group forecasts are not necessarily more accurate. I am not advocating that you limit your consensus forecast to only companies like yours, since biases may well exist within the peer group. I'm suggesting that spending time understanding the particular players in the consensus forecast will make your discussion with your CEO go easier.

Explain Sensitivities to Changes in Independent Variables as Thumb Rules, Not Coefficients

No matter how complex your actual analysis is, it's worth dumbing down your analysis into *thumb-rules* of demand that are easy to remember and make the CFO look smart in front of investors.

Carol Tome, CFO of Home Depot, does an exceptional job communicating with Wall Street analysts. Tome was questioned by a Wall Street analyst about the effect of an aging housing stock. (Housing stock is a slow-moving, structurally shifting driver with imperfect historical data, since homes in prior spending cycles were generally younger.) A tough question, with a lot of analysis.

This is how she used some of our work (emphasis mine) in their Feb. 23, 2016 earnings call: "As you know, 35% of the homes in the United States are older than 30 years, and there's external research that shows that spending on older homes is higher. *John Burns would suggest it's something like 7.5% higher*, our own internal research suggests 8% higher. So this aging housing stock bodes very well for us."

In the above instance, the actual analysis that we conducted was much more nuanced and caveat-riddled. However, we boiled the takeaway into a "close enough" thumb-rule that could directionally answer the questions investors were asking about. Her communication of a very complex and nuanced piece of research occurred in just a few words, because the thumb-rule was clear and easy to remember.

Arm your CEO/CFO with useful thumb-rules, and they will be able to pull those learnings out during important meetings with other execs or investors. Your relationship with the C-Suite will improve as your insights become easier to remember.

Your Forecast Will Be Wrong – Be Ready to Explain If Error Looks More Likely to the Upside or Downside

Your model should have equal upside/downside bias, but thinking through possible *direction* of error is worth your time. The CEO will have more confidence in you if you can articulate what other factors are on your radar that may be blind spots in your model. It also is good practice to think through how the relevance of your independent variables may be shifting.

Here is an example of a directional blind spot that I am facing today. We monitor home equity loan activity (HELOC) as one indicator of remodeling spending. However, new financial innovations are starting to appear right now that offer consumers equity financing rather than a loan. Here's the catch: technically, none of these new dollars count as HELOC because they are not a loan. For example, for Unison Home Owner

Loans, Unison will write a check to homeowners for up to 20% of the value of their home, in exchange for 30–75% of the home-price appreciation when owners sell years in the future. No payments are made, and the money is not counted as a loan. This means that data we rely on to monitor home equity lending, which we use in our forecast models, are not capturing financing dollars from UNISON. *If consumers begin to use this new type of financing, our forecast model will systemically underestimate demand.* Because the relevance of our independent variables is changing, capturing less information than they used to, our forecast may have a blind spot.

When communicating our forecast, I often mention the Unison issue and candidly explain the possibility of underestimating demand based on home equity lending. The bias may not be large enough to warrant a change in our forecast, but a CEO will be comforted to know that we are always thinking about those factors we need to be thinking about.

The predictive value of demand drivers can change over time. If you make sure you deeply understand the limitations of your model, you will not shy away when you are asked if your risk is to the upside or the downside – you will readily admit a possible blind spot, even if you can't quantify the exact impact quite yet.

References

Foote, C. L., Gerardi, K. S., and Willen, P. S. (2012). *Why did so many people make so many ex-post bad decisions? The causes of the foreclosure crisis, 2012–7.* Federal Reserve Bank of Atlanta, Working Paper Series.

Mello, J. (2009). The impact of sales forecast game playing on supply chains. *Foresight* 13 (Spring): 13–22.

5.6 HOW TO IDENTIFY AND COMMUNICATE DOWNTURNS IN YOUR BUSINESS*

Larry Lapide

Larry Lapide is a longtime columnist for the *Journal of Business Forecasting*, and in 2012 was the first recipient of the Institute of Business Forecasting's Lifetime Achievement Award. In this two-part series, Lapide explores the issue of identifying turning points in your business, how to sell your analysis to management, and how to survive the organizational fallout of a "bad news" forecast.

Forecasting can be relatively easy in a long-running consistent, stable business environment. But potential downturns (or upturns) are much harder to forecast – and if a downturn, providing unwelcome news to management may even threaten your career.

* This article originally appeared in two parts in the *Journal of Business Forecasting* (Spring and Summer 2020) and appears here courtesy of Dr. Chaman Jain, editor in chief.

These two columns suggest ways to detect turning points, and also show ways to convince the organization what is happening. These ideas are extremely relevant for today's forecasters and planners amid an economic downturn caused by the Covid-19 pandemic. Lapide presents valuable lessons learned from surviving in an organization living through the realities of a "bad news" annual forecast.

Part 1: Forecasting Heroes Catch Turning Points

I was a business forecaster for five years of my life, and without trying to boast, had a pretty good track record in forecast accuracy. However, most of that time I was dealing with a growth business that did not vary a lot because there was a lot of repeat business each year. Interestingly, I consider my best forecasting year to be the one that had the worst forecast accuracy. Why?

In that year, revenues took a downturn and turned from growing to declining. And while I was less than perfect – I forecasted flat revenue growth after having grown for many years – I caught a turning point in the business, and that was more important than forecast accuracy. Indeed, the mark of a good forecaster is whether he/she is able to project a drastic shift in the business climate, since catching a turning point in a business is important for all of a company's planning activities.

If the pundits are right about an impending economic downturn, these might be times that truly test the mettle of forecasters and planners. So I'm dedicating this column to offering advice on how to forecast a turning point in your company's business – both in terms of methods to identify it and advice on getting organizational buy-in, so that people believe in it enough to incorporate it into their planning.

Ways to Forecast a Turning Point

In contrast to forecasting constant growth, or for that matter even a declining business climate, forecasting a turning point requires a greater understanding of what is really driving a business. In a constant growth environment, you can't be too far off, nor have a significant adverse effect on operational planning activities, by just extrapolating trends from historical data. In order to forecast a drastic shift in a business, such as from growth to decline and vice versa, you require knowledge of what is going to make it so. That is, what factors will drive the drastic business change.

There are at least four methods that can be used to identify turning points, which are as follows:

1. **Leading Indicators:** The best method for identifying when a turning point might occur in a business are leading factors that impact the future. Often these are economic or demographic in nature. For example, a decline in corporate capital spending might impact future consumer purchases as companies downsize to adjust costs to revenues. Also, trends on age and birth rates might indicate future

declines in school populations, affecting back-to-school spending. These types of leading indicators are extremely useful if you are lucky enough to find them since cause-effect forecasting methods can be used to project future turning points.

2. **Econometrics:** The next useful method involves the use of economic projections to forecast business shifts. While similar to leading indicators, this approach differs in that the economic factors are not leading indicators, but are actually responsible for business changes – such as in the demand for luxury items that are bought with a consumer's disposable income, or for the materials and components used to manufacture these items. As in the leading indicator approach, this type of forecasting also involves cause-effect methods, but is harder to do, since projecting a turning point in a business is predicated on forecasting a turning point in the economy.

3. **Adoption Models:** These methods are useful for catching turning points in the sales of new products and technologies. In these cases, what drives a product's demand is the extent to which customers adopt or try the item for the first time added to replacement and repeat purchases. For durable items without repeat purchases, demand peaks occur at the point in time where the "majority" of customers start buying them, while sales decline as "laggard" customers buy them after most others have already done so. For consumable items with repeat purchases, demand peaks occur when the total of first time and (potentially multiple) repeat purchases start to decline following early growth in demand. This type of forecasting involves building quantitative models of first time and repeat purchases, often using life cycle curves.

4. **Decomposition Methods:** These methods involve gaining a deep understanding of what drives a business in terms of underlying factors. For example, I caught the turning point mentioned above using this type of method. I was forecasting revenues that were comprised of recurring monthly billings and back bills. It turned out that revenue growth in one year was due to an exorbitant amount of back billings that year, and recurring monthly billings growth had been flat. I detected that back bills had distorted revenues, masking a real business slowdown that year. Had I not done that, I would have forecast growth the following year. Generally, these decomposition methods can uncover declining underlying factors that, over time, dominate the business, causing a turning point. Another example of this type of approach uses multitier forecasting methods that incorporate data from downstream supply chain customers. One can project a product's demand turning point, for example, by uncovering a surplus or shortage of inventories in its distribution channel.

Getting Organizational Buy-In

Detecting and forecasting a turning point is really only half the forecasting battle. When you forecast a big change in business activities, especially a downturn, no one will believe you. Sales and marketing personnel will deny it could happen, finance people will panic about margins, and the CEO will have doubts.

I offer the following three bits of advice to help you get people to buy into your turning-point forecasts, especially useful for downturns:

- *Stick to your guns*: Clearly state that your forecasts are based on facts, figures, and assumptions. The fact and figures can't be questioned. However, subjective inputs (such as the assumptions) to the forecast will be questioned to a great extent when a forecast goes against common wisdom. Therefore, be prepared to defend your position with hard facts and data, and reasonable subjective estimates that are hard to refute. Remember these will be all you have to rely on because the enemies you'll have made will vehemently argue against a turning point forecast.

- *Force others to justify forecast changes*: Many people in the organization will provide you with new program ideas for generating additional revenues to support a growth forecast, rather than a declining revenue forecast. Force them to prove that these will really generate additional sales. Business-as-usual activities, such as annual promotions, are questionable. Why would they generate any more revenues than they did in prior years? Accept additional revenues into a forecast only from new innovative promotional ideas that have some merit.

- *Get executive support*: While hard to do, getting executive support after forecasting a downturn is paramount. You'll need all the help you can get in sticking to your guns. You will be a persona non grata for a while, so you'll need friends – especially in high places. Getting executive support for a downturn forecast will require you to explain it in a clear, unemotional, and unbiased fashion.

In summary, I believe it is important to live through at least one downturn to test your mettle as a forecaster. You only have to forecast one in advance to establish long-term credibility within your company. After it, you'll be a company hero and your credibility will rarely be questioned.

However, forecasting a downturn and sticking to that forecast is hard. It requires special methods and a lot of courage, in contrast to just going along with the majority and denying that it could occur. In the long run, however, don't take the easy path, and heed the words of Mark Twain when he stated, "Always do what is right: This will gratify some people and astonish the rest."

Part 2: The Best and Worst Forecasting Year

Charles Dickens's novel, *A Tale of Two Cities*, begins with the phrase "It was the best of times, it was the worst of times. . . ." I believe it was required reading in one of my high school English classes but I'm sure I merely skimmed it, at best. While I would have been interested in its historical context, I was a student in a vocational electricity and electronics program, more interested in electrical circuits, motors and generators than literature. I did, however, remember Dickens's phrase many years later during a dark period in my five-year tenure of managing the forecasting function for the field service division of a Fortune 500 computer manufacturer. The period started about three years into my forecasting tenure. It was the "best of times" because, up to that time, we'd had a pretty good track record in forecast accuracy – I was in the prime of my forecasting years. It wasn't that hard because of the nature of computer-service revenues, which are largely predicated on the installed base of computers on service contracts. Every year more than 90% of existing customers renewed their contracts. Revenue growth largely came from contracts on new computer sales and represented a minor portion of future yearly revenues.

While new contract revenue represents a minor portion of yearly revenues, it does represent a significant portion of revenue growth. This was the aspect that made the dark period the "worst of times." Historically, the division had double-digit percent revenue growth, so this was the expectation the executives initially had in mind for next year's growth. However, a slowdown in new computer sales that year was a harbinger of a slowdown in service revenue growth. Preliminary forecasts generated in support of next year's financial budget planning process showed that service revenue was taking a turn for the worse. The initial forecast projected flat (or zero) growth in revenues next year versus the prior year's rate of about 15% growth. Since service revenues don't typically change that drastically in one year, the division's executives were shocked, as well as skeptical of the forecasts. This was the start of a year-long struggle for our forecasting organization.

I first mentioned this experience in my JBF Fall 2001 column titled "Forecasting Heroes Catch Turning Points." The premise of that column is that the most difficult forecasting is one in which demand is expected to change drastically down – especially turning points in demand that historically had experienced significant growth, and then switched to negative growth or none at all. Since the economy in 2001 was in a funk, due to the dot-com stock market crash (yet prior to 9/11), I used the experience to offer advice to business forecasters on how to predict future turning points.

Since today's economic conditions are volatile and will be in a funk for quite some time, in this column I share the experience because many forecasters and planners have, and still experience similar business environments. I offer advice on how to survive and maybe even thrive in an environment where you are the harbinger of bad news. That is, when next year's revenues will not be very rosy.

The Forecasting Process

In that 2001 column, I wrote that "detecting and forecasting a turning point is really only half the forecasting battle. When you forecast a big change in business activities, especially a downturn, no one will believe you. Sales and marketing personnel will deny it could happen, the finance people will panic about margins, and the CEO will have doubts." A full account of my difficult year is described below and was one that began with the preliminary revenue forecast for the following year's budget planning process.

Our group had a good forecasting reputation that had been established over the years by always experiencing high forecast accuracy. We were also always open and candid about the facts, figures, and assumptions incorporated in our forecasts; so luckily, our credibility never wavered throughout the budget planning process that ensued. However, our division's executive team was skeptical of the forecast that showed revenue would go from 15% growth to no growth. They wanted further explanation as to why it would. In order words, they wanted to be convinced. To do this, we spent many weeks working with our finance group delving into more detail than ever before.

The final conclusion related to recent increases in contract back-billing revenue. (A back-bill is generated when a piece of contracted equipment retroactively gets put onto a service contract.) The year showed that our installed base of revenues was basically flat because of a slow-down in computer sales, yet revenue growth was 15%. The lion's share of that growth, however, was attributed to back-bill revenue, and resulted from a special field operations program conducted to make sure that contracts were accurate, showing all the equipment that was being serviced.

Back-bill revenue growth, however, would not replicate the following year for two reasons. The first was that the program was completed, so large back-bills would not reoccur. The second was the fact that (unbeknownst to our division for quite some time) the corporate-run Account Receivables group was experiencing substantial bad-collection debt and write-offs from customers refusing to pay for a portion of the larger-than-expected back-bills.

An Awkward, Unsettling, and Politicized Environment

Once the executive team was convinced that revenues would likely be flat the next year, the cost-side of the budgeting process began. As we had always done for forecasts generated, we collaborated with a host of other managers to ascertain what was happening and being planned for in the business, to see if any substantial changes would impact future revenues and costs. Historically, this group was our growing network of "friends." Unfortunately, during the budgetary process, its numbers gradually sank.

Once a flat revenue number was put in place, everyone recognized that next year's cost budget would shrink commensurably. This meant that there would likely be no new hiring, layoffs might happen, and very few employees would get salary raises and promotions. Prior to this time, whenever we bumped into these "friends," they would always ask, "How are we doing in revenue?" When we had given them the same bad news a few times, they stopped asking. This created an unsettling and uncomfortable working environment for the forecasting group.

We had quickly become personae non gratae no one really wanted to talk to—not even for small talk. In addition, company politics reached an unprecedented high as many employees tried to jockey and position themselves to prove their worth in order to keep their jobs, should there be layoffs.

Early the next year, a new SVP of the field service organization was brought in from another tech company to run the division. When he was briefed on the revenue picture, he was extremely skeptical of the forecast and the process, being unfamiliar with it. The revenue forecast prevailed throughout the year because it turned out to be relatively accurate (instead of flat growth, revenue actually shrunk by 1%). However, during each monthly revenue meeting, he would be disappointed by the fact that nothing was changing the revenue picture, despite all his efforts to improve it. My annual performance review (conducted by my managing VP) was not good. When I probed why – arguing that I had predicted the turning point – he said that the new SVP had concerns about me despite that fact.

Eventually after the year was over, I was (luckily) vindicated. During one executive briefing, the SVP said, "Larry was the only one in the division who would tell me what he really believed."

Thus, our forecast credibility with the SVP was eventually enhanced after having gone through a dark period!

Lessons Learned

What are the lessons I learned from the experience in surviving a downturn, as well as thriving in the end? The major ones are summarized below:

- **Do Opinion-less Forecasting:** A forecast must be devoid of any opinions – especially during a downturn. There is a lot of wishful thinking from others that is brought into a forecasting process during tough times. Fight the urge to go along with these, and base forecasts solely on the facts, figures, and assumptions used as inputs to your forecasting models. If needed, use only subjective estimates that would be difficult to dispute by a reasonable person. This is important in order to counter naysayers that are of the opinion that the forecast numbers are not right for no other reason than that they "just aren't!" Take the position that the forecast numbers are "innocent until proven guilty." The forecast is incorrect if it can be proved that some of the facts, figures, and assumptions are incorrect. If that turns out to be the case, then (and only then) updated forecast numbers should be generated using the corrected data.

- **Provide an Estimate of Forecast Accuracy:** Since we all know that forecasts are not perfect and are fraught with unavoidable errors, an estimate of error (such as a confidence range) should accompany each forecast. This is important so that planners can use the estimates to mitigate risks associated with the uncertainties. In addition, it might placate those naysayers whose forecast opinions are consistent with the uncertainties (such as when their opinions fall within the confidence range provided).

- **Be Professional:** The most successful forecasting organizations are those that are the most credible, not necessarily the most accurate. A longstanding reputation of credibility (such as we had) can go a long way toward getting a forecasting group through the most difficult of times. Most of it comes from always acting in a professional manner when it comes to your job. The executive team needs to believe that despite forecast accuracy erratically going up and down (as well as always being less than it would like) the forecast organization provides a greater accuracy than anyone else can. Moreover, they need to believe that no one inside or outside of the company could do a better job of forecasting. Basically, the executive team needs to fully trust the organization and believe – like my former SVP eventually believed about me – that the forecasting organization is the only one that executives can trust to tell them what's really going on.

■ **Stay Out of Politics:** A forecasting organization should always be viewed as unbiased, unemotional, and without hidden agendas. This is especially true during business downturns. Forecasters should always be viewed as "wearing their corporate hats" and not siding with one side or the other when it comes to forecasting. While there are some organizations in which political people get promoted and thrive, these environments are such that people come and go, depending upon which corporate regime is in place. Generally, a "trusted politician" is an oxymoron.

Today, some forecasters and planners might find themselves in an environment that has become awkward, unsettling, and politicized from the turbulent economic environment. Perhaps, following the lessons I learned might help them survive, and maybe even thrive!

5.7 COMMON S&OP CHANGE MANAGEMENT PITFALLS TO AVOID*

Patrick Bower

Nearly 40 years since its conception in the 1980s, Sales and Operations Planning remains a vibrant concept today. Yet despite our learnings from innumerable S&OP successes (as well as failures), implementing S&OP is still a major challenge. Why is this the case?

Patrick Bower argues that Implementing S&OP is as much a change management process as it is a technical supply chain process. But unfortunately, many process owners fail to manage the critical nuances of change required for success. In their excited exuberance, process owners oftentimes publish positive metrics without understanding the negative impact it can have on the success and sustainability of the process. This poor handling of early metric improvements – creating the appearance of "mission accomplished" when the mission has just begun – can stall or damage the S&OP implementation.

This article focuses on how to finesse the communication of these positive results, the appropriate metrics to use when gauging success, and key factors to be aware of throughout the implementation process.

---

* This article originally appeared in the *Journal of Business Forecasting* (Spring 2020) and appears here courtesy of Dr. Chaman Jain, editor in chief.

We have all observed it – the leader of an important S&OP initiative proclaims an exciting improvement in a key performance indicator (KPI) early in a project's life cycle. The good news is typically announced via an email to a large group within the organization, highlighting a quick win or success. Then everyone reflexively applauds the results while quietly questioning whether something has really been achieved or the leader is simply tooting their own horn. And as easy as clicking the send button, a seemingly innocuous email has jeopardized the long-term prospects of the entire project.

Don't get me wrong. I love to celebrate interim positive results and I like to be informed of project progress. But I have learned that short-term gains or singular results are often fleeting and rarely sustainable. Thus, I tend to be cautious when it comes to any self-praise of a project I lead. And before I go public with any results, I really need to be able to internalize the improvements in any measure. This requires monitoring many data points over an extended period of time to ensure results are both positive and consistent. More important, the metric you use to gauge success really matters. Quick hits or short-term improvements of tangential KPIs offer little cause for celebration and smack of braggadocio. Years of change management experience have proven over and over – at least to me – that project leaders weaken the overall likelihood of success by calling out positive results too early or with the wrong KPI.

Unfortunately, I have observed this tendency too often in many S&OP implementations. With rare exception it becomes clear that a project leader does not understand the potential of S&OP as a catalyst for substantive organizational transformation and thus requires a heightened level of change management finesse. For example, after a couple of months working to incorporate the right people, measures and data into the demand consensus process, it is very common to achieve improvements in forecast accuracy. Sometimes the improvement is the result of good design. But often it is nothing more than the Hawthorne Effect, a phenomena by which the mere act of observation (in this case simply paying attention to the demand plan) results in improvement. Unfortunately, there is no simple way of distinguishing the former from the latter, or to measure the viability or sustainability of the improvement. As you might expect, however, most S&OP project teams are elated by such improved results, and it is completely understandable to want to shout one's improvements from the rooftops, but it is often unwise. What if the real organizational pain points are product fill levels or inventory utilization? What if, despite the improvement in forecast accuracy, the inventory and fill metrics did not improve one iota? The result would be analogous to declaring victory in a basketball game because your team made 75% of shots from the floor yet failed to score the most points. This is a very common mistake I have seen time and time again.

In my experience, it is a major project risk to call out early victories or even quick-hit wins. And change-management theory tells us that process development is most at risk from prematurely touting improvements in performance metrics. In his seminal work on Transformational Change, John Kotter writes "While celebrating a win is fine, declaring the war won can be catastrophic. Until changes sink deeply into a company's culture, a process that can take five to ten years, new approaches are fragile and subject to regression." Over the past 25 years I have developed a few corollaries of my own with respect to Kotter's work. Specifically, I think there is danger in mentioning improvements in any specific metric early on. Variances and improvements in metrics are not always clear cut and can be misunderstood, as can the intentions and outcomes attached to the metrics. Someone reading a preliminary (or premature) communication might simply infer the wrong message – that the war has been won – when that is not the case. For this reason, the reporting of results should be very circumspect – less is more.

Here are some of my fundamental concerns about over-messaging positive results:

It reduces the sense of urgency. S&OP implementations demand a sense of urgency, heightened awareness and respect. Usually this is the result of some burning platform or missed customer expectations, a feeling that the business planning process is misaligned or downright out of control. And the transformational effort required to resolve such problems can be stunted the moment someone says "All good" or "We fixed the problem." Declaring an early victory creates a perception that the problem has been solved, making it harder to sustain the ongoing organizational commitment, resources (including funding), and focus that are necessary for progress. Even when a battle is not won, calling out early successes can easily be misinterpreted as a sign of victory. And it is even worse if you declare victory in the wrong battle, such as a measure or a result that does not matter all that much.

It shows that S&OP measures have not been aligned. A good S&OP process does not have one measure but a number of measures that, taken together, should align to the organization's pain points or strategy. In CPG businesses these measures are often fill rate, inventory, and forecast accuracy. It would be silly to declare victory in any one of these measures individually since fill rate can be altered subjectively, by carrying excess inventory or inflating a forecast. The more objective measure of success would be for all critical metrics to be in control – for some period of time – before any shouting from the rooftops occurs. Further, objectives and approximate timelines for each measure should be set in advance of the process implementation so that targets are decided in advance and not merely accepted as some arbitrary net measure of improvement. Kotter even suggests that these quick hits – and the broadcasting thereof – should be planned in advance. A better announcement might be to say, "Forecast accuracy has improved ahead of timeline expectations, enabling us to advance the scope of our process implementation. As we move forward, we will expand our focus to now evaluate fill rates."

Obstacles may still exist. There are many ways to improve forecast accuracy but few of them are easy and many of them are not sustainable, often requiring significant manual effort and countless Excel spreadsheets. If you find yourself in such a circumstance, your next step should be to spin off a sub-team to consider ways to automate some data feeds, reporting, or tool development and expansion. Of course, resources to complete such steps will be much harder to obtain if everyone believes the problem is already solved because of a premature announcement. That is why, among their many other roles and responsibilities, S&OP leaders must fight to eliminate process obstacles, including declaring early victories. In fact, any statement of results and outcomes might benefit from some stipulation about how the results were obtained. For example: "While we were able to demonstrate our ability to improve forecast accuracy results, the task required intense manual effort that is not sustainable over the long term. So, though our effort validates the proof of concept, we have put together a subteam to examine what resources are needed to sustain such a change over the long haul."

You will frustrate key stakeholders. If you are not addressing key pain points – e.g., the utilization of working capital – and instead appear to be addressing something completely different without explicitly mentioning the connection, you will frustrate your stakeholders and risk losing their confidence. In such cases it sometimes helps to announce the improvement of one measure while preemptively acknowledging that the effort is far from over: "We tackled forecast accuracy first since that is the top of the planning stack. However, to really achieve a reduction in inventory we need to examine the master planning process, safety stock calculations, capacity planning, and materials planning. We felt that establishing a reliable, low-error forecast would give us the best chance to address these other issues but we have a long way to go." The key to keeping stakeholders engaged is to help them understand your ongoing game plan for improvement.

Proclaiming early victories will shorten your project timeline and raise expectations. And this caveat warrants a big "Of course!" If your actions prematurely engender a feeling of success, it is only a matter of time before your project team members are redeployed to new assignments, thereby damaging your initiative and prospects for ongoing success. You also risk elevating expectations for additional improvements. For example, if you were able to reduce forecast accuracy by 15% in three months, surely you should be able to squeeze out some more gains over the next year.

So, how do you effectively showcase improvements in metrics without torpedoing your entire S&OP project? Set expectations up front. In the case of our working-capital utilization scenario, stakeholders should have been informed that forecast accuracy would be the first of many metrics focused on addressing the primary pain point of working capital utilization. Forecast accuracy is just one of many means to an end, after all. I would also have noted that every subsequent process step requires some examination of tools, people, and processes, to help ensure sustainable results.

And finally, while quick wins should be celebrated – carefully and strategically – they are just that: short-term results that will be fleeting if ongoing effort and support is not provided to sustain them. This is why nearly every mention of early wins and performance improvements must include a robust proviso. And if an announcement of early improvements seems to be at all self-serving, leadership should quickly reevaluate whether the S&OP leader is indeed the right person for the job.

S&OP leaders should be perceived as fulfilling a role devoid of ego and requiring an exceptional level of emotional maturity. It often takes years to develop and mature an S&OP process and effective initiatives will not thrive under the guidance of needy individuals who require the adrenaline rush of announcing short-term quick hits. Folks with this sort of need for constant ego-gratification won't likely be strong advocates for the systemic change necessary to be successful in their S&OP role. The caution is simple: tread lightly and strategically when you announce good news pertaining to a metric. Otherwise, you may be snatching defeat from the jaws of victory.

5.8 FIVE STEPS TO LEAN DEMAND PLANNING*

John Hellriegel

The basic concepts of Lean Manufacturing have been around for decades – often traced back over 100 years to Henry Ford's assembly line, or to the Toyota Production system. More recently, the lean principle of eliminating process waste underscores Forecast Value Added (FVA) analysis, which seeks to identify process activities that are failing to improve forecast accuracy.

This article describes a five-step process about how the philosophy of Lean Manufacturing can be applied to demand planning. The steps include what customers truly value (valuable products being those customers are willing to pay for); mapping the value stream (i.e., how a product is delivered to the customer); evaluating opportunities for improvement; working on activities that are requested by customers; and aiming for continuous improvement.

As a trainer and advisor for IBF, I have worked for several amazing companies with talented people. As part of the 3-day training program we deliver, we always spend time thinking about the improvement areas that will help the team to implement demand planning best practices. The Start/Stop/Continue format is used. What will the company start doing? What will they stop doing? What will they continue and improve? For most groups in our training programs, this list comes readily and most people agree on what to change.

But then a funny thing happens. When we start to discuss how and when these changes can happen, the teams face a common challenge. Their resources are often spread amazingly thin, and therefore can't devote the time to start working in a new

---

* This article originally appeared in the *Journal of Business Forecasting* (Spring 2020) and appears here courtesy of Dr. Chaman Jain, editor in chief.

area. Even more frustrating, Demand Planners often do not feel they're able to stop activities that take up precious time.

Fortunately, there is a proven methodology we take from Operations used to improve focus, effectiveness and efficiency. The Lean philosophy provides an approach to evaluating an operation to reduce waste, providing resources that can be applied to value added activities. The approach to Lean Demand Planning is fairly simple and we can adapt this methodology for the purpose of improvement and freeing up time. Here are five steps:

1. Identify value
2. Map value stream
3. Create flow
4. Establish pull
5. Seek perfection

Step 1: Identify Value

In a traditional Lean approach, one focuses on the end customer. The key is to understand clearly what the customer values (i.e., what they will pay for) and what they will not. This helps the organization to focus on what is important, and strip away work that is not important or just superfluous.

For demand planning, the customers are internal. And our internal customers want an accurate demand plan. Although that statement is true, it needs to be refined. There are different uses of forecasts, and different people need different forecasts. SKU level accuracy may be important for replenishment planning over the next 8 weeks, but, for capacity planning, we need accuracy at a more aggregate level, and for a much longer timeframe.

Beyond the core of forecast accuracy, it is the information that is generated through the demand planning process that should also be valued within the organization. Highlighting forecast variance from the plan and the reasons why is also important for making decisions. Other examples include analysis of new product sales performance to provide business insight to the organization.

Step 2: Map the Value Stream

In a typical Lean program, it is important to understand the process used to deliver a product to a customer. A visual map is used to mark each process step for a given scope, usually led by a Lean process expert with process participants. Other elements such as resources required, waiting time, and hand-offs are added to the value stream map. In many cases, after a current state map is developed, an ideal state or future state map is also created to highlight areas of change.

For demand planning processes, companies can use the same methodology. Instead of a product being delivered, it is information that is being shared. For example, teams can review the information that is prepared for a consensus meeting, or how new product forecasts are developed. Each step can be documented, including handoffs, wait times, and resources needed. Some teams may need to perform simple time studies to see where the work hours are going. In larger projects, it may be helpful to create a value stream map of the entire monthly cycle for demand planning. Again, an ideal state or future state can also be helpful.

During this step, it is critical to see which steps are really adding value. According to the Lean Enterprise Institute, these criteria truly add value if:

- The customer is willing to pay for it.
- The activity transforms a product or service in some way.
- The activity is done correctly the first time.

These steps are important not only for Lean Supply Chain Planning but also for Lean demand planning.

Step 3: Create Flow

In the end, the value stream map is used to evaluate opportunities for improvement. This is known as creating flow. Non-value-added steps are identified and then removed. Processes that have bottlenecks are solved through improved processes and/or more resources. Continuous improvement projects and kaizen (improvement) events are used to streamline the process and get more output with less waste.

Using the value stream map to create better flow is essential in the demand planning world. Too often we implement a tool, set up a consensus meeting, and ask for reports, without having a good process to support these requirements. Demand Planners do their best to figure it out but can greatly benefit from the support of others. In most cases, there are several quick wins that free up a Planner's time, and other projects that spin off to gain even greater efficiency. Some specific ways to create better flow in demand planning are:

- Automate repetitive tasks. Data entry is often a key area of opportunity, as are accuracy metrics and other reports.
- Create standard work flows. For process steps like exception management, forecast allocation, and others, best practices should be documented and followed. Work flow tools can help to organize hand-offs between groups and further document time between steps.
- Clean up and organize data. Factories use "5S" principles to make tools and materials available for seamless operation. Demand Planners should make sure that data files are easy to access and are clean and up to date.
- Remove non-value-added steps. Every action should have a purpose. Lean promotes the ruthless pursuit to eliminate waste, and demand planning is no exception.

Step 4: Establish Pull

The idea of pull in the Lean philosophy is very simple. Operations should not spend time on activities that are not directly requested by the customer. Pull process for materials mean that operations do not start until the need is signaled through a consumer shipment or material consumption in a factory. Pull helps to avoid unnecessary work along the way, and also synchronizes activities whenever needed.

In demand planning, we can apply this idea in a different way. Because demand planning is an analytical group with access to data, it is often called on to generate lots of reports and ad hoc analysis. I recently advised a company where most of their time was spent publishing current month sales trends, which didn't add any value to the core of demand planning.

A simple solution is to take an inventory of reports and analysis done by a Planner. Some reports can be discontinued ASAP (one Demand Planner in my previous company produced a weekly report for a general manager that left the business years ago). The best way is to ask our internal customers whether certain reports are needed. Per our Lean methodology, our work is adding value if the customer is willing to pay for it. This is the one way to assess whether to keep certain activities, discontinue them, or get budget for more staff.

Step 5: Seek Perfection

The final step in the Lean methodology is not the end of story, but rather just the beginning. Continuous improvement is at the heart of the Lean approach. Individuals and work teams are encouraged to improve well after the original value stream map has identified opportunities. Teams meet regularly to discuss progress and may often have specific kaizen events to focus on new areas of change.

For demand planning groups, this is absolutely critical to sustainable improvement. There are ways to improve statistical forecasting, gathering market intelligence, planning new products, managing consensus, and so on. Of course, the market is also changing, so our approach must adapt and improve to stay relevant.

As managers, we need to instill the culture of continuous improvement in our teams. Planners who seek new approaches and challenge the status quo need to be recognized and rewarded. And managers need to free up some "thinking time" for our Planners, so they don't get trapped in the habits of the monthly process.

The concept of Lean is not new; its roots are found in the operating systems of Toyota and other large manufacturers. These companies saw the need to eliminate waste and sustain reliable and effective delivery while reducing the resources needed to provide them. Demand planning is an operational role, with core process steps and customers who expect services at the lowest cost. If we apply some of the concepts of Lean, we can meet our organizational needs and support our teams in the way they work.

5.9 THE MOVE TO DEFENSIVE BUSINESS FORECASTING*

Michael Gilliland

Despite continuing technological advances that take us to the limits of achievable accuracy, most companies still struggle with forecasting. Not only do these organizations fail to reach the potential accuracy that could be achieved, they squander resources doing so, often forecasting worse than a no-cost naïve model.

More data and more complex statistical modeling, by themselves, don't seem to have solved the business forecasting problem. Focusing solely on technology does not address the political, psychological, and process issues that ultimately determine forecasting performance.

Instead of trying to fix forecasting with technology alone, meaningful improvement can come from a "defensive" approach – eliminating bad practices before trying to emulate good practices. Using tools like Forecast Value Added (FVA) analysis, a defensive approach lets organizations identify and eliminate the "worst practices" that waste resources and degrade forecasting performance. Only then can they achieve the full potential of technological advances.

The modern era of business forecasting began in 1956, with publication of Robert G. Brown's short monograph, "Exponential Smoothing for Predicting Demand." Brown's innovation was Step One in a 60+ year pursuit of increased forecast accuracy – pursued mainly through the development of more sophisticated modeling methods and forecasting software, more powerful computers, more availability of data, and more elaborate forecasting processes.

There is no denying it has made big headway, particularly in the large-scale automation of business forecasting by the most advanced analytics software. It is now possible for millions of time series to be forecast automatically, in a timely manner, with customized models for each series.

Today's technology allows us to generate forecasts that are as accurate as can reasonably be expected. Yet this fabulous technology, by itself, has not solved the business problem. Surveys show that forecasting remains a major concern for business managers and executives.

The Limits of Forecast Accuracy

There is no stopping the advance of forecasting technology. We can expect the invention of even more complex methods, utilizing more data elements, and exploiting more

---

* This article originally appeared in *Journal of Business Forecasting* (Winter 2017–2018) and appears here courtesy of Dr. Chaman Jain, editor in chief.

computational power. But is it reasonable to expect these future advances will deliver significantly more accurate forecasts than what we achieve today? (And in particular, sufficiently accurate to satisfy the needs and wishes of business management?)

There are limits to the forecast accuracy that can be achieved. Accuracy is ultimately limited by the nature of the behavior we are attempting to forecast. For example, we'll be correct 50% of the time (over a large number of trials) in forecasting heads or tails when tossing a fair coin. The 50% limit is due entirely to the nature of the behavior – the tossing of a coin. While the accuracy limit is not obvious (or even precisely determinable) for the "real life" demand patterns we seek to forecast, we can assume such a limit exists. Even a forecasting beginner recognizes that products with smooth, stable, and repeating demand can be forecast more accurately than products with wild, erratic, and volatile demand.

The Naïve Model

It is generally acknowledged that the naïve "no-change" model provides the lower bound worst-case forecast accuracy you should achieve. (The no-change model forecasts imply no change from the latest observation. If you sold 100 last month, you'd forecast 100 for this month, and so on.) For real life demand patterns (as opposed to the coin tossing example), the best accuracy we should be able to achieve is not readily apparent. But the naïve model informs us of the worst accuracy we will achieve. The shocking reality is that despite today's technological and process sophistication, organizations fail to outperform the naïve forecast at an alarming rate. Research conducted by Steve Morlidge of CatchBull found that 30–50% of real-life forecasts – forecasts companies were using to make decisions and run their organizations – were less accurate than the no-change model!

How can this be? How can organizations spend time and resources generating forecasts that, a large portion of the time, are worse than doing nothing and just using the naïve model? And what can be done about this abysmal state of affairs?

The Next Stage of Forecasting Advancement

I suggest that the next major advancement in forecasting performance will not come from more advanced modeling and technology, or from more elaborate forecasting process. Instead, the best opportunity to improve performance is through a "defensive" approach to business forecasting – by ending the bad practices that just make the forecast worse. Business forecasting is often conducted in a politicized environment. While the forecast should be an unbiased "best guess," often this is not case. Instead, what we see is the result of a statistical forecasting model (which may or may not be appropriate, depending on the capabilities of the software and the competence of the user), and step-by-step adjustments made through the organization's forecasting process.

With adjustments, we often deteriorate a forecast because those who do it try to shape the forecast to their own personal advantage.

The defensive approach entails a fundamental shift in how organizations go about addressing their forecasting issues. The traditional approach, in vogue for the last 60 years, was to focus on enhancing statistical algorithms as the way to improve forecasting. However, this approach may be reaching its limits. And even if the initial statistical forecast is sound, too many human adjustments – like too many cooks in a kitchen—can just make it worse. This is the problem exposed by Forecast Value Added (FVA) analysis.

Defensive Business Forecasting

FVA analysis is the primary tool in a defensive approach to business forecasting. FVA is defined as the change in a forecasting performance metric (such as accuracy or MAPE) that can be attributed to a particular step or participant in the forecasting process. So, if the statistical forecast turns out to be more accurate than a naïve forecast, it has a positive "value added." If an analyst's adjustment to a statistical forecast ends up making it worse, the value added is negative.

FVA is used to identify process steps and participants that are failing to add value to the forecast, or are even making it worse. Traditional metrics like accuracy and MAPE, when used alone to report forecasting performance, provide no indication of the efficiency and effectiveness of your forecasting efforts. To say "I forecasted this product with a MAPE of 20%" tells nothing about the quality of a forecast – whether it was better or worse than just using a no-cost, no-effort naïve forecast.

In the spirit of a lean supply chain, process activities that fail to improve the forecast are process waste. Such activities may rightly be considered "worst practices." The defensive approach relies largely on FVA analysis to identify, and then eliminate non-value-adding activities.

Opportunities for Improvement

When worst practices are eliminated, forecasting performance should naturally improve. The process becomes streamlined, and the organization spends fewer resources to generate more accurate forecasts. The greatest opportunity for forecasting improvement may not be at the top end (making our good forecasts better), but at the bottom end (making our worst forecasts less bad!). If we can just get companies to stop shooting themselves in the foot and move their worst forecasts from terrible to not-too-bad, that would be a tremendous step.

Continuing advances in time series modeling, software sophistication, data availability, and computational power have brought us closer to the practical limits of forecast accuracy. Yet misguided adjustments and ineffective forecasting process often take value away. Where is the next opportunity for improvement? It is through a defensive approach. Researchers and software vendors can help in this effort, mainly through improved automation of forecast modeling, and better tools (like FVA) to evaluate performance. Automation speeds up the process and reduces costly human efforts needed to build appropriate models. Also, if automated models prove their credibility to management, there may be less temptation to make manual adjustments. More sophisticated performance evaluation can prescriptively guide improvement efforts.

Better forecasts deliver their benefit by driving better decisions – that in turn drive better business outcomes. As the defensive mindset takes hold, companies will worry less about becoming great at forecasting. Instead, they will achieve meaningful improvement by becoming less bad at forecasting.

Afterwords

I f you had 1,000 words to tell the world something important about forecasting – something you think everyone should know – what would that be? That is the question we posed to a diverse pool of academics, consultants, vendors, and industry practitioners – all recognized and influential contributors to the forecasting profession. This compilation of 16 "Afterwords" delivers their response.

There is generally much to learn from the perspectives of others, and the more varied the perspectives the better. Thus, we purposely sought to avoid anchoring contributors to any specific subject area. Just like combinations of forecasts tend to perform better than an individual model, so do these varied perspectives provide a collective value greater than the individual parts.

These Afterwords were not meant to follow the formality and rigor one would find in a peer-reviewed journal. Instead, we encouraged the contributors to write in the form of an "opinion-editorial" piece, with the freedom to share thoughts on any topic they deemed worthy of sharing. We are gratified with their participation, and the breadth of topics they covered.

OBSERVATIONS FROM A CAREER PRACTITIONER: KEYS TO FORECASTING SUCCESS

Carolyn Allmon, Teleflex, Inc.

Introduction

I have been forecasting for businesses since 1994. In that year, an enlightened leader of a company making industrial cleaning machines, parts, and floor coatings, dissatisfied with the current forecasting results, hired me to develop a process to forecast product demand using statistical methods. As a forecasting practitioner in a wide variety of industries over the years since, for private and public corporations of varying sizes and with some consulting in between, I share the following observations about what makes companies successful at forecasting. It goes without saying that these opinions are mine only, based on my experience, and in no way can be extrapolated to the state of the profession elsewhere or necessarily reflect the opinions of my current employer. Since the bulk of my experience has been in forecasting customer demand for the Supply Chain, my observations and issues relate accordingly.

Characteristics of Companies Successful at Forecasting

1. **Enlightened leadership.** The most important component of forecasting success in any company, however success is defined, is the leader of the area in which forecasting responsibility resides. Forecasters cannot develop successful outcomes without his/her support. This support includes: role and desired outcomes clarity, understanding and provision of tools needed, understanding of basic forecasting principles and limitations, best practices, and time required for analysis.

   Without the ability to make budgetary decisions for improved forecasting tools, the forecaster may struggle to achieve the "best" forecasting outcomes with existing tools. Beyond budgetary considerations, leaders need to champion the forecasting function so that it is given the priority needed for "best" forecast fundamentals from data integrity to modeling tools to judgmental input.

2. **Placement of the forecasting function within the organization where it can be the most independent and objective.** My experience has found placing the forecasting function in Marketing or in an independent department fosters more accurate forecasting. A recent trend seems to be placing it under Supply Chain/Operations but since the focus of Supply is execution to requirements, forecasting has a lower priority and its leaders traditionally are not interested in the details of how to create the best demand forecast or the resources required to do so.

3. **Collaboration with all those who influence and have knowledge about customer demand for the forecasted products.** Collaboration is critical. Presentations tailored to various company functions and interests can be effective. "People support what they understand." The forecaster must have credibility and support among all stakeholders so that they will share what they know that may affect the forecast.

   Every effort must be made to encourage domain knowledge input from "those who know the territory" despite possible physical distance challenges.

4. **Meaningful metrics regularly monitored and publicized.** The organization needs to develop meaningful, achievable forecast accuracy targets based on its experience and determine the root cause of consistent over- or under-forecasting. When developing acceptable forecast accuracy goals, it should be acknowledged that longer lead-times due to moving to offshore suppliers are likely to make accurate prediction more difficult.

   In some organizations, forecasts are adjusted to the organization's financial requirements without clarity about what will cause change from historical trends. This leads to overforecasting bias. The best organizations were clear about the initiatives that would result in the attainment of the forecast if higher than historical trends. These initiatives were monitored and periodically reviewed and removed from the forecast if not achieved.

Measuring the cost of inaccurate forecasting can also be revealing and encourage the allocation of resources to the forecasting function.

5. **Structuring the system and process to achieve clear goals and objectives.** Items that have no forecasting value-added, or are inappropriate to forecast (made-to-order, for example), or cannot be forecasted accurately due to other factors, should be excluded from the forecast, and handled in a different manner. The forecaster does not have a crystal ball to exactly predict the future. Tools should be appropriate to the task and priorities based on testing. For example, though Production needs a SKU-level forecast, sometimes forecasting at a higher level and disaggregating to the SKU level will increase accuracy. If one is tied to an inflexible forecasting system configured to forecast at the SKU level only, this option is not available to the forecaster without investing in additional tools or reconfiguring the existing system, which can be costly to change.

6. **Skilled and responsive IT personnel who support existing tools and systems needed for forecasting with the expertise to customize them for effectiveness.** In my experience, these people are worth their weight in gold! Because of their support, I was able to reconfigure an ERP system installed with little consideration of what was needed for forecasting, adapt an SAP tool to accumulate demand in real time with the ability to easily view orders behind the demand and increase the length of time series to more acceptable lengths for statistical forecasting. These are but a few examples of forecasting system enhancements I made over the years with their help.

7. **Inclusion of the forecaster in decision-making about purchasing new or enhancing old tools.** The forecaster needs the best tools at his/her disposal for forecasting excellence including software with a full cache of appropriate models available. An example of the positive way in which this was handled in one of my companies follows:

Before deciding to purchase the SAP ERP system, I was asked if it could be used for forecasting. After testing the functionality on a sample, using it and two other forecasting tools, I responded that it could be used for two of the major product lines, but the functionality was not sophisticated enough to use for the third. My decision was accepted, supported, and implemented with an opportunity to configure the system for the most effective forecasting of the product lines for which this tool would be used and the appropriate data capture for the products to be forecast independently.

Software should be a tool, not a driver. ERP systems, though great at integration, are generally limited in forecasting capability and inflexible to change once initially set up. Exploring the use of other specialized forecasting drivers in conjunction with the ERP system can increase forecasting accuracy and should be encouraged.

8. **A regular well-defined, disciplined process customized to business needs and focused on products most important to the business.** For

most, this will be a variation of the classic Sales and Operations Planning process. However, the process need not be classic to be effective. For example, early in my experience, forecast changes incorporating marketing and sales information were made using a modified Delphi method without holding meetings. I conferred about reasons for suggested forecasting changes with those whose domain knowledge differed substantially from the statistical forecast and the judgment of others, and consensus was reached. Purpose and expectations of all meetings and the accountability of their participants must be clear to be effective.

9. **Personnel educated and trained in best forecasting practices and modeling techniques, focused on forecasting.** There appears to be a trend in the profession toward more training in Supply Chain generally than in Demand Forecasting. Along with this comes the expectation that forecasters should also be skilled in inventory analysis and supply planning, diluting their forecasting efforts. Continued education and certification programs in the discipline and practice of forecasting should be encouraged.

10. **Incentives for good forecasting.** Incentives can make a big difference in achieving desirable forecast accuracy. Forecast accuracy increased dramatically after the VP of Sales added "quality forecasting input" to the performance appraisals of his reps during my tenure at one company. Most companies do not reward their forecasters or collaborators for good forecasting or acknowledge how improvements have helped their "bottom line."

11. **Execution of the forecast by Supply.** I was asked this question at one company, "Why is Supply short when your forecast is so accurate?" A forecast (even if perfect) without execution is worthless. Customer fulfillment should be the goal of the entire supply chain. If there are discontinuities in this chain, they need to be acknowledged and fixed to achieve customer satisfaction.

Concluding Thoughts

As attributed to Yogi Berra (and others) "Forecasting is difficult, especially about the future." But, to satisfy customers and minimize costs, demand forecasting must be as accurate as possible. In the foregoing, I have listed the factors which support best forecasting based on my experience across a variety of industries. The overarching key to success is the leader who is engaged in the process, has realistic expectations about what is possible and supports the effort with the environment needed to foster the best forecasting outcomes. Without this support, true success is not possible.

DEMAND PLANNING AS A CAREER

Jason Breault, LifeWork Search

In the June/July 2015 edition of *Inside Supply Management* (Breault 2015), I reflected on Demand Planning as a place to start one's career. Feeling as passionate about this as when I wrote the original article, I wanted to offer my updated thoughts.

I graduated college with a Bachelor's degree in Electrical Engineering and German. I definitely wasn't the strongest engineer in my graduating class. I quickly found that I was better suited for marketing and selling technical services. Not unlike today, I found myself trying to differentiate myself from thousands of others that were ready to take on the business world. I tried to figure out where I could provide the most value.

The internet was barely mainstream in 1995, so I wrote to the German embassy and bought two books: one listing all of the German-headquartered companies that had a major presence in the United States, and another that listed all of the U.S.-head-quartered companies with a major presence in Germany. I mailed resumes to well over 100 companies and quickly learned that I had a skill (speaking German) that was very valuable to these organizations. I accepted a role with Siemens, and I loved my tenure there. Due to my being the only American within my division that spoke German, I got exposure to executives and found myself moving up the ladder much quicker than I would have had the opportunity to do otherwise. This was the perfect place for me to start my career.

Fast forward 25 years. For the past 15 years, my team and I have recruited in the area of supply chain. In my short recruiting tenure, trends have come and gone. When I first started and was still trying to figure out what to specialize in, people I trusted said I should be recruiting in the area of international logistics. It seemed that everyone was outsourcing production to places like China, Mexico, and other locations. Others suggested recruiting in global sourcing for similar reasons. That would have been a great way to go, however, like in every bull market, things eventually slow down. In China's case, labor prices increased, VAT incentives that China had been providing went away, fuel costs started to rise again and local consumers constantly questioned the quality of the products coming from overseas – factors that had companies rethinking their decisions.

During that run, having experience in purchasing/sourcing *and* having the ability to speak Chinese was priceless. It felt like every company that made any sort of hard good had a need for at least one, if not more, sourcing analyst, manager, and so on. We saw many universities expanding their language major offerings to include Chinese. This was a great path to getting high-level exposure earlier than normal. However, things can change quickly. Universities graduated record number of students and companies brought over their own Chinese-speaking sourcing specialists, so the need for this skill set quickly leveled off. Add to that the more recent trade war with China and the need for this skill set has declined significantly as companies diversify to other countries.

There are quite a few other trends like this that were hot and then not. Don't get me wrong – there will always be a need for individuals with strong supply chain execution and procurement skills. These are areas critical to any business. However, when it comes to an area of supply chain that allows for a newer graduate to rise up in the organization and get exposure early in their career, I wholeheartedly believe *the best place to start is in Demand Planning*!

My eyes were really opened to this in the 2009–2010 timeframe. In the run up to the recession, many companies had become, as we say, fat, dumb, and happy. They kept making things, consumers kept buying them and everyone thought this was the new norm. Then the recession hit. When everyone woke up from their recessionary hangovers, companies quickly realized that they needed to get more responsible about looking into the future. Cash was king again and the leading indicator of a good cash position was the forecast.

I was really surprised how few companies at the time had a strong planning process in place. Clients – well-known brands – shut down half of their plants, and the other half were at 50% capacity. These companies realized that they missed signs that others hadn't. To remedy this, they all built up demand planning teams – offering much better job security than other areas of supply chain.

A demand planner is expected to have strong analytical skills, as well as the outgoing personality (some might call it emotional intelligence) to help drive business decisions. They are required to leverage both left- and right-brain skills. A demand planner works cross-functionally with sales, marketing, product development, finance, other parts of the supply chain – and in some instances, also with the customers. In some industries, this might be a weekly interaction; in others it is a monthly cycle. Regardless, the exposure within the organization is tremendous when compared to the roles in other parts of the supply chain that are a bit more siloed.

Advanced planning software has always played an important role in the life of a demand planner. Setting up models and interpreting the results so that you can be a value-added contributor to the cross-functional meetings is critical. As data sets get larger, however, cutting through all of the information to make sense of the data has become ever more challenging.

To get through this challenge, data scientists are leveraging artificial intelligence (AI) and machine learning to help make sense of the data. Some people question whether these new technologies and the introduction of the data scientist will decrease the importance of the demand planner similar to the role of a sourcing specialist becoming a commodity (pun intended!).

The recent Covid-19 pandemic is showing that not to be the case. Although advanced technologies help us cut through the clutter, the demand planner is still needed to interpret the data and help the business drive decisions forward.

Demand planning as a career is ever evolving. We're even seeing more and more VP-level roles in this area. Regardless of whether your aspiration is to make a lifetime commitment to demand planning, or simply to use it as a stepping stone, after 15 years of recruiting in this space – and seeing the constant ups and downs in other parts of supply chain – I remain convinced that this is the best place to start your supply chain career.

REFERENCE

Breault, J. (2015). A career path in demand. *Inside Supply Management* 26 (5): 8–9. https://content. malakye.com/media/portfolios/originals/jerrett_chambers_425126.pdf

HOW DID WE GET DEMAND PLANNING SO WRONG?

Lora Cecere, Supply Chain Insights

In the 1990s, I was very excited to implement a simple form of demand planning. The algorithm used historic order patterns to generate a forward-looking product-based mix-level forecast. Three decades later, despite an abundance of market data, companies are applying similar techniques. The practice of forecasting, based on my work with manufacturers, regressed with the evolution of Advanced Planning in the last three decades. Here I share my observations on why:

- **The Role of the Budget.** Companies are enamored with tight coupling of a financial forecast with a supply chain forecast. In the process, there is little realization that the only thing that the two have in common is the word "forecast." Best-in-class companies use the budget as a comparative input while laggards tightly couple the forecasts and clamp-down on the supply chain to meet the budget. The attempts create many problems including that the financial forecast lacks the mix-level detail to run the supply chain and the budget is wrong and out of pace with the market on the date that it is published. The rise of Integrated Business Planning in Sales and Operations Planning (S&OP) degraded S&OP success by 25% over the last decade due to botched attempts to tightly integrated supply chain forecasting to financial budgets.

- **Chasing Shiny Objects.** One of the worst issues is the continued chasing of shiny objects in the evolution of the demand plan. Two decades ago, it was Vendor Managed Inventory and CPFR. Today, none of these programs connect to the central demand plan. Now the focus is on machine learning and cognitive computing. However, what good is a new technique if we are not clear on the goal?

- **Focus on Implementation of Technology.** In the last decade, most forecasting projects were treated as an IT project. The Select, Purchase, and Implement cycles went on and on. However, the processes of model tuning, data cleansing and forecast refinement were not included. Most companies side-stepped the processes of backcasting and lacked the understanding of forecast measurement. I am working with a company today that has implemented three different technologies and instead of model tuning, backcasting, and refinement, they built a technology on top of the three demand planning systems to evaluate which system to use for which item to write to the system of record. The problem? We get enamored with technology and lose our way.

- **Market Shifts.** Supply Chains were unprepared for the pandemic. Despite an abundance of market data—consumption, rating/review and activity—only 1% of companies changed their models to be more market-driven. The shifts were different by industry—a shift from restaurants to eating at home, buying lounge wear versus formal apparel, and the delay of elective surgery—yet, the majority of organizations continued to focus on the output of traditional models using order data as the basis for the modeling. Market-driven forecasting versus enterprise-focused modeling will be the downfall of many organizations.

- **Governance.** Governance is an ongoing issue. I work with a $35 Bn food manufacturer that has 35 instances implemented for demand planning. Each is custom and there is no discipline on demand planning metrics. The organization spins constantly on the upgrade cycles and refinement of the many instances. Upon closer evaluation, each instance averaged a negative 20% Forecast Value Added. In contrast, P&G, a $65 Bn global leader in demand planning, has one instance with well-defined demand management goals and objectives. The planners at P&G average 12 years in the position with a clear career path while the planners at the food company change jobs frequently with no clear career path in demand planning. The issue? Lack of clear governance and definition of a good demand planning solution.

In closing, one client that I work with stated that, "The Company will never be good at demand planning. Why should she try? Shouldn't she just focus on driving an agile response and give up on demand planning?" In response, I hung my head. In the statement, there was a lack of understanding of the need for demand planning in the organization that required leadership. The Company will be forever snarled in the quagmire of the issues listed until there is enlightened leadership. Unfortunately, in my experience, the understanding of demand planning and the role in supply chain excellence is not well understood.

Let me end by sharing my point of view. Demand is a river that flows through the organization. The river starts with the customer and winds through the value chain with each step of ordering and replenishment introducing the bullwhip effect. Forecasting is a time-phased snapshot of the river at a place in time. Laggards get enamored with the snapshot attempting to be very precise on imprecise numbers. The art of sensing, translating, and shaping demand is understood by very few manufacturers. In the last decade, despite the increase of new and promising technologies and techniques, the industry went backwards. The largest issue? The lack of understanding of the role of demand management in the delivery of supply chain excellence.

BUSINESS FORECASTING: ISSUES, CURRENT STATE, AND FUTURE DIRECTION

Simon Clarke, Argon & Co

In Sir Arthur Conan Doyle's "The Adventure of the Reigate Squire," Dr. Watson takes Sherlock Holmes to a friend's estate to rest after a previous case. Trouble, as is often the case with Sherlock Holmes, is not far away. A murder occurs at a nearby house requiring his attention. The case is solved but not before the following observation:

It is of the highest importance in the art of detection to be able to recognize, out of a number of facts, which are incidental and which are vital. Otherwise, your energy and attention must be dissipated instead of being concentrated.

In some respects, the practice of business forecasting has suffered from a similar lack of focus on the vital. Foundational processes are often underdeveloped or neglected. Instead there is often a focus on seeking the "smoother pebble" or "prettier shell," all at the expense of maximizing the benefits of a well-run, organized and calibrated process.

In many organizations there remains a lack of consideration of how to most effectively leverage forecasting in the business operating model. Very often there is a clear lack of distinction between the forecast, plan and budget. As a consequence, the forecast can become easily politicized and struggles over who owns the forecast, organization structure and decision-rights come to the fore. These battles are a distraction and obscure the more important work of aligning the forecast process to support the overall business vision and mission.

At the heart of many poorly performing business forecasts are fundamental issues of solution design. Too little focus is applied on the mundane, but critical process of hierarchy design, selection of appropriate units of measure, calendars and time buckets. Failure to get these correct disables effective cross-functional collaboration and alignment and, at worst, can drive partisan efforts to discredit or promote an alternative narrative.

Allied to issues with design can be problems with the process itself. There is often a lack of consideration of what processes the output is supporting and what detail is really required for each. For instance, a supply chain function is typically interested in the level of detail that is consumed in supply chain planning process. This is likely to be at a location and SKU level. The finance function is interested in a more aggregate level of detail. They are less likely to be interested in the lowest level detail and more interested in the level at which products are priced or costed. In addition, the "right" forecast horizon should be considered. There is no point in a 5-year ahead forecast if the decisions to be made are focused on a 12-month ahead horizon. Only once consideration of this has been made should there be focus on the forecasting method (Judgmental, Statistical, or Combination) and the methods, aggregation and inputs most appropriate. Too often these decisions are made prior to understanding the goal.

Sadly, Forecast Support Systems are often seen as a "silver bullet," which has resulted in inflated expectations and subsequent disappointment in many organizations. While the quality of systems does matter, even the most capable systems will be unable to transform a broken process or design. Systems that have been successfully implemented are often found in those organizations where the selection process has been business led (not IT), often as part of a broader transformation program. Selection criteria has included technical considerations, but also as importantly usability and forecast value-add. This has often been accomplished through comprehensive proof-of-concept pilots that pitch competing software against each other on a data set relevant to the organization. With those criteria, the software that is able to support both in-sample and out-of-sample forecast evaluation, effective integration of judgmental methods, effective aggregation/disaggregation routines, inclusion of exogenous variables and point and range forecasts often rise to the top.

Despite good solution, process and systems design, sustaining change can be elusive for many. In many instances, management have unrealistic expectations, often with little consideration of the degree of difficulty of the task. Goals are largely arbitrary and disconnected from the supporting process metrics. There is also only a focus on end results, versus metrics like forecast value-add, that focus on the health of the process. In addition, the role of the forecaster has become consumed with the administration of the S&OP process, more time is being spent on assembling the data for the demand review, building the presentation and consolidating inputs and changes than is spent on essential forecasting tasks. It is very rare that the forecaster has the time to be able to review historical data, model selections and their results and experiment with alternative approaches.

A focus on fundamentals must remain high on the priorities of those wishing to advance their performance. There must be a fact-based, detailed and objective assessment of processes, people and metrics to identify gaps and assist in the development of a set of priorities. The output must provide an understanding of how mature the end-to-end process is, where improvements are required, how to structure the improvements and what benefits should be expected and tracked. Only once these improvements are made and a solid foundation created can some of the emerging and more advanced capabilities be fully leveraged.

Some the more advanced capabilities that should be expected to become more widely adopted in the future will include demand sensing, shifting and shaping. Demand sensing serves real opportunity in the near-term to anticipate and react, in close to real-time, to changes in patterns of demand. This will place increasing importance on the ability to store and process large quantities of consumption, social media and IOT data. To fully capitalize on these data sources there will be an increasing emphasis on cloud computing, artificial intelligence and machine learning.

Demand shifting and shaping is reliant on the ability to be able to manage the trade-offs between customers and model the effects of typically price, promotion and display. This will require excellence in not just extrapolative, but also explanatory methods. It will also require the forecaster to be able to make persuasive, factual and perhaps visual business cases of the different scenarios under consideration. With a clear distinction between short-range and mid- to long-range forecasting there will be an increasing focus on how to optimally organize data temporally and align the construction of the forecast with the intended usage.

To avoid becoming distracted with the "smoother pebble" or the "prettier shell," and instead focus on the most impactful actions, the following should be considered:

- Complete a full audit of the existing capabilities – process, people and metrics.
- Prioritize the improvements based on the degree of difficulty of making the change and benefits.

▪ Focus on people and process first and systems second.

▪ Look to the future only once the present is secure.

STATISTICAL ALGORITHMS, JUDGMENT AND FORECASTING SOFTWARE SYSTEMS

Robert Fildes, Lancaster University

Within the business forecasting community of practitioners, software developers and researchers these last few years have seen increased interest in machine learning methods. In part, this has been stimulated within the forecasting community by the M4 competition (Gilliland, this volume). Excitingly, evidence of the success of ML methods has also been accumulating with applications in retailing for example, with Walmart data in 2020's M5 competition (Kaggle 2020).

Going hand in hand with the developments of ML, big data availability has offered the opportunity to apply these methods. One consequence is that incorporating multiple leading indicators (Sagaert et al. 2018) or social media and search data (Schaer, Kourentzes, and Fildes 2019) have both increased the number of possible demand drivers to consider for inclusion in the forecasting models. In turn, this enlargement has presented technical challenges which the latest algorithms have overcome. But as yet the evidence of major benefits of big data is limited with skepticism remaining (Snapp, this volume) though others, e.g., Boone et al. (2019 and in this volume), are more optimistic with "potential but gains are yet to be delivered."

In short, we've discovered that some of these new machine learning methods work well on business forecasting problems, some better than others, and the better methods are apparently quite robust for many applications. We do seem to be identifying "winning" methods and that not all ML methods are equally successful and cannot be applied out-of-the-box. But that extending the range of data to be considered to individual consumer pathways to purchase (including the internet) adds little (Kolassa, this volume).

Judgment remains a major part of the business forecasting activity but gathers little attention from researchers and software designers. As the new ML methods come into play, some claim, this should make the need for judgment less relevant. This proposition we can dismiss. The Covid crisis has for most business forecasters posed a major problem: the data that all algorithms rely on from exponential smoothing to deep learning has suddenly become close to irrelevant. Spikes in demand (toilet paper, pasta), precipitous falls (luxuries sold to restaurants), and stock outs have all undermined the historical pattern and the integrity of the data series itself. Forecasters have had to resort to that well-known fix: thumb in the air. But judgmental research in business forecasting continues to be neglected. This does not mean that the role of judgment in practice has diminished despite some machine learners claims. Ignoring the effects of the Covid disruption, even in normal times the adjustment of statistical model-based forecasts, and the role of judgment in new products, remains crucial and ill-understood.

For most practicing forecasters, their judgments, the software, its capabilities and limitations, are at the fulcrum where forecasting processes, statistical algorithms, data and personnel all come together. In the five years since the initial volume of *Business Forecasting*, we've learned quite a lot about these interactions. The core issue facing a business forecasting team is how to get the best overall from integrating these three components.

Good Judgment: Can Software Help?

If judgment is going to keep its central role in business forecasting, we need to examine how to get the best out of expert forecasters. Let's start by seeing how the recommendations from Fildes and Goodwin (2007) hold up; selectively,

1. **Don't adjust without an explicitly recorded reason.** The S&OP process underlying the production of the final operational forecast is designed to stimulate the sharing of information, some of which will have a direct impact on the expected demand. But despite the exhortations over the last five or more years, there is little evidence of software companies making such formalized information sharing easy or companies successfully integrating the baseline statistical forecasts with the myriad of reasons that sales might exceed or fall below the baseline. What we have learnt is that forecasters will misinterpret "soft" information, giving it too much weight. This leads to recommendation 2.

2. **Beware the enthusiasms of marketing and sales colleagues.** The more enthusiasm behind a judgmental intervention, unjustified by the data, the greater the damage done to accuracy. Perhaps if the historical record to adjustments, for a promotion, say, were made available then there would be less of a response to individuals hyping the forthcoming success of their latest idea and a greater reliance on the data. But this is where the software design comes in. In principle it is straightforward to summarize past promotions and any adjustment errors. In practice this is seldom done. For example, with SAP's Forecasting and Replenishment support system the dummy variables categorizing different types of promotions could provide explanations of the errors. But the system is not set up to do this.

3. **Use all the data. Discard the data only with good reason.** In the early days of computers storage limitations precluded the storage of much more than two years' records. No longer a constraint, some of the ad hoc rules of yesteryear, compounded by relabeling of ongoing products, still leave us data short. We also face out-of-stock events that require adjustment. Data cleansing still remains a problem that with large data bases requires an automatic approach and an analysis of its effectiveness. The ML results show the potential of using a large cross-section of continuous time series to produce individual product forecasts (Ma and Fildes 2020) and the need to maintain a consistent data base.

4. **Collect information on key drivers, learn from large errors.** S&OP continues to attract attention from practitioners, more so than ever in this new volume of *Business Forecasting*. For most supply chain organizations it is at the heart of the information collection and interpretation process, supplementing the more formal sources that are embedded in the forecasting support system software itself. The papers in this volume focus on communication – but that neglects the core issue of what needs to be communicated. And in particular the perils of over-emphasizing, hyping if you will, the good news. What we have learnt in the last five years is that demand planners undoubtedly continue to misinterpret "news." Laboratory experiments and a small number of case studies have shown how experts respond to information on future events that may be helpful in operational forecasting – they typically underweight the statistical forecast and overweight the news, particularly when it is hyped up. Even when the algorithm behind the demand forecast includes some of the factors such as a promotion driving future outcomes, forecasters will add more weight to these factors. They also seem to ignore the base lines that should be applied. More disturbing, they will react to large past errors trying to compensate, with unfortunate effects, perpetuating the errors (Petropoulos, Fildes, and Goodwin 2016). For many forecasters they are reliant on just the stored data history, rather than a dashboard-style evaluation of accuracy and the effects of past events.

Can software help forecasters avoid these pitfalls? We have limited evidence. Offering software-based guidance as to how to interpret news events such as weather and promotions effects can help (Lee et al. 2007). However, we don't yet know how best to offer experts' guidance, particularly in complex situations such as multiple promotional types. While software suppliers claim to offer support for judgmental interventions (Fildes, Schaer, and Svetunkov 2018; Fildes et al. 2020), these offerings have yet to be evaluated. Without improved software designed to get the best out of judgment we will continue to live with the consequences of impaired expert judgment: unnecessary bias and forecasts less accurate than they could be.

Machine Learning and Judgment

Can ML methods with appropriate software be made compatible with expert judgment? And should it, cannot we just rely on ML methods alone as some software companies claim? The short answer is, we don't know. Analysis of the studies on expert adjustment tell a mostly negative story but these studies are old and are not based on modern S&OP processes or up-to-date software. Companies such as Beiersdorf have told a more positive story where gains of up to 2.4% have been claimed, equivalent to what has been delivered by improved modeling. Perhaps more important, these were consistent across regions. In on-going academic research, the jury is also hung. Chase (this volume) provides a successful case study where ML is complemented by a dashboard guiding the demand planners' adjustments. A speculative conclusion from the limited evidence is that "ML + Expert adjustment" outperforms an adjusted Exponential smoothing forecast. But the adjustments to machine learning forecasts are often going to be damaging; can such interventions be discouraged? Baker (this volume) describes a classification tree to influence adjustment behavior by providing what behavioral economics calls a "nudge."

The challenge, even greater than when a baseline simple smoothing forecasting method is used, is when to adjust and how to get the best out of the adjustments. All too often the larger positive adjustments don't help, and the software does not support the forecasting process to analyze persistent errors. As the contributions in this book illustrate, new ideas have gained currency and shown their effectiveness in some practical situations. But there remain serious gaps in integrating these new methodologies with demand planning expertise into available software.

REFERENCES

Boone, T., Ganeshan, R., Jain, A., and Sanders, N. R. (2019). Forecasting sales in the supply chain: Consumer analytics in the big data era. *International Journal of Forecasting* 35, 170–180.

Fildes, R., and Goodwin, P. (2007). Good and bad judgment in forecasting: Lessons from four companies. *Foresight: The International Journal of Applied Forecasting* 8, 5–10.

Fildes, R., Schaer, O., and Svetunkov, I. (2018). Software survey: Forecasting 2018. *OR/MS Today* 45.

Fildes, R., Schaer, O., Svetunkov, I., and Yusupova, A. (2020). Software survey: Forecasting 2020. *OR/MS Today* 47.

Kaggle Competition (2020). M5 Forecasting – Accuracy: Estimate the unit sales of Walmart retail goods. https://www.kaggle.com/c/m5-forecasting-accuracy

Lee, W. Y., Goodwin, P., Fildes, R., Nikolopoulos, K., and Lawrence, M. (2007). Providing support for the use of analogies in demand forecasting tasks. *International Journal of Forecasting* 23, 377–390.

Ma, S., and Fildes, R. (2020). Retail sales forecasting with meta-learning. *European Journal of Operational Research* 288 (1): 111–128.

Petropoulos, F., Fildes, R., and Goodwin, P. (2016). Do "big losses" in judgmental adjustments to statistical forecasts affect experts' behaviour? *European Journal of Operational Research* 249, 842–852.

Sagaert, Y. R., Aghezzaf, E.-H., Kourentzes, N., and Desmet, B. (2018). Temporal big data for tactical sales forecasting in the tire industry. *Interfaces* 48, 121–129.

Schaer, O., Kourentzes, N., and Fildes, R. (2019). Demand forecasting with user-generated online information. *International Journal of Forecasting* 35, 197–212.

THE <<EASY BUTTON>> FOR FORECASTING

Igor Gusakov, GoodsForecast

We see in many industries that there is simultaneous movement in two different directions: complexity of what is inside and simplicity of the user interface. Have a look at the smartphone – it's extremely complex inside, but so easy to use even little children can do it. Business forecasting is going in the same direction.

People might think that in any large or medium company there is a forecasting department, but it's not necessarily so. Many companies have forecasting and data science teams. But in other companies there are no forecasters at all, and forecasts are produced by the sales, marketing or finance departments. These people are not familiar with advanced forecasting methods, and their forecasting is more about process than about math.

This situation is understandable – it's pretty hard to seduce a professional data scientist to work for a company which produces something simple (although useful) for everyday life. So, in many companies there is a need for a large red «Easy Button», pressing which gets you the «best forecast» without any efforts.

There are basically two ways to get such a forecast. First is *forecasting as a service*, when a team of professional forecasters and data scientists provides services for different companies. In accordance with the well-known economic principle of division of labor, forecasting as a service is becoming more popular.

The second and most popular way is with *forecasting software*. But software itself is just a tool providing you with advanced forecasting methods. If you don't know how to use the methods, you still face the same problem.

So how can a forecasting tool help to automate the forecasting process? When we think about forecasting, our first thought is about a set of numbers from the past (e.g., a time series of sales of a product to a particular client), and how can we extrapolate it into the future? In automation of this task there is only one serious question: Which forecasting method (and with what parameters) should be used for this particular set of numbers? Without going into details, the question has a simple solution: One needs to test several methods on the hold-out sample and chose the method which provides lower error.

For most companies, the challenge is more than just forecasting one or more *independent* time series. Sales data typically have a structure: Products can be grouped into categories and brands, clients into channels, and so on. Generally, both products and clients have *attributes* (color, size, shape, taste, and so on for products, and type, size, location, etc. for clients). Thus, both products and clients can be organized in *hierarchies*. In other words, sales data represents a cube.

There are several ways to forecast hierarchical data. All time series at the lowest level (i.e., product-client level) can be forecasted independently (bottom-up approach) and then aggregated. Or, the, top level only can be forecasted and then prorated to the lower levels (top-down). Or, some level in the middle can be selected, and then prorated to the lower levels and aggregated to the upper ones (middle-out). But either way, we've introduced another complexity. In addition to the problem of automated method selection for each time series, we encounter the problem of automating selection of the level at which to forecast.

The level selection problem can be solved in a way similar to the automated method selection. Suppose we have a low-level forecast and can check its error on a hold-out sample. If we next take some forecast from the upper level and split it to the lower level proportionally to the low-level forecast, we can again check its error, and compare it with the original low-level forecast error. Sequentially checking all possible levels, we will find one giving lowest error on the hold-out sample and will use it thereafter as the best forecasting level.

Another approach to this problem is to create forecasts at all levels, but instead of choosing the best one, use all the data to reconcile low-level forecasts. That is, change them as little as possible for its aggregates to coincide with upper level forecasts. This is called multi-dimensional reconciliation – an approach proposed by this author in a *Foresight* article, "Data Cube Forecasting for the Forecasting Support System" (Gusakov 2014). It's based on the assumption that upper-level data is generally more "forecast-able" — smooth and less sparse, while low-level demand is often intermittent. As a consequence, these upper-level data can often be forecasted by traditional time-series forecasting techniques.

Let's consider a simple example. Suppose we have some products and clients and create four types of forecasts: low-level forecast (product-client), forecasts by products (aggregated by clients), forecasts by clients (aggregated by products), and an aggregate forecast of all products and clients. Of course, these initial forecasts do not reconcile – the forecasted sums do not coincide. So, we first must adjust products and clients to be equal to the total forecast, and then solve the optimization problem with transportation-type restrictions and a quadratic objective function. (This is also known as QTP for Quadratic Transportation Problem.)

When the structure of the data-cube is more complex than described above, we need to solve several QTPs sequentially. At every step, the dimension of the optimization task is relatively small due to the hierarchical structure of the data, so every QTP can be solved quickly (Rotin et al. 2019).

The same approach is valid for three dimensions, but instead of forecasting one 2-dimensional matrix and two vectors, we now need to forecast one 3-dimensional matrix and three 2-dimensional matrices. For every 2-dimensional matrix previously described, a 2-dimensional reconciliation procedure can be applied.

Importantly, the third dimension can be the "time" dimension. This solves another problem: What time-bucket should be used for forecasting? Indeed, should we use days for forecasting and then aggregate by weeks or months? Or vice versa, forecast by weeks (or months) and disaggregate to days? Modern techniques propose to forecast both by days and weeks (or months) and then reconcile the forecasts. But the approach described above incorporates this time-bucket reconciliation procedure into the overall multidimensional reconciliation.

As we can see, traditional statistical forecasting methods are not quite ready to be sent to the scrap heap by modern machine learning techniques. Traditional methods can still be successfully used if appropriately applied. We also see that traditional forecasting is being *augmented* by both machine learning and optimization methods. As frequently happens, best results are achieved at the border of various fields of knowledge. There is no doubt that we will continue to see more advances in the area of automation of the business forecasting process.

REFERENCES

Gusakov, I. (2014). Data-cube forecasting for the forecasting support system. *Foresight: The International Journal of Applied Forecasting* 35, 25–32.

Rotin, S. V., Gusakov, I. V., and Gusakov, V. Ya. (2019). A simple parallelizable method for the approximate solution of a quadratic transportation problem of large dimension with additional constraints. https://arxiv.org/abs/1909.02334

THE FUTURE OF FORECASTING IS ARTIFICIAL INTELLIGENCE (AI) COMBINED WITH HUMAN FORECASTERS

Jim Hoover, University of Florida

The future of forecasting is artificial intelligence (AI) combined with human fore-casters. Many who read that statement may find it difficult to believe. The reason for this skepticism is that the promise of AI as a replacement for many human activities has been oversold by many in the technology sector. However, the recent, more realistic view, is that humans and AI working together can achieve better forecasting.

There are several major factors that impact the future integration of AI and human forecasting. They include: (1) the impact of AI on forecasting algorithms; (2) the impact of humans on AI methods and algorithms; (3) environmental factors which are enabling the AI/human forecaster combination; and (4) the emergence of evidence that AI combined with human forecasters achieves better forecasting results than exist-ing approaches.

The Impact of AI on Forecasting Algorithms

While AI is not a panacea capable of replacing your human forecaster, its inherent capa-bilities offer methods which can enable better forecasts. Two specific capability areas where AI excels are related to pattern recognition and early anomaly detection. One of AI's strongest application areas is in pattern recognition (Walch 2019). Most algorithms used in forecasting are simplistic models to detect patterns. By increasing the sophistica-tion and accuracy of pattern recognition, AI can determine demand patterns across time for a single product, across hierarchies of similar products, and across products that would not normally be considered in the same hierarchy, but which share similar demand pat-terns. Existing forecasting systems require a forecaster to determine and assign any hier-archies to take advantage of these patterns. AI-detected patterns would not require the pre-designation of the hierarchies to take advantage of discovered patterns.

AI-enabled forecasting can also incorporate other variables that may have patterns influencing a forecasted item. Examples include data from Internet of Things (IoT)-capable devices and data from sources outside of typical forecasting systems. For example, data from internet weather sources can be extracted from the web and included as an explanatory data pattern with demand forecasting. Incorporating weather information in typical demand forecasting algorithms requires substantial model changes, testing and integration to determine the relationship of the variable to selected demand forecasts. These steps are not required for some AI models.

Another AI capability related to the strength of AI pattern recognition is the ability to detect anomalies in demand forecasts rapidly (Improve Operations 2020). Early detection of forecasts diverging from actual values is a task every human forecaster has to perform. When tasked with running hundreds, thousands or millions of forecasts every period, it can be difficult to identify and prioritize specific forecasts for improvement. Automating this task with AI potentially provides the human forecaster with earlier opportunities to address errant forecasts more rapidly than traditional algorithmic methods.

The Impact of Humans on AI Algorithms for Forecasting

Despite the hype, artificial intelligence can't think like a human. So, what are the human activities that influence the effectiveness of AI forecasting? First is the design of the forecasting problem. In other words, there are some choices about how to expose data to an AI model that greatly impact the ability of the AI model to achieve accurate forecasts. For example, one choice is how demand will be recorded. Should demand be recorded on a daily, monthly, quarterly or annual period? This is a human choice. That choice is usually driven by data collection mechanisms and decision timeframes related to the forecasts.

For example, data are collected in real time for many stock-keeping units (SKUs). The data exist in individual transactions. However, the decision to record that demand by day, by store, by region, by category influences how the data are presented to an AI forecasting model. Humans usually tie the collection and presentation of information to forecasting models based on the need to provide the output forecasts to other models like demand planning or ordering/replenishment systems. The decisions about the collection and aggregation of the original data to be forecasted then influence the collection of other potential explanatory data. For example, if you aggregate demand data by day and by store location, you can include weather information that is localized and summarized by date (e.g., average temperature, high temperature, low temperature, cloud cover percentage, rain/snow in inches per day).

Another set of decisions that humans make that influence the effectiveness of AI models includes the collection and cleansing of other data that will be incorporated into the AI model. The creation of additional variables (known as features) is a key step in the development of AI models. Examples include the development of dummy variables related to the dates of sales promotions, advertising campaigns, and special events (e.g., shutdowns due to weather events like hurricanes and flooding). These can be added to a data set exposed to an AI model.

Next, there are human decisions about the AI model itself that influence the accuracy of forecasts. Does the model utilize time series techniques, random forests, or neural networks? What are the parameters and hyper-parameters used by the AI model? Currently, these are choices not made by the AI model or algorithm, but rather are selected by the human forecaster. They can have dramatic impacts on forecast accuracy. The skill of selecting the right models and parameters are driven by the skilled human forecaster.

Finally, the human forecaster that is responsible (and accountable) for the resulting AI forecasts has to make a decision about whether to release the forecasts into production and utilize the forecasts for decision-making. The downstream applications and decision-makers that incorporate the forecasts rely upon the human to review the output and make sure that the outputs are reliable and accurate. AI systems are not designed to self-assess their outputs. Human forecasters will continue to be responsible for those outputs as they were with earlier systemic forecast outputs.

Technological Advances Are Enabling More Effective AI/Human Forecasting

Technological advances are enabling more effective utilization of AI forecasting by their human forecasters. One key advancement is the ability to store substantially more data for forecasting. Some of the original forecasting algorithms like exponential smoothing were designed and utilized because the algorithm itself required very little storage. This made sense in the 1980s when the cost to store a gigabyte of data exceeded $100,000 (Komorowski 2014). In 2020, the cost to locally store a gigabyte of data is approximately $0.03 (Western Digital 2020). Furthermore, cloud-based storage per gigabyte can be virtually free for a gigabyte of data. Higher storage capacity at a lower cost is important to store the data to feed AI models. As storage costs (in the limit) approach 0, the ability to store more demand history, at more locations, becomes possible. Likewise, the ability to store additional predictive variables with the same periodicity as the demand data becomes possible.

The increased digitization of data sources is also creating opportunities to add new variables to AI models. Examples include online weather information and information from Internet of Things (IoT) capable devices.

Another technological advancement is the emergence of democratized tools for building AI forecasting models. Previously, only specialized forecasting software firms and enterprise resource planning software companies could build forecasting solutions implemented by forecasters. More recently forecasting tools that enable AI forecasting models have been developed utilizing an open source software approach. Open source AI software packages have been developed for R and Python. Facebook has developed an open source forecasting tool – Prophet – that is available across multiple open source software platforms. These open source modeling tools (or packages) are available for free and allow forecasters to implement customized AI models that utilize all of the increased data mentioned earlier.

Emerging Evidence of the Positive Impact on Forecasting Outcomes Resulting from the Integration of AI Models and Human Forecasters

Until recently, forecasting competitions like the M-competition had demonstrated that simpler forecasting methods like exponential smoothing performed better on out-of-sample forecasts than more complex methods. However, in the M4 Competition, those simpler methods were bested by more complex machine learning methods (a type of AI technique) (Taleb 2020).

The latest forecasting competition (the M5 Competition) being conducted in 2020 (M5 Forecasting 2020) will test the thesis that more complex AI models can further improve on forecasting outcomes. In this competition, the organizers added hierarchies, promotions and weather data to the competition data set. My forecast is that the AI models combined with the skills of the human modelers will perform the best and win the competition.

Other commercial evidence illustrates that AI models developed and directed by skilled human forecasters have resulted in more accurate forecasts than the simpler earlier approaches. One example is Amazon's patent on forecasting locations of anticipated shipments (Spiegel et al. 2013) to lower shipping times. A second example is Walmart's implementation of machine learning models. Their forecasting model implementation takes a simplistic exponential smoothing demand forecast and decomposes the high-level forecasts into store level increments of demand to drive down stockouts and increase sales (Woodie 2019).

Taken together these developments point to the future of forecasting. Skilled human forecasters using their new AI tools and increased data will be developing more accurate forecasts. This isn't hype. It is a new era of forecasting that takes advantage of the convergence of tools and capabilities that now are available to forecasts at all levels.

REFERENCES

Improve Operations with Anomaly Detection. (2020). https://www.tibco.com/solutions/anomaly-detection

Komorowski, M. (2014). A history of storage cost. https://mkomo.com/cost-per-gigabyte-update

M5 Forecasting – Accuracy. (2020). https://www.kaggle.com/c/m5-forecasting-accuracy

Spiegel, J., McKenna, M., Lakshman, G., and Nordstrom, P. (2013). Method and system for anticipatory package shipping. U.S. Patent No. 8,615,473. U.S. Patent and Trademark Office.

Taleb, N. (2020). Forward to the M4 competition. *International Journal of Forecasting* 36 (1): 1–2. https://doi.org/10.1016/j.ijforecast.2019.05.003

Walch, K. (2019). The seven patterns of AI. https://www.forbes.com/sites/cognitiveworld/2019/09/17/the-seven-patterns-of-ai/#58261b5312d0

Western Digital Elements Desktop Drive, 3 TB. (2020). https://shop.westerndigital.com/products/external-drives/wd-elements-desktop-usb-3-0-hdd#WDBWLG0030HBK-NESN

Woodie, A. (2019). How Walmart uses Nvidia GPUs for better demand forecasting. Retrieved from https://www.datanami.com/2019/03/22/how-walmart-uses-gpus-for-better-demand-forecasting/

QUANTILE FORECASTING WITH ENSEMBLES AND COMBINATIONS

Rob J. Hyndman, Monash University

Forecasting Using Possible Futures

One way to think about forecasting is that we are describing the possible futures that might occur.

Suppose we are interested in forecasting the total sales in Australian cafés and we train an exponential smoothing (ETS) model and an ARIMA model (Hyndman and Athanasopoulos 2020) on the data to the end of 2018. Then we can simulate sample paths from these models to obtain many possible "futures." Figure A.1 shows the last four years of training data and five futures generated from each of the two fitted models.

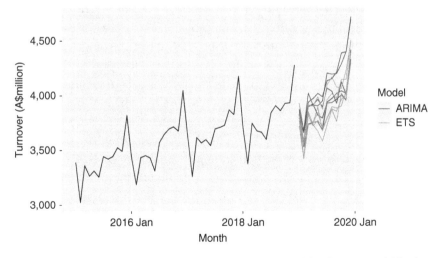

Figure A.1 Future Sample Paths Obtained Using an ARIMA Model and an ETS Model for the Australian Monthly Café Turnover

If we repeat this procedure thousands of times for each model, we can obtain a very clear picture of the probability distribution for each future time period. The means of these sample paths are the traditional point forecasts. Traditional 95% prediction intervals are equivalent to finding the middle 95% of the futures at each forecast horizon.

Simulated future sample paths also allow us to answer many more interesting questions. For example, we may wish to find prediction intervals for the total turnover for the next 12 months. This is surprisingly difficult to handle analytically but trivial using simulations – we just need to add up the turnover for each of the simulated sample paths, and then compute the relevant percentiles. We might also want to forecast the maximum turnover in any month over the next year. Again, that is a difficult problem analytically, but very easy using simulations. I expect that simulating future sample paths will play an increasingly important role in forecasting practice because it makes difficult problems relatively easy, and allows us to explore what the future might be like in ways that would otherwise be almost impossible.

Using simulations in forecasting requires a generative statistical model to be used. This is easy using an ARIMA or ETS model, but more difficult if something like a neural network or random forest has been used.

Quantile Forecasting

Almost everyone needs probabilistic forecasts whether they realise it or not. Without some kind of probabilistic forecast or other measure of uncertainty, a point forecast is largely useless as there is no way of knowing how wrong it is likely to be. A simple version of a probabilistic forecast is a prediction interval which is intended to cover the true value with a specified probability. Another use of a probabilistic forecast is the notion of "safety stock," which is the additional stock to be ordered above the point forecast in order to meet demand with a specified probability.

A more sophisticated way of producing probabilistic forecasts is to generate quantile forecasts. For example, a 90% quantile forecast is a value which should exceed the true observation 90% of the time, and be less than the true value 10% of the time. Median forecasts are equivalent to 50% quantile forecasts. Prediction intervals are often constructed in this way – an 80% prediction interval can be based on the 10% and 90% quantile forecasts. Safety stock can also be computed from quantile forecasts – set the stock order to be the 95% quantile to ensure your probability of being out-of-stock is 5%.

Any statistical forecasting method can be used to produce quantile forecasts by simulation. We simply need to compute the quantiles at each time from the simulated sample paths. Figure A.2 shows the deciles for the ETS forecasts (i.e., the 10th, 20th, and 90th percentiles).

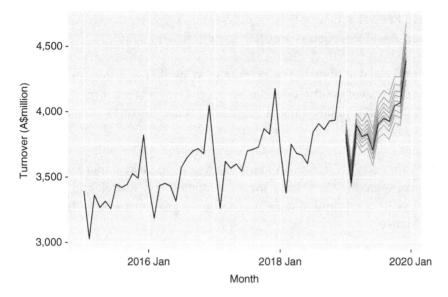

Figure A.2 Gray: Deciles for the ETS Forecasts for the Australian Monthly Café Turnover (Black: Observed Values)

Evaluating Quantile Forecasts

Most businesses doing forecasting will be familiar with computing accuracy measures for point forecasts such as MAPE or RMSE values. With quantile forecasts, we need to use some alternative measures.

Quantile scores provides a measure of accuracy for each quantile of interest. Suppose we are interested in the quantile forecast with probability p at future time t, and let this be denoted by $f_{p,t}$. That is, we expect the observation at time t to be less than $f_{p,t}$ with probability p. For example, an estimate of the 95th percentile would be $f_{0.95,t}$. If y_t denotes the observation at time t, then the quantile score is

$$Q_{p,t} = \begin{cases} 2(1-p)(f_{p,t} - y_t), & \text{if } y_t < f_{p,t} \\ 2p(y_t - f_{p,t}), & \text{if } y_t \geq f_{p,t} \end{cases}$$

This is sometimes called the "pinball loss function" because a graph of it resembles the trajectory of a ball on a pinball table. The multiplier of 2 is often omitted, but including it makes the interpretation a little easier. A low value of Q_p indicates a better estimate of the quantile.

In Figure A.2, the 90% quantile forecast for December 2019 is $f_{0.9,t} = 4680$ and the observed value is $y_t = 4389$. Then $Q_{0.9,t} = 2(1-0.9)(4680-4389) = 58$.

The quantile score can be interpreted like an absolute error. In fact, when $p = 0.5$, the quantile score $Q_{0.5,t}$ is the same as the absolute error. For other values of p, the "error" $(y_t - f_{p,t})$ is weighted to take account of how likely it is be positive or negative.

If $p > 0.5$, $Q_{p,t}$ gives a heavier penalty when the observation is greater than the estimated quantile than when the observation is less than the estimated quantile. The reverse is true for $p < 0.5$.

Often we are interested in the whole forecasting distribution (not just a few quantiles), and then we can average the quantile scores over all values of p. This gives what is known as the "Continuous Ranked Probability Score" or CRPS (Gneiting and Katzfuss 2014).

In the Australian café example, we can compute the CRPS values over the 12 months of 2019 for each of the ARIMA and ETS models. To make it more interpretable, we can also compute the CRPS for a simple seasonal naive model, and then we can calculate the "skill score" equal to the percentage improvement for ARIMA and ETS over seasonal naive.

Model	CRPS	Skill Score
SNAIVE	68.6	0.0
ARIMA	32.9	52.0
ETS	31.5	54.0

Here, ETS is providing the best quantile forecasts with a skill score of 54.0.

Ensemble Forecasting

Ensemble forecasting involves using multiple models and combining the future sample paths to produce the final forecast. If a weighted ensemble is needed, we can make the number of simulations from each model correspond to the required weight.

Ensemble forecasting has been used in weather forecasting for many years, but is not so widespread in other domains. The logic behind ensemble forecasting is that no model is perfect, and the data did not come from a model. As George Box has put it, "all models are wrong, but some are useful" (Box 1976). Ensembles allow the good features of various models to be included, while reducing the impact of any specific model. It also allows the uncertainty associated with selecting a model to be incorporated into the quantile forecasts.

For the Australian café data, we can combine 10,000 simulated sample paths from each of the ETS and ARIMA models, and compute the resulting quantile forecasts from the 20,000 sample paths.

Model	CRPS	Skill Score
ENSEMBLE	31.4	54.3

The ensemble forecasts are slightly better than either the ETS and ARIMA forecasts in this case. When the component models use very different information, the benefit of using ensemble forecasts is greater.

Combination Forecasting

Combination forecasting is a related idea that is more widely used in the general forecasting community. This involves taking a weighted average of the forecasts produced from the component models. Often a simple average is used. For more than 50 years we have known that combination forecasting improves forecast accuracy (Bates and Granger 1969; Clemen 1989). One of the reasons for this is that the combination decreases the variance of the forecasts (Hibon and Evgeniou 2005) by reducing the uncertainty associated with selecting a particular model.

Combinations are almost always used to produce point forecasts, not probabilistic forecasts. A weighted average of several component forecasts gives a point forecast that is identical to taking the mean of the sample paths from the corresponding weighted ensemble.

However, the idea can be used more generally to obtain quantile forecasts as well. Quantiles cannot simply be averaged, so we need to take account of the correlations between the forecast errors from the component models when producing quantile forecasts. This is implemented in the fable package for R. For the Australian café data, this gives the following result.

Model	CRPS	Skill Score
COMBINATION	30.9	54.9

Further improvement has been obtained by taking account of the similarity of the ETS and ARIMA forecasts, rather than simply combining the sample paths as with ensemble forecasting.

Conclusions

I have described several tools for forecasting that are likely to be increasingly used in business forecasting in the future.

- Simulated future sample paths allow us to study how the future might evolve, and allow us to answer more complicated forecasting questions than is possible with analytical methods.

- Quantile forecasts can be produced from these simulated future sample paths and provide a way of quantifying the forecast distributions.

- Quantile scores allow us to evaluate quantile forecasts. Averaging quantile scores gives the CRPS which allows us to evaluate the whole forecast distribution.

- Forecast ensembles combine information from multiple models and often provide a better estimate of future uncertainty than any individual model.

- Forecast combinations are similar to ensembles but also take account of the relationships between the component models. The best forecasts often come from combining models in this way.

Supplements

All the forecasts and calculations produced in this chapter were obtained with the fable package for R. The code used is available at https://github.com/robjhyndman/quantile_ensembles.

REFERENCES

Bates, J. M., and Granger, C.W.J. (1969). The combination of forecasts. *Journal of the Operational Research Society* 20 (4): 451–468.

Box, G. E.P. (1976). Science and statistics. *Journal of the American Statistical Association* 71 (356): 791–799.

Clemen, R. (1989). Combining forecasts: A review and annotated bibliography with discussion. *International Journal of Forecasting* 5: 559–608.

Gneiting, T., and Katzfuss, M. (2014). Probabilistic forecasting. *Annual Review of Statistics and Its Application* 1 (1): 125–151.

Hibon, M., and Evgeniou, T. (2005). To combine or not to combine: Selecting among forecasts and their combinations. *International Journal of Forecasting* 21 (1): 15–24.

Hyndman, R. J., and Athanasopoulos, G. 2020. *Forecasting: Principles and practice* (3rd ed.). Melbourne, Australia: OTexts. OTexts.org/fpp3.

MANAGING THE DEMAND FOR NEW PRODUCTS

Dr. Chaman L. Jain, St. John's University

New products are now the lifeline of businesses. They are the ones that provide margin, but competition kills that margin by turning new products into commodities. And that competition is getting more and more intense. It is coming not only from within the industry but also from the outside. Uber is not in the taxi business yet competes with it. Airbnb is not a part of the hotel industry yet competes with big hotel chains. Globalization has further intensified the competition. Michael Dell, founder and CEO of Dell, Inc., once remarked that the key to success depends on the willingness to take a calculated risk and staying one step ahead of competition. What we do today, our competitors will be doing tomorrow. To stay ahead of competition, we need to come up with more and more new products. But new products are a risky business, only a small percentage of them succeed – 25%, the most widely quoted number.

Businesses are now coming out with increasing numbers of new products. As such, a significant amount of revenue comes from new products – 18%, according to the latest survey by the Institute of Business Forecasting. Apple gets almost 60% of its revenue from products that are less than four years old. McCormick USIG gets 35% to 45% of its revenue from new products. About 60% of the LEGO sets that company sells every year are new. The success of new products depends on how a product idea is conceived and developed, how it is launched and, after the launch, how its demand is managed. The strategy to manage the demand for new products – to optimize revenue and profit – requires a dedicated New Product team and a four-step process:

1. Align supply with demand.
2. Fix problems that are fixable.
3. Look for additional opportunities.
4. Develop an exit strategy.

Align Supply with Demand

Like any other product, it is important to align supply with demand. For that, we need a fairly good forecast and agile supply chain. Because of lack of history, we often experience large errors in new product forecasting, which must be managed. The errors mostly result from overforecasting. However, there are a number of instances where demand was much more than expected. For example, when Nintendo launched the Wii console in November 2006, it could not produce enough to meet the demand. The same thing happened in 2017 when it launched the Switch console.

The best way to manage forecasts of new products, according to Patrick Bower, Senior Director of Global Supply Chain Planning & Customer Services at Combe Incorporated, is to prepare forecasts for three different zones: Liquid (18–24 months ahead), Slushy (6–18 months ahead) and Frozen (1–6 months ahead). Forecast for the Liquid zone is simply for capacity planning, the Slushy zone is for supply-chain planning where some changes can be made, and for the Frozen zone, where commitment is firm, no change can be made. To minimize the supply risk, companies may like to negotiate flexible contracts with their vendors that let them make some changes in the order after a certain number of weeks or months of launches. The other way to do is to go for two different contracts with suppliers—fixed and flexible—based on range forecasts. Have a fixed contract for the low-end forecast, and flexible for the high-end forecast. Several companies like Hewlett-Packard use this type of contract. It goes even one step further by creating a flexibility in the labor force. It keeps three types of workers—full time, part time and temporary. This enables the company to quickly adjust the labor force to its needs.

Fix Problems That Are Fixable

There are times when new products fail, not because consumers did not like them, but because of some problems that could be easily fixed. When fixed, the products take off. The problem may be that consumers are emotionally attached to a product you want to replace; instructions are not clear; product is incorrectly positioned; and so on. The best thing, therefore, is to find the problem and fix it.

The company can determine the problem by going over the feedback received directly from consumers in the form of letters, e-mails and telephone calls, as well as from social media, including tweets, blogs and posts, users' product ratings, and online reviews. Artificial Intelligence (AI) tools, such as Natural Language Processor, Computer Vision, and Machine Learning, can even let you listen to the conversations in videos and audio recording to know what customers are saying about your products.

When the Coca-Cola Company launched its New Coke in 1985, it was surprised to learn about the bond consumers had developed with the old Coke. The company changed the formula after 99 years of research and spent millions of dollars in developing and promoting it, but consumers rejected the new formula. The company was so obsessed with New Coke, it took 77 days to recognize the problem and fix it. Pepsi experienced a similar problem with Diet Pepsi when, in August 2015, it replaced aspartame sweetener with sucralose to reverse the declining trend in sales. The swap, instead of helping, accelerated the decline. Despite all the signals coming from the market, it took almost one year for the company to switch back to the older sweetener. The outcome would have been different if the company recognized earlier and acted on it.

The product may be doing poorly because instructions on how to use are not clear. Newell Rubbermaid learned this lesson in 2008 when it launched Produce Saver, a food storage container. The food storage container was supposed to extend the life of fruits and vegetables by 33%, but it was not happening. The problem was the way people were using the product. They were washing the fruits and vegetables before storing, and then putting them wet into the container. When Rubbermaid realized the issue, it quickly responded by clarifying instructions that contents must be stored dry. With that, the product became a huge success. P&G had a similar experience when it launched Crest White strips. It was surprised to learn that consumers were not buying because they could not find instructions on how to use it. Instructions were hidden inside the box.

The poor performance of a product may be the result of poor positioning. This is what happened at a consumer goods company with a failed product launch. They recognized the problem and repositioned the product in a different segment with a new label. With that, sales picked up.

What competitors do, or plan to do, in response to newly launched products, also makes a difference. Competitors may lower their price, accelerate their promotional activities, offer products in a different class of trade, and/or launch competitive products. It is, therefore, important to watch what competitors are planning. When Chrysler learned in 1993 that Ford was introducing the new Windstar minivan, it ran an aggressive price promotion. This brought back many buyers who would have otherwise waited for the Windstar. It also tweaked some interest in Chrysler's own new minivan scheduled for the following year. Such proactive response is possible with a dedicated new product team – monitoring the market, making plans, and taking action.

Look for Additional Opportunities

Another thing the New Product team needs to do is to see whether a new product offers an additional opportunity. Some products do. P&G got an additional opportunity when it launched NyQuil as a cold and flu medicine. It found that people also use it as a sleeping aid, which led to the launch of ZzzQuil. This provided additional revenue to the company. The strange part is, it took 21 years for the company to recognize this opportunity and act on it. In the meantime, many competitors had also launched their own products as sleeping aids – Ambien by Sanofi-Aventis and Rozerm by Takeda.

Avon found a new opportunity when it launched its bath oil, Skin So Soft. People were also using it as a bug repellent. When the company learned, it rolled out Skin So Soft Bug Guard, which provided millions of dollars in additional revenue.

Develop an Exit Strategy

Although successful new products generate a significant amount of revenue, a large number of new products fail. To minimize losses, we must decide quickly to get rid of those that are not performing well. Doing so avoids being left with obsolete inventory, whether it is of finished products or raw materials. This is especially important for products that require specialized materials which cannot be used anywhere else. However, in some cases, businesses may decide to hold on to a product even though it is not doing well, because they foresee a bright future. Tastykake, producer of bakery products, is currently holding on to the category of sugar- and gluten-free cakes even though it is not generating any profit, according to Jeff Marthins, former Director of Supply Chain. To see how new launches are doing, the team must review them weekly, if not daily.

Strategy Implementation

To implement the strategy outlined above, we need a dedicated New Product team who constantly watch the market trends as well as the performance of new launches. Whether the team works within the S&OP process or as an independent body is up to a company. One thing is a must: because of the high level of uncertainly associated with new products, their performance must be reviewed and acted on quickly.

More and more companies are now going for an independent team. The recent IBF survey shows that more than half of the companies (54%) manage new products outside the S&OP process. To speed up the process, companies like Hollister Incorporated, Campbell Soup, Pinnacle Foods, and Tempur-Pedic review new products weekly, even though their S&OP process is on a monthly cycle.

Coca-Cola handles product life cycle management through specific teams of managers and planners, each dedicated to a region. According to Mark Covas, former Group Director of TPW Midterm Planning at Coca-Cola, each Regional Team manages the setup of new items for distribution across the 200+ warehouse network for pipeline and re-sell for the first six months of sales. (After six months, the forecasting and replenishment process is handed over to the Franchise Demand Planners using traditional forecasting tools.) The Regional Teams' work is layered into the monthly S&OP process. At Bayer Consumer Healthcare, new launches are reviewed weekly, at least, for the first four months, according to John Gallucci, Vice President, Demand Planning.

To conclude, new products are necessary for a company's survival and growth, but they are highly risky. The strategy described above will help to minimize the risk and maximize the sales and profit.

SOLVING FOR THE IRRATIONAL: WHY BEHAVIORAL ECONOMICS IS THE NEXT BIG IDEA IN DEMAND PLANNING

Jonathon Karelse, NorthFind Management

In classical economics, forecasts and predictive models are based on the underlying premise that humans, when faced with clear value-based decisions, naturally choose the option with the greatest value. When they don't, they are acting "irrationally." Unfortunately, in reality every human carries with them some degree of this irrationality. This is why, despite the growth and development of business forecasting being primarily the story of advances in mathematics, and in the tools facilitating ever-increasing scopes and scales of modeling and prediction, the need for understanding the human component remains as critical as ever.

For SKUs with a statistically stable demand profile, there is little question that, provided there are no substantive changes in demand in the future, forecast automation may yield a significant improvement in both performance and cycle time. Nearly all businesses, however, have SKUs whose demand profiles do not lend themselves to autoregressive forecasting, and there is no business that can't under the appropriate circumstances benefit from the judicious application of human insight.

Whatever the profile of a company's demand, and whatever its degree of automation, there are nevertheless multiple touchpoints whereby human intervention can either consciously or unconsciously transmit biases into the Demand Planning process. It is our position, therefore, that the greatest overarching issue facing a Demand Planning organization is not which software to use; what algorithms to select; whether or not to integrate particular inputs; or what metrics to report with; but rather, the need to clearly identify every human touchpoint in the process, and mitigate the effect of the biases that come with them through screening, training, and a robust planning framework.

Nobel laureate Daniel Kahneman, in his seminal work *Thinking, Fast and Slow*, explores how in many of the decisions that we assume are being made rationally, it is actually our most primitive reactive brain – popularly known as the "reptilian brain" or "lizard brain" – that is making the decision. This quick-thinking part of the brain serves us well when nearby dangers require immediate action, but in situations requiring careful and abstract consideration, the heuristic or "instinct"-based reactions often lead to suboptimal and heavily biased results. The prefrontal cortex, which is a late evolutionary development and is responsible for, among other things, future value considerations, takes conscious effort to engage, and too few actually do.

What does this mean for Demand Planning, then; since nearly every aspect of it is subject to human decision-making? To begin with, there is a certainty that without proper intervention and screening, every aspect of Demand Planning will be flawed.

But it also means that by properly understanding the prevalence and causes of these biases, every aspect of Demand Planning has the potential to see improvement.

From the very outset of the Demand Planning process – Demand Sensing – unconscious biases and heuristics influence what sources of data planners may consider or exclude as part of the demand plan. For example, if the prevailing wisdom in an organization holds that the business is very unique – a sentiment held by many companies – there may be a reluctance to invest the effort into mining syndicated sales data for additional insights into demand, because the organization believes it is too different to be able to make use of market-wide information. In this case, two prevailing biases – Availability Heuristic and Groupthink – would be unconsciously biasing the demand planner and, as a result, directly influencing the entire Demand Planning process.

The generation of a statistically driven forecast may seem, by its nature, less prone to the influence of biases and heuristics, but here, too, there are numerous human touchpoints. When a planner selects or overrides algorithms in a forecast engine, it is entirely possible the decision has been influenced by the presence of a bias. Likewise, parametric adjustments of particular algorithms – the gamma variable, for instance, on the nearly ubiquitous Holt-Winters algorithm – is more frequently the result of a planner influenced by the Cluster Illusion and False Seasonality Bias than some bona fide mathematical insight. When one considers that in a study of nearly 500 demand planners around the world by my company NorthFind Management, 80% were four times as likely to adjust a trend-neutral forecast up than down, there can be no question that even in what should be the most objective component of Demand Planning, human biases exert a considerable impact on performance.

Where and when to integrate judgment has long been a point of debate in the Demand Planning community, because it is here especially that cognitive dysfunctions are most frequently on display. Although Kahneman and his long-time collaborator Amos Tversky showed conclusively by the 1980s that the judicious integration of judgment into a statistically driven forecasting process would yield greater performance over time than either single method, many organizations fail to recognize the importance of strict guidelines for forecast adjustment. Others miss the opportunity for performance improvements by mitigating against biases too heavy-handedly and ignoring judgment integration altogether. Whatever the policy, the point at which any inputs are added to the already biased statistical baseline subjects a company's Demand Planning process to a host of biases and heuristics, many of which can even be conscious.

Most Demand Planners and forecasters approach their jobs with some peripheral knowledge that biases exist – most frequently, they think, in the forecasts provided to them by salespeople – but that they personally are able to execute their functions as coldly-rational and objective arbiters, free from these encumbrances. The reality is just the opposite. Not only do Demand Planners suffer from the same biases and heuristics, they are more likely to be affected by some biases – such as the Dunning Kruger effect – than non-Demand Planners. Consequently, not only will forecasts and plans be influenced by these biases; without testing for them, the opportunities for improvement will remain, for many, undiscovered.

Given the level of human involvement in the vast majority of planning and forecasting processes, it is crucially important that the effect of the biases and heuristics influencing them be identified and mitigated. Below are four Demand Planning Behavioral Economics best practices that will not only mitigate biases and heuristics, but improve overall forecasting and planning performance:

1. **Don't Use What You Don't Measure.** It is never good enough to assume or trust that inputs – whether a customer forecast, a syndicated data source, or an individual planner adjustment – are adding value. Every input should be measured. Consider Forecast Value Add (FVA) analysis as a framework to facilitate this.

2. **Show Your Bias.** The effect of biases and heuristics is as pervasive as it is precisely because most are unconscious. By periodically measuring for biases and heuristics in contributors to your Demand Planning process, they are identified and can be mitigated.

3. **Never Stop Learning.** It should go without saying that Demand Planners should have the benefit of standardized best practices training, ideally created specifically for your organization, but many companies don't take this basic step. Ensuring that all stakeholders have the same framework to work from, especially when it includes a component of Behavioral Economics to reduce bias, raises awareness and improves performance across the organization.

4. **Value Diversity.** There are great benefits to having multiple viewpoints available in planning. Be careful not to create a homogenous team, as Groupthink and Availability Heuristics are a likely result.

BUSINESS FORECASTING IN DEVELOPING COUNTRIES

Bahman Rostami-Tabar, Cardiff University

The use of accurate forecasting to inform decision-making processes is essential in every organization regardless of whether it is based in a developed or a developing country. In this study, we aim to explore the status of business forecasting in developing countries and how it might differ from that in developed countries. By business forecasting, we mean any type of forecasting that is used to inform a decision no matter in which domain of application. Regarding the term "developing countries," although there are various ways to categorize countries based on development, we are relying on the World Bank classification by income and region (World Bank 2020a).

Data and Method

In order to explore the status of business forecasting in developing countries, we follow the data analysis process depicted in Figure A.3.

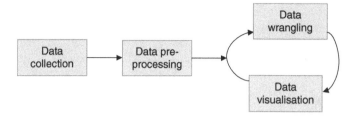

Figure A.3 Data Analysis Process

We first collected data from three different sources:

1. **World Bank data** (World Bank 2020b): We use country names, their population and classification by income and region based on the World Bank's 2020 regional and income classification of economies (World Bank 2020c, 2020d).

2. **Scopus:** We use Scopus (www.scopus.com) to collect two data sets related to the number of published documents in the area of forecasting from 2000 to 2019. To create the first data sets, we search for the term "forecast" and its variations, i.e., we search for "forecast*" in the title, abstract, and keywords for all types of document published on any subject, and in any language. To create the second data set, we restrict our search to peer-reviewed articles published in the *International Journal of Forecasting* and *Journal of Forecasting*.

   Both data sets include the following fields for each document: authors' affiliation, country and year. Documents/articles with multiple co-authors from different countries are counted separately for each country of origin.

3. **M competition:** We use two data sets from M4 and M5 competitions that include the number of teams and the country of origin of participants based on IP addresses for M5 and the country of residence of the first author for M4. (We wish to thank Evangelos Spiliotis for providing M-competitions data.)

After collecting the data, we preprocess them to resolve inconsistencies between the name of the countries in the three data sets and deal with any missing values. We then remove documents with undefined countries, such as those that no longer exist, e.g., Yugoslavia, and then we turn implicit missing values into explicit ones for the combination of the year and the region/income to get a complete data set. Finally, we replace missing values with zeros. After that, we join them with the population data and manipulate them to count the total number of documents for Scopus data and teams for M-competition data by income and by region. For the Scopus data, we divide the number by population for each category of income/region and multiply it by 10 million to obtain the number of documents/articles per 10 million of population. Finally, we visualize the result, which is presented in the next section

Key Findings

In this section, we analyze the collected data to summarize and discuss the status of business forecasting in developing countries.

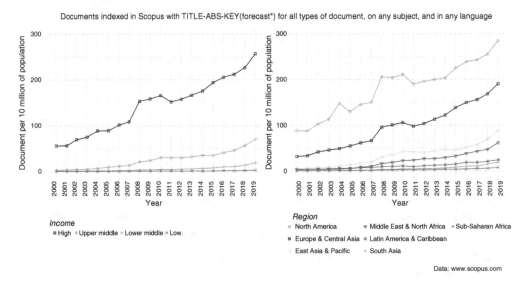

Figure A.4 Total Number of Documents per 10 Million of Population Indexed in Scopus for the Term "Forecast*" in the Title/Abstract/Keyword

Figure A.4 shows the distribution of indexed documents in Scopus from 2000 to 2019 per 10 million of population by income and by region. This figure reveals two key insights. First, we observe a strong incremental trend for virtually every income category and region. However, countries with low and lower middle income and those located in South Asia, the Middle East and North Africa, Latin America and Caribbean, and Sub-Saharan Africa still lag substantially in the number of documents published over the last two decades.

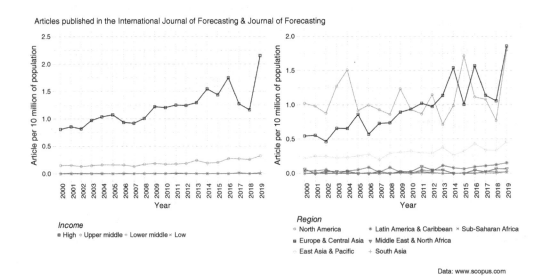

Figure A.5 Total Number of Articles per 10 Million of Population Published in *the International Journal of Forecasting* and *Journal of Forecasting*

Figure A.5 indicates the distribution of peer-reviewed articles published in the *International Journal of Forecasting and Journal of Forecasting* from 2000 to 2019 by income and by region. This figure shows that the contribution from low and lower middle-income countries and those located in South Asia, Middle East and North Africa, Latin America and Caribbean and Sub-Saharan Africa is negligible, and has grown little over the last two decades. These patterns are similar to what we found in Figure A.4.

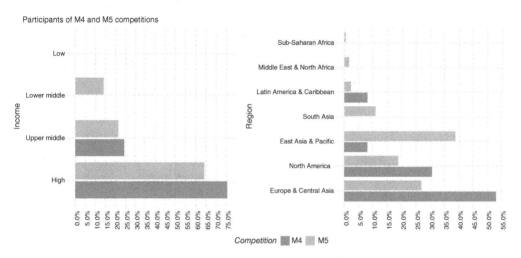

Figure A.6 M4 and M5 Competitions

Figure A.6 explores the percentage of teams that participated in M4 and M5 competitions by income and by region. While there is no team from any low- and lower-middle-income countries or those located in Sub-Saharan Africa, Middle East and North Africa, and South Asia in M4 Competition, we observe that those countries participate in M5 Competition, which might be due to the fact that it has been hosted on Kaggle. However, we still observe a similar gap discussed in Figures A.5 and A.6.

By exploring data from three different sources, our analysis produces two main results. First, we find that there is a substantial gap in the area of business forecasting between the developed and developing world. Second, we find that very little progress has been made over the past two decades to reduce this gap. While there is a substantial increment trend for developed countries, a similar pattern remains beyond the expectations for the rest of the world. There is no reason for the status of business forecasting in developing countries to be lower than that in developed countries. We know that there are barriers such as a lack of infrastructure, resources, funds, skills, trained academic and practitioners, access to research, data availability, and access to policymakers. However, there are many situations in developing countries where forecasting can be helpful in informing decisions to tackle grand challenges.

Therefore, in order to advance the current status and help reduce the gap, there is an urgent need from the forecasting community to take concrete actions to enhance the knowledge and the practice of business forecasting in developing countries.

Suggestions to Close the Gap

In order to improve the status of business forecasting in developing countries, we provide the following suggestions:

- **Increase awareness.** A greater awareness of the benefits of business forecasting is needed to foster more practical use. First, an overall understanding of the forecasting tools and techniques and their links to decision-making processes should be provided. Second, a showcase of how forecasting has been used to inform decisions and evidence for decision makers in various domains is necessary. This could be achieved through training, organizing workshops and international conferences in developing countries.

- **Improve access to resources.** The availability of free, open access resources is of great value to many in low and lower middle-income countries who may otherwise not be able to afford resources such as books, journals and software. In the past few years, we have seen the availability of open source software (R Project 2020) and free online books (Hyndman and Athanasopoulos 2020) that facilitate the training and use of forecasting for those in developing countries. These efforts need to be expanded.

- **Promote real problem solving.** A large number of studies fail to address the real problems facing society and its environment. To address this issue, there must be more studies focusing on real problems with clear statements that demonstrate the investigation is driven by real challenges. Moreover, it is important to ensure that business forecasting is integrated as an essential component of decision support systems. This may also help to increase government participation.

- **Establish a forecasting for development network.** Often increasing awareness is not enough to have a lasting impact in developing countries. Establishing an international network that partners academics and researchers in developing countries with mentors or collaborators in developed countries could be highly effective in closing the gap and providing mutual learning benefits.

- **Organize forecasting competitions for developing countries** (Global Innovation Exchange, 2020). Forecasting competitions, and in particular those dedicated to the challenges in developing countries, can help to advance knowledge, foster collaborations between researchers and practitioners in developing and developed countries, and benefit developing countries by providing solutions to challenges.

REFERENCES

Global Innovation Exchange (2020). USAID's intelligent forecasting: A competition to model future contraceptive use. https://competitions4dev.org/forecastingprize

Hyndman, R. J., and Athanasopoulos, G. (2020). *Forecasting: Principles and practice* (3rd ed.). OTexts: Melbourne, Australia. OTexts.com/fpp3

R Project (2020). The R Project for Statistical Computing. https://www.r-project.org/

World Bank (2020a). Country and lending groups. https://bit.ly/2XbCncg

World Bank (2020b). Population, total. https://data.worldbank.org/indicator/SP.POP.TOTL

World Bank (2020c). The World by Income. https://bit.ly/3hRFdLx

World Bank (2020d). The World by Region. https://bit.ly/2Dk5cwx

DO THE PRINCIPLES OF ANALYTICS APPLY TO FORECASTING?

Udo Sglavo, SAS

As the industry has broadened from statistics and analytics to big data and artificial intelligence, some things have remained constant. At SAS, we call these foundational truths the Principles of Analytics. They inform our approach to data and analytics, and they manifest themselves in our products and services.

At SAS, the principles of analytics have significantly influenced our approach to data and analytics as a company in general. If we consider forecasting as an activity that fits well under the broader term of analytics, can we claim that these principles apply to it as well? My answer is yes, and I would like to guide you through these principles and explain how they apply to modern forecasting based on analytical thinking.

But first, let's list the principles of analytics:

1. Analytics follows the data; analytics everywhere.

2. Analytics is more than algorithms.

3. Democratization of analytics; analytics for everyone.

Principle 1: Analytics Follows the Data; Analytics Everywhere

---

Data are a resource. If you are not analyzing it, it is an unused resource. At SAS, we often say, "Data without analytics is value not yet realized."

The first principle of analytics is about bringing the right analytics technology to the right place at the right time. Forecasters knew big data before it got famous. Early on they faced challenges turning transactional data into formats suitable for analytical methods. In today's times of smart edge devices, network routers, machines, health care equipment, cars, phones, and more, we have to reconsider the traditional approach of moving all data to a central database. Instead, we can take advantage of the computational power of these devices, and such a "hybrid" approach will be at the forefront of forecasting systems.

As companies recognize the advantages of cloud computing and cloud storage, forecasting ecosystems have to support cloud-native environments natively. An emphasis on data integration, data quality, data privacy, and data security will be at the center of these systems. To provide a seamless experience and help organizations accelerate their cloud transformation initiatives, SAS and Microsoft are working together to ensure that SAS products and solutions can be successfully deployed and run effectively on Azure.

Principle 2: Analytics Is More Than Algorithms

> You should pay great attention to the quality, robustness, and performance of your algorithms. But the value of analytics is not in the features and functions of the algorithm – not anymore. The value is in solving data-driven business problems.

If your forecasting team is mostly concerned with competing on which particular algorithm works best for all your data at hand, you have a problem. Yes, algorithms are at the core of forecasting efforts, but they are only a means to an end: to make the correct decision at the right time. Organizations need to adjust the choice of algorithm to the amount of data, the frequency of data, and the forecasting horizon. And of course, this should happen as automatically as possible.

If you are not yet considering forecasting as a process – which starts with accessing and managing data, all the way to feeding downstream systems used for planning and budgeting – you might as well stop using algorithms in the first place.

Solving data-driven business problems can provide the advantage your organization is aiming for, but how can you gain that advantage? Probably not with algorithms alone, especially when they are a commodity. The organization will gain an advantage with enterprise-grade analytics processes that are scalable, flexible, integrated, governed, and operational. These characteristics are just as important as the algorithms themselves.

Principle 3: Democratization of Analytics; Analytics for Everyone

> Digital transformation is an ongoing challenge that almost all organizations face. Data and analytics now play a strategic role in digital transformation. But you will not benefit from its impact unless data and analytics can scale beyond the data science team.

In an ideal world, your forecasting processes are fully automated and fit seamlessly into your business processes. Similar to not having to worry about shifting gears in an automatic engine, you should not have to worry about number crunching. However, you may not be able to switch so easily to this approach, as reality kicks in fairly quickly: new products, assortment changes, unforeseen data issues, hardware problems, you name it. The concept of Forecast Value Added is an excellent tool for focusing where to put your efforts. But still, you need to enable analytics skills at all tiers of the organization, especially in those areas that have more domain knowledge that can be applied to analytics.

Making data and analytics available to everyone is crucial for successful forecasting efforts. We can refer to this as "the democratization of analytics," and it manifests itself in many ways:

- Availability of visualization tools to everyone for ad-hoc analysis.
- Augmented analytics to support users through natural language processing and automation.
- Automation of data management and modeling.
- Analytics and AI as supporting technology.
- Educational programs that broaden analytic skills.

Conclusion

In a world where everyone has data, it's what you do with that data that matters.

How can your organization differentiate with analytics? One way is to use analytics to identify what data has the most value. For example, what if a data stream is just noise and features no signal at all? This may reveal a flaw in an organizational process, or a gap in the kind of data needed.

When an automatic forecasting engine tells you that a naïve model gives the best forecast, why is this the case? Are our demand patterns truly "almost random," meaning too complex for a model to detect any pattern?

Maybe you discover that you don't keep sufficient historical data, or other types of potentially useful data, because of IT restrictions. You can ask what's the value of keeping additional data? What further analysis could we do, and what better decisions could we make? Organizations should consider additional data feeds, such as social media streams or macro-economic indicators.

Most important, the organization needs to keep asking: Where can we improve with analytics? What markets can we disrupt? Where can we automate and support performance breakthroughs?

The principles of analytics manifest themselves in many ways:

- Analytics applied to areas of the business where it will have the most impact.
- Data and analytics strategies that expand the successful use of analytics projects throughout the organization.
- A culture dedicated to digital transformation and analytical thinking.
- New business opportunities from monetizing data and disrupting existing systems with analytics.

Why do these principles matter? Because even as analytics evolves and industries transform, these principles stay the same. They provide an internal compass that can inform an organization's approach to data and analytics and fuel its successful digital transformation.

GROUPTHINK ON THE TOPIC OF AI/ML FOR FORECASTING

Shaun Snapp, Brightwork Research & Analysis

Ever since progress was made using neural networks, and IBM's Watson performed well in *Jeopardy*, there has been an unceasing promotion of AI/ML for forecasting, in addition to just about everything else. This "third wave" of the AI/ML boom has essentially carried forward the promises made by Big Data and analytics, but which never matched what both of those areas said that they would provide. In the example of Big Data, Hadoop – the centerpiece tool for Big Data – is now sidelined as other tools have become more popular, and analytics have not led to perceptibly better decisions. Yet almost no one talks about this. Vendors like Tableau told us that if we just had enough pie charts and bar charts, we would begin to make better decisions. Tableau and other vendors and consulting companies left out the part about it still being humans reading the graphs. And humans come with their own set of limitations in interpreting information. Humans also have the financial bias to not act on data, no matter how complete and convincing, if it is against their financial interests.

The marketing mills of software vendors and consulting firms, however, must continue to churn. So, there seems nothing inappropriate with simply grafting the previous assertions onto a new vehicle – in this case AI/ML. I have tracked how one vendor, SAP, exactly copied promises from "predictive analytics" neatly over to AI/ML.

Everyone Agrees!

Of course, the problem is that all of the opinion shapers – vendors, consulting firms, IT media, IT analysts – all agree that AI/ML is the answer to everything that we need. And generally, the less one has hands-on experience with AI/ML, the more exciting it seems. We are at a point where a very significant proportion of the people that talk about AI/ML (executives, salespeople, journalists) have never run an ML algorithm. For those who have, there may be nothing more boring or less eventful than running through a series of algorithms against data that took forever to arrive from the client and that you are not even sure are accurate.

Let Us Agree Not to Worry about History

What else is curious is how AI's terrible history of failing to meet expectations has been left out of the most recent AI bubble. In my historical analysis of AI pioneer Marvin Minsky, I found him to be wrong about virtually every projection he made in the field of AI. Why a person who exaggerated what AI would be able to do is held in such high regard seems to have something to do with how personally likable he was. Minsky predicted HAL in 2001 (actually before 2001, in his notes to *2001: A Space Odyssey* director Stanley Kubrick). And in 2002, we instead got Roomba.

Yet regardless of Minsky's mispredictions, he continues to be considered the father of AI. How you can be the father of something you are consistently wrong about is beyond me.

AI/ML as Secret Sauce

AI/ML has become a way to say, "I am doing something intelligent," without describing what you are doing. In discussions with several vendors, the further I get into the discussion of what the vendor is doing, the less interesting it appears, the more it looks like something that has been around for a while – the less correspondence it has to the claims on their website. I am frequently told, "This is just how it is now. Investors want to hear you are using AI. And customers also want to know that you use AI."

And this is, of course, how bubbles get started and how they persist.

The Larger Problem

The problem with AI generalizes to other things that become hot topics in IT. Many financial forces are pushing on AI promotion, and close to no forces pushing back. Vendors and consulting companies don't want to advertise in media that is realistic. They want PR outlets for their products. Buyers of software don't want reasonable claims – the decision-makers want software that will allow them to perform "digital transformation." In IT, the best way to minimize your income is to question the validity of whatever the hot topic du jour is. And this is why there is nothing to stop a bubble once it picks up steam.

The Benefits of AI/ML to Forecasting

There can be benefits of ML to forecasting. However, something that is nearly always left out is that it requires more investment in data acquisition and forecast processing than traditional time series forecasting. The reality is that very few companies have data other than sales history on which to base forecasts. The data they could use to perform multivariate forecasting, which ML requires, exists somewhere in the company, but it is not readily available.

As is always the case, the benefits of something should not be considered without weighing the costs. For example, following the right exercise and diet regime, any forecaster can attain the body of an Adonis. However, there are very few people that look like Adonis walking around the forecasting department. Why? Because the energy input to obtain this goal is enormous. With ML, it is normalized to discuss the benefits, or potential benefits, without considering the costs. Companies, except for tech giants that have virtually unlimited resources and accumulate heaps of multivariate data as part of their daily operations, are in extreme denial if they think they will be able to adhere to a regiment of ML in their forecasting. Nearly all the companies I have consulted for tap out at energy input levels that allow them only to achieve a portion of the benefits of univariate forecasting. Few of my clients have been interested in even funding extensive forecast error measurements that compared different forecasting methods.

Conclusion

In the next few years, the AI/ML bubble will be replaced by some other fad. No one will admit to their inaccurate projection in the space. What will be left over for forecasting is a large number of projects that massively failed to meet expectations, and that will be conveniently buried by the IT decision-makers that approved them. At that time, there will be no discussion of AI/ML promises, because as with the unrealized projections of Big Data and analytics, there will be a new thing to hype and discuss, and conversation will move to that topic.

TAKING DEMAND PLANNING SKILLS TO THE NEXT LEVEL

Nicolas Vandeput, SupChains

Based on my experience as a consultant working with clients on forecasting models and teaching forecasting to master students, I see three main ideas that will take any demand planner to the next level. After discussing those ideas, I will show you how to get started to use machine learning for demand forecasting.

1. **Machine Learning is easy to use. You can do it.** While the first machine learning models date back to the 1960s with the work of Morgan and Sonquist (1963) on decision trees, and Rosenblatt (1957) on perceptrons (the inner neurons of a neural networks), the revolution of machine learning in forecasting started in the mid-2010s.

Conventional wisdom attributes this revolution to the increase in computation power along with the availability of bigger datasets. But this would be missing two other trends that made this revolution possible. First, there are better machine algorithms developed in the last years, as we find in papers by authors such as Kingma and Ba (2015) who proposed a better optimization technique for neural networks, and Ke et al. (2017) and Tianqi and Guestrin (2016), who proposed efficient and powerful methods for boosting decision trees. And second, there is an improved ease-of-use that made machine learning usable by non-experts, for example with scikit-learn (Pedregosa et al. 2011).

Today, as shown in my book *Data Science for Supply Chain Forecasting* (Vandeput 2021), you need only around 60 lines of code in Python to format your data, train and optimize a neural network (using only free and open software). With online learning platforms developing since the mid-2010s (such as edx and coursera)[1,2], learning new skills is easier than ever.

In short, today you can train and optimize state-of-the-art machine learning models using only your own laptop and a simple software (either free or with a commercial software like SAS). You do not need to have a PhD in computer science to do so. Intellectual curiosity is enough.

2. **Data is essential: Promote a data-driven culture.** Machine Learning algorithms can learn complex relationships using external variables to better forecast

demand. External variables such as pricing, marketing expenses, weather, and holidays can be taken into account. Unfortunately, as I witnessed in many projects, using those external features is often wishful thinking. Is your supply chain keeping track of the pricing of every single historical sale? Did you note down the sort and the budget of every marketing event? Of every promotion (per sales channel)?

Collecting a massive amount of clean data still remains a challenge – or even a dream – for many companies. Developing a data-driven culture in your organization should be a first step toward collecting proper data. Nevertheless, there is unfortunately no silver bullet on how to create a data-driven culture in a supply chain. E-commerce companies are often much better at this, thanks to their close ties with the internet, whereas old industries struggle to appropriately capture and use data.

A first step toward developing a data-driven culture would be to show the potential of machine learning to your team. Another idea would be to teach (basic) coding skills to as many team members as possible. They will often be able to automate their repetitive tasks in Excel using their new favorite programming language. Each new team member using coding skills rather than repetitive manual work to do mundane tasks is another step toward a data-driven culture.

3. **An efficient forecast process is the road to excellence.** As forecast models become more and more accurate, demand planners will have to adapt by challenging the way they work. The "Forecast Value Added framework" (Gilliland 2010) will help them focus on where they add value while covering the baseline forecast delivered by the forecast engine. As ML models will be able to use more and more information (including external features such as pricing, historical out-of-stocks, promotions, etc.), demand planners will have to use their communication and networking skills to add value to their forecast. In many fields, teams of humans together with AI (called cyborgs) have shown better accuracy than AI alone or humans alone. It is time that we do the same with demand planning by training the planners to understand where they can add value.

How to Create Your First ML-Driven Forecast? Where to Start?

If you start from scratch and want to use ML to populate your baseline forecast, I advise you to take the following steps:

1. Start your journey by taking introductory training in a programming language (such as Python, R, or SAS).

2. As soon as you feel confident enough with a programming language (i.e., you can load data from a .csv file, analyze and clean it), you can start to follow training on data science and machine learning.

3. Simultaneously to your training, start collecting historical demand data (at least five years).

4. Once you have created a first data set, start using simple machine learning models (such as random forests) to predict the demand.

5. You can then refine your model by either including new features (pricing, promotions, historical stock-outs, etc.) or by using more advanced ML techniques. Remember: to succeed you have to test a lot of ideas.

NOTES

1. https://www.edx.org/
2. https://www.coursera.org/

REFERENCES

Gilliland, M. (2010). *The business forecasting deal: Exposing myths, eliminating bad practices, providing practical solutions*. Hoboken, NJ: Wiley.

Ke, G., Meng, Q., Finley, T., et al. (2017). LightGBM: A highly efficient gradient boosting decision tree. *Advances in Neural Information Processing Systems* 30 (NIPS 2017): 3149–3157.

Kingma, D. P., and Ba, J. (2015). Adam: A method for stochastic optimization. International Conference on Learning Representations, 1–13.

Morgan, J. N., and Sonquist, J. A. (1963). Problems in the analysis of survey data and a proposal. *Journal of the American Statistical Association*, 415–434.

Pedregosa, F., Varoquaux, G., Gramfort, A., et al. (2011). Scikit-learn: Machine Learning in Python. *Journal of Machine Learning Research*, 2825–2830.

Rosenblatt, F. (1957). The perceptron, a perceiving and recognizing automaton. Project Para. Cornell Aeronautical Laboratory.

Tianqi, C., and Guestrin, C. (2016). XGBoost: A scalable tree boosting system. Proceedings of the 22nd ACM SIGKDD International Conference on Knowledge Discovery and Data Mining, 785–794.

Vandeput, N. (2021). *Data science for supply chain forecasting*. Berlin/Boston: De Gruyter.

UNLOCK THE POTENTIAL OF BUSINESS FORECASTING

Eric Wilson, Institute of Business Forecasting

Forecasting is the life blood of an organization and can make or break a company. Every business decision is based on a lag between an event or action and the awareness and assumptions of that looming event or action. In other words, anything you plan is generally based on an assumption of something happening in the future which, by definition, is a forecast. Mind you, not all these forecasts are created equal. Depending on your mindset, this is your challenge or opportunity.

If done well, a forecast can provide valuable insights that drive a myriad of business decisions. It can reform an organization and becomes a game changer within an industry. If done poorly, it can cost an organization time, money, and reputation. For companies left behind or not focused on quality forecasting, it can handicap them, and they will eventually see their competitors pass them by.

There is a myth that you cannot predict the future, or if you do it is always wrong. Forecasting is about more than just an educated guess that we will sell "x" number of widgets next month. Business Forecasting can encompass anything that identifies the likelihood of a future outcome, provides comparative information using analytics, or drives analytic-driven business decisions. Forecasting is understanding the data, understanding the process, and understanding the audience or users of your projections. The people who excel are not just managing a number but managing assumptions and managing expectations.

To succeed and thrive, organizations look to innovative demand planners and predictive analytics professionals that understand the corporate strategy or a concrete business question as the starting point. They manage a process and bring together various inputs to meet multiple business needs. They track and monitor results and are storytellers that use numbers as their language. A good forecaster is the cornerstone for delivering customer service, lowering costs, and increasing asset turnover.

Take, for example, forecasting improvements. Improvements in forecast accuracy can enable efficiencies and improve responsiveness to market conditions. More accurate business forecasts facilitate better plans, resulting in lower inventory levels (increasing inventory turnover) while simultaneously improving customer service levels. For marketing, better predictions of consumer demand enable higher customer satisfaction increasing top line growth, and for operations facilitate the staging of inventories at key locations in the supply chain.

Forecasting can help make sense of new information and help turn new sources of data into insights as well. Those customer reviews and comments on websites, all of that social media data, metadata on consumers and macro data on markets – all of this is bound to be useful for something. There is an arms race to leverage this new data and use forecasting and predictive analytics to glean better insights. The sheer volume and complexity of today's data are challenging, but top organizations turn this data into useful insights quicker to support faster and better decision making. This supports not only supply chains but marketing, finance, and top management, too.

Business forecasting is much more than a sales projection. It is solving problems, exploring data, and transforming understandings. There are businesses that are not only breaking new ground, they are creating an evolution in the business forecasting field. With this new wave of predictive analytics, machine learning, and artificial intelligence, it is fundamentally changing the way we forecast and make decisions. Business forecasting is reforming planning functions into centers of insights and unlocking their capabilities as masters of orchestration.

Companies that unlock the potential of forecasting and predictive analytics are making smarter and faster decisions, as well as redefining business operations. Strategically, predictive analytics allows for a quantitative foundation for quick identification and objective, unbiased evaluation of information to help pursue new opportunities.

Tactically, predictive analytics can allow companies to micro target a market with precise accuracy, as well as help determine whom to reach and when, and how to shape demand. And operationally in almost real time, predictive analytics allows you to sense and react immediately across an entire supply chain to signals and changes.

It is up to businesses how they approach and what they think about forecasting. Business is constantly changing, and portfolios are becoming more complex. Consumer preferences, season, and disruptive events are becoming more difficult to predict. Strong forecasting and predictive analytics capabilities provide the key to unlock and understand what may happen and shape the future. Forecasting helps manage assumptions and brings the right information and insights so organizations can make better analytical-driven decisions and find a competitive advantage.

BUILDING A DEMAND PLAN STORY FOR S&OP: THE BUSINESS VALUE OF ANALYTICS

Dr. Davis Wu, Nestlé

The Demand Plan is one of the key inputs to all planning processes and executions. But it often fails to inspire acceptance in the S&OP (Sales and Operational Planning) process. Heads of Sales and other key business managers may wonder why they should believe the numbers that are being presented to them in the Demand Plan. Thus, Demand Planners face a constant battle for trust, and for getting their voices heard.

To be most effective, the Demand Plan should read like an inspiring story, full of fact-based analysis, insights and predictions supported by the right data and technology. Demand Planners can then tell their story convincingly. With the explosion of available data sources and the arrival of new technology such as analytics and machine learning, it is finally possible to make the Demand Plan more trustworthy and accepted, and really start to drive a more fact-based S&OP process.

An inspiring Demand Plan Story should consist of the following key elements.

A Demand Plan Story: The Setting

A Demand Plan Story should first provide a broad context of the current setting, consisting of Market Conditions, Category Trend, and Sales Performance:

1. **Market Conditions.** Market Conditions relates to broad market context such as government regulations, policies and macro-economic conditions that affect the given product segment. For example, the product segment of Baby Infant Formula is highly regulated by government policies on product specification, quality control and consumer communications. Macro-economic conditions such as affordability are also an important factor. Any potential material impact due to change in market conditions should be articulated to set out the context of a Demand Plan Story.

2. **Category Trend.** Category Trend is mostly driven by the competition landscape, demographic composition, and ongoing evolution in a given market. How the factors will lead to change of market share is an important element of the overall Demand Plan Story. Both tactical and strategic planning horizons must be considered to ensure supply with the right capacity available in factories, warehouses and transportation.

3. **Sales Performance.** Sales Performance is a matrix of performance measures that indicate how well the sales outputs have (or have not) met company's expectations. The matrix consists of both financial and volumetric indicators. From a demand planning perspective, it should include a forecast accuracy measure with the right planning lags. Focus should be given to performance-related key events such as new product launches, promotions, media campaigns, etc. A Demand Plan Story should start with how well the given product is performing, what worked, and what didn't.

These three elements provide the story setting. Demand Planners must incorporate and articulate this broader setting as first agenda item for S&OP collaborations and meetings.

From a technology perspective, the setting is enabled by Descriptive Analytics, focusing on a summary of current status and past performance measures. Visualization of the information is critical to help articulate the story setting in the S&OP.

A Demand Plan Story: The Actors

Like actors in a story who have their own characteristics and play different roles, a Demand Plan Story consists of a few fundamental building blocks (actors). Each building block contributes differently to the overall Demand Plan Story and must be clearly addressed and articulated in all key S&OP collaborations and meetings.

The building blocks are Demand Pattern, Activity Plans, and Assumptions:

1. **Demand Pattern.** The demand pattern incorporates the underlying trend, seasonality, and shifts. Statistical algorithm should be used to get to the true underlying demand pattern. It excludes the volumetric influences related to promotion events in the trade and media. A key skillset for a Demand Planner is to be able to state clearly how much the demand plan is influenced by seasons, trends, and shifts.

2. **Activity Plans.** The timing and mechanics of activity (or event) plans can be statistically modelled. The models result in incremental estimates based on past occurrences of similar activities. Activity-related sales can represent a significant part of the overall sales volume, and therefore must be prioritized by Demand Planners. It is one of the key focus areas for S&OP processes and should be articulated with facts, backed up by modern statistical/analytical technologies.

3. **Assumptions.** New product launches, customer or distribution gains or losses, and cannibalization or halo effects are other examples that must be factored into the total demand plan. They are often provided by Marketing and Sales managers as assumptions, rather than being statistically modelled. They form another important part of the total demand plan, and are a key focus area for S&OP.

Demand Pattern, Activity Plan, and Assumptions are the main actors of a Demand Plan Story. Demand Planners must learn and master the analysis and communication of each building block in the context of S&OP collaborations and meetings. To do this, Demand Planners are often assisted by specialized analysts – data scientists with the right statistical/analytical skillsets.

From technology perspective, the data scientists are enabled by Predictive Analytics – deeper statistical/analytical analysis methods that can predict the most likely outcomes. They do this using modern technology such as advanced analytics models, machine learning, and artificial intelligence.

A Demand Plan Story: The Plot

Where the story becomes thrilling is in the plot – what goes behind the demand plan. This includes Forecast in a Range, Impactor Analytics, "What-if" Scenarios, and sometimes additional components.

These plot components drive tremendous value for companies in shaping the optimal plan, which includes the right activities at the right time with the right pricing strategy. They also drive efficiencies in the overall S&OP process.

1. **Forecast in a Range.** All demand plans (forecasts) must come with a range representing a certain confidence level. This range is also known as a confidence corridor, or prediction interval. A fixed number (point forecast) by itself is not enough, as it only represents the most probable prediction within a range.

   The prediction interval is an important concept that brings the Demand Plan alive. The behavior of constantly adjusting and readjusting a demand plan for small variations within the interval does not add value at all. It is wasted effort for Demand Planners, and also wastes the time of cross-functional teams around the S&OP processes. The Forecast in a Range concept helps avoid a lot of those bad practices.

2. **Impactor Analytics.** When a Demand Plan is generated using advanced analytics algorithms, and it is based on rich data sets such as point-of-sales, pricing, promotions, media and spends, the results are valuable for much more than just the future Demand Plan. The analysis can provide rich insights, for example, into the effectiveness of promotion mechanics, seasonal impacts, media contribution to volume, and other areas. All these insights give Demand Planners the elements to build a powerful story about the Demand Plan, increasing their credibility.

3. **"What-if" Scenarios.** A natural evolution of proper Impactor Analytics is "What-if" Scenarios.

Often, a Demand Plan will not match business expectation or targets in its first iteration within the S&OP process. The gap between plan and target can be material. By reassessing the effectiveness of each main impactor, Demand Planners can provide the best possible options to reduce the gap, or even create a positive gap where possible. This obviously requires true collaboration with Sales and Marketing colleagues to ensure the feasibility of executing such a new plan.

All the above elements, together, can make a Demand Plan Story inspiring. Demand Planners become true copilots of the overall business plan, building and articulating the full story of What, Why, and How to achieve better outcomes in the context of the S&OP process.

From a technology perspective, Demand Planners are enabled here by Prescriptive Analytics, utilizing optimization, and/or machine learning and AI technologies.

Conclusion

The S&OP process should not be boring. It should be grounded in reality and enhanced with facts, the right data, and the right technology. Demand Planners play a critical role in building and telling the story – a story consisting of the setting and the full characteristics of the actors, all packed into a fascinating plot.

The Demand Plan Story is built on the right analytics technology, with each part of the story relying on a specific type of analytics capabilities as illustrated in the diagram.

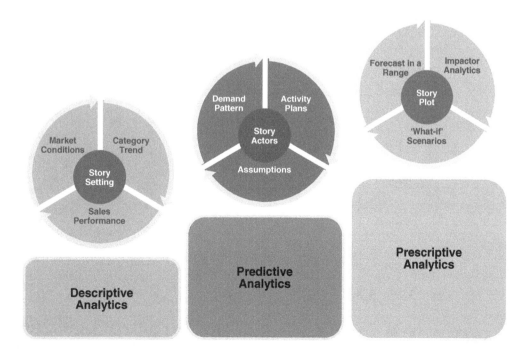

About the Editors

Michael Gilliland is Marketing Manager for SAS forecasting software, Associate Editor of *Foresight: The International Journal of Applied Forecasting*, author of *The Business Forecasting Deal*, and editor of *Forecasting with SAS®: Special Collection*. He is on the Board of Directors of the International Institute of Forecasters, and in 2017 received the Lifetime Achievement Award from the Institute of Business Forecasting. Mike holds a BA in Philosophy from Michigan State University, and Master's degrees in Philosophy and Mathematical Sciences from Johns Hopkins University. Follow his blog *The Business Forecasting Deal* at blogs.sas.com/content/forecasting.

Len Tashman is the founding editor of *Foresight: The International Journal of Applied Forecasting*, now in its 16th year of publication. He serves on the Board of Directors of the International Institute of Forecasters, and is organizer and chair of the *Foresight* Practitioner Conferences and the Forecasting in Practice Track at the annual International Symposium on Forecasting. Len is an emeritus professor of business administration at the University of Vermont and Director of the Center for Business Forecasting.

Udo Sglavo is Vice President of Analytics R&D at SAS, leading a team of highly skilled individuals responsible for building and testing the SAS analytical ecosystem. He has a diploma in mathematics from the University of Applied Sciences, Darmstadt, Germany, and holds several patents in the area of advanced analytics. Udo served on the practitioner advisory board of *Foresight*, and is currently on the analytics advisory board of Oklahoma State University. He has published in *Analytics* magazine, and joined Mike Gilliland and Len Tashman in editing the original volume of *Business Forecasting: Practical Problems and Solutions*.

Index